THE
ART
OF
PUBLIC
SPEAKING

FIFTH EDITION

THE
ART
OF
PUBLIC
SPEAKING

STEPHEN E. LUCAS
University of Wisconsin–Madison

McGraw-Hill, Inc.

New York   St. Louis   San Francisco   Auckland
Bogotá   Caracas   Lisbon   London   Madrid
Mexico City   Milan   Montreal   New Delhi
San Juan   Singapore   Sydney   Tokyo   Toronto

THE ART OF PUBLIC SPEAKING

Photo Credits appear on page 469 and on this page by reference.

This book is printed on acid-free paper.

1 2 3 4 5 6 7 8 9 0   VNH   VNH   9 0 9 8 7 6 5 4

ISBN 0-07-039015-0

This book was set in Veljovic Book by Monotype Composition Company.
The editors were Hilary Jackson, Bob Greiner, and Peggy Rehberger;
the designer was Carol A. Couch;
the production supervisor was Leroy A. Young.
The photo editor was Debra Hershkowitz.
Von Hoffmann Press, Inc., was printer and binder.

Cover photo by Bob Henriques.
Cover photo hand-colored by Carol A. Couch.

Library of Congress Cataloging-in-Publication Data

Lucas, Stephen.
    The art of public speaking / Stephen E. Lucas.—5th ed.
      p.   cm.
    Includes bibliographical references (p.) and index.
    ISBN 0-07-039015-0
    1. Public speaking.   I. Title.
PN4121.L72   1995   94-30496
808.5'1—dc20

INTERNATIONAL EDITION

About the Author

Stephen E. Lucas is Professor of Communication Arts at the University of Wisconsin–Madison, where he has taught since 1972. Born in New York and raised in California, he received his bachelor's degree from the University of California, Santa Barbara, and his master's and doctorate degrees from Penn State University.

Professor Lucas has been recognized for his work as both a scholar and a teacher. His first book, *Portents of Rebellion: Rhetoric and Revolution in Philadelphia, 1765–1776,* received the Golden Anniversary Award of the Speech Communication Association in 1977 and was nominated for a Pulitzer Prize. His major articles include "The Schism in Rhetorical Scholarship" (1981), "The Renaissance of American Public Address: Text and Context in Rhetorical Criticism" (1988), and "Justifying America: The Declaration of Independence as a Rhetorical Document" (1989). He is currently writing a book on Booker T. Washington's Atlanta Exposition Address.

Professor Lucas has received a number of teaching awards, including the Chancellor's Award for Excellence in Teaching at the University of Wisconsin. His lecture course on "The Rhetoric of Campaigns and Revolutions" is among the most popular on campus and has twice been selected for statewide broadcast in its entirety by Wisconsin Public Radio.

In addition, Professor Lucas has directed the introductory public speaking course at the University of Wisconsin–Madison since 1973. Over the years he has been responsible for numerous teaching innovations and has supervised the training of hundreds of graduate assistants. He has also participated in public speaking workshops and colloquia at schools throughout the United States.

Stephen Lucas lives in Madison, Wisconsin, with his wife Patty and his sons Jeff and Ryan. His interests include travel, sports, art, and photography.

v

Preface

If it is true, as Walter Pater said, that "a book, like a person, has its fortunes," then fortune has indeed smiled upon *The Art of Public Speaking*. I am deeply appreciative to the students and teachers who have made it the leading textbook on its subject at colleges and universities across the United States.

In preparing this, the fifth edition, I have retained what readers have identified as the main strengths of previous editions. The book continues to be informed by classical and contemporary theories of rhetoric but does not present theory for its own sake. Keeping a steady eye on the practical skills of public speaking, it offers full coverage of all major aspects of speech preparation and presentation.

Throughout *The Art of Public Speaking* I have followed David Hume's advice that one "who would teach eloquence must do it chiefly by examples." Whenever possible I have tried to *show* the principles of public speaking in action in addition to telling about them. Thus you will find in the book a large number of narratives and extracts from speeches—set off from the text in a contrasting typeface. There are also many speech outlines and sample speeches. All these are provided so students can *see* how to formulate specific purpose statements, how to analyze and adapt to audiences, how to organize ideas and construct outlines, how to assess evidence and reasoning, how to use language effectively, and so forth.

Because the immediate task facing students is to present speeches in the classroom, I have relied heavily on examples that relate directly to students' classroom needs and experiences. The speech classroom, however, is a training ground where students develop skills that will serve them throughout life. Therefore, I have also included a variety of illustrations drawn from the kinds of speaking experiences students will face after they graduate—in their careers and in their communities.

As in previous editions, I have been guided by the belief that a book intended for students who want to speak more effectively should never lose sight of the fact that the most important part of speaking is thinking. The ability to think critically is vital to a world in which personality and image too often substitute for thought and substance. While helping students become capable, responsible speakers, *The Art of Public Speaking* also aims at helping them become capable, responsible thinkers.

FEATURES OF THE FIFTH EDITION

Given the favorable response of teachers and students to the first four editions of *The Art of Public Speaking,* I have kept the basic philosophy and approach of the book intact. At the same time, I have made a number of improvements in response to suggestions from readers. The most important of these improvements provide fuller coverage of ethics, of diversity and multiculturalism, and of persuasive speaking. Let me explain a bit about each.

Ethics

In previous editions, the ethics of speechmaking was discussed as part of Chapter 1. Now it is the subject of Chapter 2. After explaining the importance of ethics, this new chapter presents guidelines for ethical speaking, discusses the problem of plagiarism and how to avoid it, and explains guidelines for ethical listening. Reviewers have responded to the chapter with great enthusiasm, and I hope instructors and students alike will find it a valuable addition to the new edition.

Diversity and Multiculturalism

The Art of Public Speaking has long been a leader in recognizing and adapting to the diversity of contemporary life. As society has changed since the first edition in 1983, so has the book. In each edition, I have sought to relate the principles of effective speechmaking to students of diverse backgrounds, values, and aspirations. This new edition continues my efforts to make sure *The Art of Public Speaking* is respectful of and applicable to all of its readers.

Most important in this regard, I have added a new section to Chapter 1 on public speaking in a multicultural world. This section places public speaking in the context of today's global multiculturalism, explores the impact of cultural diversity on speechmaking, and offers basic strategies for addressing culturally diverse audiences. The placement of this section in the opening chapter reflects its importance to the book as a whole. Given the nature of the modern world, students need to know from the outset that many of the speaking situations they enter will involve people from a variety of cultural backgrounds.

Expanded attention to diversity and multiculturalism is also evident in every chapter—including the range of potential speech topics presented in Chapter 4, the treatment of audience analysis in Chapter 5, the discussion of reference materials in Chapter 6, the addition of a new section on nonsexist language in Chapter 11, and the inclusion of a new section on dialect in Chapter 12. There are also dozens of fresh examples throughout the book that reflect the diversity of life in our modern world and that encourage an inclusive approach to the art of public speaking.

Persuasion

In keeping with recommendations from readers of the fourth edition, I have strengthened the treatment of persuasion and divided it into two chapters. In previous editions, speaking to persuade was discussed in Chapter 14. Now it is presented in Chapters 15 and 16. After exploring the psychology of persuasion, Chapter 15 explains the kinds of persuasive speeches and how to organize them most effectively. Chapter 16 deals with the methods of persuasion and focuses on credibility, evidence, reasoning, and emotional appeals.

Among the specific improvements in these two chapters are greater attention to the psychological factors of persuasion, fuller discussion of evidence and reasoning, and expanded consideration of the strategies and ethics of emotional appeal. Taken together, the chapters offer the same clear approach to persuasion that was so well received by readers of past editions while updating and improving the text to keep it as current, useful, and readable as possible.

Other Improvements

In addition to the major changes described above, I have made a number of other improvements, including:

- Updated treatment of library research in Chapter 6.

- A fresh sample outline with commentary in Chapter 10.

- A new section on nonsexist language in Chapter 11.

- Expanded treatment of dialect in Chapter 12.

- A new unit on overhead transparencies in Chapter 13.

- Thorough reworking of examples throughout the book to keep the material clear, interesting, and relevant to today's readers.

- Four new speeches in the Appendix for analysis and discussion, including Mary Fisher's highly acclaimed speech on AIDS at the 1992 Republican National Convention.

In addition to these revisions, I have tried in every chapter to make sure the footnote references reflect current theory and research. My aim has been to maintain the readability of the text while using the footnotes to help students understand that the principles of effective speechmaking have been confirmed by substantial contemporary scholarship as well as by centuries of practical experience.

PLAN OF THE BOOK

One of the biggest challenges in writing a textbook is deciding what to include and in what order to present it. I have tried to structure *The Art of Public Speaking* so its coverage of material and its sequence of chapters will fit the introductory public speaking class as it is offered at most colleges and universities. Still, only rarely does a textbook line up exactly with an instructor's established syllabus. For this reason I have made each chapter as self-contained as possible. Instructors should have little difficulty adapting the book to their own emphases and teaching methods.

Part One, "Speaking and Listening," introduces the basic principles of speech communication and the respective responsibilities of speakers and listeners. The opening chapter explains the value of a course in public speaking, identifies the basic elements of the speech communication process, and seeks to ease the stage fright that is nearly always uppermost in students' minds at the beginning of the class. Chapter 2 deals with the ethics of public speaking, while Chapter 3 explores the importance of listening and offers practical tips to help students become better listeners.

Part Two, "Speech Preparation: Getting Started," takes up the initial steps of speech preparation. Chapter 4 guides students through the crucial process of selecting a speech topic, formulating a specific purpose, and phrasing an effective central idea. Chapter 5 introduces the basic principles of audience analysis and explains how to adapt a speech to an audience. Chapter 6 shows how students can gather materials for a speech by drawing on their own experience, by interviewing other people, and by conducting library research. Chapter 7 looks at the basic kinds of supporting materials and offers guidelines for using them effectively.

Part Three is titled "Speech Preparation: Organization and Outlining." After surveying the basic patterns of speech organization in Chapter 8, students learn in Chapter 9 how to construct effective introductions and conclusions. Chapter 10 explains the principles of outlining and exemplifies them with a model preparation outline. A sample speaking outline is also provided to show how a detailed preparation outline is transformed into a brief set of speaker's notes. Taken together, Chapters 8–10 provide a solid foundation upon which students can build their skills of speech organization.

Part Four is titled "Presenting the Speech" and focuses on language, delivery, and visual aids. Chapter 11 discusses the importance of language and offers a number of practical guides for using words accurately, clearly, vividly, and appropriately. Chapter 12 deals with the basic methods of speech delivery, the use of the speaker's voice, and the role of nonverbal communication in speechmaking. Chapter 13 explains the advantages of visual aids, the kinds of visual aids, and the ways to use visual aids most effectively.

Part Five, "Varieties of Public Speaking," takes up different types of discourse. In Chapter 14 the subject is informative speaking. The first part of this chapter explains how to analyze and organize informative speeches; the second part offers guidelines for effective informative presentations. Chapters 15 and 16 deal with speaking to persuade. They seek to give students the knowledge they most need to create effective persuasive speeches—without bogging them down in hazy theoretical issues or excessive jargon. Chapter 17 deals with several kinds of speeches for special occasions, while Chapter 18 is designed for instructors who include a unit on group discussion in their classes.

■ RESOURCES FOR INSTRUCTORS

The Art of Public Speaking has a number of instructional resources to help students learn and apply the principles of effective speechmaking. Chapters 7, 14, 15, and 16 contain sample speeches with commentary. Chapter 10 has complete preparation and speaking outlines, both with commentary. The Appendix consists of seven additional speeches for discussion and analysis.

A set of Application Exercises accompanies each chapter. The exercises are written assignments that students can complete on their own in conjunction with reading assignments. They can also be used as the basis for classroom activities and discussion. In keeping with the importance of critical thinking and the experiential nature of speechmaking, these exercises require that students *work with* (rather than simply memorize) the principles presented in the book. The wide range of exercises—in the text and in the *Instructor's Manual*—should give instructors maximum flexibility in choosing those best suited for their students.

A special feature of the fifth edition is the *Speaker's Helper,* an innovative computer program that guides students through the sometimes daunting task of outlining their speeches. This program, which is fully compatible with IBM and MacIntosh computers, utilizes the principles of interactive learning and has been developed exclusively for use with *The Art of Public Speaking.*

To give teachers as much assistance as possible, I have developed a four-volume *Instructional Resource Program.* The first volume is the *Instructor's Manual,* which contains chapter outlines; discusses the Application Exercises in the textbook; furnishes supplementary exercises, speeches, and classroom activities; offers suggested course outlines and speaking assignments; provides synopses of the Appendix speeches; and gives a bibliography of additional teaching and learning resources.

The second volume of the *Instructional Resource Program* is the *Test Bank,* which furnishes more than 1,200 examination questions based on *The Art of Public Speaking.* As a special feature the *Test Bank* offers preconstructed chapter quizzes for each chapter in the book, as well as several complete final examinations. The *Test Bank* is also available on disc for computerized test construction.

The third and fourth volumes of the *Instructional Resource Program* consist of two anthologies of material from *The Speech Communication Teacher.*

Taken together, these anthologies reprint more than 150 brief articles (1–2 pages each) relative to all aspects of teaching public speaking. Written by teachers for teachers, these articles offer a wealth of practical ideas for classroom use.

There are several videotapes of sample student speeches that accompany *The Art of Public Speaking.* A number of these speeches are printed in the book, so students can see on tape some of the same speeches they are studying in class. Instructors who adopt *The Art of Public Speaking* can also select from a wide range of "Great Speeches" videotapes that accompany the book. Among the selections on these tapes are Martin Luther King's "I Have a Dream" and Barbara Bush's 1990 commencement speech at Wellesley College, both of which are reprinted in the textbook.

Finally, I have produced a unique videotape entitled "Introductions, Conclusions, and Visual Aids." This tape contains excerpts from speeches by students and public figures that illustrate the principles of effective speech introductions and conclusions in action. It also contains examples of speakers using visual aids such as charts, graphs, drawings, photographs, and videotapes. Developed in conjunction with the fourth edition of *The Art of Public Speaking,* "Introductions, Conclusions, and Visual Aids" has been received with great enthusiasm at schools throughout the country and is available with the fifth edition as well.

ACKNOWLEDGMENTS

Ralph Waldo Emerson said, "'Tis the good reader that makes the good book." I have been fortunate to have very good readers indeed, and I would like to thank the following reviewers for their comments and suggestions: Mary Eleanor Anderson, Memphis State University; Sandy Berkowitz, University of Minnesota; R. B. Bookwalter, Marshall University; Jackie Buckrop, Ball State University; Carl Burgchardt, Colorado State University; David Droge, University of Puget Sound; Thomas B. Harte, Southeast Missouri State University; Richard Haven, University of Wisconsin–Whitewater; Robert Heath, University of Houston; Susan Hellweg, San Diego State University; Susan Huxman, Wichita State University; J. Vernon Jensen, University of Minnesota; Richard Johannesen, Northern Illinois University; Jack Kay, Wayne State University; Jayne Landon, Bakersfield College; Ron Lustig, San Diego State University; Mary Y. Mandeville, Oklahoma State University; Judith S. Mish, Springfield Technical Community College; Robert J. Myers, Baruch College; Steve Neilson, University of Nevada; Terry Perkins, Eastern Illinois University; Laura Rouzan, Xavier University of Louisiana; Deanna Sellnow, North Dakota State University; Melody Templeton, Villanova University; Denise Vrchota, Iowa State University; and Kent Zimmerman, Sinclair Community College.

I am also grateful to the following people who used the fourth edition and offered their reactions: Jerry Agent, Althea Allard, Floyd D. Anderson, Georgia Anstine, Eija Ayravainen, Barbara Battenberg, Dale A. Bertelsen, Kenneth Blume, Sue L. Brooks, Louvincey Brown, David Burke, Paul A. Chambers, Beverly S. Christofferson, Susan Collie, Linda Cooper, Joseph S.

Coppolino, M. V. Crowley, Roberta Davilla, Betty Dillard, Natalie R. Dudchock, Eugenie H. Dye, Eunice R. Eifert, Susan Redding Emel, Ronald A. Gaiz, Ruth L. Goldfarb, Catherine Gragg, Steven Grant, Denise Halbach, Kate Hastings, Anthony Hatcher, Margaret Hazel, Barbara Horn, Susan Schultz Huxman, Deryl Johnson, Virginia E. Judge, Shayne Kellogg, Laura L. Kinzinger, Marcia S. Kuehl, David Lawless, Shelly Lutzweiler, Laurie McBride, Patricia Macvaugh, Rod McVetta, Phoebe P. Mallory, Vicki Marie, Edward Martin, Paul Marx, Sharon Mason, Ronnie Miller, A. R. Montanaro, Jr., Michael Moriarty, Marjorie Morris, Maureen O'Brien, Mabry M. O'Donnell, James S. O'Rourke, IV, Annemarie Penick, Samuel Perry, Thomas Peters, Tony Peyronel, Janet Pickler, R. W. Platt, Betty Popper, Gaut Ragsdale, Closepet N. Ramesh, Kellie W. Roberts, Louis Rutherford, Monique Sacay, Vaughn Schutz, Kathy Shipley, Janet Simpson, Alan Sivell, Amy R. Slagell, Yvonne Souliere, Mary Steffancin, Carla Stevens, Gary Sullivan, Barbara Taylor, Dencil R. Taylor, Eleanor Tucker, Stan W. Tucker, Anita J. Turpin, Catherine Egley Waggoner, William B. Wetherbee, Carol Winkler, Alan Winson, and "Kat" Doran Wood.

In addition, I would like to express my gratitude to the students at the University of Wisconsin whose speeches provided the material for so many of the examples in the text; to Susan Zaeske, whose expertise and judgment improved the book in numerous ways; to Karen Johnson, who helped sharpen my thinking on dialect and the special problems faced by non-native speakers of English; to Anne Mackinnon, who contributed to several parts of the book; to Roger Axtell and Rudy Wright, who generously shared their insights about public speaking in the international arena; and to Carl Burgchardt, Doug Pedersen, and Diana Ivy, who provided wise counsel on a variety of issues.

Members of the Communication Arts 101 and 105 teaching staffs at the University of Wisconsin–Madison have helped me by collecting sample speeches, by identifying rough spots in the fourth edition, and by piloting new assignments and exercises in the classroom. I would especially like to thank Maggie Censky, Franklin Billerbeck, Kris Harrison, Kelly Wolff, Jim Brentar, Jennifer Fay, David Henningsen, Donald Meckiffe, Lisa Parks, Pradeep Sopory, Alastair Thorne, and Tania Bikerman.

In addition, there are many people at McGraw-Hill who contributed to this edition of *The Art of Public Speaking.* I am especially indebted to Hilary Jackson, who provided outstanding editorial support and direction; Bob Greiner, whose dedication, discernment, and attention to detail is evident on every page; Carol Couch, who created a striking design and cover; Leroy Young, who supervised the production and scheduling; Debra Hershkowitz, who once again did a superb job of photo research; and Peggy Rehberger, who guided the book through the final stages of production.

As always, I owe a deep debt of gratitude to my family—Patty, Jeff, and Ryan—who have improved the book (and the life of its author) in countless ways. Finally, I would like to dedicate this edition in memory of my father, who believed deeply in the importance of sound thinking, clear writing, and effective speaking.

Stephen E. Lucas

Contents

Presentation
"Talk"
Class #/ Prut

PART TWO: SPEECH PREPARATION: GETTING STARTED

Lecture for Class #2

Lecture for Class #3

Lecture for Class #5

Lecture for Class #5

CHAPTER 7

Lecture for Class #7

SUPPORTING YOUR IDEAS   143

PART THREE: SPEECH PREPARATION:
ORGANIZING & OUTLINING

CHAPTER 8

Lecture for Class #6

ORGANIZING THE BODY OF THE
SPEECH   173

Lecture for Class #8

PART FIVE: VARIETIES OF PUBLIC SPEAKING

CHAPTER 14   SPEAKING TO INFORM   309

CHAPTER 15   SPEAKING TO PERSUADE   335

CHAPTER 16   METHODS OF PERSUASION   367

CHAPTER 17   SPEAKING ON SPECIAL OCCASIONS   401

THE
ART
OF
PUBLIC
SPEAKING

Chapter 1

Speaking in Public

1

An old English proverb says "talk is cheap." Whoever coined that phrase obviously did not anticipate the 1990s. Nowadays, talk—good talk—can be very expensive indeed. The burden of this expense falls heavily both on those who wish to hear accomplished speakers and on those who wish to become accomplished speakers.

Throughout the history of the United States there have been people who earned a living by working the lecture circuit—traveling from city to city, town to town, delivering speeches as a form of entertainment or information to paying audiences. Today, however, the pay for such speechmaking has reached new heights. A polished speaker with expertise in some area of interest can command thousands of dollars for a single speech. Top-ranked stars of the lecture circuit—such as Barbara Walters, Larry King, and Ted Koppel—are paid $35,000 or more per speech.

How do such people learn the art of public speaking? A few are "naturals" who seem to be born with the talent. Some have had the benefit of public speaking courses in college, like the one you are taking now. Others do it the expensive way. They seek private instruction in speechmaking, which can cost up to $4,500 for six hours of individual work. No, talk is not cheap.

We should not be surprised that people place such a high value on public speaking. Throughout history this art has been a vital means of communication. What the Greek leader Pericles said nearly 2,500 years ago is just as true today: "One who forms a judgment on any point but cannot explain" it clearly "might as well never have thought at all on the subject."[1] In modern times many women and men have spread their ideas and influence largely by public speaking. The list would include Susan B. Anthony, Franklin Roosevelt, Billy Graham, Barbara Jordan, Martin Luther King, Margaret Thatcher, Ronald Reagan, and Jesse Jackson.

As you read these names, you may think to yourself, "That's fine. Good for them. But what does that have to do with me? I don't plan to be a president or a preacher, or a crusader for any cause." Nevertheless, the need for effective public speaking will almost certainly touch you sometime in your life— maybe tomorrow, maybe not for five years. Can you imagine yourself in any of these situations?

You are a management trainee in a large corporation. Altogether, there are seven trainees in the program. One of you will get the lower-management job that has just opened. There is to be a large staff meeting at which each of the trainees will discuss the project he or she has been developing. One by one your colleagues make their presentations. They have no experience in public speaking and are intimidated by the higher-ranking managers present. Their speeches are stumbling and awkward. You, however, call upon all the skills you learned in your public speaking course. You deliver an informative talk that is clear, well reasoned, and articulate. You get the job.

You are married and have three children. One of your children has a learning disability. You hear that your local school board has decided, for budget reasons, to eliminate the special teacher who has been helping your child. At an open meeting of the school board, you stand up and deliver a thoughtful, compelling speech on the necessity for keeping the special teacher. The school board changes its mind.

You are the assistant manager in a branch office of a national company. Your immediate superior, the branch manager, is about to retire, and there will be a retirement dinner. All the executives from the home office will attend. As his close working associate, you are asked to give a farewell toast at the party. You prepare and deliver a speech that is both witty and touching—a perfect tribute to your boss. After the speech, everyone applauds enthusiastically, and a few people have tears in their eyes. The following week you are named branch manager.

Fantasies? Not really. Any of these situations could occur. Study after study has shown that communication skills—including public speaking—are among the most prized assets job recruiters look for when hiring college graduates.[2] This is true across the board—for accountants and architects, teachers and engineers, scientists and stockbrokers. Regardless of your profession, you will almost surely need the art of public speaking. As business leader Midge Costanza says, you must have "the ability to stand on your feet, either on a one to one basis or before a group, and make a presentation that is convincing and believable."[3]

The same is true in community life. Look back for a moment at the second of our three hypothetical situations, the one in which you persuade the school board to keep the special teacher who has been helping your child. Why did the school board change its mind? Not simply because the facts were on your side (though they may have been) or because you know more about education than the school board (which you probably do not). The school board changed its mind because of your *speech*—in which you presented a convincing case for keeping the special teacher.[4]

The point is that public speaking can—and often does—make a difference in things you care about very much. The key phrase here is "make a difference." That is what most of us want to do in life—to make a difference, to change the world in some small way. Public speaking offers you at least three possibilities for making a difference—by *persuading* people to do something you feel is right; by *informing* people about things they do not know; or by *entertaining* people and making them feel happy and good about themselves. These are the three major goals of public speaking—to persuade, to inform, to entertain. They are also the three major goals of everyday conversation.

■ SIMILARITIES BETWEEN PUBLIC SPEAKING AND CONVERSATION

How much time do you spend each day talking to other people? The average adult spends about 30 percent of her or his waking hours in conversation. As you will see, there are many similarities between daily conversation and public speaking.

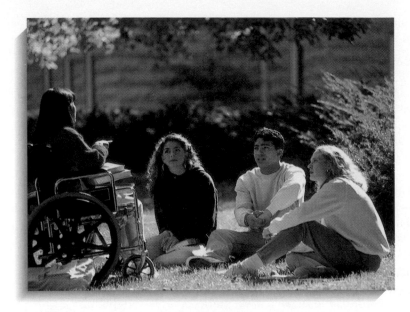

Many skills used in conversation also apply in public speaking. As you learn to speak more effectively in public, you may also learn to communicate more effectively in other situations.

Children learn the art of conversation by trial and error. A baby cries to inform its parents that the diaper needs changing. A toddler says "Cookie!" to persuade her father to give her a snack. A five-year-old tells a little story to entertain Grandma and gain admiration. If none of these things works—the diaper stays wet, the cookie isn't forthcoming, Grandma is not amused—well, back to the drawing board. Next time the child will try it a slightly different way.

By the time you read this book, you will have spent much of your life perfecting the art of conversation. You may not realize it, but you already employ a wide range of skills when talking to people. These skills include the following:

1. *Organizing your thoughts logically.* Suppose you were giving someone directions to get to your house. You wouldn't do it this way:

When you turn off the highway, you'll see a big diner on the left. But before that, stay on the highway to Exit 67. Usually a couple of the neighbors' dogs are in the street, so go slow after you turn at the blinking light. Coming from your house you get on the highway through Maple Street. If you pass the taco stand, you've gone too far. The house is blue.

Instead, you would take your listener systematically, step by step, from his or her house to your house. You would organize your message.

2. *Tailoring your message to your audience.* You are a geology major. Two people ask you how pearls are formed. One is your roommate; the other is your nine-year-old niece. You answer as follows:

To your roommate: "When any irritant, say a grain of sand, gets inside the oyster's shell, the oyster automatically secretes a substance called nacre, which is principally calcium carbonate and is the same material that lines the oyster's shell. The nacre accumulates in layers around the irritant core to form the pearl."

To your niece: "Imagine you're an oyster on the ocean floor. A grain of sand gets inside your shell and makes you uncomfortable. So you decide to cover it up. You cover it with a material called mother-of-pearl. The covering builds up around the grain of sand to make a pearl."

3. *Telling a story for maximum impact.* Suppose you are telling a friend about a funny incident at last week's football game. You don't begin with the punch line ("Cheryl fell out of the stands right onto the field. Here's how it started. . . ."). Instead, you carefully build up your story, adjusting your words and tone of voice to get the best effect.

4. *Adapting to listener feedback.* Whenever you talk with someone, you are aware of that person's various reactions—verbal, facial, and physical. For example:

You are explaining an interesting point that came up in biology class. Your listener begins to look confused, puts up a hand as though to stop you, and says "Huh?" You go back and explain more clearly.

A friend has asked you to listen while she practices a speech. At the end you say, "There's just one part I really don't like—that quotation from the attorney general." Your friend looks very hurt and says, "That was my favorite part!" So you say, "But if you just worked the quotation in a little differently it would be wonderful."

Each day, in casual conversation, you do all these things many times without thinking about them. You already possess these communication skills. And these are among the most important skills you will need for public speaking.

To illustrate, let's return briefly to one of the hypothetical situations at the beginning of this chapter. When addressing the school board about the need for a special teacher:

- You *organize* your ideas to present them in the most persuasive manner. You steadily build up a case about how the teacher benefits the school.

- You *tailor your message* to your audience. This is no time to launch an impassioned defense of special education in the United States. You must show how the issue is important to the people in that very room—to their children and to the school.

- You tell your story for *maximum impact.* Perhaps you relate an anecdote to demonstrate how much your child has improved. You also have statistics to show how many other children have been helped.

■ You *adapt to listener feedback.* When you mention the cost of the special teacher, you notice sour looks on the faces of the school board members. So you patiently explain how small that cost is in relation to the overall school budget.

In many ways, then, public speaking requires the same skills used in ordinary conversation. Most people who communicate well in daily talk can learn to communicate just as well in public speaking. By the same token, training in public speaking can make you a more adept communicator in a variety of situations such as conversations, classroom discussions, business meetings, and interviews.

DIFFERENCES BETWEEN PUBLIC SPEAKING AND CONVERSATION

Despite their many similarities, public speaking and everyday conversation are not identical. Let's consider an example in which casual conversation expanded gradually into a true—and vital—public speaking situation. Here the speaker originally had no intention of becoming a *public* speaker and had not trained formally for that role. She was forced to learn by trial and error—in circumstances where the outcome has affected one of the vital issues of our time:

Mary Fisher's life changed forever on July 17, 1991. Two weeks earlier, her ex-husband had called to say he had tested positive for the HIV virus. Now, as Fisher listened to her doctor, she learned that she, too, was HIV-positive.

Born into one of Detroit's most prominent families, Fisher was a successful artist, onetime television producer, and former staff assistant to President Gerald Ford. She was used to meeting challenges. But this was different. At the age of forty-three, the mother of two young sons, she felt a sense of shock "so great," she recalls, "that it took every ounce of energy for me to move."

For the next several months, Fisher wrestled with her grief and fear. In conversations with friends and family she wondered, "Why me?" and "What will happen to my children?" But as she came to terms with her condition, she also asked, "Can any good come out of this?" and "Is there anything I can do in the fight against AIDS?" Knowing that conversations with a few people would not solve the problem, in February 1992 she told her story to a reporter from the *Detroit Free Press.* The story made headline news and launched Fisher's career as an AIDS activist.

As Fisher moved more and more into the public eye, she found herself in many public speaking situations—from high-school auditoriums around Detroit to the International AIDS Conference in Amsterdam. In the process, she had to adapt her conversational abilities to larger audiences and more structured occasions. The spontaneous give-and-take of conversation and informal interviews evolved into speeches prepared carefully in advance.

In April 1992 Fisher created the Family AIDS Network, a nonprofit organization devoted to expanding public understanding and resources in the battle against AIDS. Four months later, she presented a deeply moving speech at the Republican National Convention in Houston, Texas. The speech mesmerized delegates in the Astrodome and won the hearts of millions who saw it on television.

Again Fisher had to adapt—this time to the glare of national publicity. After Houston, her audience became the whole nation. Soon she was criss-crossing the land, speaking to church and community groups, health-care providers, educators, students, and government officials. Today she delivers about 75–80 speeches a year—not including radio, television, and newspaper interviews—to spread her message of awareness, compassion, and caring. She will continue, she says, as long as her health allows.[5]

What a long road Mary Fisher has traveled in the past few years. If someone had asked her before July 17, 1991, "Do you see yourself as a major public speaker?" she would have laughed at the idea. Yet today she has become a compelling advocate for HIV-positive people of all ages, hues, and classes. Along the way, she has had to adapt to three major differences between conversation and public speaking:

1. *Public speaking is more highly structured.* It usually imposes strict time limitations on the speaker. In most cases, the situation does not allow listeners to interrupt with questions or commentary. The speaker must accomplish her or his purpose in the speech itself. In preparing the speech, the speaker must anticipate questions that might arise in the minds of listeners and answer them. Consequently, public speaking demands much more detailed planning and preparation than ordinary conversation.

2. *Public speaking requires more formal language.* Slang, jargon, and bad grammar have little place in public speeches. When Mary Fisher addressed the Republican National Convention, she didn't say, "We damn well better change our attitudes about people who are HIV-positive!" Instead, she delivered an eloquent appeal to "lift the shroud of silence which has been draped over the issue of HIV/AIDS." Despite the increasing informality of all aspects of American life, listeners usually react negatively to speakers who do not elevate and polish their language when addressing an audience. A speech is supposed to be "special."

3. *Public speaking requires a different method of delivery.* When conversing informally, most people talk quietly, interject stock phrases such as "you know" and "I mean," adopt a casual posture, and use what are called vocalized pauses ("uh," "er," "um"). Effective public speakers, however, adjust their voices to be heard clearly throughout the audience. They assume a more erect posture. They avoid distracting mannerisms and verbal habits.

With study and practice, you will be able to master these differences and expand your conversational skills into speechmaking. Your speech class will provide the opportunity for this study and practice.

■ DEVELOPING CONFIDENCE: YOUR SPEECH CLASS

One of the major concerns of students in any speech class is stage fright. We may as well face the issue squarely. Many people who converse easily in all kinds of everyday situations become frightened at the idea of standing up before a group to make a speech.

If you are worried about stage fright, you may feel better knowing you are not alone. A survey conducted in 1973 asked more than 2,500 Americans to list their greatest fears. To the surprise of the researchers, the largest number of people—41 percent—listed speaking before a group among their greatest fears. By contrast, only 18 percent included death as one of their greatest fears.[6] Amazing as it may seem, many Americans appear to consider public speaking a fate worse than death.

In a more recent study, researchers concentrated on social situations and, again, asked their subjects to list their greatest fears. Here is how they responded:[7]

GREATEST FEAR	PERCENT NAMING
A party with strangers	74
Giving a speech	70
Asked personal questions in public	65
Meeting a date's parents	59
First day on a new job	59
Victim of a practical joke	56
Talking with someone in authority	53
Job interview	46
Formal dinner party	44
Blind date	42

Again, speechmaking ranks near the top in provoking anxiety.

Nervousness Is Normal

Actually, most people tend to be anxious about doing anything important in public. Actors are nervous before a play; politicians are nervous before a campaign speech; athletes are nervous before a big game. The ones who succeed have learned to use their nervousness to their advantage. Listen to figure skater Nancy Kerrigan, speaking the night before the women's competition at the 1994 Winter Olympic Games in Lillehammer, Norway: "Of course, I'm nervous. You get nervous every time you skate. You just want to make it work for you when you're out on the ice." Putting her butterflies to good use, Kerrigan skated the best performance of her life to trounce arch-rival Tonya Harding and win the silver medal.

Much the same thing happens in speechmaking. Surveys show that 76 percent of experienced speakers have stage fright before taking the floor.[8] But their nervousness is a healthy sign that they are getting "psyched up" for a good effort. Novelist and lecturer I. A. R. Wylie explains: "Now after many years of practice I am, I suppose, really a 'practiced speaker.' But I rarely rise to my feet without a throat constricted with terror and a furiously thumping heart. When, for some reason, I *am* cool and self-assured the speech is always a failure."[9]

In other words, it is perfectly normal—even desirable—to be nervous at the start of a speech. The question is: How can you control your nervousness and make it work for you rather than against you?

Dealing with Nervousness

You have already taken the first step. You are enrolled in a public speaking course, where you will learn about speechmaking and gain speaking experience. Think back to your first day at kindergarten, your first date, your first day at a new job. You were probably nervous in each situation because you were facing something new and unknown. Once you became accustomed to the situation, it was no longer threatening. So it is with public speaking. For most students, the biggest part of stage fright is fear of the unknown. The more you learn about public speaking and the more speeches you give, the less threatening speechmaking will become.

Your speech class will provide knowledge and experience to help you speak with confidence. Of course, the road to confidence will sometimes be bumpy. Learning to give a speech is not much different from learning any other skill—it proceeds by trial and error. The purpose of your speech class is to shorten the process, to minimize the errors, to give you a nonthreatening arena—a sort of laboratory—in which to undertake the "trial." Your teacher recognizes that you are a novice and is trained to give the kind of guidance you need to get started. In your fellow students you have a highly sympathetic audience who will provide valuable feedback to help you improve your speaking skills. As the class goes on, your fears about public speaking will gradually recede until they are replaced by only a healthy nervousness before you rise to speak.[10]

Another key to gaining confidence is to pick speech topics you truly care about—and then to prepare your speeches so thoroughly you cannot help but be successful. Here is how one student combined enthusiasm for her topic with thorough preparation to score a triumph in speech class:

Tia Betances was concerned about taking a speech class. Not having any experience as a public speaker, she got butterflies in her stomach just thinking about talking in front of an audience. But when the time came for Tia's first speech, she was determined to make it a success.

Tia chose the Special Olympics as the topic for her speech. Her younger brother was mentally retarded and for the past five years Tia had worked as a volunteer at the local Special Olympics competition. The purpose of her speech was to explain the origins, events, and philosophy of the Special Olympics.

As Tia spoke, it became clear that she cared deeply about her subject and genuinely wanted her audience to care about it too. Because she was intent on communicating with her audience, she forgot to be nervous. She established eye contact with her listeners and spoke clearly, fluently, and dynamically. Soon the entire class was engrossed in her speech.

Afterward, Tia conceded that she had surprised even herself. "I could hardly believe it," she said. "Once I got through the introduction, I didn't think about being nervous—I just concentrated on what I wanted to say. It was even sort of fun."*

A speech is much like a play. While the actual performance of a play may take no more than two hours, those two hours represent the final, polished product of hundreds of hours of work. Of course, you will not spend hundreds of hours preparing a speech. But like an actor who rehearses a role until it is just right, you will find that your confidence as a speaker increases when you work on a speech until it is just right.[11]

If you follow the techniques suggested by your teacher and in the rest of this book, you will stand up for every speech fully prepared. Imagine that the day for your first speech has arrived. You have studied your audience and selected a topic you know will interest them. You have researched the speech thoroughly and practiced it several times until it feels absolutely comfortable. You have even tried it out before two or three trusted friends. The subject is one you feel strongly about. How can you help but be confident of success?

Besides stressing the importance of being fully prepared, your teacher will probably give you several tips for dealing with nervousness in your first speeches. They may include:

- Think positively. Visualize yourself giving a strong, effective speech. Confidence is mostly the well-known power of positive thinking. If you think you can do it, you usually can do it.

- Be at your best physically and mentally. It is not a good idea to stay up until 4:00 A.M. partying with friends or cramming for an exam the night before your speech. A good night's sleep will serve you better.

- Concentrate on communicating with your audience rather than on worrying about your nervousness. If you get caught up in your speech, your audience will too.

---

* Like most of the examples in the book, this one is based on a true story. Usually the names have been changed and the situations altered slightly to protect privacy.

- Take a couple of deep breaths before you start to speak. It really does help to get a healthy dose of oxygen into your system.

- Work especially hard on your introduction. The butterflies in your stomach will be most active at the start of a speech. A good introduction will help calm them down and build your confidence for the rest of your speech.

- Make eye contact with members of your audience. Remember they are individual people, not a blur of faces. And they are your friends.

- Use visual aids. They create interest, draw attention away from you, and make you feel less self-conscious.[12]

It may also help you to know that your listeners probably won't realize how tense you are—especially if you do your best to act confident on the outside. Most of the time when students confess after a speech "I was so nervous I thought I was going to die," their classmates are surprised. To them the speaker looked calm and self-assured.[13]

Even if you do make a mistake during a speech, that is no catastrophe. Consider the plight of Princess Diana of England. During her wedding to Prince Charles, faced by platoons of cameras and lights and microphones, with virtually the whole world listening, she managed to garble the names of her almost-husband. Nobody thought she had made a fool of herself. Instead, that one small error in an otherwise flawless performance only made her seem more human.

If you are like most students, you will find your speech class to be a very positive experience. As one student wrote on her course evaluation form at the end of the class:

I was really dreading this class. The idea of giving all those speeches scared me half to death. But I'm glad now that I stuck with it. It's a small class, and I got to know a lot of the students. Besides that, this is one class in which I got to express *my* ideas, instead of spending the whole time listening to the teacher talk. I even came to enjoy giving the speeches. I could tell at times that the audience was really with me, and that's a great feeling.

Over the years thousands of students have developed confidence in their speechmaking abilities. As your confidence grows, you will be better able to stand before other people and tell them what you think and feel and know—and to make them think and feel and know those same things. The best part about confidence is that it nurtures itself. After you score your first triumph, you will be that much more confident the next time. And as you become a more confident public speaker, you will likely become more confident in other areas of your life as well.[14]

■ PUBLIC SPEAKING AND CRITICAL THINKING

That guy at the party last night really demolished me when we got into a discussion. I know my information is right, and I'm sure there was something wrong with his argument, but I can't put my finger on it.

I need a word processor, and every advertisement says its brand is state-of-the-art. But which is really the best buy for me?

I've worked hard on my term paper, but I'm not satisfied. It just doesn't seem to hang together, and I can't figure out what's wrong.

Political speeches are so one-sided. The candidates talk and talk, and they make everything sound rosy, but I still don't know whom to vote for.

Do any of these situations sound familiar? Have you ever found yourself in similar situations? If so, you may find help in your speech class. Besides building confidence, a course in public speaking can develop your skills as a critical thinker. Those skills can make the difference between the articulate debater and the pushover, the careful consumer and the easy mark, the A student and the C student, the thoughtful voter and the coin-tosser.

What is critical thinking? To some extent, it is a matter of logic—of being able to spot weaknesses in other people's arguments and to avoid them in your own. It also involves such related skills as distinguishing fact from opinion, judging the credibility of statements, and assessing the soundness of evidence.

In the broadest sense, critical thinking is focused, organized thinking—the ability to see clearly the relationships among ideas. It has often been said that there are few new ideas in the world, only reorganized ideas. The greatest thinkers, scientists, and inventors have often taken information that was readily available and put it together differently to produce new insights. That, too, is critical thinking.[15]

If you are wondering what this has to do with your public speaking class, the answer is quite a lot. As the class proceeds, for example, you will probably spend a good deal of time organizing your speeches. While this may seem like a purely mechanical exercise, it is closely interwoven with critical thinking. If the structure of your speech is disjointed and confused, odds are your thinking is also disjointed and confused. If, on the other hand, the structure is clear and cohesive, there is a good chance your thinking is too. Organizing a speech is not just a matter of arranging the ideas you already have. Rather, it is an important part of shaping the ideas themselves.

What is true of organization is true of many aspects of public speaking. The skills you learn in your speech class can help you become a more effective thinker in a number of ways. As you work on expressing your ideas in clear, accurate language, you will enhance your ability to think clearly and accurately. As you study the role of evidence and reasoning in speechmaking, you will see how they can be used in other forms of communication as well.

As you learn to listen critically to speeches in class, you will be better able to assess the ideas of speakers (and writers) in a variety of situations.[16]

To return to the four examples at the beginning of this section:

That guy at the party last night—would sharpened critical thinking have helped you pounce on the flaws in his argument?

Buying a word processor—are advertisements a reliable source of information, or should you try to find out more about prices and the features you need?

The term paper—would better organization and a clear outline help pull it together?

The politicians—once you filter out the fluff, are they drawing valid conclusions from sound evidence?

If you take full advantage of your speech class, you will be able to enhance your skills as a critical thinker in many circumstances. This is one reason public speaking has been regarded as a vital part of education since the days of ancient Greece.

THE SPEECH COMMUNICATION PROCESS

As you begin your first speeches, you may find it helpful to understand what goes on when one person talks to another. Regardless of the kind of speech communication involved, there are seven elements—speaker, message, channel, listener, feedback, interference, and situation. Here we shall focus on how these elements interact when a public speaker addresses an audience.

Speaker

Speech communication begins with a speaker. If you pick up the telephone and call a friend, you are acting as a speaker. (Of course, you will also act as a listener when your friend is talking.) In public speaking, you will usually present your entire speech without interruption.

Your success as a speaker depends on *you*—on your personal credibility, your knowledge of the subject, your preparation of the speech, your manner of speaking, your sensitivity to the audience and the occasion. But successful speaking is more than a matter of technical skill. It also requires enthusiasm. You can't expect people to be interested in what you say unless you are interested yourself. If you are truly excited about your subject, your audience is almost sure to get excited along with you. You can learn all the techniques of effective speechmaking, but before they can be of much use, you must first have something to say—something that sparks your own enthusiasm.

The powers of critical thinking you develop in researching and organizing public speeches can also be applied in many other forms of communication.

Message

The message is whatever a speaker communicates to someone else. If you are calling a friend, you might say, "I'll be a little late picking you up tonight." That is the message. But it may not be the only message. Perhaps there is a certain tone in your voice that suggests reluctance, hesitation. The underlying message might be "I really don't want to go to that party. You talked me into it, but I'm going to put it off as long as I can."

Your goal in public speaking is to have your *intended* message be the message that is *actually* communicated. Achieving this depends both on what you say (the verbal message) and on how you say it (the nonverbal message).

Getting the verbal message just right requires work. You must narrow your topic down to something you can discuss adequately in the time allowed for the speech. You must do research and choose supporting details to make your ideas clear and convincing. You must organize your ideas so listeners can follow them without getting lost. And you must express your message in words that are accurate, clear, vivid, and appropriate.

Besides the message you send with words, you also send a message with your tone of voice, appearance, gestures, facial expression, and eye contact. Imagine that one of your classmates gets up to speak about student loans. Throughout her speech she slumps behind the lectern, takes long pauses to remember what she wants to say, stares at the ceiling, and fumbles with her visual aids. Her intended message is "We must make more money available for student loans." But the message she actually communicates is "I haven't prepared very well for this speech." One of your jobs as a speaker is to make sure your nonverbal message does not distract from your verbal message.

Channel

The channel is the means by which a message is communicated. When you pick up the phone to call a friend, the telephone is the channel. Public speakers may use one or more of several channels, each of which will affect the message received by the audience.

Consider a speech to Congress by the President of the United States. The speech is carried to the nation by the channels of radio and television. For the radio audience the message is conveyed entirely by the President's voice. They can hear him, but they can't see him. For the television audience the message is conveyed by both the President's voice and the televised image of the President and his surroundings. The people in Congress have a more direct channel. They not only hear the President's voice as amplified through a microphone, but they see him and the setting at firsthand.

In a public speaking class your channel is the most direct of all. Your classmates will see you and hear you without any electronic intervention.

Listener

The listener is the person who receives the communicated message. Without a listener, there is no communication. When you talk to a friend on the phone, you have one listener. In public speaking you will have many listeners.

Everything a speaker says is filtered through a listener's *frame of reference*—the total of his or her knowledge, experience, goals, values, and attitudes. Because a speaker and a listener are different people, they can never have exactly the same frame of reference. And because a listener's frame of reference can never be exactly the same as a speaker's, the meaning of a message will never be exactly the same to a listener as to a speaker.

You can easily test the impact of different frames of reference. Ask each of your classmates to describe a chair. If you have fifteen classmates, you'll probably get fifteen different descriptions. One student might picture a large, overstuffed easy chair, another an elegant straight-backed chair, yet another an office chair, a fourth a rocking chair, and so on. Even if two or more envision the same general type—say a rocking chair—their mental images of the chair could still be different. One might be thinking of an early American rocker, another of a modern Scandinavian rocker—the possibilities are unlimited. And "chair" is a fairly simple concept. What about "patriotism" or "freedom"?

Because people have different frames of reference, a public speaker must take great care to adapt the message to the particular audience being addressed. To be an effective speaker, you must be *audience-centered*. You must do everything in your speech with your audience in mind. You cannot assume that listeners will be interested in what you have to say. You must understand their point of view as you prepare the speech, and you must work to get them involved. You will quickly lose your listeners' attention if your presentation is either too basic or too sophisticated. You will also lose your audience if you do not relate to *their* experience, interests, knowledge, and values. When you make a speech that causes listeners to say "That is important to *me,*" you will almost always be successful.

Feedback

When the President addresses the nation on television, he is engaged in one-way communication. You can talk back to the television set, but the President won't hear you. Most situations, however, involve *two-way* communication. Your listeners don't simply absorb your message like human sponges. They send back messages of their own. These messages are called feedback.

For example, when you phone your friend to say you will be late, you may hear, "Oh, no you don't! I don't care *what* your problem is; you get here on time!" That is feedback.

This kind of verbal give-and-take is unusual in public speaking. Still, there is always plenty of feedback to let you know how your message is being received. Do your listeners lean forward in their seats, as if paying close attention? Do they applaud in approval? Do they laugh at your jokes? Do they have quizzical looks on their faces? Do they shuffle their feet and gaze at the clock? The message sent by these reactions could be "I am fascinated," "I am bored," "I agree with you," "I don't agree with you," or any number of others. As a speaker, you need to be alert to these reactions and adjust your message accordingly.

Like any kind of communication, feedback is affected by one's frame of reference. How would you feel if, immediately after your speech, all your classmates started to rap their knuckles on the desks? Would you run out of the room in despair? Not if you were in a European university. In many parts of Europe, students rap their knuckles to show great admiration for a classroom lecture. You must understand the feedback to be able to deal with it.

There are still two more elements we must consider to understand fully what happens in speech communication.

Interference

Interference is anything that impedes the communication of a message. When you talk on the telephone, sometimes there is static, or wires get crossed so that two different conversations are going on at once. That is a kind of interference. Many classrooms are subject to interference—from traffic outside the building, the clatter of a radiator, students conversing in the hall. Any of these can distract your listeners from what you are saying.

There are also other sources of interference. Many of them come from *within* your audience rather than from the outside. Perhaps one of your listeners has a bad mosquito bite or a patch of poison ivy. She may be so distracted by the itch that she doesn't pay attention to your speech. Another listener may be worrying about a test coming up in the next class period. Yet another could be brooding about a fight he had with his girlfriend.

As a speaker, you must try to hold your listeners' attention despite these various kinds of interference. In the chapters that follow you will find many ways to do this.

Situation

The situation is the time and place in which speech communication occurs. Conversation always takes place in a certain situation. Sometimes the situation helps—as when you propose marriage over an intimate candlelight dinner. Other times it may hurt—as when you try to speak words of love in competition with a blaring stereo. When you have to talk with someone about a touchy issue, you usually wait until the situation is just right.

Public speakers must also be alert to the situation. Certain occasions—funerals, church services, graduation ceremonies—require certain kinds of speeches. Physical setting is also important. It makes a great deal of difference whether a speech is presented indoors or out, in a small classroom or in a gymnasium, to a densely packed crowd or to a handful of scattered souls. When you adjust to the situation of a public speech, you are only doing on a larger scale what you do every day in conversation.

Now let us look at a complete model of the speech communication process, as shown in Figure 1.1.[17]

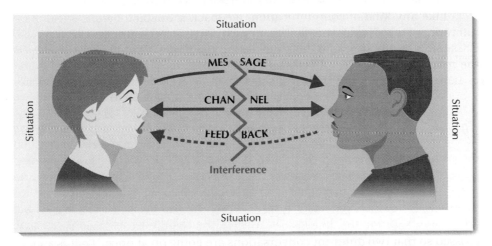

FIGURE 1.1

The Speech Communication Process: Example with Commentary

The following example shows how the various components of the speech communication process interact:

Situation   *The afternoon was warm and sunny, perfect for the first annual Pacific Culture Festival.* Up and down the plaza, families were busy making Japanese paper cranes, watching Indonesian puppeteers and Mexican dancers, tasting foods from Thailand, Vietnam, and other countries of the Pacific Rim.

Speaker   But *Migdalia Rivera,* the festival organizer, was worried. The president of the festival's main corporate sponsor had just arrived—almost an hour late. A large crowd had gathered in front of the stage, waiting for the opening ceremonies, which Migdalia had delayed until the president got there.

Listeners   As Migdalia led the president toward the stage, she saw that *the audience was made up mainly of families, many with toddlers.* Most were the parents and siblings of children who were scheduled to perform in the opening ceremonies. Many had grown impatient, but

Message   *Migdalia hoped to recapture their interest with her opening speech. She wanted the crowd to give the president a warm reception.* Funding for next year's festival might depend on it.

Channel   Migdalia stepped to the *microphone* and began her speech. As
Feedback she spoke, *she could see people looking at their watches and whis-*
Interference *pering to one another. A number of young children were out of their seats, making if difficult for others in the audience to hear.* Migdalia knew she had to act quickly.

Dealing with   *"I'm glad to see so many children here today,"* she said, *"because*
Interference *our opening show is going to be a special treat. Are you ready for a treat?* I know I am. The reason we're running late is because I wanted one very special guest to arrive before we began. I wanted him to see these wonderful opening ceremonies. I wanted him to see what our children can do. Because once he does, I think he'll be as proud as we are of their talents and accomplishments. Personally, I'm glad we waited, and I think once you meet our guest, you'll be glad too."

Feedback   *Most of the audience, including the children, were now listening intently, and quite a few were smiling.* Migdalia could see their mood had changed. When she introduced the president, he was greeted with enthusiastic applause. The president was visibly pleased. As he took the microphone, he apologized for being late and promised his support for future festivals. When he had finished speaking, he sat down next to Migdalia. "Thanks," he said to her as he took his seat. "That was very, very nice."

◼ PUBLIC SPEAKING IN A MULTICULTURAL WORLD

Cultural Diversity in the Modern World

The United States has always been a diverse society. In 1673, more than three centuries ago, a visitor to what is now New York City was astonished to find that eighteen languages were spoken among the city's 8,000 inhabitants.[18] By the middle of the nineteenth century, so many people from so many lands had come to the United States that novelist Herman Melville exclaimed, "You cannot spill a drop of American blood without spilling the blood of the whole world."[19]

One can only imagine what Melville would say today! The United States has become the most diverse society on the face of the earth. For more than a century, most immigrants to the U.S. were Europeans—Irish, Germans, English, Scandinavians, Greeks, Poles, Italians, and others. Together with African Americans, they made America the "melting pot" of the world. Today another great wave of immigration—more than 1 million people a year, mostly from Asia and Latin America—is transforming the United States into what one writer has called "the first universal nation," a multicultural society of unmatched diversity.[20]

The diversity of life in the United States can be seen in cities and towns, schools and businesses, community groups and houses of worship all across the land. Consider the following:

- Forty percent of first-year students at UCLA are of Asian descent; 17 percent of the total student population is Hispanic.

- New York City has over 170 distinct ethnic communities.

- More than 127 languages and dialects are spoken by students in the Washington, D.C., school system.

- Los Angeles has more people of Mexican origin than any city in the world except Mexico City.

- More than 60 percent of the people in Miami were born outside the United States.

- If current trends continue, people of European descent will become a minority of U.S. citizens sometime after the middle of the next century.

Nor are these kinds of changes limited to the United States. We are living in an age of international multiculturalism. Fax machines and computer networks allow almost instant communication around the world. CNN is broadcast in more than 140 countries. International air travel has made national boundaries almost meaningless. All nations, all people, all cultures are becoming part of a vast global village. For example:[21]

- In Brussels, the center of the European Community, one in every four new babies is Arabic.

- Korean neighborhoods abound in the South American city of Asunción, the capital of Paraguay.

- There are more than 40,000 Canadians living in Hong Kong.

- Restaurants in coastal towns of Queensland, Australia, print their menus in both Japanese and English.

- More than 5,000 foreign businesses have offices in the United States, and foreigners own 13 percent of all U.S. industrial assets.

- Over 8,000 U.S. firms operate abroad, and more than 2.5 million American citizens live and work in foreign lands.

Cultural Diversity and Public Speaking

"That's all very interesting," you may be saying to yourself, "but what does it have to do with my speeches?" The answer is that diversity and multiculturalism are such basic facts of life in today's world that they can play a role in almost any speech you give. Consider the following situations: A business manager briefing employees of a multinational corporation. A lawyer presenting her closing argument to an ethnically mixed jury. A minister sermonizing to a culturally diverse congregation. An international student explaining the customs of his land to students in a U.S. university. A teacher addressing parents at a multiethnic urban school. These are only a few of the countless speaking situations affected by the cultural diversity of modern life.

As experts in intercultural communication have long known, speechmaking becomes more complex as cultural diversity increases. Part of the complexity stems from the differences in language from culture to culture. As we shall see in Chapter 11, language and thought are closely linked. So, too, are language and culture. Nothing separates one culture from another more than language. Not only do words change from language to language, but so do ways of thinking and of seeing the world. Language and culture are so closely bound that "we communicate the way we do because we are raised in a particular culture and learn its language, rules, and norms."[22]

The meanings attached to gestures, facial expressions, and other nonverbal signals also vary from culture to culture. Even the gestures for such basic messages as "yes" and "no," "hello" and "goodbye" are culturally based. In the United States people nod their heads up and down to signal "yes" and shake them back and forth to signal "no." In Thailand the same actions have exactly the opposite meaning! To take another example, the North American "goodbye" wave is interpreted in many parts of Europe and South America as the motion for "no," while the Italian and Greek gesture for "goodbye" is the same as the U.S. signal for "come here."[23]

Many stories have been told about the fate of public speakers who fail to take account of cultural differences between themselves and their audiences. Consider the following scenario:[24]

The sales manager of a U.S. electronics firm is in Brazil to negotiate a large purchase of computers by a South American corporation. After three days of negoti-

The diversity of modern life can affect almost any public speaking situation. If you are to be successful as a speaker, you must be responsive to the cultural values and expectations of your listeners.

ations, the sales manager holds a gala reception for all the major executives to build good will between the companies.

As is the custom on such occasions, time is set aside during the reception for an exchange of toasts. When it is the sales manager's turn to speak, he praises the Brazilian firm for its many achievements and talks eloquently of his respect for its president and other executives. The words are perfect, and the sales manager can see his audience smiling in approval.

And then—disaster. As the sales manager closes his speech, he raises his hand and flashes the classic U.S. "Okay" sign to signal his pleasure at the progress of the negotiations. Instantly the festive mood is replaced with stony silence; smiles turn to icy stares. The sales manager has given his Brazilian audience a gesture with roughly the same meaning as an extended middle finger in the United States.

The next day the Brazilian firm announces it will buy its computers from another company.

As this scenario illustrates, public speakers can ill afford to overlook their listeners' cultural values and customs. This is true whether you are speaking at home or abroad, in Atlanta or Rio de Janeiro, in a college classroom or at a meeting of community volunteers. Because of the increasing diversity of modern life, many—perhaps most—of the audiences you address will include people of different cultural backgrounds.

As you read the rest of this book, you will learn the methods of effective public speaking. Almost all of those methods will be helpful to you in speaking to culturally diverse audiences. Here we need to stress the importance of avoiding the ethnocentrism that often blocks communication between speakers and listeners of different cultural, racial, and ethnic backgrounds.

Avoiding Ethnocentrism

Ethnocentrism is the belief that our own group or culture—whatever it may be—is superior to all other groups or cultures. Because of ethnocentrism, we identify with our group or culture and see its values, beliefs, and customs as "right" or "natural"—in comparison to the values, beliefs, and customs of other groups or cultures, which we tend to think of as "wrong" or "unnatural."[25]

Ethnocentrism is part of every culture. If you were born and raised in the United States, you may find it strange that most people in India regard the cow as a sacred animal and forego using it as a source of food. On the other hand, if you were born and raised in India, you might well be shocked at the use of cows in the United States for food, clothing, and other consumer goods. If you are Christian, you most likely think of Sunday as the "normal" day of worship. But if you are Jewish, you probably regard Saturday as the "correct" sabbath. And if you are Muslim, you doubtless see both Saturday and Sunday as unusual times for worship. For you, Friday is the "right" day.

Ethnocentrism can play a positive role in creating group pride and loyalty. But it can also be a destructive force—especially when it leads to prejudice and hostility toward different racial, ethnic, or cultural groups. To be an effective public speaker in a multicultural world, you need to keep in mind that all people have their special beliefs and customs.[26]

Avoiding ethnocentrism does not mean you must agree with the values and practices of all groups and cultures. At times you might try to convince people of different cultures to change their traditional ways of doing things—as speakers from the United Nations seek to persuade farmers in Africa to adopt more productive methods of agriculture, as Muslim parents in the United States urge public school officials to accommodate Muslim customs for children who adhere to Islam, or as delegates from the U.S. and Japan attempt to influence the other country's trade policies.

If such speakers are to be successful, however, they must show respect for the cultures of the people they address. They cannot assume that their cultural assumptions and practices will be shared—or even understood—by all members of their audience. They need to adapt their message to the cultural values and expectations of their listeners.

When you work on your speeches, keep in mind the growing diversity of life in the modern world and be alert to how cultural factors might affect the way listeners respond to your speeches. As we shall see in Chapter 5, for classroom speeches you can use audience-analysis questionnaires to learn about the backgrounds and opinions of your classmates in regard to specific speech topics. For speeches outside the classroom, the person who invites you to speak can usually provide information about the audience.

Once you know about any cultural factors that might affect the audience's response to your speech, you can work on adapting the speech to make it as effective and appropriate as possible. As you prepare the speech, try to put yourself in the place of your listeners and to hear your message through their ears. If there is a language difference between you and your audience, avoid any words or phrases that might cause misunderstanding. When researching the speech, keep an eye out for examples, comparisons, and other supporting materials that will relate to a wide range of listeners. Also, consider using visual aids in your speech. As we shall see in Chapter 13, they can be especially helpful in bridging a gap in language or cultural background.

When delivering your speech, be alert to feedback that might indicate the audience is having trouble grasping your ideas. If you see puzzled expressions on the faces of your listeners, restate your point to make sure it is understood. With some audiences, you can encourage feedback by asking, "Am I making myself clear?" or, "Did I explain this point fully enough?" If you pose such questions, however, be aware that listeners from various cultures may respond quite differently. Most Arabs, North Americans, and Europeans will give you fairly direct feedback if you ask for it. Listeners from Asian and Caribbean countries, on the other hand, may not respond out of concern for showing disrespect for the speaker. (See Chapter 5 for a full discussion of audience analysis and adaptation.)

Finally, we should note the importance of avoiding ethnocentrism when listening to speeches. As we shall see in Chapters 2 and 3, speech audiences have a responsibility to listen courteously and attentively. When you listen to a speaker from a different cultural background, be on guard against the temptation to judge that speaker on the basis of her or his appearance or manner of delivery. Too often we form opinions about people by the way they look or speak rather than by listening closely to what they *say*. No matter what the cultural background of the speaker, you should listen to her or him as attentively as you would want your audience to listen to you.

SUMMARY

The need for effective public speaking will almost certainly touch you sometime in your life. When it does, you want to be ready. But even if you never give another speech in your life, you still have much to gain from studying public speaking. Your speech class will give you training in researching topics, organizing your ideas, and presenting yourself skillfully. This training is invaluable for every type of communication.

There are many similarities between public speaking and daily conversation. The three major goals of public speaking—to inform, to persuade, to entertain—are also the three major goals of everyday conversation. In conversation, almost without thinking about it, you employ a wide range of skills. You organize your ideas logically. You tailor your message to your audience. You tell a story for maximum impact. You adapt to feedback from your listener. These are among the most important skills you will need for public speaking.

Public speaking is also different from conversation. First, public speaking is more highly structured than conversation. It usually imposes strict time limitations on the speaker, and it requires more detailed preparation than does ordinary conversation. Second, public speaking requires more formal language. Listeners react negatively to speeches loaded with slang, jargon, and bad grammar. Third, public speaking demands a different method of delivery. Effective speakers adjust their voices to the larger audience and work at avoiding distracting physical mannerisms and verbal habits.

One of the major concerns of students in any speech class is stage fright. Actually, most successful speakers are nervous before making a speech. Your speech class will give you an opportunity to gain confidence and make your nervousness work for you rather than against you. You will take a big step toward overcoming stage fright if you think positively, choose speech topics you really care about, prepare thoroughly, and concentrate on communicating with your audience. Like other students over the years, you too can develop confidence in your speechmaking abilities.

Besides building your confidence, a course in public speaking can help develop your skills as a critical thinker. Critical thinking is the ability to perceive relationships among ideas. It can help you spot weaknesses in other people's reasoning and avoid them in your own. Critical thinking can make a difference in many areas of your life, from your schoolwork to your activities as a consumer to your responsibilities as a citizen.

The speech communication process as a whole includes seven elements—speaker, message, channel, listener, feedback, interference, and situation. The speaker is the person who initiates a speech transaction. Whatever the speaker communicates is the message, which is sent by means of a particular channel. The listener receives the communicated message and provides feedback to the speaker. Interference is anything that impedes the communication of a message, while the situation is the time and place in which speech communication occurs. The interaction of these seven elements is what determines the outcome in any instance of speech communication.

Because of the growing diversity of modern life, many—perhaps most—of the audiences you address will include people of different cultural, racial, and ethnic backgrounds. When you work on your speeches, be alert to how such factors might affect the responses of your listeners and take steps to adapt your message accordingly. Above all, avoid the ethnocentric belief that your own culture or group—whatever it may be—is superior to every other culture or group. Also keep in mind the importance of avoiding ethnocentrism when listening to speeches. Accord every speaker the same courtesy and attentiveness you would want from your listeners.

REVIEW QUESTIONS

After reading this chapter, you should be able to answer the following questions:

1. In what ways is public speaking likely to make a difference in your life?

2. How is public speaking similar to everyday conversation?

3. How is public speaking different from everyday conversation?

4. Why is it normal—even desirable—to be nervous at the start of a speech?

5. How can you control your nervousness and make it work for you in your speeches?

6. What are the seven elements of the speech communication process? How do they interact to determine the success or failure of a speech?

7. What is ethnocentrism? Why do public speakers need to avoid ethnocentrism when addressing audiences with diverse cultural, racial, or ethnic backgrounds?

APPLICATION EXERCISES

1. Think back on an important conversation you had recently in which you wanted to achieve a particular result. (*Examples:* Trying to convince your parents you should live in off-campus housing rather than in a dormitory; asking your employer to change your work schedule; explaining to a friend how to change the oil and filter in a car; trying to persuade a professor to accept your term paper a week late; attempting to talk your spouse into buying the VCR you like rather than the one he or she prefers.) Work up a brief analysis of the conversation.

   In your analysis, explain the following: (1) your purpose in the conversation and the message strategy you chose to achieve your purpose; (2) the communication channels used during the conversation and how they affected the outcome; (3) the interference—internal or external—you encountered during the conversation; (4) the steps you took to adjust to feedback; (5) the strategic changes you would make in preparing for and carrying out the conversation if you had it to do over again.

2. Divide a sheet of paper into two columns. Label one column "Characteristics of an Effective Public Speaker." Label the other column "Characteristics of an Ineffective Public Speaker." In the columns, list and briefly explain what you believe to be the five most important characteristics of effective and ineffective speakers. Be prepared to discuss your ideas in class.

3. On the basis of the lists you developed for Exercise 2, candidly evaluate your own strengths and weaknesses as a speaker. Identify the three primary aspects of speechmaking you most want to improve.

NOTES

[1] Quoted in Richard Whately, *Elements of Rhetoric,* 7th ed. (London: John W. Parker, 1846), p. 10.

[2] Dan B. Curtis, Jerry L. Winsor, and Ronald D. Stephens, "National Preferences in Business and Communication Education," *Communication Education,* 38 (1989), 6–14.

[3] Quoted in Sharon Nelson, "Address for Success," *Nation's Business* (February 1991), pp. 43–44.

[4] A number of studies have shown the importance of public speaking to people in all walks of life. See, for example, Kathleen Edgerton Kendall, "Do Real People Ever Give Speeches?" (Paper presented at Eastern Communication Association meeting, May 1985).

[5] Compiled from Daniel Shaw, "The Messenger," *Town and Country* (December 1992); Frank Bruni, "Coming Out against AIDS," *Detroit Free Press* (February 13, 1992); and materials provided by Family AIDS Network, Inc., Grand Rapids, Michigan. For the full text of Fisher's August 1992 speech to the Republican National Convention, see the Appendix, pages 439–462.

[6] "What Are Americans Afraid Of?" *The Bruskin Report,* 53 (July 1973).

[7] Daniel Goleman, "Social Anxiety: New Focus Leads to Insights and Therapy," *New York Times* (December 18, 1984).

[8] Jeffrey C. Hahner, Martin A. Sokoloff, and Sandra L. Salisch, *Speaking Clearly: Improving Voice and Diction,* 4th ed. (New York: McGraw-Hill, 1993), p. 368.

[9] Quoted in Bert E. Bradley, *Fundamentals of Speech Communication: The Credibility of Ideas,* 6th ed. (Dubuque, Iowa: W.C. Brown, 1991), p. 31.

[10] A number of studies have shown that taking a public speaking course is effective in reducing stage fright. Among the most recent are Lynne Kelly and James Keaten, "A Test of the Effectiveness of the Reticence Program at the Pennsylvania State University," *Communication Education,* 41 (1992), 361–374; Heidi M. Rose, Andrew S. Rancer, and Kenneth C. Crannell, "The Impact of a Basic Course in Oral Interpretation and Public Speaking on Communication Apprehension," *Communication Reports,* 6 (1993), 54–60.

[11] For research on this point, see Kent E. Menzel and Lori J. Carrell, "The Relationship Between Preparation and Performance in Public Speaking," *Communication Education,* 43 (1994), 17–26.

[12] For fuller discussion of these and other approaches to reducing stage fright, see William J. Fremouw and Joseph L. Breitenstein, "Speech Anxiety," in Harold Leitenberg (ed.), *Handbook of Social and Evaluation Anxiety* (New York: Plenum Press, 1990), pp. 455–474; Joe Ayres and Tim S. Hopf, *Coping with Speech Anxiety* (Norwood, N.J.: Ablex, 1993).

[13] Marianne Martini, Ralph R. Behnke, and Paul E. King, "The Communication of Public Speaking Anxiety: Perceptions of Asian and American Speakers," *Communication Quarterly,* 40 (1992), 279–288.

[14] See, for example, Wendy S. Zabava Ford and Andrew D. Wolvin, "The Differential Impact of a Basic Communication Course on Perceived Competencies in Class, Work, and Social Contexts," *Communication Education,* 42 (1993), 215–223.

[15] For a review of various concepts of critical thinking, see Joanne Gainen Kurfiss, *Critical Thinking: Theory, Research, Practice, and Possibilities* (Washington, D.C.: Association for Study of Higher Education, 1988).

[16] Virginia P. O'Keefe, *Affecting Critical Thinking Through Speech* (Urbana, Ill.: ERIC Clearinghouse on Reading and Communication Skills, 1986); Paul A. Fritz and Richard L. Weaver II, "Teaching Critical Thinking in the Basic Speaking Course: A Liberal Arts Perspective," *Communication Education,* 35 (1986), 174–182.

[17] For other models of the speech communication process, see Brent D. Ruben, *Communication and Human Behavior,* 3rd ed. (Englewood Cliffs, N.J.: Prentice-Hall, 1992), pp. 20–49; Em Griffin, *A First Look at Communication Theory,* 2nd ed. (New York: McGraw-Hill, 1994).

[18] John Elson, "The Great Migration," *Time* (Fall 1993), p. 30. For a detailed look at the cultural diversity of colonial America, see Bernard Bailyn and Philip D. Morgan (eds.), *Strangers Within the Realm: Cultural Margins of the First British Empire* (Chapel Hill, N.C.: University of North Carolina Press, 1991).

[19] Quoted in Ronald Takai, *A Different Mirror: A History of Multicultural America* (Boston: Little, Brown, 1993), p. 427.

[20] Ben J. Wattenberg, *The First Universal Nation: Leading Indicators and Ideas About the Surge of America in the 1990s* (New York: Free Press, 1991). Also see Lawrence H. Fuchs, *The American Kaleidoscope: Race, Ethnicity, and the Civic Culture* (Hanover, N.H.: University Press of New England, 1990).

[21] Pico Iyer, "The Global Village Finally Arrives," *Time* (Fall 1993), pp. 86–87.

[22] William B. Gudykunst and Young Yun Kim, *Communicating with Strangers: An Approach to Intercultural Communication,* 2nd ed. (New York: McGraw-Hill, 1992), p. 4. For more detail, see Larry A. Samovar and Richard E. Porter, *Communication Between Cultures* (Belmont, Calif.: Wadsworth, 1991), pp. 151–158.

[23] For an entertaining look at nonverbal signals in different cultures, see Roger E. Axtell, *Gestures: The Do's and Taboos of Body Language Around the World* (New York: Wiley, 1991).

[24] Adapted from Roger E. Axtell (ed.), *Do's and Taboos Around the World,* 3rd ed. (New York: Wiley, 1993), p. 41.

[25] Myron W. Lustig and Jolene Koester, *Intercultural Competence: Interpersonal Communication Across Cultures* (New York: HarperCollins, 1993), pp. 92–96.

[26] Gudykunst and Kim, *Communicating with Strangers,* p. 5. Also see Donald W. Klopf, *Intercultural Encounters: The Fundamentals of Intercultural Communication,* 2nd ed. (Englewood, Co.: Morton, 1991), pp. 95–100.

Chapter 2

Ethics and
Public Speaking

THE IMPORTANCE OF ETHICS

GUIDELINES FOR ETHICAL SPEAKING
Make Sure Your Goals Are Ethically Sound
Be Fully Prepared for Each Speech
Be Honest in What You Say
Avoid Name-Calling and Other Forms of Abusive Language
Put Ethical Principles into Practice

PLAGIARISM
Global Plagiarism
Patchwork Plagiarism
Incremental Plagiarism

GUIDELINES FOR ETHICAL LISTENING
Be Courteous and Attentive
Avoid Prejudging the Speaker
Maintain the Free and Open Expression of Ideas

Sharon Rakove is assistant director of public relations for a large land development firm. On this particular evening, she is speaking to a packed meeting of the city planning board in an effort to gain approval for a controversial new industrial complex near a residential neighborhood. Although a private study has shown that the complex will reduce property values in the neighborhood by as much as 20 percent, Sharon, who has read the study, tells the board there is no evidence the complex will harm home owners. The board, which does not know about the study, accepts Sharon's word and votes for the project.

Two years later, after the industrial complex has been built, property values in the neighborhood are down 17 percent. Home owners with young children are strapped with mortgages larger than the value of their houses. Older residents, who had planned to sell their homes to help finance their retirements, are forced to change plans. And Sharon Rakove? Once a rising star in the land development firm, she has been denounced by the press and fired by her company. She has moved to another city where she hopes to find work in a different occupation.

This is not a happy story, but it shows why speechmaking needs to be guided by a strong sense of integrity. Sharon Rakove was persuasive when speaking to the city planning board, but she was unethical in not disclosing the impact of the commercial complex on home owners. As a result, hundreds of people have suffered—including Sharon herself.

You might be saying to yourself, "Yes, that's very unfortunate. But lots of people lie and cheat, and many of them don't get caught." And you would be correct—many people don't get caught. But that doesn't make their behavior right. In public speaking, as in other areas of life, there are standards for ethical conduct.

The goal of public speaking is to gain a desired response from listeners—but not at any cost. Speechmaking is a form of power and therefore carries with it heavy ethical responsibilities. As the Roman rhetorician Quintilian stated 2,000 years ago, the ideal of commendable speechmaking is the good person speaking well. In this chapter, we explore that ideal by looking at the importance of ethics in public speaking, the ethical obligations of speakers and listeners, and the practical problem of plagiarism and how to avoid it.

THE IMPORTANCE OF ETHICS

Ethics is the branch of philosophy that deals with issues of right and wrong in human affairs. Questions of ethics arise whenever we ask whether a course of action is moral or immoral, fair or unfair, just or unjust, honest or dishonest.[1]

We face such questions daily in almost every part of our lives. The parent must decide how to deal with a child who has been sent home from school for unruly behavior. The researcher must decide whether to shade her data "just a bit" in order to gain credit for an important scientific breakthrough. The shopper must decide what to do with the $5 extra change mistakenly given by the clerk at the grocery store. The student must decide whether to say anything about a friend he has seen cheating on a final exam.

Questions of ethics also come into play whenever a public speaker faces an audience. In an ideal world, as the Greek philosopher Plato noted, all public speakers would be truthful and devoted to the good of society. Yet history tells us that the power of speech is often abused—sometimes with disastrous results. Adolf Hitler was unquestionably a persuasive speaker. His oratory galvanized the German people into following one ideal and one leader. But his aims were horrifying and his tactics despicable. He remains to this day the ultimate example of why the power of the spoken word needs to be guided by a strong sense of ethical integrity.

As a public speaker, you will face ethical issues at every stage of the speechmaking process—from the initial decision to speak through the final presentation of the message. This is true whether you are speaking in the classroom or the courtroom, whether you are participating in a business meeting or a religious service, whether you are addressing an audience of two people or two thousand people. And the answers will not always be easy. Consider the following example:

Felicia Robinson is running for school board in a large eastern city. Her opponent is conducting what Felicia regards as a highly unethical campaign. In addition to twisting the facts about school taxes, the opponent is pandering to racial prejudice by raising resentment against African Americans and newly arrived immigrants.

Five days before the election, Felicia, who is slightly behind in the polls, learns that the district attorney is preparing to indict her opponent for shady business practices. But the indictment will not be formally issued until after the election. Nor can it be taken as evidence that her opponent is guilty—like all citizens, he has the right to be presumed innocent until proven otherwise.

Still, news of the indictment could be enough to throw the election Felicia's way, and her advisers urge her to make it an issue in her remaining campaign speeches. Should Felicia follow their advice?

There are creditable arguments to be made on both sides of the ethical dilemma faced by Felicia Robinson. She has tried to run an honest campaign, and she is troubled by the possibility of unfairly attacking her opponent—despite the fact that he has shown no such scruples himself. Yet she knows that the impending indictment may be her last chance to win the election, and she is convinced that a victory for her opponent will spell disaster for the city's school system. Torn between her commitment to fair play, her desire to be elected, and her concern for the good of the community, she faces the age-old ethical dilemma of whether the ends justify the means.

"So," you may be saying to yourself, "what is the answer to Felicia Robinson's dilemma?" But in complex cases such as hers there are no cut-and-dried answers. As Richard Johannesen, a leader in the study of communication ethics, states, "We should formulate meaningful ethical guidelines, not inflexible rules."[2] Your ethical decisions will be guided by your values, your conscience, your sense of right and wrong.

But this does not mean such decisions are simply a matter of personal whim or fancy. Sound ethical decisions involve weighing a potential course of action against a set of ethical standards or guidelines. Just as there are guidelines for ethical behavior in other areas of life, so are there guidelines for ethical conduct in public speaking. These guidelines will not automatically solve every ethical quandary you face as a speaker, but knowing them will provide a reliable compass to help you find your way.

GUIDELINES FOR ETHICAL SPEAKING

Make Sure Your Goals Are Ethically Sound

Not long ago, I spoke with a former student—we'll call her Melissa—who had turned down a job in the public relations department of the American Tobacco Institute. Why? Not because of the salary (which was generous) or the work schedule (which was ideal). Melissa declined the job because it would have required her to lobby on behalf of the cigarette industry. Knowing that cigarettes are the number-one health hazard in the United States, Melissa did not believe she could ethically promote a product that she saw as responsible for thousands of deaths and illnesses each year.

Given Melissa's view of the dangers of cigarette smoking, there can be no doubt that she made an ethically informed decision to turn down the job with the American Tobacco Institute. On the other side of the coin, someone with a different view of cigarette smoking could make an ethically informed decision to *take* the job. The point of this example is not to judge the rightness or wrongness of Melissa's decision (or of cigarette smoking), but to illustrate how ethical considerations can affect a speaker's choice of goals.

Your first responsibility as a speaker is to ask whether your goals are ethically sound. During World War II, Hitler stirred the German people to condone war, invasion, and genocide. More recently, we have seen politicians who betray the public trust for personal gain, business leaders who defraud investors of millions of dollars, preachers who lead lavish lifestyles at the expense of their religious duties. There can be no doubt that these are not worthy goals.

But think back for a moment to the examples of speechmaking given in Chapter 1. What do the speakers hope to accomplish? Report on a business project. Improve the quality of education. Pay tribute to a fellow worker. Stop the plague of drug use among young Americans. Support the Special Olympics. Few people would question that these goals are ethically sound.

As with other ethical issues, there can be gray areas when it comes to assessing a speaker's goals—areas in which reasonable people with well-defined standards of right and wrong can legitimately disagree. But this is not a reason to avoid asking ethical questions. If you are to be a responsible public speaker, you cannot escape assessing the ethical soundness of your goals.

Be Fully Prepared for Each Speech

"A speech," as Jenkin Lloyd Jones noted, "is a solemn responsibility." You have an obligation—to yourself and to your listeners—to prepare fully every time you stand in front of an audience. The obligation to yourself is obvious: The better you prepare, the better your speech will be. But the obligation to your listeners is no less important. Think of it this way: The person who makes a bad 30-minute speech to an audience of 200 people wastes only a half-hour of her or his own time. But that same speaker wastes 100 hours of the audience's time—more than four full days. This, Jones exclaimed, "should be a hanging offense!"

At this stage of your speaking career, of course, you will probably not be facing many audiences of 200 people. And you will probably not be giving many speeches in which the audience has come for the sole purpose of listening to you. But neither the size nor the composition of your audience changes your ethical responsibility to be fully prepared. Your speech classmates are as worthy of your best effort as if you were addressing a jury or a business meeting, a union conference or a church congregation, the local Rotary Club or even the United States Senate.

Being prepared for a speech involves everything from analyzing your audience to creating visual aids, organizing your ideas to rehearsing your delivery. Most crucial from an ethical standpoint, though, is being fully informed about your subject. Why is this so important? Consider the following story:

Several years ago Manuel Higuera, a student at a large California university, gave a classroom speech demonstrating how to use the Heimlich maneuver to dislodge a piece of food trapped in a person's windpipe. Manuel had learned the maneuver from his mother, a Red Cross worker, but he did not rely on that knowledge alone in preparing his speech. He read several magazine articles about the Heimlich maneuver, and he picked up a pamphlet from the local fire department explaining how to perform the maneuver.

In addition to his research, Manuel gave a lot of thought to organizing and delivering his speech. He even got a friend to serve as a volunteer on whom he could demonstrate the steps of the Heimlich maneuver for his classmates. By the day of his speech, Manuel was thoroughly prepared—and he gave an excellent presentation.

No more than a week later, one of Manuel's classmates, Alison Bartlett, was eating dinner in her apartment when her roommate began choking on a piece of food. Remembering Manuel's speech, Alison went into action with the Heimlich maneuver. First she got her roommate to stand up. Then she put her arms around her roommate's waist, made a fist with one hand, pressed it into her roommate's abdomen, and exerted several quick upward thrusts until the food popped out. Alison saved her roommate's life, thanks to Manuel's speech.

This is an especially dramatic case, but it demonstrates how your speeches can have a genuine impact on your listeners' lives. As a speaker, you have an ethical responsibility to consider that impact and to make sure you prepare fully so as not to communicate erroneous information or misleading advice. Imagine what might have happened if Manuel had not done such a thorough job researching his speech. He might have given his classmates faulty instructions about the Heimlich maneuver—instructions that might have had tragic results.

No matter what the topic, no matter what the audience, you need to explore your speech topic as thoroughly as possible. Investigate the whole story, learn about all sides of an issue, seek out competing viewpoints, get the facts right. Not only will you give a better speech, you will also fulfill one of your major ethical obligations.

Be Honest in What You Say

Nothing is more important to ethical speechmaking than honesty. Public speaking rests on the unspoken assumption that "words can be trusted and people will be truthful."[3] Without this assumption, there is no basis for communication, no reason for one person to believe anything that another person says. Once the bond of trust between a speaker and listener is broken, it can never be fully restored.

Does this mean *every* speaker must *always* tell "the truth, the whole truth, and nothing but the truth"? We can all think of situations in which this is impossible (because we do not know the whole truth) or inadvisable (because it would be tactless or imprudent). Consider a presidential press secretary who denies the existence of secret diplomatic negotiations because she does not know they are taking place. Or a parent who tells his two-year-old daughter that her screeching violin solo is "beautiful." Or a speaker who tells a falsehood in circumstances when disclosing the truth might touch off mob violence. Few people would find these actions unethical.[4]

In contrast, think back to the case of Sharon Rakove at the start of this chapter. Sharon knew, from a private study, that the industrial complex she was backing would reduce property values in the nearby residential neighborhood. Yet she told the planning board there was "no evidence" the complex would harm home owners. The planning board accepted her word and voted for the project. There is no way to excuse Sharon's conduct. She told a flat-out lie for personal gain without regard to its consequences on the audience.

Such blatant contempt for the truth is one kind of dishonesty in public speaking. But there are more subtle forms of dishonesty that are just as unethical. They include juggling statistics, quoting out of context, misrepresenting the sources of facts and figures, painting tentative findings as firm conclusions, portraying a few details as the whole story, citing unusual cases as typical examples, and substituting innuendo and half-truths for evidence and proof. All of these violate the speaker's duty to be accurate and fair in presenting information.

While on the subject of honesty in speechmaking, we should also note that ethically responsible speakers do not present other people's words as their own. They do not plagiarize their speeches. This subject is so important that we devote a separate section to it later in this chapter.

Avoid Name-Calling and Other Forms of Abusive Language

"Sticks and stones can break my bones, but words can never hurt me." This popular children's chant could not be more wrong. Words may not literally break people's bones, but they are powerful weapons that can leave psychological scars as surely as sticks and stones can leave physical scars. As one writer explains, "Our identities, who and what we are, how others see us, are greatly affected by the names we are called and the words with which we are labelled."[5] This is why almost all communication ethicists warn public speakers to avoid name-calling and other forms of abusive language.

Name-Calling and Personal Dignity   Name-calling is the use of language to defame, demean, or degrade other individuals or groups. When applied to ethnic and religious groups in America, it includes such epithets as "kike," "nigger," "wop," "jap," "chink," and "spic." Such terms have been used to debase people of Jewish, African, Italian, Japanese, Chinese, and Hispanic ancestry. These words dehumanize the groups they are directed against. They imply that the groups are inferior and do not deserve to be treated with the same dignity and respect as other members of society.

The same is true of sexist language. We have come to understand in recent years how the English language is riddled with sexism. Most blatant is the generic "he," which excludes women from whatever group is being discussed—as in, "When a college student studies for an exam, he should be sure to review all his lecture notes." Not only does this imply that women do not attend college, but it overlooks the fact that women now outnumber men on most campuses. There are also countless words and phrases that convey negative, stereotyped, or misleading views of women. Some disparage, patronize, or ridicule ("little woman," "chick," "dumb blonde"); others imply second-class status ("the other sex," "the weaker sex"); still others classify women in ways that are seldom applied to men ("coed," "woman pioneer," "unchaste").[6]

In Chapter 11 we will look at ways you can avoid sexist language in your speeches. For now the point to remember is that, contrary to what some people claim, avoiding racist, sexist, and other kinds of abusive language is not simply a matter of "political correctness." Such language is ethically suspect because it devalues the people in question and stereotypes them in ways that assume the innate superiority of one group over another. This principle applies whether the group is being maligned for its gender, religion, ethnic background, sexual orientation, or physical or mental disability. The issue is not one of politics, but of respecting the dignity of the diverse groups in contemporary society.

Questions of ethics arise whenever a speaker faces an audience. Among current public speakers, Barbara Jordan is highly regarded for her combination of ethical integrity and powerful audience appeal.

Name-Calling and Free Speech   Name-calling and abusive language also pose ethical problems in public speaking when they are used to silence opposing voices. A democratic society depends upon the free and open expression of ideas. In the United States, all citizens have the right to join in the never-ending dialogue of democracy. As a public speaker, you have an ethical obligation to help preserve that right by avoiding tactics such as name-calling that automatically impugn the accuracy or respectability of public statements made by groups or individuals who voice opinions different from yours.[7]

This obligation is the same regardless of whether you are black or white, Asian or Hispanic, male or female, Republican or Democrat, liberal or conservative. An office seeker who castigates everyone opposed to her election as "blatant sexists" regardless of the reasons for their opposition would be on as thin ice ethically as a politician who labels his adversary a "wild-eyed feminist" when he knows full well the charge is untrue. No matter what your stand on particular issues, you have an ethical responsibility to avoid name-calling and other tactics that harm the free and open expression of ideas.

Like other ethical questions in public speaking, name-calling raises some thorny issues. Although name-calling can be hazardous to free speech, it is still protected under the free speech clause of the Bill of Rights. This is why the American Civil Liberties Union, a major defender of constitutional rights, has opposed broadly worded codes against abusive speech on college campuses. Such codes usually prohibit threatening or insulting speech against racial or religious minorities, women, gays and lesbians, and people with physical disabilities. To date, these codes have not survived legal challenges, and a number of schools are now developing more narrowly focused regulations that they hope will stand up in court.[8]

But whatever the legal outcome may be, it will not alter the ethical responsibility of public speakers—on or off campus—to avoid name-calling and other kinds of abusive language. Legality and ethics, though related, are not identical. There is nothing illegal about falsifying statistics in a speech, but there is no doubt that it is unethical. The same is true of name-calling. It may not be illegal to cast racial, sexual, or religious slurs at people in a speech, but it is still unethical. Not only does it demean the dignity of the groups or individuals being attacked, but it undermines the right of all groups in the U.S. to be fairly heard.

Put Ethical Principles into Practice

We are all familiar with people who say one thing and do another. It is easy to pay lip service to the importance of ethics. It is much harder to act ethically. Yet that is just what the responsible public speaker must do. As one popular book on ethics states, "Being ethical means behaving ethically *all the time*—not only when it's convenient."[9]

As you work on your speeches, you will ask yourself such questions as, "Is my choice of topic suitable for the audience?" "Are my supporting materials clear and convincing?" "How can I phrase my ideas to give them more punch?" These are *strategic* questions. As you answer them, you will try to make your speech as informative, as persuasive, or as entertaining as possible.

But you will also face moments of *ethical* decision—similar, perhaps, to those faced by Sharon Rakove, Felicia Robinson, and the other speakers in this chapter. When those moments arrive, don't simply brush them aside and go on your way. Take your ethical responsibilities as seriously as your strategic objectives. Keep in mind the guidelines for ethical speechmaking we have discussed and do your best to follow them through thick and thin.

 PLAGIARISM

"Plagiarism" comes from *plagiarius,* the Latin word for kidnapper. To plagiarize means to present another person's language or ideas as your own—to give the impression you have written or thought something yourself when you have actually taken it from someone else.[10] We often think of plagiarism as an ethical issue in the classroom, but it can have repercussions in other situations:

In 1987, Senator Joe Biden of New Jersey was emerging as a strong candidate for the Democratic Party's presidential nomination. Handsome, articulate, and a dynamic speaker, Biden seemed ready to make a serious run for the nomination when it was reported that his eloquent conclusion to a speech at the Iowa State Fair was lifted, almost word for word, from an address by British political leader Neil Kinnock.

Biden claimed the similarity between his speech and Kinnock's was purely accidental, but it was soon discovered that in an earlier speech he had pirated, almost verbatim, the words of Robert Kennedy. Even more damage was done a few days later when Biden admitted he had been found guilty of plagiarism while a law student at Syracuse University.

Although Biden tried to pass the whole matter off as "much ado about nothing," his standing in the polls plummeted and his presidential campaign never recovered. In the view of many experts, Biden's credibility was so damaged as to permanently injure any hopes he might have of becoming President.

As this story shows, plagiarism is a serious matter. If you are caught plagiarizing a speech in class, the punishment can range from a failing grade to expulsion from school. If you are caught plagiarizing outside the classroom, you stand to forfeit your good name, to damage your career, or, if you are sued, to lose a large amount of money. It is worth your while, then, to make sure you know what plagiarism is and how to avoid it.[11]

Global Plagiarism

Global plagiarism is stealing your speech entirely from another source and passing it off as your own. The most blatant—and unforgivable—kind of plagiarism, it is grossly unethical.

When global plagiarism takes place in a college classroom, it is sometimes the result of deliberate dishonesty. More often it happens because a student puts off the assignment until the last minute. Then, in an act of desperation, the student gets an old speech from a friend or roommate, a fraternity or sorority file, and hands it in as his or her own. Or the student dashes to the library, finds a suitable magazine article or encyclopedia entry, copies it more or less verbatim, and turns that in as the assigned speech.

The best way to avoid this, of course, is not to leave your speech until the last minute. Most teachers explain speech assignments far enough in advance that you should have no trouble getting an early start. By starting early, you will give yourself plenty of time to prepare a first-rate speech—a speech of your own.

If, for some reason, you fail to get your speech ready on time, do not succumb to the lure of plagiarism. Whatever penalty you suffer from being late will pale in comparison with the consequences if you are caught plagiarizing. Here, as in other aspects of life, honesty is the best policy.

give a speech, not download it!!

Patchwork Plagiarism

Unlike global plagiarism, in which a speaker pirates an entire speech from a single source, patchwork plagiarism occurs when a speaker pilfers from two or three sources. Here's an example:

Kevin Moss chose "The Paintings of Georgia O'Keeffe" as the topic for his first informative speech. In his research, Kevin found three especially helpful sources. The first was a pamphlet about O'Keeffe published by the local art center, which was showing an exhibit of her work. The second was an entry in the *Encyclopaedia Britannica.* The third was an article in *Art Digest.* Working from these sources, Kevin put together a speech dealing with O'Keeffe's early life, the major features of her paintings, and her contributions to modern art.

Unfortunately, instead of using his research materials creatively to generate a speech in his own words, Kevin lifted long passages from the pamphlet, the encyclopedia entry, and the magazine article and patched them together with a few transitions. When he was finished, he had a speech that sounded wonderful—but it was not truly *his* speech since it was composed almost entirely of other people's words.

As it turned out, Kevin's teacher had been to the same art show and thought parts of his speech sounded very familiar. After checking her copy of the art center's pamphlet at home that evening, her suspicions were confirmed. Fearful that Kevin might have filched from more than the pamphlet, she stopped at the library the next morning. In a short while, she found both the encyclopedia entry and the magazine article. Kevin was caught red-handed.

This story illustrates an important point about plagiarism. Kevid did not take his speech from a single source. He even did a little research. But copying word for word from a few sources is no less plagiarism than is copying from a single source. When you give a speech, it is just like putting your name on a paper in your English class. You declare that the speech is your work—that it is the product of your thinking, your beliefs, your language. Kevin's speech did not contain any of these. Instead it was cut and pasted wholly from other people's ideas, other people's words.

"But," you may be thinking, "not many students are experts on their speech topics. Why should they be expected to come up with new ideas that even the experts haven't thought of?" The answer is they aren't. The key is not whether you have something absolutely original to say, but whether you do enough research and thinking to come up with your own slant on the topic.

How can you do this? There is no formula, but perhaps an example will help. At the end of Chapter 14, you will find an informative speech titled "Dandelions: The Uncommon Weed" (pages 329–331). The speaker, Susan Hirsch, an English major, is hardly an expert on dandelions. The inspiration for her topic came from a statement by her botany professor that the dandelion, which most people think of as an obnoxious weed, is actually a very useful plant.

Speakers who consult a wide range of research materials are less likely to fall into the trap of plagiarism than are speakers who rely on a limited number of sources.

As Susan did her research she learned a number of important facts about dandelions—many more than she could ever include in a six-minute speech. Noticing that much of what she found dealt with the dandelion's medical and culinary uses, she decided to focus her speech on those two areas. From all the materials she gathered in her research, she selected for her speech those that best illustrated her ideas. Because those ideas were truly hers, she had no trouble expressing them in her words. By the time she was done, she had blended the raw materials amassed during her research into a speech that was distinctively her own.

As with global plagiarism, one key to averting patchwork plagiarism is to start working on your speech as soon as you possibly can. The longer you work on it, the more apt you are to come up with your own approach. It is also vital to consult a large number of sources in your research. If you have only two or three sources to turn to for inspiration, you are far more likely to fall into the trap of patchwork plagiarism than if you consult a wide range of research materials.

Incremental Plagiarism

In global plagiarism and patchwork plagiarism the entire speech is cribbed more or less verbatim from a single source or a few sources. But plagiarism can still exist even when the speech as a whole is not pirated. This is called incremental plagiarism. It occurs when the speaker fails to give credit for particular parts—increments—of the speech that are borrowed from other people. The most important of these increments are quotations and paraphrases.

Quotations Whenever you quote someone directly, you must attribute the words to that person. Suppose you are giving a speech on Malcolm X, the famous African-American leader of the 1960s. While doing your research, you run across the following passage from Bruce Perry's acclaimed biography, *Malcolm: The Life of a Man Who Changed Black America:*

> Malcolm X fathered no legislation. He engineered no stunning Supreme Court victories or political campaigns. He scored no major electoral triumphs. Yet, because of the way he articulated his followers' grievances and anger, the impact he had upon the body politic was enormous.[12]

This is a fine quotation that summarizes the nature and importance of Malcolm's impact on American politics. It would make a strong addition to your speech—as long as you acknowledge Perry as the author. The way to avoid plagiarism in this instance is to introduce Perry's statement by saying something like:

> In his 1991 biography, *Malcolm: The Life of a Man Who Changed Black America,* historian Bruce Perry says the following about Malcolm's impact on American politics. . . .

Or,

> According to historian Bruce Perry in his 1991 book, *Malcolm: The Life of a Man Who Changed Black America,* . . .

Now you have clearly identified Perry and given him credit for his words rather than presenting them as your own.

Paraphrases When you paraphrase an author, you restate or summarize her or his ideas in your own words. Suppose, once again, that your topic is Malcolm X. But this time you decide to paraphrase the statement from Bruce Perry's biography rather than quoting it. You might say:

> Malcolm X was not a politician. He did not pass any laws, or win any Supreme Court victories, or get elected to any office. But he stated the grievances and anger of his followers so powerfully that the whole nation took notice.

Even though you do not quote Perry directly, you still appropriate the structure of his ideas and a fair amount of his language. Thus you still need to give him credit—just as if you were repeating his words verbatim.

It is especially important in this case to acknowledge Perry because you are borrowing his opinion—his judgment—about Malcolm X. If you simply recount basic facts about Malcolm's life—he was born in Omaha, Nebraska, converted to the Nation of Islam while in prison, traveled to Mecca toward the end of his life, was assassinated in February 1965—you do not have to report the source of your information. These facts are well known and can be found in any standard reference work on Malcolm X.

On the other hand, there is still considerable debate about Malcolm's views of other African-American leaders, the circumstances surrounding his death, and what he might have done had he lived. If you were to cite Perry's views on any of these matters—regardless of whether you quoted or paraphrased—you would need to acknowledge him as your source. If you did not, you could very well be charged with plagiarism.

As more than one speaker (and writer) has discovered, it is possible to commit incremental plagiarism quite by accident. This is less offensive than deliberate plagiarism, but it is plagiarism nonetheless. There are two ways to guard against incremental plagiarism. The first is to be careful when taking research notes to distinguish among direct quotations, paraphrased material, and your own comments. (See Chapter 6 for a full discussion of research methods.) The second way to avoid incremental plagiarism is to err on the side of caution. In other words, when in doubt, cite your source. This way, you cannot go wrong.

GUIDELINES FOR ETHICAL LISTENING

So far in this chapter we have focused on the ethical duties of public speakers. But speechmaking is not a one-way street. Listeners also have ethical obligations. They are (1) to listen courteously and attentively; (2) to avoid prejudging the speaker; and (3) to maintain the free and open expression of ideas. Let us look at each.

Be Courteous and Attentive

Imagine that you are giving your first classroom speech. You have put a great deal of time into writing the speech, and you have practiced your delivery until it is just right. You have not had much experience giving speeches, but you are confident you can do well—especially once you get over the initial rush of stage fright.

You have worked hard on your introduction, and your speech gets off to a fine start. You are pleased to see that most of your classmates are paying close attention. But you also notice that some are not. One appears to be doing homework for another class. Another keeps sneaking glances at the school newspaper. Two or three are gazing out the window, and one is leaning back in his chair with his eyes shut!

You try to block them out of your mind—especially since the rest of the class seems interested in what you are saying—but the longer you speak, the more concerned you become. "What am I doing wrong?" you wonder to yourself. "How can I get these people to pay attention?" The more you think about your inconsiderate and inattentive listeners, the more your confidence and concentration waver.

When you momentarily lose your place halfway through the speech, you start to panic. Your nerves, which you have held in check so far, take the upper hand. Your major thought now becomes, "How can I get this over as fast as possible?" Flustered and distracted, you rush through the rest of your speech and sit down.

How would you feel if this happened to you? Angry? Frustrated? Discouraged? Certainly you would not regard your speech as a positive experience. Nor would you be brimming with confidence as you work on your next speech. Perhaps you would be soured on speechmaking altogether.

Just as public speakers have an ethical obligation to prepare fully for each speech, so listeners have a responsibility to be courteous and attentive during the speech. This responsibility—which is a matter of civility in any circumstance—is especially important in speech class. You and your classmates are in a learning situation in which you need to support one another. Professional speakers are trained to deal with inconsiderate or unresponsive audiences, but novices need encouraging, sympathetic listeners to help maintain their morale and confidence.

When you listen to speeches in class, give your fellow students the same courtesy and attention you want from them. Come to class prepared to listen to—and to learn from—your classmates' speeches. As you listen, be conscious of the feedback you are sending the speaker. Sit up in your chair rather than slouching; maintain eye contact with the speaker; show support and encouragement in your facial expressions. Keep in mind the power you have as a listener over the speaker's confidence and composure, and exercise that power with a strong sense of ethical responsibility.

Avoid Prejudging the Speaker

We have all heard that you can't judge a book by its cover. The same is true of speeches. You can't judge a speech by the name, race, lifestyle, appearance, or reputation of the speaker.

As we shall see in Chapter 3, jumping to conclusions about a speaker's ideas before hearing the speech is one of the major barriers to effective listening. But it also has ethical implications. If a speaker has fulfilled her or his responsibility to prepare fully and conscientiously, the audience has an obligation to listen to that speaker before deciding whether to accept or reject what she or he is saying.

This does not mean you must agree with every speaker you hear. You do not want to be a "rubber-stamp" listener any more than you want to be a closed-minded one. Your aim is to listen carefully to the speaker's ideas, to assess the evidence and reasoning offered in support of those ideas, and to reach an intelligent judgment about the speech. In Chapter 3, we will discuss specific steps you can take to improve your listening skills. For now it is enough to know that if you prejudge a speaker—either positively or negatively—you will fail in one of your ethical responsibilities as a listener.

Maintain the Free and Open Expression of Ideas

As we saw earlier in this chapter, a democratic society depends on the free and open expression of ideas. The right of free expression is so important that it is protected by the First Amendment to the U.S. Constitution, which declares, in part, that "Congress shall make no law . . . abridging the freedom of speech." Without the right of individual citizens to speak their minds on public issues, free government cannot survive. Just as public speakers need to avoid name-calling and other tactics that can undermine free speech, so listeners have an obligation to maintain the right of speakers to be heard.

As with other ethical issues, the extent of this obligation is open to debate. Disputes over the meaning and scope of the First Amendment arise almost daily in connection with issues such as abortion, pornography, and hate speech on college campuses. The question underlying such disputes is whether *all* speakers have a right to be heard.

There are some kinds of speech that are not protected under the First Amendment—including defamatory falsehoods that destroy a person's reputation, threats against the life of the President, and inciting an audience to illegal action in circumstances where the audience is likely to carry out the action. Otherwise, the Supreme Court has held—and most experts in communication ethics have agreed—that public speakers have an almost unlimited right of free expression.[13]

In contrast to this view, it has been argued that some ideas are so dangerous, so misguided, or so offensive that society has a duty to suppress them. But who is to determine which ideas are too dangerous, misguided, or offensive to be uttered? Who is to decide which speakers are to be heard and which are to be silenced?

No matter how well-intentioned they may be, efforts to "protect" society by restricting free speech usually end up repressing minority viewpoints and unpopular opinions. In U.S. history such efforts were used to keep women off the public platform until the 1840s, to stop abolitionist orators from exposing the evils of slavery before the Civil War, to muzzle labor organizers during the 1890s, and to impede civil rights leaders in our own century. Imagine what American society might be like if these speakers had been silenced!

It is important to keep in mind that ensuring a person's freedom to express her or his ideas does not imply agreement with those ideas. You can disagree entirely with the message but still support the speaker's right to express it. In the long run, there is no better way to maintain liberty and human dignity than to protect the free and open expression of ideas. As the Speech Communication Association states in its Credo for Free and Responsible Communication, "much good and little harm can ensue if we err on the side of freedom, whereas much harm and little good may follow if we err on the side of suppression."[14]

SUMMARY

Because public speaking is a form of power, it carries with it heavy ethical responsibilities. Today, as for the past 2,000 years, the good person speaking well remains the ideal of commendable speechmaking.

There are five basic guidelines for ethical public speaking. The first is to make sure your goals are ethically sound—that they are consistent with the welfare of society and your audience. The second is to be fully prepared for each speech. Every audience you address—in class and out—deserves your best effort. You do not want to waste their time or mislead them through shoddy research or muddled thinking. The third guideline is to be honest in what you say. Responsible speakers do not distort the truth for personal gain. They are accurate and fair in their message and in their methods.

The fourth guideline for ethical speaking is to avoid name-calling and other forms of abusive language. Name-calling is the use of language to defame or degrade other individuals or groups. It is ethically suspect because it demeans the dignity of the people being attacked and because it can undermine the right of all groups in American society to be fairly heard. The final guideline is to put ethical principles into practice—to follow them through thick and thin, not just when it is convenient.

Of all the ethical lapses a public speaker can commit, few are more serious than plagiarism. Global plagiarism is lifting a speech entirely from a single source and passing it off as your own. Patchwork plagiarism involves stitching a speech together by copying more or less verbatim from a few sources. Whenever you give a speech, you must be sure it represents your work, your thinking, your language. You must also take care to avoid incremental plagiarism, which occurs when a speaker fails to give credit for specific quotations and paraphrases that are borrowed from other people.

In addition to your ethical responsibilities as a speaker, you also have ethical obligations as a listener. The first is to listen courteously and attentively. The second is to avoid prejudging the speaker. The third is to support the free and open expression of ideas. In all these ways, your speech class will offer a good testing ground for questions of ethical responsibility.

REVIEW QUESTIONS

After reading this chapter, you should be able to answer the following questions:

1. What is ethics? Why is a strong sense of ethical responsibility vital for public speakers?

2. What are the five guidelines for ethical speechmaking discussed in this chapter?

3. What is the difference between global plagiarism and patchwork plagiarism? What are the best ways to avoid these two kinds of plagiarism?

4. What is incremental plagiarism? How can you steer clear of it when dealing with quotations and paraphrases?

5. What are the three basic guidelines for ethical listening discussed in this chapter?

APPLICATION EXERCISES

1. Look back at the story of Felicia Robinson on page 31. Evaluate her dilemma in light of the guidelines for ethical speechmaking presented in this chapter. Explain what you believe would be the most ethical course of action in her case.

2. The issue of insulting and abusive speech—especially slurs directed against people on the basis of race, religion, gender, or sexual orientation— is extremely controversial. Do you believe society should punish such speech with criminal penalties? To what degree are colleges and universities justified in trying to discipline students who engage in such speech? Do you feel it is proper to place any boundaries on free expression in order to prohibit insulting and abusive speech? Why or why not? Be prepared to explain your ideas in class.

3. All of the following situations could arise in your speech class. Identify the ethical issues in each and explain what, as a responsible speaker or listener, your course of action would be.

   a. You are speaking on the topic of prison reform. In your research, you run across two public opinion polls. One of them, an independent survey by the Gallup poll, shows that a majority of people in your state oppose your position. The other poll, suspect in its methods and conducted by a partisan organization, says a majority of people in your state support your position. Which poll do you cite in your speech? If you cite the second poll, do you point out its shortcomings?

   b. When listening to an informative speech by one of your classmates, you realize that much of it is plagiarized from a magazine article you read a couple of weeks ago. What do you do? Do you say something when your instructor asks for comments about the speech? Do you mention your concern to the instructor after class? Do you talk with the speaker? Do you remain silent?

c. While researching your persuasive speech, you find a quotation from an article by a highly respected expert that will nail down one of your most important points. But as you read the rest of the article, you realize the author does not in fact support the policy you are advocating. Should you still include the quotation in your speech?

NOTES

[1] James A. Jaska and Michael S. Pritchard, *Communication Ethics: Methods of Analysis,* 2nd ed. (Belmont, Calif.: Wadsworth, 1994), pp. 3–6.

[2] Richard L. Johannesen, *Ethics in Human Communication,* 3rd ed. (Prospect Heights, Ill.: Waveland Press, 1990), p. 17.

[3] Johannesen, *Ethics in Human Communication,* p. 15. Also see Sissela Bok, *Lying: Moral Choice in Public and Private Life* (New York: Knopf, 1989).

[4] See, for example, David Nyberg, *The Varnished Truth: Truth Telling and Deceiving in Ordinary Life* (Chicago: University of Chicago Press, 1993).

[5] Haig A. Bosmajian, *The Language of Oppression* (Washington, D.C.: Public Affairs Press, 1974), p. 5.

[6] The discussion in this and the preceding paragraph is modeled on William Zinsser, *On Writing Well,* 4th ed. (New York: HarperCollins, 1990), p. 117.

[7] Donald K. Smith, *Man Speaking: A Rhetoric of Public Speech* (New York: Dodd, Mead, 1969), p. 244.

[8] Thomas L. Tedford, *Freedom of Speech in the United States,* 2nd ed. (New York: McGraw-Hill, 1993), pp. 180–186. Also see Cass R. Sunstein, *Democracy and the Problem of Free Speech* (New York: Free Press, 1993), pp. 197–204.

[9] Kenneth Blanchard and Norman Vincent Peale, *The Power of Ethical Management* (New York: Ballantine Books, 1988), p. 64.

[10] Joseph Gibaldi and Walter S. Achtert, *MLA Handbook for Writers of Research Papers,* 3rd ed. (New York: Modern Language Association of America, 1988), p. 21.

[11] For a fascinating look at the history of plagiarism in a variety of contexts, see Thomas Mallon, *Stolen Words: Forays into the Origins and Ravages of Plagiarism* (New York: Penguin Books, 1991).

[12] Bruce Perry, *Malcolm: The Life of a Man Who Changed Black America* (Barrytown, N.Y.: Station Hill, 1991), p. 380.

[13] See, for example, Rodney A. Smolla, *Free Speech in an Open Society* (New York: Knopf, 1992); Franklyn S. Haiman, *"Speech Acts" and the First Amendment* (Carbondale, Ill.: Southern Illinois University Press, 1994).

[14] The entire credo is printed in Thomas L. Tedford, *Public Speaking in a Free Society* (New York: McGraw-Hill, 1991), p. 46. For further discussion of free speech and its place in a system of communication ethics, see Ronald C. Arnett, "The Practical Philosophy of Communication Ethics and Free Speech as the Foundation for Speech Communication," *Communication Quarterly,* 38 (1990), 208–217.

Chapter 3

Listening

I t had been a long day at the office, and the going-home traffic was bumper to bumper. By the time Jason Whitehawk pulled his late-model car into the driveway at home, he was exhausted. As he trudged into the house, he routinely asked his wife, "How did things go with you at work today?"

"Oh, pretty well," she replied, "except for the terrorist attack in the morning and the outbreak of bubonic plague in the afternoon."

Jason nodded his head as he made his way toward the sofa. "That's nice," he said. "At least someone had a good day. Mine was awful."

This story illustrates what one research study after another has revealed—most people are shockingly poor listeners. We fake paying attention. We can look right at someone, appear interested in what that person says, even nod our head or smile at the appropriate moments—all without really listening.

Not listening doesn't mean we don't hear. *Hearing* is a physiological process, involving the vibration of sound waves on our eardrums and the firing of electrochemical impulses from the inner ear to the central auditory system of the brain.[1] But *listening* involves paying close attention to, and making sense of, what we hear. Even when we think we are listening carefully, we usually grasp only 50 percent of what we hear. After two days we can remember only half of that—or 25 percent of the original message.[2] It's little wonder that listening has been called a neglected art.

LISTENING IS IMPORTANT

Although most people listen poorly, there are exceptions. Top-flight business executives, successful politicians, brilliant teachers—nearly all are excellent listeners. So much of what they do depends on absorbing information that is given verbally—and absorbing it quickly and accurately. If you had an interview with the president of a major corporation, you might be shocked (and flattered) to see how closely that person listened to your words. One business executive admitted, "Frankly, I had never thought of listening as an important subject by itself. But now that I am aware of it, I think that perhaps 80 percent of my work depends upon my listening to someone, or upon someone listening to me."[3]

In our communication-oriented age, listening is more important than ever. This is why, in most companies, effective listeners hold higher positions and are promoted more often than people who are ineffective listeners.[4] When business managers are asked to rank-order the communication skills most crucial to their jobs, they usually rank listening number one.[5] Listening is so important that in one survey of America's Fortune 500 companies, almost 60 percent of the respondents said they provide some kind of listening training for their employees.[6]

Even if you don't plan to be a corporate executive, the art of listening can be helpful in almost every part of your life. This is not surprising when you realize that people spend more time listening than doing any other communicative activity—more than reading, more than writing, more even than speaking.[7]

Think for a moment about your own life as a college student. Close to 90 percent of class time in U.S. colleges and universities is spent listening to discussions and lectures. A number of studies have shown a strong correlation between listening and academic success. Students with the highest grades are usually those with the strongest listening skills. The reverse is also true—students with the lowest grades are usually those with the weakest listening skills.[8]

There is plenty of reason, then, to take listening seriously. Employers and employees, parents and children, wives and husbands, doctors and patients, students and teachers—all depend on the apparently simple skill of listening. Regardless of your profession or walk of life, you never escape the need for a well-trained ear.

Listening is also important to you as a speaker. It is probably the way you get most of your ideas and information—from television, radio, conversation, and lectures. If you do not listen well, you will not understand what you hear and may pass along your misunderstanding to others.

Besides, in class—as in life—you will listen to many more speeches than you give. It is only fair to pay close attention to your classmates' speeches; after all, you want them to listen carefully to *your* speeches. An excellent way to improve your own speeches is to listen attentively to the speeches of other people. One student, reflecting on her speech class, said, "As I listened to the speeches, I discovered things that seemed to work—things I could try. I also learned what didn't work—what to avoid. That helped a lot in my own speeches." Over and over, teachers find that the best speakers are usually the best listeners.

A side benefit of your speech class is that it offers an ideal opportunity to work on the art of listening. During the 95 percent of the time when you are not speaking, you have nothing else to do but listen and learn. You can sit there like a stone—or you can use the time profitably to master a skill that will serve you in a thousand ways.

▇ LISTENING AND CRITICAL THINKING

One of the ways listening can serve you is by enhancing your skills as a critical thinker. We can identify four kinds of listening:[9]

- *Appreciative listening*—listening for pleasure or enjoyment, as when we listen to music, to a comedy routine, or to an entertaining speech.

- *Empathic listening*—listening to provide emotional support for the speaker, as when a psychiatrist listens to a patient or when we lend a sympathetic ear to a friend in distress.

- *Comprehensive listening*—listening to understand the message of a speaker, as when we attend a classroom lecture or listen to directions for finding a friend's house.

- *Critical listening*—listening to evaluate a message for purposes of accepting or rejecting it, as when we listen to the sales pitch of a used-car dealer, the campaign speech of a political candidate, or the closing argument of an attorney in a jury trial.

Although all four kinds of listening are important, this chapter deals primarily with the last two—comprehensive listening and critical listening. They are the kinds of listening you will use most often when listening to speeches in class, when taking lecture notes in other courses, when communicating at work, and when responding to the barrage of commercials and other persuasive appeals you face every day in our fast-paced society. They are also the kinds of listening that are most closely tied to critical thinking.

As we saw in Chapter 1, critical thinking involves a number of skills. Some of those skills—summarizing information, recalling facts, distinguishing main points from minor points—are central to comprehensive listening. Other skills of critical thinking—separating fact from opinion, spotting weaknesses in reasoning, judging the soundness of evidence—are especially important in critical listening. When you engage in comprehensive listening or critical listening, you must use your mind as well as your ears. When your mind is not actively involved, you may be hearing, but you are not *listening*.[10] In fact, listening and critical thinking are so closely allied that one researcher has concluded that training in listening is really training in how to think.[11]

At the end of this chapter, we'll discuss steps you can take to improve your skills in comprehensive and critical listening. If you follow these steps, you may also become a better critical thinker at the same time.

FOUR CAUSES OF POOR LISTENING

Not Concentrating

The brain is incredibly efficient. Although we talk at a rate of 120 to 150 words a minute, the brain can process 400 to 800 words a minute.[12] This would seem to make listening very easy, but actually it has the opposite effect. Because we can take in a speaker's words and still have plenty of spare "brain time," we are tempted to interrupt our listening by thinking about other things. And thinking about other things is just what we do. Here's what happens:

Aaron Cappelli is the youngest member of the public relations team for a giant oil company. He is pleased to be included in the biweekly staff meetings. After two dozen or so meetings, however, he is beginning to find them tedious.

People spend more time listening than in any other communicative activity. One benefit of your speech class is that it gives you a chance to improve your listening skills.

This time the vice president is droning on about executive speech writing—an area in which Aaron is not directly concerned. The vice president says, "When the draft of a speech hits the president's desk . . ."

"Desk," thinks Aaron. "That's my big problem. It's humiliating to have a metal desk when everyone else has wood. There must be some way to convince my boss that I need a new wooden desk." In his imagination, Aaron sees himself behind a handsome walnut desk. He is conducting an interview, and his visitor is so impressed . . .

Sternly, Aaron pulls his attention back to the meeting. The vice president has moved on to a public relations problem in Latin America. Aaron listens carefully for a while, until he hears the words "especially in the Caribbean."

"Oh, if only I could get away for a winter vacation this year," he thinks. He is lost in a reverie featuring white beaches, tropical drinks, exotic dances, scuba diving, sailboats, himself tanned and windblown . . .

". . . will definitely affect salary increases this year" brings him back to the meeting with a jolt. What did the vice president say about salary increases? Oh, well, he can ask someone else after the meeting. But now the vice president is talking about budgets. All those dreary figures and percentages . . . And Aaron is off again.

His date last night, Tara, really seems to like him and yet . . . Was it something he did that made her say goodnight at the door and go inside alone? Could she have been *that* tired? The last time she invited him in for coffee. Of course, she really did have a rough day. Anybody can understand that. But still . . .

". . . an area that Aaron has taken a special interest in. Maybe we should hear from him." Uh, oh! *What* area does the vice president mean? Everyone is looking at Aaron, as he tries frantically to recall the last words said at the meeting.

It's not that Aaron *meant* to lose track of the discussion. But there comes a point at which it's so easy to give in to physical and mental distractions—to let your thoughts wander rather than to concentrate on what is being said. After all, concentrating is hard work. Louis Nizer, the famous trial lawyer, says, "So complete is this concentration that at the end of a court day in which I have only listened, I find myself wringing wet despite a calm and casual manner."[13]

Later in this chapter, we will look at some things you can do to concentrate better on what you hear.

Listening Too Hard

Until now we have been talking about not paying close attention to what we hear. But sometimes we listen *too* hard. We turn into human sponges, soaking up a speaker's every word as if every word were equally important. We try to remember all the names, all the dates, all the places. In the process we often miss the speaker's point by submerging it in a morass of details. What is worse, we may end up confusing the facts as well.

Hilary Schneider was about to see her last patient when she got a phone call from her husband, Joel. "Guess what," he exclaimed. "I left work early so I could come home and fix us a nice dinner. By the way, do you remember how your sister makes that incredible chocolate cake?"

"Sure," Hilary said. "The secret is to beat the egg whites separately. But the oven isn't working. I tried it yesterday, and the temperature control is all messed up."

"I just need to know where to find the recipe," Joel answered. "I'm sure it's in one of our cookbooks."

"If you really want to know," Hilary told him, "I think it's in the *American Regional Cookbook,* the one with the picture of an old farmhouse on the cover. It's on the second shelf of the cabinet with all the other cookbooks—just above the shelf with the cooking wine and spices."

"I'm sure I can find it." Joel declared. "There are a ton of great recipes in that book. But I've got to hustle if I'm going to get everything done by the time you get home. Bye."

"Joel, wait a minute," Hilary said. "How in heaven's name are you going to bake the cake?"

"How am I going to bake the cake?" Joel asked in surprise. "In the oven, of course." And he hung up.

This is a typical example of losing the main message by concentrating on details. Joel had set his mind to find the cookbook with the great chocolate cake recipe—period. In so doing, he blocked out everything else—including the information that the oven was not working.

The same thing can happen when you listen to a speech: you pick up the details but miss the point. It just isn't possible to remember everything a speaker says. Efficient listeners usually concentrate on main ideas and evidence. We'll discuss these things more thoroughly later in the chapter.

Jumping to Conclusions

Maura Anello, a recent college graduate, took a job as an editorial assistant in the research department of a regional magazine. Shortly after Maura arrived, the editor in charge of the research department left the magazine for another job. For the next two months, Maura struggled to handle the work of the research department by herself. She often felt in over her head, but she knew this was a good opportunity to learn, and she hated to give up her new responsibilities.

One day Seiji Tomasu, the editor in chief of the magazine, comes into Maura's office to talk. The following conversation takes place:

SEIJI: You've done a great job these last two months, Maura. But you know we really need a new editor. So we've decided to make some changes.

MAURA: I'm not surprised. I know I've made my share of mistakes.

SEIJI: Everyone makes mistakes when they're starting out. And you've been carrying a lot of responsibility. Too much. That's why . . .

MAURA: That's okay. I'm grateful to have had a chance to try my hand at this. I know I'm inexperienced, and this is an important department.

SEIJI: Yes, it is. And it's not an easy job. We really need an editor and an assistant to handle all the work. That's why I wanted to tell you . . .

MAURA: You're right, of course. I hope you've found somebody good to be the new editor.

SEIJI: I think so. But, Maura, I don't think you understand . . .

MAURA: No, I understand. I knew all along that I was just filling in.

SEIJI: Maura, you're not listening.

MAURA: Yes, I am. You're trying to be nice, but you're here to tell me that you've hired a new editor and I'll be going back to my old job.

SEIJI: No, that's not it at all. I think you've done a fine job under difficult circumstances. You've proved yourself, and I intend to make *you* the editor. But I think you'll need an assistant to help you.

Why is there so much confusion here? Clearly, Maura is unsure about her future at the magazine. Although she has worked hard, she knows she has made some mistakes that a more experienced person might have avoided. So when Seiji starts to talk about making some changes, Maura jumps to a conclusion and assumes the worst. The misunderstanding could have been avoided if, when Seiji had said, "We've decided to make some changes," Maura had asked, "What changes?"—and then *listened*.

This is one form of jumping to conclusions—putting words into a speaker's mouth. It is one reason why we sometimes communicate so poorly with people we are closest to. Because we are so sure we know what they mean, we don't listen to what they actually say. Sometimes we don't even hear them out.

Another way of jumping to conclusions is prematurely rejecting a speaker's ideas as boring or misguided. We may decide early on that a speaker has nothing valuable to say. Suppose you are passionately committed to animal rights and a speaker's announced topic is "The Importance of Animals to Scientific Research." You may decide in advance not to listen to anything the speaker has to say. This would be a mistake. You might pick up useful information that could either strengthen or modify your thinking. In another situation, you might jump to the conclusion that a speech will be boring. Let's say the announced topic is "Looking Toward Jupiter: Science and the Cosmos." It sounds dull. So you tune out—and miss a fascinating discussion of possible extraterrestrial life-forms.

Nearly every speech has something to offer you—whether it be information, point of view, or technique. You are cheating yourself if you prejudge and choose not to listen.

Focusing on Delivery and Personal Appearance

Terrence and Sabrina were looking to buy their first house. Friends of theirs had recently found a house in a great neighborhood, so one Saturday afternoon Sabrina and Terrence decided to drive over and look around. They checked the newspaper and found an ad for an open house in the area.

When they got to the house, they knew immediately it was too traditional for them, but Sabrina suggested they go in and talk with the realtor anyway. Terrence agreed. They spent almost an hour looking through the house with the realtor.

At the end of the hour, the realtor sat down with Terrence and Sabrina and talked with them about what they wanted and what they could afford. The realtor then proposed meeting the next day to see several houses in their price range. "I think I know what you're looking for," she said, "so I'll show you the more contemporary houses first."

When Terrence and Sabrina got back in the car, Sabrina was enthusiastic. "I can't wait until tomorrow," she said. "I have a feeling she's going to help us find just the right house."

"I doubt it," Terrence replied. "I'm not sure I want to go. I don't see how she could possibly know what we want."

"She was right when she said we wanted a contemporary," Sabrina reminded him. "She's a professional."

"Maybe so," Terrence said, "but to tell you the truth, I didn't pay much attention to anything she said because our tastes are obviously completely different. I mean, really, she was wearing an orange suit!"

This story illustrates a very common problem. We tend to judge people by the way they look or speak and therefore don't listen to what they *say.* Some people are so put off by personal appearance, regional accents, speech defects, or unusual vocal mannerisms that they can't be bothered to listen.

This kind of emotional censorship is less severe in the United States now than it was a decade or two ago, but we need always to guard against it. Nothing is more deadly to communication.

HOW TO BECOME A BETTER LISTENER

Take Listening Seriously

The first step to improvement is always self-awareness. Analyze your short-comings as a listener and commit yourself to overcoming them. Good listeners are not born that way. They have *worked* at learning how to listen effectively. Good listening does not go hand in hand with intelligence, education, or social standing. Like any other skill, it comes from practice and self-discipline.

You should begin to think of listening as an active process. So many aspects of modern life encourage us to listen passively. We "listen" to the radio while studying or "listen" to the television while moving about from room to room. This type of passive listening is a habit—but so is active listening. We can learn to identify those situations in which active listening is important. If you work seriously at becoming a more efficient listener, you will reap the rewards in your schoolwork, in your personal and family relations, and in your career.

Resist Distractions

In an ideal world, we could eliminate all physical and mental distractions. In the real world, however, this is not possible. Because we think so much faster than a speaker can talk, it's easy to let our attention wander while we listen. Sometimes it's very easy—when the room is too hot, when construction machinery is operating right outside the window, when the speaker is tedious. But our attention can stray even in the best of circumstances—if for no other reason than a failure to stay alert and make ourselves concentrate.

Whenever you find this happening, make a conscious effort to pull your mind back to what the speaker is saying. Then force it to stay there. One way to do this is to think a little ahead of the speaker—try to anticipate what will come next. This is not the same as jumping to conclusions. When you jump to conclusions, you put words into the speaker's mouth and don't actually listen to what is said. In this case you *will* listen—and measure what the speaker says against what you had anticipated.

Another way to keep your mind on a speech is to review mentally what the speaker has already said and make sure you understand it. Yet another is to listen between the lines and assess what a speaker implies verbally or says nonverbally with body language. Suppose a politician is running for reelection. During a campaign speech to her constituents she makes this statement:

"Just last week I had lunch with the President, and he assured me that he has a special concern for the people of our state." The careful listener would hear this implied message: "If you vote for me, there's a good chance more tax money will flow into the state."

To take another example, suppose a speaker is introducing someone to an audience. The speaker says, "It gives me great pleasure to present to you my very dear friend, Nadine Zussman." But the speaker doesn't shake hands with Nadine. He doesn't even look at her—just turns his back and leaves the podium. Is Nadine really his "very dear friend"? Certainly not.

Attentive listeners can pick up all kinds of clues to a speaker's real message. At first you may find it difficult to listen so intently. If you work at it, however, your concentration is bound to improve.

Don't Be Diverted by Appearance or Delivery

If you had attended Abraham Lincoln's momentous Cooper Union speech of 1860, this is what you would have seen:

> The long, ungainly figure upon which hung clothes that, while new for this trip, were evidently the work of an unskilled tailor; the large feet and clumsy hands, of which, at the outset, at least, the orator seemed to be unduly conscious; the long, gaunt head, capped by a shock of hair that seemed not to have been thoroughly brushed out, made a picture which did not fit in with New York's conception of a finished statesman.[14]

But although he seemed awkward and uncultivated, Lincoln had a powerful message about the moral evils of slavery. Fortunately, the audience at Cooper Union did not let his appearance stand in the way of his words.

Similarly, you must be willing to set aside preconceived judgments based on a person's looks or manner of speech. Einstein had frizzy, uncombed hair and wore sloppy clothes. Gandhi was a very unimpressive-looking man who often spoke dressed in a loincloth or wrapped in a blanket. Helen Keller, deaf and blind from earliest childhood, always had trouble articulating words distinctly. Yet imagine if no one had listened to them. Even though it may tax your tolerance, patience, and concentration, don't let negative feelings about a speaker's appearance or delivery keep you from listening to the message.

On the other hand, try not to be misled if the speaker has an unusually attractive appearance. It's all too easy to assume that because someone is good-looking and has a polished delivery, he or she is speaking eloquently. Some of the most unscrupulous speakers in history have been handsome people with hypnotic delivery skills. Again, be sure you respond to the message, not to the package it comes in.

Suspend Judgment

Unless we listen only to people who think exactly as we do, we are going to hear things with which we disagree. When this happens, our natural inclination is to argue mentally with the speaker or to dismiss everything she or he says. But neither response is fair—to the speaker or to ourselves. In both cases we blot out any chance of learning or being persuaded.

Does this mean you must agree with everything you hear? Not at all. It means you should hear people out *before* reaching a final judgment. Try to understand their point of view. Listen to their ideas, examine their evidence, assess their reasoning. *Then* make up your mind. If you're sure of your beliefs, you need not fear listening to opposing views. If you're not sure, you have every reason to listen carefully. It has been said more than once that a closed mind is an empty mind.

*nothing more dangerous
Than a definite opinion
in a closed mind*

Focus Your Listening

As we have seen, skilled listeners do not try to absorb a speaker's every word. Rather, they focus on specific things in a speech. Here are three suggestions to help you focus your listening.

Listen for Main Points   Most speeches contain from two to four main points. Here, for example, are the main points of a recent speech by Raymond W. Kelly, former Police Commissioner of New York City:[15]

1. The increasing level of crime and violence has become a serious problem throughout the United States.

2. The best way to deal with the problem at the national level is for Congress to pass strict gun control laws.

3. The best way to deal with the problem at the local level is by instituting community policing programs.

These main points are the heart of Kelly's message. As with any speech, they are the most important things to listen for.

Unless a speaker is terribly scatterbrained, you should be able to detect his or her main points with little difficulty. Often at the outset of a speech, a speaker will give some idea of the main points to be developed. For example, in his introduction Kelly said, "My premise today is that we have gotten far too accustomed to, and accepting of, crime and violence." He also stated that "the vehicles to help us regain some ground over violent crime are there. One is gun control and the other is community policing." Noticing this, a sharp lis-

Focusing your listening includes listening for main points and evidence. In addition, focusing on an effective speaker's techniques can help you improve your own speaking.

tener would have been prepared for a speech with three main points—one dealing with the problem of crime and violence, one dealing with gun control, and one dealing with community policing.

Listen for Evidence   Identifying a speaker's main points is not enough. You must also listen for supporting evidence. By themselves, Kelly's main points are only assertions. You may be inclined to believe them because they come from a respected law-enforcement official. Yet a careful listener will be concerned with evidence no matter who is speaking. Had you been listening to Kelly's speech, you would have heard him support his point about the problem of crime and violence with an abundance of verifiable evidence. Here's an excerpt:

> There's no doubt about how violent we've become. The annual homicide rate in America is now about 22 for every 100,000 Americans. In Canada the rate is 3 for every 100,000 Canadians. In Japan it is less than 1. . . .
>
> The number of guns in private hands about doubles in America every 20 years—to the point that there are now over 200 million guns in circulation. That compares to 54 million in 1950. . . . We confiscated nearly 20,000 illegal guns in New York City last year. . . .
>
> The fact is we have become too tolerant of murder. In New York City there has somehow arisen a new benchmark for homicides. Over 2,000 homicides is considered bad. Up to 2,000 is, well, somehow "expected," or acceptable. The old chestnut of laying things end-to-end to get a sense of proportion becomes frighteningly macabre when you realize that 2,000 bodies end-to-end would stretch for over two miles.

There are four basic questions to ask about a speaker's evidence:

Is it *accurate*?

Is it taken from *objective* sources?

Is it *relevant* to the speaker's claims?

Is it *sufficient* to support the speaker's point?

In Kelly's case, the answer to each question is yes. His figures about guns in the United States, murders in New York City, and homicide rates for the U.S., Canada, and Japan are well established in the public record and can be verified by independent sources. The figures are clearly relevant to Kelly's claim about the seriousness of crime and violence, and they are sufficient to support that claim. If Kelly's evidence were inaccurate, biased, irrelevant, or insufficient, you should be wary of accepting his claim.

We will discuss these—and other—tests of evidence in detail in Chapters 7 and 16. For now, it is enough to know that you should be on guard against unfounded assertions and sweeping generalizations. Keep an ear out for the speaker's evidence and for its accuracy, objectivity, relevance, and sufficiency.

Listen for Technique   We said earlier that you should not let a speaker's delivery distract you from the message, and this is true. However, if you want to become an effective speaker, you should study the methods other people use to speak effectively. When you listen to speeches—in class and out—focus above all on the content of a speaker's message; but also pay attention to the techniques the speaker uses to get the message across.

Analyze the introduction: What methods does the speaker use to gain attention, to relate to the audience, to establish credibility and goodwill? Assess the organization of the speech: Is it clear and easy to follow? Can you pick out the speaker's main points? Can you follow when the speaker moves from one point to another?

Study the speaker's language: Is it accurate, clear, vivid, appropriate? Does the speaker adapt well to the audience and occasion? Finally, diagnose the speaker's delivery: Is it fluent, dynamic, convincing? Does it strengthen or weaken the impact of the speaker's ideas? How well does the speaker use eye contact, gestures, and visual aids?

As you listen, focus on the speaker's strengths and weaknesses. If the speaker is not effective, try to determine why. If he or she is effective, try to pick out techniques you can use in your own speeches. If you listen in this way, you will be surprised how much you can learn about successful speaking.

This is why many teachers require students to complete evaluation forms on their classmates' speeches. To fill in such forms conscientiously, you must listen carefully. But the effort is well worth the rewards. Not only will you provide valuable feedback to your classmates about their speeches, you will also find yourself becoming a much more efficient listener.

Develop Note-Taking Skills

Speech students are often amazed at how easily their teacher can pick out a speaker's main points, evidence, and techniques. Of course, the teacher knows what to listen for and has had plenty of practice. But the next time you get an opportunity, watch your teacher during a speech. Chances are she or he will be listening with pen and paper. When note taking is done properly, it is a surefire way to improve your concentration and keep track of a speaker's ideas.[16]

The key words here are *when done properly.* Unfortunately, many people don't take notes effectively. Some try to write down everything a speaker says. They view note taking as a race, pitting their handwriting agility against the speaker's rate of speech. As the speaker starts to talk, the note taker starts to write. But soon the speaker is winning the race. In a desperate effort to keep up, the note taker slips into a scribbled writing style with incomplete sentences and abbreviated words. Even this is not enough. The speaker pulls so far ahead that the note taker can never catch up. Finally, the note taker concedes defeat and spends the rest of the speech grumbling in frustration.[17]

Some people go to the opposite extreme. They arrive armed with pen, notebook, and the best of intentions. They know they can't write down everything, so they settle comfortably in their seats and wait for the speaker to say something that grabs their attention. Every once in a while the speaker rewards them with a joke, a dramatic story, or a startling fact. Then the note taker seizes pen, jots down a few words, and leans back dreamily to await the next fascinating tidbit. By the end of the lecture the note taker has a set of tidbits—and little or no record of the speaker's important ideas.

As these examples illustrate, most inefficient note takers suffer from one or both of two problems: they don't know *what* to listen for, and they don't know *how* to record what they do listen for. The solution to the first problem is to focus on a speaker's main points and evidence. But once you know what to listen for, you still need a sound method of note taking.

Although there are a number of systems, most students find the *key-word outline* best for listening to classroom lectures and formal speeches. As its name suggests, this method briefly notes a speaker's main points and supporting evidence in rough outline form. Suppose a speaker says:

Elephants have long been hunted for their ivory tusks. In the 1920s thousands of elephants were killed to meet demand in the United States for 60,000 ivory billiard balls every year and hundreds of thousands of piano keys. Today the ivory trade is centered in the Far East, where ivory ornaments are highly prized. Hong Kong is the world's ivory marketplace. According to *Time* magazine, more than 3,900 tons of ivory were imported into Hong Kong during the 1980s. That represents the death of more than 400,000 elephants.

How serious is this problem? The Associated Press notes that just ten years ago, 1.3 million elephants roamed Africa. Now that number has been cut in half. In

Kenya, the elephant population has been reduced by 70 percent over the past ten years. *U.S. News & World Report* states that if the carnage continues, elephants could be threatened with extinction.

A key-word note taker would record something like this:

> Elephants long hunted
> >   1920s—U.S.
> >   Today—Far East
> > >   Hong Kong ivory marketplace
> > >   400,000 elephants killed in 1980s
>
> How serious a problem?
> >   African elephants down 50 percent
> >   Kenya reduced 70 percent
> >   *U.S. News:* could threaten extinction

Notice how brief the notes are. They contain only 35 words (compared to the speaker's 148), yet they accurately summarize the speaker's ideas. Also notice how clear the notes are. By separating main points from subpoints and evidence, the outline format shows the relationships among the speaker's ideas.

Perfecting this—or any other—system of note taking requires practice.[18] But with a little effort you should see results soon. As you become a better note taker, you will become a better listener. There is also a good chance you will become a better student. Common sense and experience suggest that students who take effective notes usually get higher grades than those who do not.

SUMMARY

Most people are poor listeners. Even when we think we are listening carefully, we usually grasp only half of what we hear, and we retain even less. Improving your listening skills can be helpful in every part of your life— including speechmaking. The best speakers are often the best listeners. Your speech class gives you a perfect chance to work on your listening skills as well as your speaking skills.

The most important cause of poor listening is giving in to physical and mental distractions. Many times we let our thoughts wander rather than concentrating on what is being said. Sometimes, however, we listen *too* hard. We try to remember every word a speaker says, and we lose the main message by concentrating on details. In other situations, we may jump to conclusions and prejudge a speaker without hearing out the message. Finally, we often judge people by their appearance or speaking manner instead of listening to what they say.

You can overcome these poor listening habits by taking several steps. First, take listening seriously. Think of listening as an active process and commit yourself to becoming a better listener. Second, resist distractions. Make a conscious effort to keep your mind on what the speaker is saying. Third, try not to be diverted by appearance or delivery. Set aside preconceived judgments based on a person's looks or manner of speech. Fourth, suspend judgment until you have heard the speaker's entire message—even if you think you are going to disagree. Fifth, focus your listening by paying attention to main points, to evidence, and to the speaker's techniques. Finally, develop your note-taking skills. When done properly, note taking is an excellent way to improve your concentration and to keep track of a speaker's ideas. It almost forces you to become a more attentive and creative listener.

REVIEW QUESTIONS

After reading this chapter, you should be able to answer the following questions:

1. What is the difference between hearing and listening?
2. Why is listening important to you as a public speaker?
3. What are the four main causes of poor listening?
4. What are six ways to become a better listener?

APPLICATION EXERCISES

1. Which of the four causes of poor listening do you consider the most important? Choose a specific case of poor listening in which you were involved. Explain what went wrong.
2. Write a candid evaluation of your major strengths and weaknesses as a listener. Explain what steps you need to take to become a better listener. Be specific.
3. Watch the lead story on "60 Minutes" this week. Using the key-word method of note taking, record the main ideas of the story.
4. Choose a lecture in one of your other classes. Analyze what the lecturer does most effectively. Identify three things the lecturer could do better to help students keep track of the lecture.

NOTES

[1] Hayes A. Newby and Gerald R. Popelka, *Audiology,* 6th ed. (Englewood Cliffs, N.J.: Prentice-Hall, 1992), pp. 5–59.

[2] Lyman K. Steil, Larry L. Barker, and Kittie W. Watson, *Effective Listening* (Reading, Mass.: Addison-Wesley, 1983), pp. 38, 51.

[3] Quoted in Ralph G. Nichols and Leonard A. Stevens, *Are You Listening?* (New York: McGraw-Hill, 1957), p. 141.

[4] Beverly Davenport Sypher, Robert N. Bostrom, and Joy Hart Seibert, "Listening, Communication Abilities, and Success at Work," *Journal of Business Communication,* 26 (1989), 293–303.

[5] See the studies cited by Andrew D. Wolvin and Carolyn Gwynn Coakley, "A Survey of the Status of Listening Training in Some Fortune 500 Corporations," *Communication Education,* 40 (1991), 153.

[6] Wolvin and Coakley, "Survey of the Status of Listening Training," 152–162.

[7] The classic study on this subject is Paul T. Rankin, "The Importance of Listening Ability," *English Journal,* 17 (1928), 623–630. For a review of the scholarly literature on listening, see Kittie W. Watson and Larry L. Barker, "Listening Behavior: Definition and Measurement," in Robert N. Bostrom and Bruce Westley (eds.), *Communication Yearbook 8* (Beverly Hills, Calif.: Sage, 1984), pp. 178–197.

[8] Carolyn Coakley and Andrew Wolvin, "Listening in the Educational Environment," in Deborah Borisoff and Michael Purdy (eds.), *Listening in Everyday Life: A Personal and Professional Approach* (Lanham, Md.: University Press of America, 1991), pp. 163–164.

[9] Andrew W. Wolvin and Carolyn Gwynn Coakley, *Listening,* 4th ed. (Dubuque, Iowa: W.C. Brown, 1992), pp. 223–396.

[10] Mortimer J. Adler, *How to Speak, How to Listen* (New York: Macmillan, 1983), pp. 85–86.

[11] Thomas G. Devine, "Listening: What Do We Know after Fifty Years of Research and Theorizing?" *Journal of Reading,* 21 (1978), 296–304.

[12] Florence I. Wolff and Nadine C. Marsnik, *Perceptive Listening,* 2nd ed. (Fort Worth, Texas: Harcourt Brace Jovanovich, 1992), p. 66.

[13] Louis Nizer, *My Life in Court* (New York: Doubleday, 1961), pp. 297–298.

[14] George H. Putnam, *Abraham Lincoln* (New York: Putnam, 1909), pp. 44–45.

[15] Raymond W. Kelly, "Toward a New Intolerance: Gun Control and Community Policing," *Vital Speeches,* 60 (1993), 332–334.

[16] For a review of studies on the efficacy of note taking as an aid to listening, see Robert N. Bostrom and D. Bruce Searle, "Encoding, Media, Affect, and Gender," in Robert N. Bostrom (ed.), *Listening Behavior: Measurement and Application* (New York: Guilford Press, 1990), pp. 28–30.

[17] Nichols and Stevens, *Are You Listening?,* pp. 113–114.

[18] See Wolff and Marsnik, *Perceptive Listening,* pp. 132–143, for several alternative note-taking systems.

Chapter 4

Selecting a Topic and Purpose

CHOOSING A TOPIC

DETERMINING THE GENERAL PURPOSE

DETERMINING THE SPECIFIC PURPOSE
Tips for Formulating the Specific Purpose Statement
Questions to Ask About Your Specific Purpose

PHRASING THE CENTRAL IDEA

A s you read through this book, you will find examples of hundreds of speeches that were delivered in classrooms, in the political arena, in community and business situations. Here is a very small sample of the topics they cover:

acupuncture	Navajo sandpainting
bicycles	organ donation
Cesar Chavez	Passover
DNA testing	Quinceanera
E-mail	right of privacy
fiber optics	Special Olympics
gambling addiction	tenants' rights
hypnosis	UFOs
India	virtual reality
jai alai	women in business
kites	x-rays
lasers	Yucatán peninsula
Malcolm X	zoos

Undoubtedly you noticed that the list runs from A to Z. This array of topics wasn't planned. It happened naturally in the course of presenting many different kinds of speeches. The list is given here simply to show you that there are literally endless possibilities for speech topics—from A to Z.

CHOOSING A TOPIC

The first step in speechmaking is choosing a topic. For speeches outside the classroom this is seldom a problem. Usually the speech topic is determined by the occasion, the audience, and the speaker's qualifications. When Janet Reno lectures on a college campus, she is invited to speak about crime and law enforcement. Connie Chung will discuss news and current events. Gene Siskel might share his views about the latest in filmmaking. The same is true of ordinary citizens. The doctor is asked to speak with high-school athletes and their parents about sports injuries. The stockbroker discourses on investment procedures, the florist on how to grow thriving house plants.

In a public speaking class the situation is different. Most of your speech assignments will not come with a designated topic. Students generally have great leeway in selecting subjects for their speeches. This would appear to be an advantage, since it allows you to talk about matters of personal interest.

Choosing a topic is the first step in speech preparation. When you look for a topic, keep in mind campus issues about which you hold strong opinions and beliefs.

Yet there may be no facet of speech preparation that causes more gnashing of teeth than selecting a topic.

It is a constant source of amazement to teachers that students who regularly chat with their friends about almost any subject under the sun become mentally paralyzed when faced with the task of deciding what to talk about in their speech class. Fortunately, once you get over this initial paralysis, you should have little trouble choosing a good topic.

There are two broad categories of potential topics for your classroom speeches: (1) subjects you know a lot about and (2) subjects that interest you and that you would like to know more about. Let's start with the first.

Most people speak best about subjects with which they are most familiar. You can't go too far wrong by drawing on your own knowledge and experience. You may think to yourself, "That's impossible. I've never done anything fascinating. My life is too ordinary to interest other people." But that isn't true. Everyone knows things or has done things that can be used in a speech.

Think for a moment about unusual experiences you may have had. Think also about special knowledge or expertise you may have acquired. You are bound to come up with something. One student, who grew up in Pakistan, presented a fascinating speech about daily life in that country. Another used her knowledge as a jewelry-store salesperson to prepare a speech on how to judge the value of cut diamonds. A third student, who had lived through a tornado, gave a gripping speech about that terrifying experience.

Too dramatic? You have nothing in your life that is as interesting? Yet another student, who described herself as "just a housewife who is returning to school to finish the education she started twenty years ago," delivered a witty and highly entertaining speech on the adjustments she had to make in coming back to college. This speaker talked about the strange feelings of sitting in class with students young enough to be her children, about the difficulty of balancing her academic work against her family commitments at home, and about the satisfaction of completing the education she had begun years earlier.

Here are a few more examples of speech topics based largely on the students' personal knowledge and experience:

Hong Kong: City of Paradox

Working in a Television Newsroom

Iguanas: The Ideal Pets

A Tour of Old Jerusalem

Jai Alai: The World's Fastest Sport

Scuba Diving: A New World Under Water

Performing with the Native American Dance Troupe

Diabetes: You Can Live with It

How to Have a Successful Job Interview

On the other hand, you may decide to make your speech a learning experience for yourself as well as for your audience. You may choose a subject about which you already have some knowledge or expertise but not enough to prepare a speech without doing additional research. You may even select a topic that hasn't touched you at all before but that you want to explore. Say, for example, you've always been interested in volcanoes but never knew much about them. This would be a perfect opportunity to research a fascinating subject and turn it into a fascinating speech.

Still another possibility—especially for persuasive speeches—is to think of subjects about which you hold strong opinions and beliefs. Imagine you are at dinner with a friend and find yourself arguing that television broadcasters should not report the projected results of presidential elections until polls have closed throughout the country. Why not give a speech in class on the same topic? Or suppose you believe your school should set up a program to help reduce burglaries on campus. Why not try to convince your classmates and get them to petition for such a program?

Like everyone else, you surely have issues about which you care deeply. They may include national or international concerns such as gun control, protection of the environment, or the spread of pornography. Or perhaps you are closely involved in a local issue, such as a teachers' strike, the campaign for mayor, or a proposal to increase tuition. Not all such topics must be "political." They can deal with anything from graduation requirements to helping people with physical disabilities, from religious cults to preserving a nature sanctuary, from dormitory regulations to building a church recreation center.

After all this you may still be thinking, "I *don't* care about volcanoes. I've *never* been to Pakistan. I'm *not* active in politics. WHAT am I going to speak about?" If you are having trouble selecting a topic, there are a number of procedures you can follow to get started. Here are three possibilities.

First, make a quick inventory of your experiences, interests, hobbies, skills, beliefs, and so forth. Jot down anything that comes to mind, no matter how silly or irrelevant it may seem. From this list may come a general subject area out of which you can fashion a specific topic. This method has worked for many students.

If the first method doesn't work, try the second. It is a technique called *brainstorming*. Take a sheet of paper and divide it into nine columns. Label the columns as follows: People, Places, Things, Events, Processes, Concepts, Natural Phenomena, Problems, and Plans and Policies.[1] Then list in each column the first five or six items that come to mind. The result might look like this:

I AM vs I AM NOT

PEOPLE	PLACES	THINGS
Jesse Jackson	Miami	virtual reality
Hillary Clinton	Los Angeles	computers
my parents	Sahara Desert	cellular phones
David Letterman	my hometown	Bible
Whitney Houston	New York City	Koran

EVENTS	PROCESSES
Passover	Getting a tattoo
World Cup	Buying a personal computer
job interview	How fiber optics work
Olympic Games	Investing in the stock market
graduation	What happens when people dream
Cinco de Mayo	Adapting to a different culture

CONCEPTS	NATURAL PHENOMENA
free trade	hurricanes
Afrocentrism	earthquakes
chaos theory	lightning
conservatism	rain forests
multiculturalism	global warming

PROBLEMS	PLANS AND POLICIES
teenage gun use	balancing the federal budget
sexual harassment	reducing infant mortality
water shortage	building a new library
illiteracy	immigration regulations
campus crime	genetic testing in the workplace
prison overcrowding	changing Native American team names

Very likely, several items on your lists will strike you as potential topics. If not, take the items you find most intriguing and compose sublists for each. Try to free-associate. Write down a word or an idea. What does that trigger in your mind? Whatever it is, write that down next, and keep going until you have six or seven ideas on your list. For example, working from the brainstorming lists printed above, one student composed sublists for cartoons, campus crime, and lightning:

CARTOONS	CAMPUS CRIME	LIGHTNING
television	vandalism	thunder
movies	police	noise
Academy Awards	fingerprints	traffic
prizes	hands	air pollution
lotteries	gloves	gasoline
gambling	cold weather	motorcycles

Can you follow her trail of association? In the first column cartoons made her think of television. Television reminded her of movies. Movies suggest the Academy Awards. The Academy Awards are prizes. Prizes reminded her of lotteries. Lotteries are a form of gambling. Suddenly, this student remembered a magazine article she had read on the growing problem of gambling addiction in America. The idea clicked in her mind. After considerable research she developed an excellent speech entitled "Gambling Addiction: Why You Can't Beat the Odds."

That's a far cry from cartoons! If you started out free-associating from cartoons, you would doubtless end up somewhere completely different. This is what brainstorming is all about.

By brainstorming, most people are able to come up with a topic rather quickly. But if you are still stymied, don't despair. There is a third technique you can use as a last resort. Go to the reference room of the library and browse through an encyclopedia, the *Reader's Guide to Periodical Literature,* the *New York Times Index,* or some other reference work until you stumble across what might be a good speech topic. As an experiment, one student decided to try flipping through the dictionary, limiting herself to the letter "m." Within ten minutes she had come up with these potential topics:

Mexico City	meteors	mummies	Mafia
macramé	Mozart	mythology	miracles
metric system	Mojave Desert	mastodons	Medal of Honor
Morse code	monkeys	Mohammed	milk
malaria	marimbas	Mount Vernon	modern jazz

With proper research and development, any one of these could make an exciting speech.

Whatever means you use for selecting a topic, *start early.* The major reason students have difficulty choosing speech topics is that, like most people, they tend to procrastinate—to put off starting projects for as long as possible. Since choosing a topic is your first step in the process of speech preparation, it is only natural to postpone facing up to it. But if you postpone it for too long, you may dig yourself into a hole from which you cannot escape.

Start thinking about your topic as soon as each assignment is announced. Pay attention to interesting subjects in class and conversation, on the radio and television, in newspapers and magazines. Jot down in your notebook ideas for topics as they occur to you. Having an inventory of possible topics to choose from is much better than having to rack your brain for one at the last minute. If you get an early start on choosing a topic, you will have plenty of time to pick just the right one and prepare a first-rate speech.

▌ DETERMINING THE GENERAL PURPOSE

Along with choosing a topic, you need to determine the *general purpose* of your speech. Usually it will fall into one of two overlapping categories—to inform or to persuade. (As noted in Chapter 1, there is a third possible category—the speech to entertain. But classroom speeches are rarely of this type.)

When your general purpose is to *inform,* you act as a teacher or lecturer. Your goal is to convey information—and to do so clearly, accurately, and interestingly. If you give an account of your trip to Spain, describe how to lift weights, narrate the major events of the war in Bosnia, report on your sorority's financial position, or explain how genetic testing for hereditary diseases works, you are speaking to inform. Your aim is to enhance the knowledge and understanding of your listeners—to give them information they did not have before.

When your general purpose is to *persuade,* you act as an advocate or a partisan. You go beyond giving information to espousing a cause. You want to *change* or *structure* the attitudes or actions of your audience. The difference between informing and persuading is the difference between "explaining" and "exhorting."[2] If you try to convince your listeners that they should start a regular program of weight lifting, that the United States should have done more to prevent the tragedy in Bosnia, that more students should take advantage of the study-abroad program, that your sorority should start a fund-raising drive to balance its budget, or that the federal government should prohibit businesses from using genetic testing when hiring employees—then you are speaking to persuade. In doing so, you cannot help but give information; but your primary goal is to win over your listeners to your point of view—to get them to believe something or do something as a result of your speech.

In speech classes, the general purpose is usually specified as part of the speech assignment. For speeches outside the classroom, however, you have to make sure of your general purpose yourself. Usually this is easy to do. Are you going to explain, report, or demonstrate something? Then your general purpose is to inform. Are you going to sell, advocate, or defend something? Then your general purpose is to persuade. But no matter what the situation, you must be certain of exactly what you hope to achieve by speaking. Knowing your general purpose is the first step. The next step is determining your specific purpose.

▦ DETERMINING THE SPECIFIC PURPOSE

Once you have chosen a topic and a general purpose, you must narrow your choices to determine the *specific purpose* of your speech. The specific purpose should focus on one aspect of a topic. You should be able to state your specific purpose in a single infinitive phrase (to inform my audience about . . . ; to persuade my audience to . . .) that indicates *precisely* what you hope to accomplish with your speech. Perhaps an example will help to clarify the process of choosing a specific purpose.

Keith Williams, a student at the University of Wisconsin, decided to give his first classroom speech on a topic from his personal experience. Like many people, Keith had started saving baseball cards when he was in elementary school. Unlike most people, however, he had become a serious collector over the years. By the time he went to college, he owned thousands of cards, subscribed to *Sports Collectors Digest,* attended card shows throughout the Midwest, and made enough money selling cards to help pay his expenses at school. So he planned to speak about baseball cards. This gave him a topic and a specific purpose, which were:

Topic: Baseball cards.

General Purpose: To inform.

So far, so good. But what aspect of baseball cards would Keith discuss?

The history of baseball cards? The different kinds of cards? The thrill of discovering a rare card? He had to choose something interesting that he could cover in a five-minute speech. Finally, he settled on explaining the factors that determine the value of a baseball card. He stated his specific purpose this way:

Specific Purpose: To inform my audience of the major factors that determine the value of a baseball card.

This turned out to be an excellent choice, and Keith's speech was among the best in the class.

Notice how clear and concise the specific purpose is. Notice also how it relates the topic directly to the audience. That is, it states not what the *speaker* wants to *say,* but what the speaker wants the *audience* to *know* as a result of the speech. This is very important, for it helps keep the audience at the center of your attention as you prepare the speech.

Look what happens when the specific purpose statement does not include the audience:

Specific Purpose: To explain the major factors that determine the value of a baseball card.

Explain to whom? To baseball-card collectors? To a group of business majors? To a delegation of exchange students from Saudi Arabia? Those would be three different speeches. The card collectors already know the basic facts about judging the value of a baseball card. For them the speaker might provide a more advanced discussion. The business majors may know something about baseball cards, but they will not have anywhere near the knowledge of the collectors. So the speaker will prepare a more general speech. The Saudi Arabian exchange students don't have the foggiest notion what baseball cards are. In this case, the speaker must design a speech that doesn't depend on the audience having any prior knowledge about baseball cards.

When the audience slips out of the specific purpose, it may slip out of the speaker's consciousness. You may begin to think your task is the general one of preparing "an informative speech," when in fact your task is the specific one of informing a particular group of people. This may seem like a small point right now, but as we shall see in the next chapter, it is almost impossible to prepare a good speech without keeping constantly in mind the *people* for whom it is intended.

Tips for Formulating the Specific Purpose Statement

Formulating a specific purpose is the most important early step in developing a successful speech. In writing your purpose statement, try to follow the general principles outlined below.

Write the Purpose Statement as a Full Infinitive Phrase, Not as a Fragment

Ineffective: Calendars.

More Effective: To inform my audience about the four major kinds of calendars used in the world today.

Ineffective: Buying a personal computer.

More Effective: To inform my audience of the best way to select a personal computer suited to their individual needs.

The ineffective statements above are adequate as announcements of the speech topic, but they are not thought out fully enough to indicate the specific purpose.

Express Your Purpose as a Statement, Not as a Question

Ineffective: What is Quinceanera?

More Effective: To inform my audience about the origins, ceremonies, and importance for young women of the traditional Quinceanera celebration in Mexico.

Ineffective: Is the U.S. space program necessary?

More Effective: To persuade my audience that the U.S. space program provides many important benefits to people here on earth.

The questions might make adequate titles, but they are not effective as purpose statements. They give no indication about what direction the speech will take or what the speaker hopes to accomplish.

Avoid Figurative Language in Your Purpose Statement

Ineffective: To persuade my audience that the university's plan to reduce the number of campus parking spaces assigned to students is a real bummer.

More Effective: To persuade my audience to petition against the university's plan to reduce the number of campus parking spaces assigned to students.

Ineffective: To persuade my audience that banning all fraternities because there have been hazing abuses at some colleges would be like throwing out the baby with the bath water.

More Effective: To persuade my audience that banning all fraternities because there have been hazing abuses at some colleges would punish the vast majority of fraternities for the actions of a few.

Although the ineffective statements indicate something of the speaker's viewpoint, they do not state concisely what he or she hopes to achieve. Metaphors, analogies, and the like are effective devices for reinforcing ideas within a speech, but they are too ambiguous for specific purpose statements.

Limit Your Purpose Statement to One Distinct Idea

Ineffective: To persuade my audience that the federal government should ban all cigarette advertising and that smoking should be prohibited in all campus buildings.

This purpose statement expresses two separate ideas. The easiest remedy is to select one or the other as a focus for your speech.

More Effective: To persuade my audience that the federal government should ban all cigarette advertising.

Or:

More Effective: To persuade my audience that smoking should be prohibited in all campus buildings.

Make Sure Your Specific Purpose Is Not Too Vague or General

Ineffective: To inform my audience about the Civil War.

More Effective: To inform my audience about the role of African-American soldiers in the Civil War.

The ineffective purpose statement above falls into one of the most common traps—it is too broad and ill-defined. It gives no clues about what aspect of the Civil War the speaker will cover. The more effective purpose statement is sharp and concise. It reveals clearly what the speaker plans to discuss.
  Here is another example, this time for a persuasive speech:

Ineffective: To persuade my audience that something should be done about the federal budget deficit.

More Effective: To persuade my audience that a national sales tax should be instituted to help reduce the federal budget deficit.

Again, the ineffective purpose statement is vague and indistinct. It gives no indication of the speaker's stance toward the topic. The "something" that "should be done" about the federal budget could include anything from raising income taxes to reducing spending for national defense or Social Security. The more effective purpose statement is crisp and clear. It does not leave us guessing about what the speaker hopes to accomplish.

The more precise your specific purpose, the easier it will be to prepare your speech. Consider this topic and specific purpose:

Topic: Astrology.

Specific Purpose: To inform my audience about astrology.

With such a hazy purpose, you have no systematic way of limiting your research or of deciding what to include in the speech and what to exclude. The ancient origins of astrology, its role in history, its current popularity—all could be equally relevant to a speech designed "to inform my audience about astrology."

In contrast, look at this topic and specific purpose:

Topic: Astrology.

Specific Purpose: To inform my audience why astrology cannot be accepted as scientifically valid.

Now it is easy to decide what is germane and what is not. The origins of astrology, its role in history, its current popularity—all are interesting, but none is essential to the specific purpose of explaining "why astrology cannot be accepted as scientifically valid." Thus you need not worry about researching these matters or about explaining them in the speech. You can spend your preparation time efficiently.

Questions to Ask About Your Specific Purpose

Sometimes you will arrive at your specific purpose almost immediately after choosing your topic. At other times you may do quite a bit of research before deciding on a specific purpose. Much will depend on how familiar you are with the topic, as well as on any special demands imposed by the assignment, the audience, or the occasion. But whenever you settle on your specific purpose, ask yourself the following questions about it.

Does My Purpose Meet the Assignment?   Students occasionally stumble over this question. Be sure you understand your assignment, and shape your specific purpose to meet it. If you have questions, check with your instructor.

Can I Accomplish My Purpose in the Time Allotted?   Most classroom speeches are quite short, ranging from four or five minutes up to ten minutes. That may seem like a lot of time if you have never given a speech before. But you will quickly find what generations of students have discovered, much to their surprise—time flies when you are giving a speech! Most people speak at an average rate of 120 to 150 words a minute. This means that a six-minute speech will consist of roughly 720 to 900 words. That is not long enough to develop a highly complex topic. Here are some specific purpose statements that

A speaker's specific purpose should be appropriate for the audience. A speech to school children on French impressionist painting would have a different specific purpose than a speech on the same topic to college art students.

would defy being handled well in the time normally allocated for classroom speeches:

> To inform my audience about the history of social reform in America.

> To inform my audience about the rise and fall of the Roman Empire.

> To persuade my audience to convert to Buddhism.

You are much better off with a limited purpose that you have some reasonable hope of achieving in the short span of four to ten minutes.

Is the Purpose Relevant to My Audience?   The price of retirement homes in Sun City might be an engrossing topic for older citizens who are in the market for such dwellings. And the quality of hot lunches in the elementary schools is of great concern to the students who eat them and the parents who pay for them. But neither subject has much relevance for an audience of college students. No matter how well you construct your speeches, they are likely to fall flat unless you speak about matters of interest to your listeners.

   This is not to say you must select only topics that pertain *directly* to the college student's daily experience—the grading system, dormitory conditions, parking spaces on campus, and the like. Most students have wide-ranging backgrounds, interests, ideas, and values. And most of them are intellectually curious. They can get involved in an astonishing variety of subjects. Follow your common sense, and make sure *you* are truly interested in the topic. Also, when speaking on a subject that is not obviously relevant to your listeners, take time in your speech to tie the subject in with their goals, values, interests, and well-being. We'll discuss how to do this in the next chapter.

Is the Purpose Too Trivial for My Audience?   Just as you need to avoid speech topics that are too broad or complicated, so you need to steer clear of topics that are too superficial. How to build a fire without matches might absorb a group of Cub Scouts, but your classmates would probably consider it frivolous. Unfortunately, there is no absolute rule for determining what is trivial to an audience and what is not. Here are some examples of specific purposes that most people would find too trivial for classroom speeches:

> To inform my audience how to make a submarine sandwich.

> To inform my audience how to tie a bow tie.

> To persuade my audience that Mountain Dew is superior to Seven-Up.

Is the Purpose Too Technical for My Audience?   Nothing puts an audience to sleep faster than a dry and technical speech. Beware of topics that are inherently technical, as well as of treating ordinary subjects in a technical fashion. Although you may be perfectly familiar with the principles and vocabulary of quantum physics, physical anthropology, generic criticism, molecular biology, clinical psychology, or constitutional law, most of your classmates probably are not. There are aspects of these and similar subjects that *can* be treated clearly, with a minimum of jargon. But if you find you can't fulfill your specific purpose without relying on technical words and concepts, you should reconsider your purpose. Here are some examples of specific purposes that are overly technical for most classroom speeches:

> To inform my audience about the solution to Fermat's Last Theorem.

> To inform my audience about the complexities of Aristotelian metaphysics.

> To inform my audience how scientists developed the process of DNA fingerprinting.

We shall discuss the details of audience analysis and adaptation in Chapter 5. For the moment, remember to make sure that your specific purpose is appropriate for your listeners. If you have doubts, ask your instructor, or circulate a questionnaire among your classmates (see pages 105–108).

▪ PHRASING THE CENTRAL IDEA

The specific purpose of a speech is what you hope to accomplish. The *central idea* is a concise statement of what you *expect to say.* Sometimes it is called the thesis statement, the subject sentence, or the major thought. Whatever the term, the central idea is usually expressed as a simple, declarative sentence that refines and sharpens the specific purpose statement.

Imagine you run into a friend on your way to speech class. She says, "I have to dash to my history lecture, but I hear you're giving a speech today. Can you tell me the gist of it in one sentence?" "Sure," you reply. "America's prison system suffers from three major problems—overcrowding of inmates, lack of effective rehabilitation programs, and high expense to taxpayers."

Your answer is the central idea of your speech. It is more precise than your topic (America's prison system) or your specific purpose statement ("To inform my audience of the three major problems facing America's prison system"). By stating exactly what the three major problems are, the central idea "sums up" your speech in a single sentence.

Another way to think of the central idea is as your *residual message*— what you want your audience to remember after they have forgotten everything else in the speech. Most of the time the central idea will encapsulate the main points to be developed in the body of the speech. To show how this works, let's take a few of the examples we had earlier in this chapter and develop them from the topic, general purpose, and specific purpose to the central idea.

We can start with the speech about baseball cards:

Topic: Baseball cards.

General Purpose.   To inform.

Specific Purpose: To inform my audience of the major factors that determine the value of a baseball card.

Central Idea: The four factors that determine the value of a baseball card are the fame of the player, the age of the card, the rarity of the card, and the physical condition of the card.

Look carefully at this example. It shows how the speaker might start with a broad subject (baseball cards) that gets narrower and narrower as the speaker moves from the general purpose to the specific purpose to the central idea. Notice also how much the central idea suggests about the content of the speech. From it we can expect the speaker to develop four main points in his speech—each corresponding to one of the four major factors that determine the value of a baseball card.

This sharpening of focus as one proceeds to the central idea is crucial. Here is another example:

Topic: Calendars.

General Purpose: To inform.

Specific Purpose: To inform my audience of the four major calendars used in the world today.

Central Idea: The four major calendars used in the world today are the Gregorian calendar, the Hebrew calendar, the Chinese calendar, and the Islamic calendar.

This central idea is especially well worded. We can assume from it that the body of the speech will contain four main points—on the Gregorian calendar, the Hebrew calendar, the Chinese calendar, and the Islamic calendar.

Much the same is true of this example:

Topic:	Campus parking.
General Purpose:	To persuade.
Specific Purpose:	To persuade my audience to petition against the university's plan to reduce the number of campus parking spaces assigned to students.
Central Idea:	The university's plan to reduce student parking spaces is an infringement of student rights and will result in widespread illegal parking.

From this central idea we can deduce that the student will develop two main points in the speech: (1) students have a right to park on campus; and (2) if this right is limited, the students' only recourse is to park illegally.

There is something else important about these examples. Notice in each case how much more the central idea reveals about the content of the speech than does the specific purpose. This is not accidental. Often you can settle on your specific purpose statement early in preparing your speech. The central idea, however, usually emerges later—after you have done your research and have decided on the main points of the speech. The process may work like this:

As an environmental science major, Marcia Esposito had learned that many experts fear the world may face a severe water shortage by the year 2000. She decided this would make a good topic for her informative speech. Tentatively, she adopted the following specific purpose statement: "To inform my audience about the seriousness of the growing international water crisis." Then Marcia started her research.

An article in *Newsweek,* which she located through the *Readers' Guide to Periodical Literature,* explained how the population in countries such as China, Egypt, and Mexico is outstripping the available supply of fresh water. According to the article, one-third of the wells in Beijing, China's largest city, have gone dry, and the water table in Mexico City is dropping at the rate of 11 feet per year.

Next Marcia found a newspaper story about the impact of pollution on the water supply. It quoted a report from Worldwatch Institute stating that, in many parts of the world, urban and industrial contamination is creating "a water supply too polluted for their people to drink."

Then Marcia hit upon the idea of interviewing one of her environmental science professors. In addition to confirming Marcia's research about the impact of population growth and pollution, the professor also mentioned the problems caused by mismanagement of water supplies. Around the world 65 to 70 percent of the water people use is lost to waste, evaporation, and other inefficiencies; the rate in the United States is about 50 percent.

Marcia digested all this information. Now she was ready to formulate her central idea: "Population growth, pollution, and mismanagement are creating a serious shortage of fresh water in many parts of the world."

What makes a well-worded central idea? Essentially the same things that make a well-worded specific purpose statement. The central idea should be expressed in a full sentence, should not be in the form of a question, should avoid figurative language, and should not be vague or overly general.

Here, for example, are four poorly written central ideas. See if you can identify the problem with each and figure out how each might be phrased more effectively:

Ineffective: Paying college athletes a salary is a good idea.

Ineffective: Problems of fad diets.

Ineffective: How does indoor soccer differ from outdoor soccer?

Ineffective: Mexico's Yucatán peninsula is a sweet place for a vacation.

Number one, of course, is too general. To say that paying college athletes a monthly salary is a "good idea" does not convey the speaker's viewpoint sharply and clearly. What does the speaker mean by a "good idea"? That paying athletes a monthly salary is justified given the millions of dollars generated for universities by sports such as football and basketball? That the salary should be paid to all athletes, or just to those in major revenue-producing sports? That the salary should be $200 a month? If so, the central idea should say as much. A revised central idea for this speech might be:

More Effective: Because college athletes in revenue-producing sports such as football and basketball generate millions of dollars in revenue for their schools, the NCAA should allow such athletes to receive a $200 monthly salary as part of their scholarships.

The second ineffective central idea is also too general, but it suffers further from not being written as a complete sentence. "Problems of fad diets" might work as a topic statement, but it does not reveal enough about the content of the speech to serve as the central idea. It should be rewritten as a full sentence that identifies the problems of fad diets to be discussed in the speech:

More Effective: Although fad diets produce quick weight loss, they can lead to serious health problems by creating deficiencies in vitamins and minerals and by breaking down muscle tissue as well as fat.

The third poorly written central idea is phrased as a question rather than as a full declarative sentence. Asking "How does indoor soccer differ from outdoor soccer?" might be a good way to catch the interest of your listeners, but it does not encapsulate the main points to be developed in the speech. A more effective central idea would be:

More Effective: Played on a smaller, enclosed field that resembles a hockey rink with artificial turf, indoor soccer involves faster action, more scoring, and different strategies than outdoor soccer.

The final ineffective central idea is flawed by its use of figurative language. To say that the Yucatán peninsula is a "sweet" place for a vacation does not state the speaker's central idea clearly and concisely. It does not indicate what characteristics of the Yucatán peninsula the speaker intends to discuss. Moreover, "sweet" could mean quite different things to different people. A better central idea might be:

More Effective: Mexico's Yucatán peninsula has many attractions for vacationers, including a warm climate, excellent food, and extensive Mayan ruins.

Notice that in all these examples the more effective central idea encapsulates or sums up the main points of the speech in a single sentence. If you are having trouble phrasing your central idea, the reason may be that you do not yet have a firm grasp on the main points of your speech. Do not worry too much about your central idea until after you have developed the body of your speech (see Chapter 8). If, at that point, you still cannot come up with a clear, concise central idea, it may be that your speech itself is not very clear or concise. Keep working on the speech until you can compose a central idea that fits the criteria just discussed. The result will be a sharper central idea and a tighter, more coherent speech.

SUMMARY

The first step in speechmaking is choosing a topic. For classroom speeches it is often best to choose a subject you know well or in which you have personal experience, but you can also succeed with a topic you research especially for the speech. If you have trouble picking a topic, you can follow at least three procedures. First, make a quick inventory of your hobbies, interests, skills, experiences, beliefs, and so forth. Second, use the technique of brainstorming and write down on a sheet of paper the first topics that come to mind in several categories. Third, if you are really stuck, browse through a reference book for ideas.

After you choose a topic, you need to settle on the general purpose of your speech. Usually the general purpose will be to inform or to persuade. When your general purpose is to inform, you act as a teacher. Your goal is to communicate information clearly, accurately, and interestingly. When your general purpose is to persuade, you act as an advocate. You go beyond giving information to espousing a cause. Your goal is to win listeners over to your point of view.

Once you know your topic and general purpose, you must narrow in on a specific purpose that you can express as a single infinitive phrase. The phrase should indicate precisely what your speech seeks to achieve; for example, "To inform my audience of the major kinds of canoe races." The specific purpose statement should (1) be a full infinitive phrase, not a fragment; (2) be phrased as a statement, not a question; (3) avoid figurative language; (4) concentrate on one distinct idea; (5) not be too vague or general.

In addition, keep several questions in mind as you formulate your specific purpose statement: Does my purpose meet the assignment? Can I accomplish my purpose in the time allotted? Is the purpose relevant to my audience? Is the purpose too trivial or too technical for my audience?

The central idea refines and sharpens your specific purpose. It is a concise statement of what you will say in your speech, and it usually crystallizes in your thinking after you have done your research and have decided on the main points of your speech. An example of a central idea is "The three major kinds of canoe races are marathon races, white-water races, and flat-water races." As you can see, the central idea usually encapsulates the main points to be developed in the body of your speech.

REVIEW QUESTIONS

After reading this chapter, you should be able to answer the following questions:

1. What three procedures can you follow if you are having trouble choosing a topic for your speech?

2. What are the two general purposes of most classroom speeches? How do they differ?

3. Why is determining the specific purpose such an important early step in speech preparation? Why is it important to include the audience in the specific purpose statement?

4. What are five tips for formulating your specific purpose?

5. What are five questions to ask about your specific purpose?

6. What is the difference between the specific purpose and the central idea of a speech? What are four criteria for checking the effectiveness of your central idea?

APPLICATION EXERCISES

1. Using the method of brainstorming described in the chapter, come up with three topics you might like to deal with in your next classroom speech. For each topic, devise two possible specific purpose statements suitable for the speech assignment. Make sure the specific purpose statements fit the guidelines discussed in the chapter.

2. Below are six topics. Choose three, and for each of the three compose two specific purpose statements—one suitable for an informative speech and one suitable for a persuasive speech.

   Example:

   Topic: School buses.

   Informative: To inform my audience of the dangerous conditions of many school buses in the United States.

   Persuasive: To persuade my audience that the federal government should impose stronger safety standards for school buses in the United States.

weight lifting	women's rights
electoral college	skin cancer
television	education

3. Here are several specific purpose statements for classroom speeches. Identify the problem with each, and rewrite the statement to correct the problem.

   To inform my audience about Thailand.

   To persuade my audience that something has to be done about the growing problem of tuberculosis in the United States.

   To inform my audience how to make perfect popcorn every time.

   What is chronic fatigue syndrome?

   To inform my audience that being a Big Brother or a Big Sister is a cool experience.

   Learn CPR.

   To inform my audience about the growth of credit-card fraud and the methods of sound financial planning.

   To inform my audience why square grooves are superior to U-shaped grooves on golf clubs.

4. Below are four central ideas for speeches. Which two are from informative speeches, and which two are from persuasive speeches?

   The five major elements of art design are shape, space, color, line, and texture.

   Our state should deal with the problem of incompetent lawyers by requiring all attorneys to pass recertification examinations every ten years.

   A comprehensive program of parental leave should be instituted because it will benefit society as a whole as well as individual workers and families.

   The three major types of sleep disorders are insomnia, narcolepsy, and apnea.

5. Below are three sets of main points for speeches. For each set supply the general purpose, specific purpose, and central idea.

General Purpose:

Specific Purpose:

Central Idea:

Main Points: I. The first major race in alpine skiing is the downhill.
    II. The second major race in alpine skiing is the slalom.
    III. The third major race in alpine skiing is the giant slalom.

General Purpose:

Specific Purpose:

Central Idea:

Main Points: I. You should support the school-bond referendum because it will improve classroom facilities.
    II. You should support the school-bond referendum because it will increase the number of teachers.
    III. You should support the school-bond referendum because it will upgrade instructional resources.

General Purpose:

Specific Purpose:

Central Idea:

Main Points: I. As a social worker, Jane Addams founded the settlement-house movement in Chicago.
    II. As a reformer, Jane Addams campaigned for child-labor laws, unemployment compensation, and better public sanitation.
    III. As a suffragist, Jane Addams fought to give women the vote.
    IV. As a writer, Jane Addams is best known for her autobiographical *Twenty Years at Hull House.*

NOTES

[1] Adapted from R. R. Allen and Ray E. McKerrow, *The Pragmatics of Public Communication,* 3rd ed. (Dubuque, Iowa: Kendall/Hunt, 1985), pp. 42–44.
[2] James C. Humes, *Roles Speakers Play* (New York: Harper & Row, 1976), p. 5.

Chapter 5

Analyzing the Audience

AUDIENCE-CENTEREDNESS

YOUR CLASSMATES AS AN AUDIENCE

THE PSYCHOLOGY OF AUDIENCES

DEMOGRAPHIC AUDIENCE ANALYSIS
>   Age
>   Gender
>   Racial, Ethnic, or Cultural Background
>   Religion
>   Group Membership

SITUATIONAL AUDIENCE ANALYSIS
>   Size
>   Physical Setting
>   Disposition Toward the Topic
>   Disposition Toward the Speaker
>   Disposition Toward the Occasion

GETTING INFORMATION ABOUT THE AUDIENCE
>   Interviewing
>   Questionnaires

ADAPTING TO THE AUDIENCE
>   Audience Adaptation Before the Speech
>   Audience Adaptation During the Speech

F or Susan Estrada, the speaking invitation could not have come at a better time. Less than a year ago, she had passed her bar exams and taken a job with a leading local law firm. Now she had been asked to address a luncheon meeting of the Optimist Club on recent developments in business law. Here was the perfect opportunity to show her expertise and perhaps attract a new client or two.

With this in mind, Susan prepared the speech carefully. After much research and practice, it seemed absolutely right. She even had a graphics company make up some computer-generated charts for visual aids.

On the day of her speech, Susan was pleased to see that the meeting room was full. After being introduced, she walked to the lectern and started to talk. Because she was an expert in tax law, her speech was filled with information about "accrual basis deductions," "pre-affiliation depreciations," "Subchapter-S corporations," and "modified accelerated cost recovery systems." After a while, Susan noticed that people were beginning to shuffle their feet and look at their watches. She started speaking more emphatically and pointed often to her visual aids. Still, she could tell that she was losing her audience.

When the speech was finished, there was a ripple of polite applause, and Susan sat down. At the end of the meeting, she sought out the director of the program committee, who had invited her to speak. "Something tells me," she said, "that my speech was not an unqualified success."

"Oh, it was a good speech," the director replied. "We could all see that you know your subject inside and out. But you approached it at too high a level for this audience. Most of the people here are in small businesses. They are not particularly concerned about Subchapter-S corporations and pre-affiliation depreciations. When you started talking about modified accelerated cost recovery systems, you could almost see their eyes glaze over."

AUDIENCE-CENTEREDNESS

This story points up an important fact about public speaking: Good speakers are audience-centered. They know the primary purpose of speechmaking is not to display one's learning or demonstrate one's superiority or blow off steam. Rather, it is to gain a *desired response* from listeners. The key to successful communication is to "translate a truth into language perfectly intelligible to the person to whom you speak."[1] Susan Estrada's desired response at the Optimist Club meeting was to have her listeners see her as a competent lawyer. But she didn't make her message meaningful to them. Instead, she talked about tax concepts far outside their experience.

Being audience-centered does not mean taking any means to an end. You need not prostitute your beliefs to get a favorable response from your audience. Nor should you use devious, unethical tactics to achieve your goals. You can remain true to yourself while adapting your message to the needs of a particular audience. When working on your speeches, you should keep several questions in mind:

To whom am I speaking?

What do I want them to know, believe, or do as a result of my speech?

What is the most effective way of composing and presenting my speech to accomplish that aim?

The answers to these questions will influence every decision you make along the way—selecting a topic, determining a specific purpose, settling on your main points and supporting materials, organizing the message, and, finally, delivering the speech.

It can be instructive to watch how political candidates deal with audience-centeredness. Suppose a person is running for Congress. To an audience of senior citizens she or he might talk about Social Security benefits; to a group of farmers the speech might emphasize agricultural price supports; to urban apartment dwellers the candidate might stress methods to counteract street crime. This strategy is perfectly legitimate, provided all the policies are part of the candidate's overall program. If the candidate were to concentrate on agricultural price supports before a group of white-collar workers, they simply wouldn't care. The speaker's aim is to adjust to the concerns of the audience, not to show how much she or he knows about a wide variety of issues.

This is not very different from what you do in your daily social contacts. A generation or two ago it was considered rude to bring up three topics in polite conversation—politics, religion, and sex. Nowadays we don't adhere to such strictures. But since these are among the most controversial topics of discussion, we are usually careful about them. Few people would walk into a party and announce, "What a jerk the President is!" Or, "You know, I think those people protesting at the administration building against Dow Chemical are just plain nuts!" If you made either of these statements, you would risk having among your listeners (a) an ardent supporter of the President, (b) someone who participated in the protest at the administration building, (c) both of the above. The resulting situation could be most embarrassing.

People usually prefer to open such topics with a fairly noncommital position, to see how their listeners respond. You might say, "Did you hear what the President did today?" Or, "What's going on at the administration building?" Then when you have heard and processed your companion's response, you can tailor your statements accordingly. (You don't have to *agree* with a viewpoint different from your own; but neither do you have to hit your listeners over the head with your own opinion.)

When you make a speech, either in class or in some other forum, you can't just wait to see how your audience responds and then change the rest of the speech. But you can find out in advance as much as possible about your listeners' positions on various subjects. Unless you know what your listeners believe *now*, you cannot hope to change their beliefs.

At this point you may be nodding your head and saying, "Of course, everyone knows that. It's only common sense." But knowing a precept and putting it into practice are two different matters. The aim of this chapter is to introduce the basic principles necessary to understanding audiences. Chapters 14–16 will deal with those features of audience analysis and adaptation unique to informative and persuasive speaking.

YOUR CLASSMATES AS AN AUDIENCE

There is a tendency—among students and teachers alike—to view the class-room as an artificial speaking situation. In a way, it is. Your speech class is a testing ground where you can develop your communication skills before ap-plying them outside the classroom. No elections, no verdicts, no business de-cisions, no promotions ride on your performance. The most serious measure of success or failure is your grade, and that is determined ultimately by your teacher.

Because of this, it is easy to lose sight of your fellow students as an au-thentic audience. But each of your classmates is a real person with real ideas, attitudes, and feelings. Your speech class offers an enormous opportunity to inform and persuade other people. As one student wrote on her evaluation form at the end of her speech class, "I thought the speeches would all be phony, but they weren't. Some of them really hit me hard. I've not only learned a lot about speaking—I've learned a lot about other things from lis-tening to the speeches in class."

The best classroom speeches are those that take the classroom audience as seriously as a lawyer, a politician, a minister, or an advertiser takes an au-dience. Public speaking is not acting. The essence of speechmaking is not to learn a role that can be played over and over without variation, but to adapt one's ideas to particular audiences on particular occasions. If you regard your audience as artificial, you will probably give a speech that sounds artificial.

One key to successful speaking is to consider every audience—inside the classroom and out—as worthy of your best efforts to communicate your knowledge or convictions. At the least you show respect for your listeners. At the most you could make a real difference in their lives. The following story demonstrates the latter:

Crystal Watkins gave an informative speech on the subject of small claims court, where ordinary people can press lawsuits involving up to $2,000 without lawyers. Part of her speech went like this: "It's two weeks after you have moved into a new apartment. A letter arrives from your old landlord. Expecting to get back your $400 security deposit, you joyfully tear open the envelope. Inside is a form letter ex-plaining why your security deposit is not being returned. What can you do about it? Nothing, right? Wrong! You can file a claim in small claims court."

Lee Callaway, one of Crystal's classmates, paid close attention. At the end of the previous term, he had run into a situation just like the one Crystal described. Not having money to hire a lawyer, he assumed he would have to forfeit his security de-posit. But now, as he listened to Crystal's speech, Lee decided he would try to get his money back in small claims court. He filed suit the next week, and within a month he had his money back—thanks in part to his classmate's speech!

Most of your classroom speeches won't have this much immediate impact. Nevertheless, any topic that you handle conscientiously can influence your listeners—can enrich their experience, broaden their knowledge, perhaps change their views about something important.

■ THE PSYCHOLOGY OF AUDIENCES

What do you do when you listen to a speech? Sometimes you pay close attention; at other times you let your thoughts wander. People may be compelled to attend a speech, but no one can make them listen unless they want to. It's up to the speaker to make the audience *choose* to pay attention.

Even when people do pay attention, they don't process a speaker's message exactly as the speaker intends. Auditory perception is always *selective.* Every speech contains two messages—the one sent by the speaker and the one received by the listener. As we saw in Chapter 1, what a speaker says is filtered through a listener's frame of reference—the sum of her or his needs, interests, expectations, knowledge, and experience. As a result, we constantly listen and respond to speeches not as they are, but as we are. Or, to borrow from Paul Simon's classic song "The Boxer," people hear what they want to hear and disregard the rest.

What do people want to hear? Very simply, they usually want to hear about things that are meaningful to them. People are *egocentric.* They pay closest attention to messages that affect their own values, their own beliefs, their own well-being. Listeners typically approach speeches with one question uppermost in mind: "Why is this important to *me?*" As Harry Emerson Fosdick, the great preacher, once said: "There is nothing that people are so interested in as themselves, their own problems, and the way to solve them. That fact is basic. . . . It is the primary starting point of all successful public speaking."[2]

What do these psychological principles mean to you as a speaker? First, they mean your listeners will hear and judge what you say on the basis of what they already know and believe. Second, they mean you must relate your message to your listeners—show how it pertains to them, explain why they should care about it as much as you do. Here's an example:

Lisa Rugirello was hired straight out of college to be marketing assistant for a major firm that manufactured greeting cards. After only a few months on the job, Lisa was assigned to present to the sales force of 150 people a brand-new line of cards. She wrote a beautiful speech, pointing out the esthetic virtues of the artwork, the high quality of the verses, the excellence of the color reproduction.

Luckily, Lisa's boss asked to hear the speech before the day of the sales meeting. Her boss said, "You really have learned a lot about the product, and that's fine. But now you have to learn about sales representatives. These people earn their living selling cards. Their commissions make the difference between steak and canned tuna on the dinner table. You have to reach them through their pocketbooks."

Lisa digested this and reworked her speech. On the day of the sales meeting, she stood up before her audience and began: "Here's a new line of cards that can increase your quarterly sales by 15 percent. Let me give you some tips on selling them that can push you over your quota." In a few moments she had everyone's attention, and her speech was off to a great start.

As Lisa's experience shows, you need some grasp of what your listeners know, believe, and care about. Saul Alinsky, the noted community organizer, advises: "People only understand things in terms of their experience," which means that to communicate with them, "you must get within their experience."[3]

Of course, you can't actually get inside another person's experience. But you can learn enough about your audience to know what you should do to make your ideas clear and meaningful. How you can do this is our next topic.

■ DEMOGRAPHIC AUDIENCE ANALYSIS

One of the ways speakers analyze audiences is by looking for observable traits such as age, gender, religious orientation, racial, ethnic or cultural background, group membership, and the like. This is called *demographic audience analysis.* It consists of two steps: (1) identifying the general demographic features of your audience; (2) gauging the importance of those features to a particular speaking situation. Here are a few of the major factors you will need to consider.

Age

Are you a teenager or a senior citizen? Twentysomething or thirtysomething? A baby boomer or a baby buster? To some extent these are merely labels. All teenagers do not think alike; all baby boomers do not buy the same products; all senior citizens do not vote for the same political candidates.

Yet, as Aristotle noted over 2,000 years ago and as researchers have confirmed many times since, few things affect a person's outlook more than his or her age. Each generation has more-or-less common values and experiences that set it apart from other generations. No matter how hard they may try, for example, most people who grew up during the 1930s will probably never be fully comfortable with rap music, men wearing earrings, and couples living together outside of marriage. On the other hand, to people in their late teens or early twenties, Pearl Harbor, Marilyn Monroe, Vietnam, John Kennedy, Watergate—all are just people and events out of the past. Whatever your age, you are a product of your world.

You can see what this means for your speeches. Suppose you address an audience of older people. If you refer offhandedly to your "roommate"—making it clear that your roommate is someone of the opposite sex—your audience may be disturbed and tune out the rest of your speech. Similarly, if you speak to an audience of young adults and casually mention Joseph

McCarthy (an anti-Communist Senator of the 1950s) or the Tet offensive (an important campaign of the Vietnam war), they may not know what you are talking about. Even if younger listeners do recognize the names, they will not have the emotional associations of older people who lived through the 1950s or the war in Vietnam.

Depending on the composition of your speech class, you may face an audience that is mostly in their late teens and early twenties. If so, you can assume a common level of age experience. On the other hand, 45 percent of college students today are age twenty-five or older, and many classrooms include students in their thirties, forties, fifties, and beyond. You may then have to tackle two or three generations. This will give you good practice for speeches outside the classroom, where age is usually a major factor in audience analysis.

Gender

Shortly after graduation from college, Peter Harrington, who had been an art major, landed a dream job. He was hired as a guide-lecturer by a major museum, which meant he would conduct tours of people through the galleries and speak about the art. His first assignment was the contemporary art collection, and he prepared his talk carefully. At one point in it he said:

"The artist of today lives in a world that would have been incomprehensible to Rembrandt or van Gogh. He can be a superstar by the time he is twenty-five. He might see his earning power increase overnight from $10 a painting to $10,000 a painting. He is lionized by the media and sought out by collectors. No longer need an artist fear he will achieve fame only after he dies."

When Peter had finished, he asked the tour group whether they had any questions. A woman raised her hand and said, "Your talk was very interesting, but I have one problem with it. You kept referring to the artist as 'he.' Right here in this gallery I see paintings by five women artists. Don't you think it's time we acknowledged that not all artists are men?"

This story illustrates a problem that continues to plague speakers in all fields. We think of our times as enlightened, but we still encounter people who automatically refer to artists or doctors as "he" and to grade-school teachers or nurses as "she." A speaker who makes such remarks is almost certain to offend some members of the audience.

In speechmaking you must be wary of making assumptions with respect to gender until you have tested those assumptions and found them to be correct. Social distinctions between the sexes have been eroding for some years. Men now cook, keep house, work as receptionists, and volunteer in their children's schools. Women work in construction trades, run corporations, enlist in the armed forces, and serve as college athletic directors. Men and women today share a much broader range of experiences, interests, and aspirations than they once did.

In addition, the "typical" composition of audiences has also changed. At one time local civic groups such as the Kiwanis and Rotary clubs were all-

Good speakers are audience-centered. They work hard to find creative ways—including the use of humor—to evoke an enthusiastic response from their listeners.

male. Today most have sizable contingents of women. Parent associations, which were once composed almost solely of women, now include plenty of interested fathers. Here, as in other areas, the old stereotypes no longer apply.

This is not to say that women and men are alike in all their values and beliefs. When it comes to politics, for instance, American women tend to be more concerned about issues such as education, health care, and social justice, whereas men tend to stress economics and military defense. But keep in mind that these are generalizations. There are lots of women who believe military defense comes first, just as there are plenty of men who give priority to social issues. As astute speaker will be equally attuned to both the differences *and* the similarities between the sexes.

An astute speaker will also take care to avoid using sexist language. As we saw in the story of Peter Harrington at the start of this section, almost any audience you address will contain people—men and women alike—who will take offense at words and phrases that convey stereotyped or demeaning views of women. In Chapter 11 we will look more closely at sexist language and how to avoid it in your speeches. For now, it is enough to know that refraining from sexist language is an important part of being an audience-centered public speaker.[4]

Racial, Ethnic, or Cultural Background

As we saw in Chapter 1, the United States is becoming more and more a multiracial, multicultural society. Twenty-five percent of all Americans identify themselves as Hispanic or nonwhite, a figure that will continue to increase in the years ahead. Despite their similarities as Americans, people of European descent, blacks, Hispanics, Asians, and others may have different customs and beliefs that bear upon your speech topic. So, too, may international students. Here's what happened to one student who forgot to allow for such differences:

Beth Pilster-Pearson was giving an informative speech about trends in the naming of children. After citing figures on the most popular first names in the past ten years, she went on to describe changes in last names.

"Combining the father's last name and the mother's last name became popular in the late 1970s and early 1980s," she said, "but it never caught on in a big way. Even though I have a hyphenated name, I don't know what I'll do if I marry someone who also has a hyphenated name. And imagine what happens a few generations down the road when the baby's name doesn't fit on the birth certificate!"

Beth expected a laugh on this line, but the reaction was lukewarm at best. At the end of class, one of her classmates approached her. "Beth," she said, "there's no reason you would know, but in Hispanic culture, all children have two last names, the first from the father and the second from the mother. It's not a crazy system, and it wasn't new in the 1970s. My name is Esmeralda Razo Portillo—Razo from my Mexican father and Portillo from my Guatemalan mother."

What happened to Beth, of course, could happen to anyone who is not familiar with Hispanic culture. Even business leaders and heads of state sometimes misstep when speaking to people of different racial, ethnic, or cultural background. During his first trip to a foreign land after being elected President of the U.S., Bill Clinton rose to make a speech during a state dinner in South Korea. He asked the translator to stand between him and South Korean President Kim Young-sam, creating an awkward moment in a country where it is an insult for anyone to stand between two heads of state. At the same dinner, Clinton also referred several times to Kim's wife as "Mrs. Kim." But Korean women keep their birth names. Clinton should have addressed President Kim's wife as "Mrs. Sohn Myong-suk," or as "Mrs. Sohn."[5]

How can you avoid these kinds of gaffes in your speeches? The first step is to recognize that some of your listeners may indeed have special racial, ethnic, or cultural orientations that bear upon your speech topic. The second step is to try to determine what those orientations are and how they are likely to affect the audience's response to your message. The third step is to adjust your message so it will be as clear, suitable, and convincing as possible given the racial, ethnic, or cultural background of your listeners—as in the following example:

Wayne Reardon, a student at a large California university, decided to address his class about the value of crisis intervention counseling. To prepare for his speech, Wayne interviewed the director of the campus hotline about crisis intervention counseling on campus. At the end of the interview, the director made a comment Wayne found very interesting.

"Don't be surprised," the director said, "if Asian students are skeptical about your speech. Western-style psychotherapy is not common in countries such as Japan, Thailand, or Cambodia. Most people in Southeast Asia consider it an invasion of privacy and believe that telling one's problems to a stranger would mean loss of face. In times of crisis, they usually turn to their families."

In planning his speech, Wayne decided to meet the possible reservations of his classmates head-on. He began by explaining how crisis intervention had helped him through a difficult time. He then said: "I know many of you would be reluctant to call a hotline or talk to a stranger about a personal problem. I certainly was. Some of us, for cultural or personal reasons, believe family and friends are the only people we can turn to in a moment of crisis. The staff at the hotline understand these feelings very well. And their services are completely confidential. So when family and friends are far away or can't help, remember the hotline. Maybe it can help you as much as it helped me."

Throughout the rest of his speech, as Wayne described the theories and methods of crisis intervention, he could see that he had the full attention of his audience. Afterward, Ellen Morishita, one of Wayne's friends in class, told him, "I don't know if I'm totally convinced about the hotline, but I really appreciate your sensitivity to my culture. It made me want to listen to what you were saying."

No matter who the speaker, no matter what the occasion, adapting one's message to people of diverse cultures is an increasingly important aspect of the art of public speaking.

Religion

Russell Middleton, the director of the town's public library, was delighted to get an invitation to address his local civic association. He needed volunteers to help paint the reading rooms, and he felt sure he could recruit some from the association.

On the evening of his speech, Russell explained the painting project, making special mention of the fact that anyone who volunteered would help the library save money for more books and better programs. "Most of our work will be on Saturdays," he said. "We might also work in the evening, or maybe on a Sunday afternoon. But don't worry. We won't work on Sunday morning because that's when everyone will be at church." He finished by asking volunteers to sign up on a clipboard near the door.

At the end of the evening, Russell was pleased to see plenty of names on his clipboard, but he also found the following note. "Mr. Middleton," it began, "your project seems excellent, and I will be pleased to help. But I think you should remember that there are people in this community who do not go to church or worship on Sunday morning. I am Muslim, and some of the people sitting near me are Jewish. Fortunately, I had a chance to hear about your project before the comment about attending church on Sunday. If I hadn't, I might have concluded that you were not interested in my help. Please give me a call when you are ready to start the painting. Hamid Shakir."

This story illustrates a factor you must take into account in all your speeches. You cannot assume that your views on religion—whatever they may be—are shared by your listeners. And religious views are among the most emotionally charged and passionately defended of all human concerns. Even your small speech class might include a wide range of faiths, as well as atheists and agnostics.

As the United States becomes more diverse culturally, it is also becoming more diverse religiously. The traditional mix of Protestantism, Catholicism, and Judaism is being enriched by growing numbers of Muslims, Buddhists, Hindus, Sikhs, Baha'is, and others. You can see this diversity in cities large and small across the land. There are seven Buddhist temples in Salt Lake City, two Sikh gurdwaras in Phoenix, a Taoist temple in Denver, five Muslim mosques in Oklahoma City, and a Jain center in Blairstown, New Jersey. Nationwide there are more than 1,100 houses of worship for Muslims, 1,500 for Buddhists, and 400 for Hindus.[6]

There is also great diversity within different faiths. You cannot assume that all Catholics support the official view of their church on such matters as birth control or women in the priesthood, any more than you can stereotype all Mormons as favoring polygamy or all Baptists as being born-again. In matters of religion, the United States is truly a nation of many faiths, many voices, many views.

Whenever you speak on a topic with religious dimensions, then, be sure to consider the religious orientations of your listeners. At the least, failure to do so can weaken your speech. At the most, you may be seriously embarrassed.

Group Membership

"Tell me thy company," says Don Quixote, "and I'll tell thee what thou art." For all of our talk about rugged individualism, Americans are very group-oriented. Workers belong to unions, businesspeople to chambers of commerce. Hunters join the National Rifle Association, environmentalists the Sierra Club, feminists the National Organization for Women. Doctors enroll in the American Medical Association, lawyers in the American Bar Association. There are thousands of such voluntary organizations in the United States.

Similar groups abound on campus. Some of your classmates may belong to fraternities or sororities, some to Campus Crusade for Christ, some to the Young Republicans, some to the film society, some to the ski club, and so forth. For speeches in the classroom, as well as for those outside the classroom, the group affiliations of your audience may provide excellent clues about your listeners' interests and attitudes.

Age, gender, religion, racial, ethnic, or cultural background, group membership—these are just a few of the variables to consider in demographic audience analysis. Others include occupation, economic position, social standing, education, intelligence, and place of residence. Indeed, *anything* characteristic of a given audience is potentially important to a speaker addressing that audience. For your classroom speeches, you may want to learn about your classmates' academic majors, years in school, extracurricular activities, living arrangements, and job aspirations.

Perhaps the most important thing to keep in mind about demographic audience analysis is that it is not an end in itself. Your aim is not just to list the major traits of your listeners but to find in those traits clues about how your listeners will respond to your speech. Once you have done that, you are ready to move on to the second stage of audience analysis.

SITUATIONAL AUDIENCE ANALYSIS

Situational audience analysis usually builds on the demographic analysis. It identifies traits of the audience unique to the speaking situation at hand. These traits include the size of the audience, attitudes influenced by the physical setting, and the disposition of the audience toward the subject, the speaker, and the occasion.

Size

Outside the classroom, the size of an audience can, with the aid of television and radio, range in the millions. Most speech classes, however, consist of between fifteen and thirty people—a small- to medium-sized audience. This is a good size for beginning speakers, most of whom are horrified at the prospect of addressing a huge crowd. As you gain more experience, though, you may welcome the challenge of speaking to larger groups. Some speakers actually prefer a large audience to a small one.

No matter what size group you are addressing, bear in mind one basic principle: The larger the audience, the more formal your presentation must be. This will have the greatest impact on your delivery, but it may also affect your language, choice of appeals, and use of visual aids.

Physical Setting

The receptivity of listeners to your speech frequently will be influenced by factors beyond their control—and sometimes beyond your control. Which of the following would you rather address?

An audience assembled immediately after lunch, crammed into an overheated room with inadequate seating

An audience assembled at 10:00 in the morning, comfortably seated in an airy, well-lighted room

Undoubtedly you chose the second option. Any of the adverse conditions listed in the first could seriously impair your audience's willingness to accept your ideas or even listen to you at all.

When you face any speaking situation, it is important to know in advance if there will be any difficulties with the physical setting. For classroom speeches, of course, you already do know. But speeches outside the classroom can confront you with many unpleasant surprises unless you do your homework beforehand.

When you are invited to speak, don't be shy about asking questions of the person who arranged the speech. If possible, look over the room yourself a few days in advance, or else arrive early on the day of your speech to give the room a quick inspection. If it is too warm or too cold, see about adjusting the thermostat. Check the seating arrangements and the location of the lectern to be sure your audience can see you properly. In short, do everything you can to control the influence of physical setting on your audience.

But, you may wonder, what about circumstances you can't control? Your speech *is* scheduled directly after lunch or dinner. The room *is* too small for the audience expected. The heat *cannot* be regulated. Then you are simply going to have to work harder to adapt to these aspects of your listeners' discomfort. When faced with an audience that is potentially hot, sleepy, and cross, do your best to make the speech as interesting and lively as you can. Above all, don't let *yourself* be influenced by the poor physical setting. If your audience sees that you are energetic, alert, and involved with your topic, chances are they will forget their discomfort and come right along with you.

Disposition Toward the Topic

As we saw in Chapter 4, you should keep your audience in mind when choosing a topic. Ideally, you will pick a topic that suits them as well as it suits you. Once you have your topic, however, you must consider in more detail how your listeners will react to it. In particular, you need to assess their interest in the topic, their knowledge about it, and their attitudes toward it.

Interest   Outside the classroom, people do not often expend the time and effort to attend a speech unless they are interested in the topic. But the members of your speech class are a captive audience. Sometimes they will be deeply interested in your topic, particularly if it relates directly to them. Most of the time they will range from fairly interested to mildly curious to downright indifferent.

One of your tasks will be to assess their interest in advance and to adjust your speech accordingly. Most important, if your topic is not likely to generate great interest, you must take special steps to get your classmates involved. Here are two brief examples of how to do this:

Ahmed planned to speak about Parkinson's disease. At the beginning of his speech, he said: "Imagine you just had five cups of coffee for breakfast at the student union. When you get to class, you decide to have two more cups just outside the door. You're probably feeling a bit disoriented, and if you held your hands out, you'd notice they were shaking. This feeling is about as close as you can get to the first symptoms of Parkinson's disease."

Megan's speech was about world hunger. Before she began to speak, she started a metronome that was set to tick at intervals of one-and-a-half seconds. Megan let the metronome tick for twenty-five seconds. Then she turned it off and said, "For each tick of this metronome, one person, somewhere in the world, has just died from starvation, malnutrition, or a malnutrition-caused disease."

In the chapters that follow, we will look closely at all the ways you can develop interest in your topic—by an arresting introduction, provocative supporting details, vivid language, dynamic delivery, visual aids, and so forth.

Knowledge   There is often a strong correlation between interest in a topic and knowledge about it. People tend to be interested in what they know about. Likewise, they are inclined to learn about subjects that interest them. But there are exceptions. Few students know much about handwriting analysis, yet most would find it an absorbing topic. On the other hand, almost all know a lot about checking books out of the library, but few would find it a fascinating subject for a speech.

Why is it important to gauge your listeners' knowledge about your topic? Quite simply, because it will to a large extent determine what you can say in your speech. If your listeners know little about your topic—whether or not they find it interesting—you will have to talk at a more elementary level. If they are reasonably well informed, you can take a more technical and detailed approach.

Attitude   The attitude of your listeners toward your topic can be extremely important in determining how you handle the material. If you know in advance the prevailing attitude among your audience, you can adjust what you say to what your audience needs to hear. Consider the experiences of the following two students—one who did not account for listener attitude and one who did:

Brad Kaminski spoke about the effects on human health of pesticides and other chemicals found in the environment. On the basis of his research, he believed that the dangers of exposure to pesticide residues in our food have been exaggerated by the popular press. His position was interesting but highly controversial. Unfortunately, rather than citing his sources and acknowledging that his point of view was unusual, Brad presented his material as though it were general knowledge.

The speech was not well received. In fact, the class found Brad's approach so inconsistent with everything they had read about pesticides and food that they couldn't accept it. As one student said after the speech, "You may be right in what you said, but I have trouble believing it. We've all heard so much about the dangers of pesticides—can it all be wrong? I think you would have been more persuasive if you had looked at both sides of the issue rather than just your own."

Had Brad taken the skepticism of his audience into account, he could have established the scientific credibility of his material, and thereby made his audience more receptive to his point of view.

Compare the approach of Kristi Nguyen, who also espoused a controversial viewpoint:

A firm believer in animal rights, Kristi decided to give her persuasive speech in favor of banning all use of animals in scientific experiments. After distributing a questionnaire among her classmates, she found that most of them favored using animals—when necessary—in scientific research. They gave two reasons. First, they believed the welfare of human beings was more important than that of animals. Second, they believed research with animals was indispensable to the fight against such maladies as AIDS, cancer, heart disease, and diabetes.

Although Kristi disagreed with these beliefs, she realized she could neither ignore them nor insult her classmates for holding them. She knew she would have to discuss these points logically and with hard evidence if she were to have any chance of persuading her audience.

As it turned out, Kristi did convince some members of the class to reconsider their beliefs. She could not have done so without first investigating what those beliefs were and then adapting her message to them.

Disposition Toward the Speaker

Let's return for a moment to Brad's speech about pesticide residues in food. Brad was a sophomore business major with no special scientific or nutritional background. It's not surprising that his classmates took his statements with a large grain of salt. But suppose Brad had been a recognized expert on pesticides and the food chain. Then his listeners would have found him much more believable. Why? Because an audience's response to a message is invariably colored by their perception of the speaker.

The more competent listeners believe a speaker to be, the more likely they are to accept what the speaker says. Likewise, the more listeners believe that a speaker has their best interests at heart, the more likely they are to respond positively to the speaker's message.

We will come back to this subject in detail when we deal with strategies for persuasive speaking in Chapter 16. For now, keep in mind that your listeners will always have *some* set of attitudes toward you as a speaker. Estimating what those attitudes are and how they will affect your speech is a crucial part of situational audience analysis.

Disposition Toward the Occasion

It was Martin Luther King Day, and the city was holding a public program celebrating King's life and legacy. More than 1,000 people, including hundreds of schoolchildren, were in attendance. All the prominent figures of the city—politicians, clergy, businesspeople, community leaders—were on the platform. Between songs and other performances, they came to the microphone to talk briefly about the great civil rights leader and what his memory meant to them.

One of the last to speak was James Irvin, the developer of a proposed business complex that he hoped to locate in one of the city's more impoverished neighborhoods. Irvin began his speech by invoking the memory of Dr. King. He then continued: "Some people say I'm out to exploit the poor people of this city and get tax breaks for myself. All I want to do is bring money into the community and make a fair profit on my investment. But to do that I need the support of every one of the people sitting up here with me today, and I want all of you to hold them accountable."

The people on the platform merely looked uncomfortable, but the audience reacted with boos and hisses.

On other occasions Irvin's comments would not have touched off such an angry response. But the Martin Luther King Day gathering was understood by the organizers—and the audience—to be an occasion for commemoration and reverence. The last thing they expected to hear was a pitch for a business project. What angered the audience was not what Irvin said, but that he exploited the occasion for his own purposes.

No matter what the situation, listeners have fairly definite ideas about the speeches they consider appropriate. They expect to hear political speeches in Congress, sermons in church, after-dinner speeches after dinner, and so forth. Speakers who seriously violate these expectations can almost always count on infuriating the audience.

Perhaps most important, the occasion will dictate how long a speech should be. When you are invited to speak, the chairperson will usually say how much time you have for your talk. If not, be sure to ask. And once you know, pare down your speech so it fits easily within the allotted time. Do not exceed that time under any circumstances, for you are likely to see your audience dwindle as you drone on. (This is one reason why most teachers insist that classroom speeches be kept within the designated time limit. It provides crucial training for speeches you will give outside the classroom.)

There are other audience expectations that apply to your classroom situation. One is that speeches will conform to the assignment. Another is that speakers will observe appropriate standards of taste and decorum. Failure to adhere to these expectations may disturb your classmates and will almost certainly damage your grade.

GETTING INFORMATION ABOUT THE AUDIENCE

Now that you know *what* to learn about an audience, the next question is *how* do you learn it? A person running for high political office can rely on hired professional pollsters. If, as is more likely, you are invited sometime to address a particular group—say a meeting of the local Rotary club—the person who invites you can usually provide a good sketch of the audience. Ask your contact with the group where you can find out more about its history and purpose. Best of all, if you know someone who has spoken to the same group, be sure to sound out that person.

In political campaigns, poll-taking helps the candidates keep track of public opinion. For classroom speeches, you can use an audience questionnaire to gauge the knowledge and opinions of your listeners.

What about your classmates as an audience? You can learn a lot about them just by observation and conversation. Still, you probably will need to know more about their backgrounds and opinions in relation to specific speech topics. Some teachers require students to do a formal audience analysis—either through interviews or through written questionnaires—for at least one of their speeches.

Interviewing

The face-to-face interview (see Chapter 6) is highly flexible and allows for in-depth questioning. When properly planned, structured, and conducted, it can be a superb way of learning about individual members of an audience. The great drawback is the cost in time and energy. Interviewing each member of a class before every speech may be the most thorough method of audience analysis, but it is seldom practical. Therefore, most teachers encourage their students to rely on questionnaires.

Questionnaires

Like interviewing, constructing a good questionnaire is an art you cannot be expected to master in a speech class. By following a few basic guidelines, however, you can learn to develop a questionnaire that will be more than adequate for analyzing your classroom audience.

There are three major types of questions to choose from: fixed-alternative questions, scale questions, and open-ended questions.[7]

Fixed-alternative questions, as their name implies, offer a fixed choice between two or more responses. For example:

Have you ever voted in a local, state, or national election?

Yes _____

No _____

Are you currently registered to vote?

Yes _____

No _____

By limiting the possible responses, such questions produce clear, unambiguous answers. They also tend to yield superficial answers. Other techniques are needed to get beneath the surface.

Scale questions resemble fixed-alternative questions, but they allow more leeway in responding. For example:

How important is it for U.S. citizens to exercise their right to vote?

very					not at all
important					important

Do you agree or disagree with this statement: People have a responsibility to vote even if they do not fully support any of the candidates.

strongly agree	mildly agree	undecided	mildly disagree	strongly disagree

Questions like these are especially useful for getting at the strength of a respondent's attitudes.

Open-ended questions give maximum latitude in responding. For example:

How would you feel if you lived in a country where you did not have the right to vote?

Briefly respond to this statement: Unhappiness with political leaders is a bad excuse for not voting; if you don't vote, you can't make things better.

Although open-ended questions invite more detailed responses than the other two types of questions, they also increase the likelihood of getting answers that do not give the kind of information you need.

Because each type of question has its advantages and disadvantages, many questionnaires contain all three types. Figure 5.1 shows a questionnaire that was distributed before a classroom speech on living wills—documents written by people to indicate how much medical intervention they would

Two fixed alternative questions establish the listeners' level of knowledge about the topic.

A third fixed-alternative question pins down the listeners' degree of involvement.

This scale question was designed to show the audience's empathy or lack of empathy toward people who have drawn up a living will.

The open-ended questions help show the listeners' disposition toward solutions. Specifically, the speaker wants to know: Will my audience support the living will even in the face of opposition?

1. Do you know what a living will is?
   Yes _____
   No _____

2. Do you know anyone who has made a living will?
   Yes _____
   No _____
   Not sure _____

3. Has anyone close to you— a relative or family friend— ever been hospitalized with a terminal illness?
   Yes _____
   No _____

4. Do you agree or disagree with this statement: Doctors and hospitals should abide by a patient's wish to refuse medical treatment when death is inevitable.

Strongly agree	Mildly agree	Undecided	Mildly disagree	Strongly disagree

5. What would you do if a close relative were gravely ill and wished to be allowed to die, but the hospital insisted on continuing "heroic" medical procedures?

6. Who do you believe should have the most say in deciding when a patient should be allowed to die?

FIGURE 5.1   Sample Questionnaire

want should they become terminally ill or incapacitated. By using all three types of questions, the student did two things—elicited specific information about the audience and probed more deeply into their attitudes toward the speech topic. The results of the questionnaire survey broke down like this:

1. Only half of the class knew what a living will is. Therefore, the speaker had to be sure to explain living wills clearly at the start of her speech.

2. Six students knew someone who had made a living will; most said they were not sure. Thus the speaker could not depend on a high degree of personal involvement among the audience.

3. Five students reported that a relative—a grandparent or elderly aunt or uncle—had been hospitalized with a terminal illness. One of these wrote movingly about a grandparent's pleas to "let me go."

4. More than 65 percent of the respondents either "strongly agreed" or "mildly agreed" that a patient's wishes should be paramount in refusing medical treatment. Another 20 percent were undecided. The speaker could therefore depend on an audience generally disposed toward the concept of a living will.

5. Responses to the fifth question—"What would you do if a close relative were gravely ill and wished to be allowed to die, but the hospital insisted on continuing 'heroic' medical procedures?"—were varied. They ranged from "I guess I'd take the doctors' word; they know best" to "I'd pull the plug myself!" Obviously, this was a charged issue. The questionnaire showed the speaker would have to handle it very carefully.

6. Again, responses varied on the question of who should have the most say in deciding about a patient's death. Most students proposed a compromise—the patient *and* the family, or the family *and* the doctors. Only two thought lawyers and judges should be involved. In combination with the answers to question 4, these responses indicated that the audience could be classified as favorable to the speaker's views.

This questionnaire worked extremely well. It revealed a great deal about the listeners' knowledge, attitudes, and concerns. You should be able to put together an equally useful questionnaire. In doing so, keep the following principles in mind:

1. Plan the questionnaire carefully to elicit precisely the information you need.

2. Use all three types of questions—fixed-alternative, scale, and open-ended.

3. Make sure the questions are clear and unambiguous.

4. Keep the questionnaire relatively brief.

ADAPTING TO THE AUDIENCE

Once you have completed the audience analysis, you should have a pretty clear picture of your listeners. You should know their relevant demographic characteristics, their interest in and knowledge about the topic, their attitudes toward the topic and the speaker, and their expectations about the occasion. Knowing all this, however, does not guarantee a successful speech. The key is how well you *use* what you know in preparing and presenting the speech.

This point deserves special attention because it poses one of the hardest tasks facing novice speakers. Most people can identify the major characteristics of their audience, but many have trouble *adapting* their ideas to the audience. There are two major stages in the process of audience adaptation—the first occurs before the speech, as part of your preparation and rehearsal; the second occurs during the presentation of the speech itself.

Audience Adaptation Before the Speech

As we have seen, you must keep your audience in mind at every stage of speech preparation. "Keep your audience in mind," however, involves more than simply remembering who your listeners will be. Above all, it means two things: (a) assessing how your audience is likely to respond to what you will say in your speech and (b) adjusting what you say to make it as clear, appropriate, and convincing as possible.

This is not always easy to do. We are all so wrapped up in our own ideas and concerns that we have trouble seeing things from other people's perspective—especially if their perspective is quite different from ours. If, for example, you speak on a subject in which you are expert, you may find it hard to put yourself in the place of someone who knows nothing about it. To step outside your own frame of reference and see things from another person's point of view is a real achievement.

Yet this is what a successful speaker eventually learns to do. You must submerge your own views so completely that you can adopt, temporarily, those of your listeners. When you do this, you will begin to hear your speech through the ears of your audience and to adjust it accordingly.

You must keep your listeners constantly in mind as you prepare your speech. Try to imagine what they will like, what they will dislike, where they will have doubts or questions, whether they will need more details here or fewer there, what will interest them and what will not.

At every point you must *anticipate* how your audience will respond. How will they react to your introduction and conclusion? Will they find your examples clear and convincing? Will your visual aids help them grasp your ideas? How will they respond to your language and manner of delivery? As you answer these questions, consciously identify with your listeners. Put yourself in their place and respond to your speech as they would.

Here is how one student worked out his problems of audience adaptation:

Juan Ruiz, a junior geology major, decided to give an informative speech about how earthquakes occur. From his audience analysis he learned that only two or three of his classmates knew much of anything about geology. To most of them, a tectonic plate would be found on a dinner table rather than below the surface of the earth. Juan realized, then, that he must present his speech at an elementary level and with a minimum of scientific language.

As he prepared the speech, Juan kept asking himself, "How can I make this clear and meaningful to someone who knows nothing about earthquakes or geological principles?" Since he was speaking in the Midwest, he decided to begin by noting that the most severe earthquake in American history took place not in California or Alaska, but at New Madrid, Missouri, in 1811. If such an earthquake happened today, it would be felt from the Rocky Mountains to the Atlantic Ocean and would flatten most of the cities in the Mississippi Valley. That, he figured, should get his classmates' attention.

Throughout the body of the speech, Juan dealt only with the basic mechanics of earthquakes and carefully avoided technical terms such as "asthenosphere," "lithosphere," and "subduction zones." He also prepared visual aids diagramming fault lines so his classmates wouldn't get confused.

To be absolutely safe, Juan asked his roommate—who was not a geology major—to listen to the speech. "Stop me," he said, "any time I say something you don't understand." Juan's roommate stopped him four times, and at each spot Juan worked out a way to make his point more clearly. Finally, he had a speech that was interesting and perfectly understandable to his audience.

As you work on your speeches, try to keep your listeners constantly in mind. Anticipate how they will respond to your ideas. Be creative in thinking about ways to adapt your message to them. Like Juan, you will give a much better speech.

Audience Adaptation During the Speech

No matter how hard you work ahead of time, it's always possible that things will not go just as you had planned on the day of your speech. For speeches in the classroom you may find that the easel for your visual aids is not available or that another student has the same topic as you. For speeches outside the classroom you might learn that the room for your speech has been changed, that the audience will be much larger (or smaller) than you had anticipated, or even that the amount of time available for your speech has been cut in half because a previous speaker has droned on for too long.

If something like this happens to you, don't panic. Find another way to present your visual aids. Modify your introduction to mention the other student's speech on your topic. Adjust your delivery to the changed audience size. And if you find you have less time for your speech than you had planned, don't simply talk twice as fast to get everything in—that would be worse than not talking at all. Instead, condense your speech to its most essential points and present them in the time available. Your listeners will sympathize with your predicament and will appreciate your regard for their time. This will more than compensate for your lost speaking time.

Finally, be sure to keep an eye out during your speech for audience feedback. If your listeners are sitting forward in their chairs, looking at you with interest, and nodding their heads in approval, you can assume things are going well. But suppose you find them frowning or responding with quizzical looks. Then you may need to back up and go over your point again, as in this example:

Michelle Voss, a business major, had worked diligently to make sure her informative speech on investing in the stock market was not too technical for her classmates, most of whom were engineering and humanities students. She explained everything from the ground up, prepared two excellent visual aids, and practiced giving the speech to her best friend, an art major and self-confessed "economics imbecile."

On the day of Michelle's speech, everything went well until she got to her second main point, when she noticed that several of her classmates seemed puzzled by the relationship between common stock and preferred stock. Knowing they would be lost for the rest of the speech if they didn't understand that relationship, Michelle paused and said, "I can see some of you are confused by my explanation. Let me try it again from another angle."

As Michelle went through the material a second time, she could see her classmates nodding their heads in understanding. She could now go on with her speech, confident that her audience was ready to go with her.

Adapting to your audience—both before the speech and during it—is one of the most important keys to successful public speaking. Like other aspects of speechmaking, it is sometimes easier said than done. But once you master it, you'll see that it pays dividends in more personal facets of your life—when you adapt to an audience of one.

SUMMARY

Good speakers are audience-centered. They know the aim of speechmaking is to gain a desired response from listeners. When working on your speeches, keep three questions in mind: To whom am I speaking? What do I want them to know, believe, or do as a result of my speech? What is the most effective way of composing and presenting my speech to accomplish that aim? Your classroom speeches will give you excellent practice in dealing with these questions, provided you always think of your classmates as a *real* audience.

To be an effective speaker, you should know something about the psychology of audiences. Auditory perception is selective. Even when people pay close attention, they don't process a speaker's message exactly as the speaker intended. People hear what they want to hear. People also are egocentric. They typically approach speeches with one question uppermost in mind: "Why is this important to *me?*" Therefore, you need to study your audience and adapt your speech directly to their beliefs and interests.

The first stage in learning about your audience is to undertake a demographic audience analysis. This involves identifying important demographic traits of your audience such as age, gender, religion, group membership, and racial, ethnic, or cultural background. The second stage in learning about your audience is to conduct a situational audience analysis. This involves identifying traits of the audience unique to the particular speaking situation at hand. These traits include the size of the audience, attitudes influenced by the physical setting, and your listeners' disposition toward the topic, toward you as a speaker, and toward the occasion.

For speeches outside the classroom, you can best get information about the audience by asking the person who invites you to speak. If possible, you should also sound out someone else who has spoken to the same group. For your classroom speeches, you can learn much about your audience by observation and conversation. You also can do a more formal audience analysis by interviewing or by circulating a questionnaire.

Once you complete the audience analysis, you must adapt your speech so it will be clear and convincing to your listeners. Keep them in mind constantly as you prepare the speech. Put yourself in their place. Try to hear the speech as they will. Anticipate questions and objections, and try to answer them in advance.

When you deliver your speech, keep an eye out for audience feedback. If you see frowns or puzzled looks on your listeners' faces, you may need to adjust your remarks in response. Like other aspects of audience adaptation, this may be difficult at first, but if you work at it, you should soon see results.

REVIEW QUESTIONS

After reading this chapter, you should be able to answer the following questions:

1. Why must a public speaker be audience-centered?

2. What does it mean to say that people are egocentric? What implications does the egocentrism of audiences hold for you as a public speaker?

3. What are the five demographic traits of audiences discussed in this chapter? Why is each important to audience analysis?

4. What is situational audience analysis? What factors do you need to consider in situational audience analysis?

5. How can you get information about an audience?

6. What are the three kinds of questions used in questionnaires? Why is it a good idea to use all three in audience analysis?

7. What methods can you use to adapt your speech to your audience before the speech? During the speech?

APPLICATION EXERCISES

1. Advertisers are usually very conscious of their audience. Choose an issue of a popular magazine such as *Time, Newsweek, Sports Illustrated,* or *Cosmopolitan.* From that issue select five advertisements to analyze. Try to determine the audience being appealed to in each advertisement, and analyze the appeals (verbal and visual) used to persuade buyers. How might the appeals differ if the ads were designed to persuade a different audience?

2. Below are three general speech topics and, for each, two hypothetical audiences to which a speech might be delivered. For each topic, write a brief paragraph explaining how you might adjust your specific purpose and message according to the demographic characteristics of the audience.

a. *Topic:* "Fiber-Optic Technology"
   Audience #1: 50% engineering majors, 30% science majors, 20% music majors
   Audience #2: 40% English majors, 30% science majors, 30% prelaw majors

b. *Topic:* "Sexual Assault: The Biggest Campus Crime"
   Audience #1: 80% female, 20% male
   Audience #2: 80% male, 20% female

c. *Topic:* "The Watergate Crisis"
   Audience #1: Day class, 70% age 18 to 22, 30% age 23 and over
   Audience #2: Evening class, 50% age 35 and over, 30% age 22 to 35, 20% age 18 to 22

3. For your next speech, design and circulate among your classmates an audience analysis questionnaire like that discussed on pages 105–108. Use all three kinds of questions explained in the text—fixed-alternative questions, scale questions, and open-ended questions. After you have tabulated the results of the questionnaire, write an analysis explaining what the questionnaire reveals about your audience and what steps you must take to adapt your speech to the audience.

4. Analyze the speech in the Appendix by Alan Alda ("A Reel Doctor's Advice to Some Real Doctors," pages 440–444). Explain the methods Alda uses to fit his message to the audience. Be specific in your analysis, and be prepared to discuss your conclusions in class.

5. Read the speech in the Appendix by Barbara Bush ("Choices and Change," pages 447–450). Focus on how Bush adapts her message to her audience in light of the controversy that preceded her speech. Be prepared to discuss your ideas in class.

NOTES

[1] Ralph Waldo Emerson, quoted in Robert T. Oliver, *History of Public Speaking in America* (Boston: Allyn and Bacon, 1965), p. 122.

[2] Quoted in Halford R. Ryan, "Harry Emerson Fosdick," in Bernard K. Duffy and Halford R. Ryan (eds.), *American Orators of the Twentieth Century* (New York: Greenwood Press, 1987), p. 148.

[3] Saul Alinsky, *Rules for Radicals* (New York: Random House, 1971), p. 81.

[4] For a broader discussion of gender issues in communication, see Diana K. Ivy and Phil Backlund, *Exploring GenderSpeak: Personal Effectiveness in Gender Communication* (New York: McGraw-Hill, 1994); Julia T. Wood, *Gendered Lives: Communication, Gender, and Culture* (Belmont, Calif.: Wadsworth, 1994).

[5] David Foster, "Cultural Concierges on Alert," *Wisconsin State Journal* (November 19, 1993).

[6] Richard N. Ostling, "One Nation under Gods," *Time* (Fall 1993), p. 62.

[7] Fred N. Kerlinger, *Foundations of Behavioral Research*, 3rd ed. (New York: Holt, Rinehart and Winston, 1986), pp. 441–445.

Chapter 6

Gathering Materials

USING YOUR OWN KNOWLEDGE AND EXPERIENCE

INTERVIEWING
Before the Interview
During the Interview
After the Interview

WRITING AWAY FOR INFORMATION

DOING LIBRARY RESEARCH
The Librarians
The Library Catalogues
The Reference Section
Computerized Research Services

TIPS FOR DOING RESEARCH
Start Early
Make a Preliminary Bibliography
Take Notes Efficiently
Think About Your Materials As You Research

Suppose you want to build an audiovisual center for your home. You need to provide space for all the components (tape player, speakers, CD player, television, VCR, etc.) as well as storage for tapes and discs. How do you go about it? You can talk to people who have built their own centers and ask them for details. You can write away to a magazine for plans. You can get books from the library and follow their instructions. On the other hand, if you've worked on an audiovisual center before, you can fall back on your experience and adapt it to your present needs. Since you want your center to be perfect, you gather as much information as you can before starting to build.

Gathering material for a speech is like gathering information for any project. Many resources are available to you if you take advantage of them. How do you get material for your speeches? There are several ways. You can interview people with specialized knowledge on a given topic. You can write to individuals or groups that collect information on your subject and are set up to provide it to the public. You can do research in the library. Sometimes you can use yourself as a resource—whenever you have personal experience or more-than-average knowledge about a subject. Let's turn first to the resource of your own experience.

USING YOUR OWN KNOWLEDGE AND EXPERIENCE

Everybody is an expert on something, whether it is auto mechanics or baking brownies or simply "Why I Failed Calculus." As we saw in Chapter 4, we usually speak best about subjects with which we are familiar. This is why teachers encourage students to capitalize on their own knowledge and experience in developing speech topics.

When you choose a topic from your own experience, you may be tempted to depersonalize it by relying solely on facts and figures from books. Such outside information is almost always necessary. But supplementing it with the personal touch can really bring your speeches to life.

One student, afflicted with diabetes, chose to explain how a person can live with the disease on a daily basis. He cited statistics on the incidence of diabetes in the United States, identified symptoms of the disease, and related how it is treated. Along the way he also illustrated his points by talking about his personal experiences. Here is part of what he said:

Being a diabetic presents a challenge one cannot afford to lose. On a personal note, I have tried not to let my diabetes affect my life style. Last year I spent nine months traveling in Central and South America. The trip was very memorable, but I had one particularly frightening experience that quickly makes you realize just how vulnerable a diabetic is. On the fifth day of a two-week excursion down the Amazon River in Brazil, our canoe tipped, dumping everything into the river.

Although I recovered my pack, part of its contents—including my insulin—were swallowed up by the river. Without insulin I could not eat any food, for if I did, my blood-sugar level would become too high and I could eventually go into convulsions, slip into a coma, and die. We returned back up the Amazon and traveled three days until we reached the first village and I could radio for more medicine. I was hot and hungry, but alive.

This speech has color and emotion. By drawing on his own experience, the speaker conveyed his point much more meaningfully than he could have in any other way.

Even if your life stories are not that dramatic, you can still put them to work for you. After all, you are the one who was there. You did, saw, felt, heard whatever it is you are speaking about. By thinking over your past experiences—gathering material from yourself—you can find many supporting details for your speeches.

 INTERVIEWING

Most people think of interviewing in terms of job interviews or conversations with celebrities. But there is another kind of interview—the research (or investigative) interview. Among journalists it is a time-honored way to collect information. It is also an excellent way to gather materials for speeches.

Suppose you are explaining the latest advances in personal computers. Why not contact a local computer dealer as one source of information? Or suppose you are dealing with the problem of alcohol abuse among college students. Why not get in touch with the dean of students to find out the situation at your school? Once you begin to think about the possibilities, you will discover many people on your campus and in your community who can contribute to your speeches.

When done well, interviewing (like many things) looks deceptively easy. In practice, it is a complex and demanding art. So before you dash off to conduct your interviews à la Larry King or Barbara Walters, you should understand a few basic principles of effective interviewing. They fall into three groups—what to do before the interview, what to do during the interview, and what to do after the interview.

To illustrate, we'll follow the entire interview process for a hypothetical speech about gender equity in college athletics.

Before the Interview

Just as the outcome of most speeches is decided by how well the speaker prepares, so the outcome of most interviews is decided by how well the interviewer prepares. Here are five steps you should take ahead of time to help ensure a successful interview.

Define the Purpose of the Interview   You have done library research about the issue of gender equity in college athletics and have begun to grasp the major points of view fairly well. At this stage you think it would be helpful to know the status of men's and women's athletics at your school. You get some information from the newspaper, and some more from a handbook put out by the athletic department. But you still have many questions. You decide the only way to get answers is to interview someone associated with the athletic program. In that decision you have begun to formulate a purpose for the interview.

Decide Whom to Interview   There are a number of possibilities—players, coaches, administrators. You elect to start at the top—with the athletic director. Isn't that a bit presumptuous? Why not begin with someone a little further down the line—an assistant director or a coach, for instance? You could. But in dealing with administrative organizations it is usually best to go to the leaders first. They are likely to have a broad understanding of the issues. And if you need more specific information than they have, they can get it for you or put you in touch with the right person.

Arrange the Interview   In this case, let's assume the athletic director is a man. The subject of gender equity may be a delicate issue. Furthermore, he is a very busy person. So you work out a plan for getting him to agree to talk with you. Knowing that it is easier to brush someone off over the telephone than in person, you go to the athletic office to request the interview. You introduce yourself, identify your exact purpose, and explain why the interview is important. The athletic director agrees, and you set up the interview for three days later.

(You are astonished to get the interview, but you shouldn't be. Nearly everyone likes to be interviewed. If your purpose is a serious one and you conduct yourself well, the person you ask to interview is likely to cooperate.)

Decide Whether or Not to Use a Tape Recorder   If your subject does not want the interview tape-recorded, then the decision is made. Otherwise, you must choose. There are two major advantages of using a tape recorder: (1) Since you don't have to spend all your time taking notes, you can concentrate on the interviewee's message and on formulating your questions. (2) Your record of the interview will be exact—there will be no possibility of misquoting or of forgetting important facts.

There are also two disadvantages to using a tape recorder during an interview: (1) Many interviewees are so uncomfortable with a recorder in the room that this may spoil the interview. (2) You will have to spend a lot of time after the interview playing the tape over and over to distill the recorded material. When you take notes, on the other hand, that distillation process takes place during the interview because you write down only the important points.

If you decide to use a tape recorder, never smuggle it in without the knowledge or consent of the person being interviewed. Not only is it unethical, but the interviewee is bound to find out and you will cause yourself more trouble than you had hoped to avoid.

Prepare Your Questions   You now face the most important of your preinterview tasks—working out the questions you will ask during the interview. Keep in mind the old adage, "Ask a stupid question, you'll get a stupid answer." You should devise questions that are sensible, intelligent, and meaningful. Here are some types of questions to *avoid:*

- Questions you can answer without the interview. (How long has the school had a women's athletic program? What sports does it include?) Queries like this just waste the subject's time and make you look foolish. Research this information yourself before the interview.

- Leading questions (You *do* think women should have as many athletic scholarships as men, *don't you?*)

- Hostile, loaded questions. (I think it's disgraceful that most of the women's athletic teams at this school are coached by men. Don't you think women can coach as well as men? Or maybe you just look at women's sports as another way to provide jobs for male coaches. What do you say to *that,* hmmm?)

You need not shy away from tough questions. Just phrase them as neutrally as possible and save them until near the end of the interview. That way, if your interviewee becomes irritated or uncooperative, you will still get most of the information you want.

When you are finished preparing, you should have a set of direct, specific, reasonable questions, such as the following:

- Gender equity seems to be the major issue facing college athletic programs today. How does our school plan to deal with recent decisions about gender equity made by the federal courts and the NCAA?

- I understand you are considering adding three additional sports for women. What sports will those be and when will they get under way?

- How does the athletic department intend to pay for the cost of reaching equity between men's and women's sports? Will any men's sports be cut in order to achieve gender equity?

- Last month the women's gymnastics team complained that while the athletic department spends a lot of money on women's basketball and volleyball, it still does not provide adequate facilities or practice time for other sports. Is the complaint justified? If so, are steps being taken to deal with it?

■ Given the controversy over gender equity, how do you see the future of intercollegiate athletics in the United States? What do you think athletic programs will look like ten years from now?

Although some experienced journalists conduct interviews with only a few key-word notes on the areas to be covered, you want to be sure not to forget anything during the interview. So you arrange your questions in the order you want to ask them and take the list with you to the interview.

During the Interview

Every interview is unique. Just as a speaker adapts to the audience during a speech, so must an interviewer adapt to the person being interviewed. Because the session will seldom go exactly as you plan, you need to be alert and flexible. Here are several steps you can take to help make the interview proceed smoothly.

Dress Appropriately and Be on Time   The athletic director has a busy schedule and is doing you a favor by agreeing to an interview, so you make every effort to show up on time. Since the interview is a special occasion, you dress appropriately. This is one way of telling the athletic director that you regard the interview as serious business. In return, he is likely to take you more seriously.

Repeat the Purpose of the Interview   The athletic director invites you into his office; you exchange a few introductory remarks. Now, before you plunge into your questions, you take a minute or two to restate the purpose of the interview. This refreshes the athletic director's memory and gives the interview a sharper focus. You are more likely to get clear, helpful answers if your subject knows why you are following a certain line of questioning.

Set Up the Tape Recorder, If You Are Using One   If your subject has agreed to the interview being recorded, keep one principle in mind: the tape-recording should be as casual and as inconspicuous as possible. Don't thrust the microphone into your subject's face. Don't fiddle endlessly with the tape or the machine. You should have practiced in advance to make sure you understand how the recorder works. Set up the recorder, start the tape, and then try to ignore it for the rest of the interview. With luck, your subject will ignore it too.

For this exercise, we'll assume the athletic director does not want the interview tape-recorded.

Keep the Interview on Track   You ask the athletic director the first question on your list. He answers it. You ask him the second question. He answers it, but in doing so he also answers question 4. What do you do now? Do you go on to question 5 or return to question 3?

Either approach is fine. As it turns out, you go back to question 3 (while also checking off question 4 from your list). Now, in answering question 3, the athletic director raises an important issue that is not covered anywhere in your list of questions. Do you pursue that issue or forge doggedly ahead with question 5?

You make the wise decision to veer slightly from your prearranged order of questioning to pursue the new issue. You pose a couple of questions about it, get helpful answers, then keep the interview on track by returning to your list of prepared questions.

This is more or less how things go for the rest of the interview. You pursue new leads when they appear, improvise probing follow-up questions when called for, then lead on again in an orderly fashion. The interview is freewheeling at times, but you never let it get out of control. When it is over, you have answers to all your prepared questions—and a lot more.

Listen Carefully   During the interview, you listen attentively while taking key-word notes (see Chapter 3). When you don't understand something, you ask for clarification. If you hear a statement you want to quote directly, you have the athletic director repeat it to make sure you get it exactly right. Chances are a prominent person like him will have been misquoted more than once in the press, so he'll be happy to oblige.

Don't Overstay Your Welcome   Try to keep within the stipulated time period for the interview, unless your subject clearly wants to prolong the session. When the interview is over, you thank the athletic director for having given of his time and his insights.

After the Interview

Although the interview is over, the interviewing process is not. You must now review and transcribe your notes.

Review Your Notes As Soon As Possible   When you leave the athletic director's office, the interview is fresh in your mind. You know what the cryptic comments and scrawls in your notes mean. But as time passes, the details will become hazy. Don't let something like this true story happen to you:

Years ago, a prominent woman—writer and diplomat—was being interviewed by a young reporter. Among other things, the reporter asked about hobbies and leisure activities. The woman replied that she enjoyed skeet shooting and raised Siamese cats. The reporter scribbled in her notes "shoots" and "cats"—but didn't bother to put a comma or a dash between the words. The interview was published. And ever since, that prominent woman has been trying to live down the reputation that she "shoots cats."

Sometimes a personal interview is the best way to get up-to-date information from people with special expertise on your speech topic. When conducting such an interview, be sure to prepare your questions carefully and to listen attentively.

In reviewing your notes, try to concentrate on two things—discovering the main points that emerged during the interview, and pulling out specific information that might be useful in your speech.

The best way to locate the main points is to decide what you would answer if someone asked you to summarize the interview in one minute or less. As you look through your notes, you see three ideas that surface over and over in the athletic director's comments: (1) Gender equity is mandated by Title IX legislation passed by Congress in 1972 and has been consistently upheld by the courts. (2) In the absence of significant new sources of revenue, your school cannot create additional sports for women without trimming men's sports. (3) To prevent harming the men's athletic program, the school should contribute money from its general funds to help pay for the achievement of gender equity.

As you review the interview, you also seize on several specific items—figures, anecdotes, quotations—that look promising as supporting details for your speech. If any of them are unclear, call the athletic director to make sure you have the facts right.

Transcribe Your Notes   After reviewing the notes, you transcribe important ideas and information onto index cards. Since this will require filling in from memory various details of the interview, you do it as soon as possible. It's important to use index cards because that is how you will record materials gathered in your library research (see pages 136–138). This way you will have all your research materials in the same format so they can be arranged and rearranged easily when you begin to organize your speech.

◼ WRITING AWAY FOR INFORMATION

If the subject of your speech is at all controversial, you can be pretty sure that somewhere there is an organization for it or against it—and probably both. Take the issue of exploring for oil in the national parks as an example. Companies like Exxon are for it; environmental groups like the Sierra Club are against it. Cigarette smoking? The American Tobacco Institute is for it; numerous organizations, including the American Cancer Society, are actively opposed to it.

There are thousands of special-interest groups in this country, and most of them offer pamphlets and other literature related to their concerns free for the asking. The *Encyclopedia of Associations*, available in the reference section of most libraries, will give you a list of these groups, along with their mailing addresses.

A bit of caution is needed in using material obtained from such groups, however. Since these organizations exist specifically to promote or oppose some cause, their information may be biased, slanted, even downright wrong. Whenever possible, check facts and statistics against a more impartial source.

Government agencies are another excellent source of information on a wide range of topics. Suppose you plan to speak on a subject related to farming. The Department of Agriculture publishes hundreds of bulletins, all available at little or no cost. A list of these can be obtained from the U.S. Government Printing Office, Washington, D.C. 20401.

If you are in doubt about which government agency is responsible for a particular subject, try calling or writing your congressional representative. His or her staff can point you in the right direction.

◼ DOING LIBRARY RESEARCH

Some students regard the library as a sinner regards a church—as a place to be entered only in the most desperate circumstances. Then they take a speech class and discover that the library is not so forbidding after all. You will get most of the materials for your speeches from the library. Thus you need to know the basic techniques of doing library research. Of course, you may know them already, in which case you need only review this section of the book.

There are quick, easy, systematic ways to find whatever you need in the library. The first step is to learn your way around. Take the orientation tour offered by your library. While on the tour, you will probably receive a brief handbook or series of leaflets explaining what is in the library and how to find it. Keep this material with your class notes. It takes only a few minutes to read and will be helpful later.

Ultimately, the only way to become adept at library research is to do it—and to do it properly. You have four important resources for finding what you need in the library: the librarians, the library catalogues, the reference section, and computerized research services. We'll look at each in turn and then consider basic research techniques.[1]

The Librarians

Thanks to movies, comic strips, and television commercials, librarians have a bad image. They are typically portrayed as cold, stuffy, bespectacled people whose main goal in life is to keep others from talking above a whisper. In fact, most librarians are friendly men and women who can be of enormous help.

Too often students waste their time wandering aimlessly in search of a source because they are afraid to ask for assistance. They don't want to appear stupid or to "bother" anyone. But would you be as sensitive about asking a doctor for help with a medical problem? Librarians are experts in their own field, trained in library use and research methods. If you have a question, don't hesitate to ask a librarian. She or he can help you find your way, locate sources, even track down a specific piece of information.

The Library Catalogues

There are two kinds of library catalogues: the card catalogue and the computer catalogue. Although many libraries now have fully computerized catalogue systems, some use both kinds of catalogues and a few rely solely on the card catalogue. Regardless of the setup at your school, one fact remains constant—the catalogues are the key to finding materials in the library. If you learn how to use the catalogues effectively, you can save yourself a great deal of time.

The Card Catalogue   In the card catalogue you will find listed alphabetically on 3 × 5 cards all the books and periodicals owned by the library. For each book there will be at least three cards—one listing it by the *author's last name,* one listing it by *title,* and one (or more) listing it by *subject.* If you know who wrote a book or know the book's title, your first step is to locate the catalogue card under the author or title. When you do not know the author or title, or when you simply want to see what books are available on a given subject, check the catalogue under the appropriate subject.

Figure 6.1 shows three sample catalogue cards that index the same book. As you can see, the catalogue cards give quite a bit of information about the book. The key to finding the book on the shelves is the call number, which is always found in the upper left-hand corner of the card. Once you have the call number, all you have to do is find the right section of the shelves (or stacks, as they are called in some libraries) and retrieve your book.

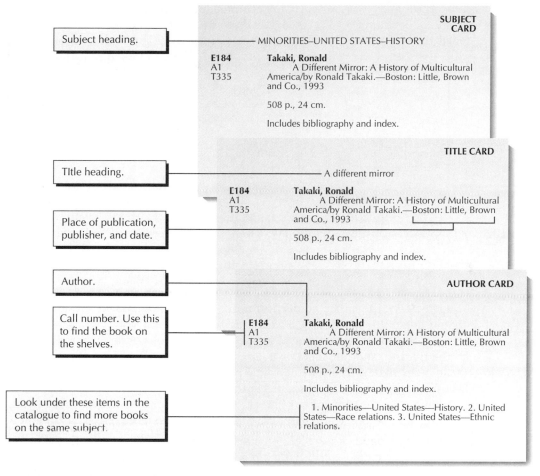

Subject heading.

SUBJECT CARD

MINORITIES–UNITED STATES–HISTORY

E184
A1
T335

Takaki, Ronald
A Different Mirror: A History of Multicultural America/by Ronald Takaki.—Boston: Little, Brown and Co., 1993

508 p., 24 cm.

Includes bibliography and index.

TITLE CARD

Title heading.

A different mirror

E184
A1
T335

Takaki, Ronald
A Different Mirror: A History of Multicultural America/by Ronald Takaki.—Boston: Little, Brown and Co., 1993

Place of publication, publisher, and date.

508 p., 24 cm.

Includes bibliography and index.

Author.

AUTHOR CARD

Call number. Use this to find the book on the shelves.

E184
A1
T335

Takaki, Ronald
A Different Mirror: A History of Multicultural America/by Ronald Takaki.—Boston: Little, Brown and Co., 1993

508 p., 24 cm.

Includes bibliography and index.

Look under these items in the catalogue to find more books on the same subject.

1. Minorities—United States—History. 2. United States—Race relations. 3. United States—Ethnic relations.

FIGURE 6.1 **Three Catalogue Cards**

Periodicals are listed by title in the card catalogue. Figure 6.2 (page 126) shows a catalogue card for a periodical. Libraries usually have a special room in which they keep the latest issues of newspapers and magazines. Bound volumes of issues from past years are kept on the book shelves.

The Computer Catalogue   At one time, the only way to find books and periodicals was to search for them by hand in the card catalogue. Today, you often can get the same information from a computer catalogue (or an on-line catalogue, as it is sometimes called). Rather than scurrying from one card catalogue file to another to find what you need, you can sit in one place and call up the titles you need on a computer screen (see Figure 6.3, page 127).

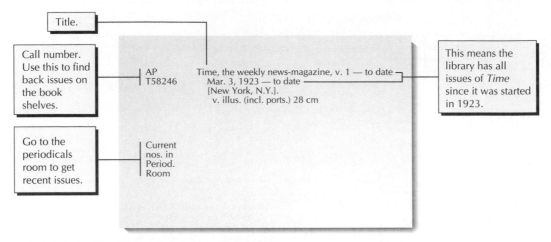

FIGURE 6.2   **Catalogue Card for a Periodical**

Because there are many different computer catalogue systems, you should check to see exactly how the system works at your library. At some schools, the computer catalogue includes all the books and periodicals owned by the library. At other schools, it contains only recent books and periodicals, while older materials are listed in the card catalogue. Because each computer catalogue system works a bit differently, you need to spend some time learning how to use the one at your library. The best time to do this is early in your speech class, before you have library assignments to complete. Learning how to use a computer catalogue *and* doing research for a speech at the same time can be a frustrating experience.

The Reference Section

The catalogues tell you what books and periodicals are in the library. But suppose you want to find a particular piece of factual information (such as the number of deaths caused by drunk drivers in the United States last year, the origins of the phrase "raining cats and dogs," or the distance from Los Angeles to Tokyo). Or suppose you are trying to locate recent magazine articles on a given topic. You could rummage through a dozen books or thumb through a batch of magazines in hopes of stumbling across what you need. But the easy, efficient way to get the information is to go to the reference section.

The reference section puts a wealth of information at your fingertips. It contains encyclopedias, yearbooks, dictionaries, biographical aids, atlases, and indexes. Here are the ones you should find most useful in preparing your speeches.

Encyclopedias   We all are familiar with general encyclopedias such as the *Encyclopaedia Britannica* and the *Encyclopedia Americana*. They seek to provide

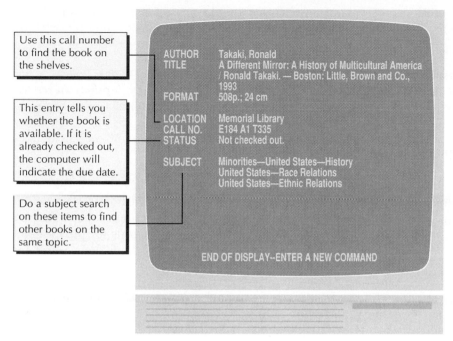

Use this call number to find the book on the shelves.

This entry tells you whether the book is available. If it is already checked out, the computer will indicate the due date.

Do a subject search on these items to find other books on the same topic.

AUTHOR   Takaki, Ronald
TITLE   A Different Mirror: A History of Multicultural America
            / Ronald Takaki. — Boston: Little, Brown and Co.,
            1993
FORMAT   508p.; 24 cm

LOCATION   Memorial Library
CALL NO.   E184 A1 T335
STATUS   Not checked out.

SUBJECT   Minorities—United States—History
            United States—Race Relations
            United States—Ethnic Relations

END OF DISPLAY--ENTER A NEW COMMAND

FIGURE 6.3   Computer Catalogue

accurate, objective information about all branches of human knowledge and are an excellent place to begin your research. Both *Britannica* and *Americana* are arranged alphabetically and publish annual supplements to update what is contained in the basic volumes.

In addition to the general encyclopedias, there are special encyclopedias devoted to particular subjects such as art, religion, science, and literature. They cover their fields in much more depth and detail than do the general encyclopedias. The most frequently used special encyclopedias are:

Encyclopedia of Philosophy

International Encyclopedia of the Social Sciences

Encyclopedia of World Art

Encyclopedia of Black America

Encyclopedia of Religion

Grove's Dictionary of Music and Musicians

Grzimek's Animal Life Encyclopedia

McGraw-Hill Encyclopedia of Science and Technology

Yearbooks   As the name implies, yearbooks are published annually. They contain an amazing amount of current information that would otherwise be all but impossible to track down. Here are three of the most valuable.

Statistical Abstract of the United States. Published since 1878 by the U.S. Bureau of the Census, the *Statistical Abstract* is the standard reference source for numerical information on the social, political, and economic aspects of American life. Among the incredible array of facts it contains are the U.S. fertility rate, death rates from various diseases, labor-union membership, median family income by state, and so on.

World Almanac and Book of Facts. Unlike the *Statistical Abstract,* the *World Almanac* is not limited to the United States or to numerical data. Among the things you can find out from it are all the Nobel Prize winners since 1901, the most-watched television shows of the previous year, records for professional and collegiate sports, the literacy rate in Afghanistan, and the natural resources of Peru.

Facts on File. This is a weekly digest of national and foreign news events. It covers politics, sports, science, medicine, education, religion, crime, economics, and the arts. At the end of the year, all the weekly issues are published together as *Facts on File Yearbook.* This is an excellent place to check up quickly on something that happened in a given year.

Dictionaries   There are several excellent dictionaries of the English language, including *Webster's* and the *Random House Dictionary.* If you are interested more in the history of a word than in its present meaning, you should turn first to the *Oxford English Dictionary.* There are also a number of more specialized dictionaries that cover a wide range of topics. Among the best are *Safire's Political Dictionary* and the *Morris Dictionary of Word and Phrase Origins.*

Books of Quotations   The best-known collection of quotations is *Bartlett's Familiar Quotations.* With more than 22,500 quotations from historical and contemporary figures, it has long been regarded as an indispensable source for speakers and writers alike. Other excellent books of quotations include:

> *The Oxford Dictionary of Quotations*
>
> *The Harper Book of American Quotations*
>
> *The New Quotable Woman*
>
> *A Treasury of Jewish Quotations*
>
> *My Soul Looks Back, 'Less I Forget: A Collection of Quotations by People of Color*

All of these works are indexed to help you locate quotations by subject as well as by author.

Biographical Aids   When you need information about people, living or dead, you should go first to the reference section, where you will find a number of excellent biographical guides. Here are the ones you are likely to find most useful:

Who's Who. Published annually since 1849, *Who's Who* is the forerunner of the biographical guides to living persons. Its information is limited mostly to men and women who reside in the British Commonwealth of Nations, and it includes a full listing of the English Royal Family.

Who's Who in America. Published every other year since 1899, these volumes give brief life and career facts about 75,000 noteworthy contemporary Americans.

Who's Who of American Women. Begun in 1958, this guide spotlights women who are making important contributions to American life.

International Who's Who. Issued annually since 1935, this reference work contains over 11,000 one-paragraph biographical sketches of people of international stature in almost every sphere of activity.

Current Biography. Initiated in 1940, this exceedingly helpful magazine is published every month except December. During each year it offers some 400 independent and highly readable articles about newsworthy people all over the world. Each article is three to four pages long, and the fields covered include politics, science, the arts, labor, sports, and industry. At the end of the year, the articles are revised and collected alphabetically in a single volume entitled *Current Biography Yearbook.* An excellent cumulative index makes it easy to find the article you want from any year. If you are looking for information about someone now in the news, this is probably your best bet.

Dictionary of American Biography. This monumental work contains first-rate biographies of more than 17,000 famous Americans—mostly men—who are no longer living.

Notable American Women. Modeled on the *Dictionary of American Biography,* this publication is limited to women in the United States.

Biography Index. This source won't give you biographical information, but it will tell you where to find it. Published four times a year, the *Biography Index* provides references to biographical material appearing in selected books and some 2,600 periodicals. Although it includes information about recent articles on historical figures, it is especially useful for locating material about contemporary women and men the world over.

Atlases and Gazetteers   Atlases, of course, contain maps. But most modern atlases also contain a variety of charts, plates, and tables that furnish information about the geography of states, regions, and countries. The leading all-purpose atlas is the *Rand McNally Cosmopolitan World Atlas,* which includes maps of the world by region, as well as maps of each state of the United States. It also gives a wealth of facts and figures about the population, politics, and geography of the U.S. and other parts of the world.

Gazetteers and geographical dictionaries. They follow the same alphabetical format as regular dictionaries, but all entries deal with geographical topics. The best-known gazetteer is *Webster's New Geographical Dictionary.* This fascinating volume lists more than 47,000 places around the world—countries, regions, states, cities, islands, lakes, mountains, rivers—and gives concise facts about each. It is where you should look to find such things as the height of Mount Everest, the state flower of Florida, and all the places in the world named Athens.

Periodical Indexes   Periodical indexes do for articles in magazines and journals what the library catalogues do for books. They include the well-known *Readers' Guide to Periodical Literature* as well as a number of more specialized indexes.

Readers' Guide to Periodical Literature. The *Readers' Guide* is the indispensable general-purpose index. It provides an up-to-date listing of more than 180 of the most widely read magazines in the United States. Included are *Time, Newsweek, Scientific American, Sports Illustrated, Aviation Week and Space Technology, Consumer Reports, Ebony, Ms., Vital Speeches, Rolling Stone,* and *Psychology Today.* Most libraries keep bound volumes of the *Readers' Guide* going back to its start in 1900. All issues since January 1983 can also be searched by computer using the Wilsondisc Information Retrieval System. You should check with your library to see whether it offers this service. (For a full discussion of computer research services, see pages 132–134.)

One of the virtues of the *Readers' Guide* is that it is easy to use. Articles are indexed alphabetically by author and subject. Each entry gives all the necessary information for finding the articles in the magazines—title of article, author, name of magazine (abbreviated), volume number, page numbers, and date. If you were giving a speech on the need to reform the U.S. public welfare system, you would look in the *Reader's Guide* under "Public Welfare." Figure 6.4 shows what you would find.

Special Indexes. Sometimes you may need more specialized information than you can find in the general magazines covered by the *Readers' Guide.* If so, check with your librarian, who will direct you to a special index. Examples are:

Applied Science and Technology Index

Art Index

Index to Black Periodicals

Business Periodicals Index

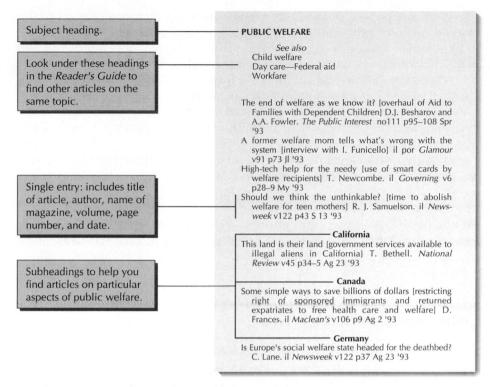

Subject heading.

Look under these headings in the *Reader's Guide* to find other articles on the same topic.

Single entry: includes title of article, author, name of magazine, volume, page number, and date.

Subheadings to help you find articles on particular aspects of public welfare.

PUBLIC WELFARE

See also
Child welfare
Day care—Federal aid
Workfare

The end of welfare as we know it? [overhaul of Aid to Families with Dependent Children] D.J. Besharov and A.A. Fowler. *The Public Interest* no111 p95–108 Spr '93
A former welfare mom tells what's wrong with the system [interview with I. Funicello] il por *Glamour* v91 p73 Jl '93
High-tech help for the needy [use of smart cards by welfare recipients] T. Newcombe. il *Governing* v6 p28–9 My '93
Should we think the unthinkable? [time to abolish welfare for teen mothers] R. J. Samuelson. il *Newsweek* v122 p43 S 13 '93

California
This land is their land [government services available to illegal aliens in California] T. Bethell. *National Review* v45 p34–5 Ag 23 '93

Canada
Some simple ways to save billions of dollars [restricting right of sponsored immigrants and returned expatriates to free health care and welfare] D. Frances. il *Maclean's* v106 p9 Ag 2 '93

Germany
Is Europe's social welfare state headed for the deathbed? C. Lane. il *Newsweek* v122 p37 Ag 23 '93

FIGURE 6.4   Sample *Readers' Guide* Entry

(*Readers' Guide to Periodical Literature* © copyright 1993 by the H.W. Wilson Company. Material reproduced by permission of the publisher.)

Education Index

Hispanic American Periodicals Index

Index to Legal Periodicals

Public Affairs Information Service Bulletin

Most of these indexes are also computerized, usually beginning with issues from the early 1980s. If you are interested in using any of them, check to see whether your library has them on computer. It might save you a great deal of time.

Newspaper Indexes   Newspapers are invaluable for research on many topics, historical as well as current. Fortunately, back issues of several major U.S. newspapers are now indexed, including the *New York Times, Wall Street Journal, Christian Science Monitor, Los Angeles Times, Washington Post, Atlanta Constitution,* and *USA Today.*

Of these papers, your library is most likely to carry back issues of the *New York Times* on microfilm or computer. To find what you are looking for in the *Times,* look under your subject in the *New York Times Index.* You will find listed all articles on that subject printed during the year.

If you are hunting for information from a newspaper, you may also be able to find it in *NewsBank.* This helpful resource reprints selected articles on a wide range of topics from more than 450 newspapers. The *NewsBank Index,* available both on computer and in bound volumes, makes it easy to track down exactly what you need.

Finally, you should know about more specialized reference sources such as *Editorials on File* and *Black Newspapers Index. Editorials on File* reprints editorials on important public issues from hundreds of newspapers across the United States and is an excellent source of informed opinion on current events. *Black Newspapers Index* provides a helpful guide to articles printed in eight leading African-American newspapers, including the *Amsterdam News, Chicago Defender,* and *Los Angeles Sentinel.*

Computerized Research Services

Most libraries now have computerized research services that can save you hours of work—especially if your speech topic involves obscure or specialized information. Suppose you need material on "bilingual education in the Southwest" or "military tactics in the battle of Gettysburg." Instead of reading through a stack of periodical or newspaper indexes until you find the citations you need, you let the computer find them for you.

Various commercial organizations have developed computerized information retrieval services. Each service contains a large set of indexes known as *databases.* Some of these databases are the same as those for printed periodical indexes, while others have been created just for use with computers and have no printed equivalent. Altogether there are hundreds of databases, covering topics from agriculture to zoology. The specific databases you can use will depend on the retrieval systems available in your library. Here are a few of the major databases you are most likely to use in preparing one of your speeches:

InfoTrac. This popular database indexes more than 100,000 articles that have appeared in general-interest and scholarly periodicals during the past five years.

ProQuest General Periodicals Index. This easy-to-use database indexes over 1,000 general-interest, business, and scholarly publications since 1987.

Readers' Guide to Periodical Literature. This computer version of the printed *Readers' Guide* goes back to January 1983.

▸ *Ethnic Newswatch.* An especially helpful database that indexes more than 100 newspapers and magazines from the ethnic press, including Spanish-language publications.

▸ *ERIC (Education Resources Information Center).* A comprehensive guide to books, articles, research findings, and unpublished materials on all aspects of education.

▸ *Newspaper Abstracts.* Indexes and provides brief abstracts of articles from ten major U.S. newspapers since 1985, including the *New York Times, Wall Street Journal, Washington Post, Los Angeles Times, Atlanta Constitution,* and *USA Today.*

You need not be a computer expert to take advantage of computer-assisted research. Using most of the databases listed above is as easy as using the computer catalogue. You simply enter the subject on which you want information, and citations of articles on your subject appear on the screen. You can choose the citations that interest you, and a printer hooked up to the computer will print them out for you. Depending on the database you are using, you may also be able to get a printout summarizing the articles on your list of citations. In some cases, the articles themselves can be called up on screen or may be available on laser discs or microfilm cassettes for immediate viewing or photocopying.

To use more specialized databases or for more complex searches, you may need to make an appointment with a reference librarian. The librarian will help you formulate a research strategy. He or she will then direct the

Library research is vital for most speeches. Knowing the resources available in your library and how to use them efficiently will make the time you spend researching much more productive.

computer through its search. In most libraries, there is a fee for this kind of service. To get maximum value for your dollar, librarians advise that you begin your research in the general indexes and avoid using expensive databases until you have a clear idea of exactly what you are looking for.

Despite their many advantages, computer research services have one important limitation. Few databases cover more than last fifteen years. If you are looking for something published before 1980, you may be able to find it only through printed indexes.

For current information, however, you cannot beat the ease, convenience, and resources of computer research services. Because such services are expanding rapidly, we can expect them to become even more widely available and easier to use in the years ahead. The day is not far off when college students will be able to do all their research—including reading books and articles—from a personal computer in their home or dorm room.

TIPS FOR DOING RESEARCH

Few people regard doing research as one of life's great joys. There are, however, ways to make it less tedious and more productive. Learning how to use the library efficiently is one way. Here are some others.

Start Early

The biggest mistake students make when faced with a research project is waiting too long to begin. The longer you wait, the more problems you will encounter. You may find that a vital book has been checked out of the library or that you no longer have time to arrange a crucial interview. Starting early also eases the tension of completing an assignment. Instead of sweating under intense time pressure, you can work at your convenience. No matter what kind of research you do, you can be sure of one thing. It will *always* take longer than you expect. So get started early and avoid the pitfalls that come from procrastinating.

Starting early also gives you plenty of time to think about what you find. In researching, you will collect much more material than you will actually use in the speech. Preparing a speech is a little like constructing a jigsaw puzzle. Once you gather the pieces, you have to decide how they fit together. The more time you give yourself, the more likely you are to get the pieces to fit just right.

Make a Preliminary Bibliography

In your research, you will run across the titles of books and magazine articles that look as if they might contain helpful information about your speech

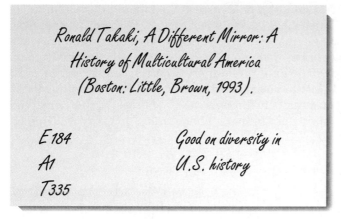

Ronald Takaki, A Different Mirror: A
History of Multicultural America
(Boston: Little, Brown, 1993).

E 184   *Good on diversity in*
A1   *U.S. history*
T335

FIGURE 6.5   **Sample Bibliography Card for a Book**

topic. When this happens, prepare a preliminary bibliography card for the book or article. Fill out a separate 3 × 5 or 4 × 6 index card for each book or article. (It is important to use index cards because they can be put in alphabetical order quickly.)

For books, record the author, title, place of publication, publisher, date of publication, and call number. You may also want to include a brief comment indicating why the book may be valuable for your speech. Figure 6.5 shows a sample bibliography card for a book.

For magazine articles, record the author (if identified), title of article, name of magazine, date of publication, and page numbers, as well as the call number. As with book entries, you may also want to include a brief comment to yourself about the article. Figure 6.6 shows a sample bibliography card for a magazine article.

Brandon S. Centerwall, "Television
and Violent Crime, Public
Interest" (Spring 1993), pp.
56–71.

AP   *Get this*
P977   *for sure.*
1615

FIGURE 6.6   **Sample Bibliography Card for a Magazine Article**

One important point needs to be stressed. You should fill out an index card for *each* book or article that looks as if it *could be* helpful in preparing your speech. As a result, you may well have fifteen or twenty preliminary bibliography cards. But remember that you have not yet seen the works listed on the cards. Of the fifteen or twenty preliminary sources, only seven or eight are likely to be of much use to you in drafting the speech. It is an inevitable fact of research that you must sift through many sources to find what you need. If you prepare a skimpy preliminary bibliography, you may well end up with a skimpy speech.

Take Notes Efficiently

Mike Simmons began his speech preparation with the best of intentions. His topic was a fascinating one: "Stone Age Peoples Today." Soon after receiving the assignment, he went to the library to start his research. Since he had no index cards with him, he took notes in the back of one of his notebooks. For two hours he industriously jotted down anything that seemed useful. Then he came upon a short book about an obscure tribe in the Philippines. The book was so engrossing that he read it straight through. He didn't bother taking notes, because he was sure he'd remember it all. The next day he returned to the library. When he got there, he saw he didn't have the same notebook with him but had one from another class. So he used that. He proceeded this way for two more days.

Then Mike remembered he had a test in another class. Somewhat panicked, he put aside his speech research to study for the test. When he got back to researching his speech, the deadline was only four days away. After a long search, he finally found the notes he had made. But what did they mean? He flipped back and forth through the pages several times, trying to make sense of them. One entry said, "Wilson—*important!!!!*" But who or what was Wilson? An author? An anthropologist? Or could it be a place? Another note was particularly frustrating. It said, "Unusual sexual customs—masks." Just the thing to spark up a speech! But where had he read it? He hadn't the faintest idea. With a sense of doom, Mike realized he would have to start all over—and finish in four days.

Sound familiar? This has happened to almost everyone at least once. But once is enough. There is a better way to take research notes. Here is a method that has worked well for many students:

1. Record notes on index cards. Many people prefer the 4 × 6 or 5 × 8 size. Both are large enough to hold quite a bit of information, yet they can be sorted easily when you start to organize the speech. The importance of using index cards cannot be overemphasized. It is the first step to more efficient note taking. Once you begin to use them, you'll be surprised at how much time and frustration they save.

2. On each card write the note, the source of the note, and a heading indicating the subject of the note (see Figure 6.7). The subject heading is particularly important, for it allows you to tell at a glance what the note is about.

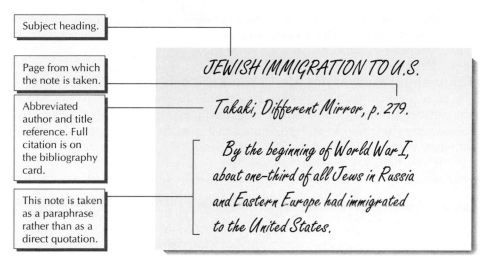

Subject heading.

Page from which the note is taken.

Abbreviated author and title reference. Full citation is on the bibliography card.

This note is taken as a paraphrase rather than as a direct quotation.

JEWISH IMMIGRATION TO U.S.

Takaki, Different Mirror, p. 279.

By the beginning of World War I, about one-third of all Jews in Russia and Eastern Europe had immigrated to the United States.

FIGURE 6.7   Sample Note on an Index Card

This simplifies the task of arranging your notes when you start to organize the speech. Use the same format for notes taken from an interview.

3. Use a separate card for each note. Many students try to write down all the information from one source on a single card. This defeats the purpose of index cards because it makes your notes almost impossible to review and organize. You can avoid this problem by making a separate card for each quotation or piece of information you record. Although you may end up with several cards from the same book or article, you will find that this method allows you to keep better track of your research.

4. Distinguish among direct quotations, paraphrases, and your own ideas. As we saw in Chapter 2, it is easy to plagiarize accidently by not taking careful research notes. As you do research for your speeches, be sure to use quotation marks on your note cards whenever you copy the exact words of a source. If you paraphrase, rather than quote verbatim, make sure to cite the source on your note card. By keeping track of quotations and paraphrases, you will be able to separate your own words and ideas from those of other people. This will help you avoid the trap of inadvertent plagiarism when you put your speech together.

5. Take plenty of notes. Few things are more aggravating than trying to recall some bit of information you ran across in your research but neglected to record on a note card. You might have said to yourself, "That's sort of interesting, but I don't know whether it's important. I'll remember it if I need it." Now, of course, you don't remember it exactly. Worse yet, you don't remember where you read it. So you head back to the library hoping you can relocate the information. Even if you do find it, you have wasted a lot of time. The moral is clear: If there is even an outside chance you may need a piece of information, jot it down. This procedure will take a little extra time in the short run, but in the long run it can save you much grief.

Think About Your Materials As You Research

Students often approach research as a mechanical routine that simply involves gathering the materials to be used in a speech or paper. But when done properly, research can be extremely creative.

If you *think about* what you are finding in your research, you will see your topic just a little bit differently with each note you take. You will find new relationships, develop new questions, explore new angles. You will, in short, begin to write the speech in your head even as you do the research. As you learn more about the topic, you will formulate a central idea, begin to sketch out main points and supporting points, experiment with ways of organizing your thoughts. You may even change your point of view, as did this student:

Barbara Lopez began her speech preparation with this central idea in mind: "Wild animals make more interesting pets than dogs and cats." She went about her research conscientiously, spending many hours in the library. On her third day she came upon some disturbing information about the capture of wild animals. She read that young chimpanzees and other apes were literally snatched out of their mothers' arms, and that the mothers were afterward heard to cry almost like humans. Back in her room that night, Barbara couldn't get her mind off the baby chimpanzees.

The next day at the library Barbara found some more disturbing material. One source told about the extraordinarily high death rate of wild animals during shipment to the United States. Again that night, Barbara brooded about the young animals dying of fear and cold in the cargo holds of airplanes.

By the time she finished her research, Barbara's central idea was completely different. When she spoke, her central idea was "The importation of wild animals for use as pets is inhumane."

This is an example of creative research—and of critical thinking. Barbara kept her mind open, read everything she could find about her topic, and thought seriously about what she found. Because of this, she changed her mind.

Your own speech preparation may not cause you to reverse your position, but it should give you new insights into your topic. If you approach research in this way, you may well find that the time you spend researching is the most productive of all the time you devote to preparing your speech.

SUMMARY

Gathering materials for a speech is like gathering information for any project. Many resources are available if you take advantage of them. When you have personal experience or more-than-average knowledge about a topic, you can use yourself as a resource. Most of the time, however, you will need outside information, which you can get in one or more of three ways. You can interview people with specialized knowledge about your topic. You can write away for information. You can do research in the library.

A personal interview takes place in three stages—before, during, and after the interview. Before the interview you should define its purpose, decide whom you are going to interview, and make an appointment with that person. You should also prepare the questions you will ask during the interview. Once the interview begins, be sure to keep it on track, to listen attentively, and to take accurate notes. Afterward, review and transcribe your notes as soon as possible, while they are still fresh in your mind.

Writing away for information is a good way to gather material if you have enough time before your speech. Government agencies, corporations, and special-interest groups all offer free or very inexpensive publications.

The library will be the major source of material for most of your speeches. There are four important resources for finding what you need in the library—the librarians, the library catalogues, the reference section, and computerized research services. Librarians are trained to help you; never hesitate to ask their advice when you cannot find something. The library catalogues list alphabetically all the books and periodicals owned by the library. The reference section contains encyclopedias, yearbooks dictionaries, biographical aids, atlases, indexes, and the like. If your library has computerized research services, you may be able to locate even obscure sources quickly and efficiently.

No matter what kinds of facilities are available to you, your research will be more effective if you start early and make a preliminary bibliography to keep track of all the books and articles that look as if they might be helpful. By learning to take research notes efficiently, you will save yourself time and energy every step of the way. And if you think about your materials while you research, you may find that gathering materials is the most creative part of your speech preparation.

REVIEW QUESTIONS

After reading this chapter, you should be able to answer the following questions:

1. Why is it important to draw on your own knowledge and experience in gathering materials for your speeches?

2. What are the three stages of interviewing? What should you do as an interviewer in each stage to help ensure a successful interview?

3. What are four important resources for finding what you need in the library?

4. Why is it important to start your speech research early?

5. What is a preliminary bibliography? Why is it helpful to you in researching a speech?

6. What are five things you should do to take research notes efficiently?

APPLICATION EXERCISES

1. Plan to conduct an interview for one of your classroom speeches. Be sure to follow the guidelines for effective interviewing discussed in this chapter. Afterward, evaluate the interview. Did you prepare for it adequately? Did you get the information you wanted? What would you do differently if you could conduct the interview again?

2. Your library probably has the *Encyclopedia of Associations* in its reference section. Using the *Encyclopedia,* find the names and addresses of three organizations you might write to for information about one of your speech topics.

3. In the *Readers' Guide to Periodical Literature* or one of the special indexes listed on pages 130–131, find three articles on the subject of your next speech. Prepare a preliminary bibliography card for each article, and track down the articles in the stacks or in the periodicals section of the library.

4. This exercise is designed to give you firsthand acquaintance with some of the major reference works discussed in this chapter. Your task is to answer each of the following questions. Some of the questions indicate where you will find the answer, and some do not. If necessary, recheck the chapter to see in which reference works you are most likely to find the answers. For each question, record both your answer and where you found it.

   Example:

   Question: What is the highest point on the Rock of Gibraltar?
   Answer: The highest point on the Rock of Gibraltar is 1,398 feet. *Webster's New Geographical Dictionary,* p. 441.

   a. According to *Facts on File,* what did four girls in Great Britain win from their parents during the week of December 31, 1992?
   b. Who said, "Who knows what women can be when they are finally free to become themselves?"
   c. In what year was nineteenth-century Native American leader Pushmataha elected chief of his Choctaw tribe?
   d. According to volume 64 of *Education Index,* what journal published an article entitled "Lost in the Crowd?" in July 1992 about class size in colleges and universities?
   e. From what school and in what year did American family studies researcher Li-Ying Hilary Wang receive her Ph.D.?

f.   According to the *Oxford English Dictionary*, what is the original meaning of the word "assassin"?

g.   Which issue of the *New York Times* in 1992 carried an article on the Pennsylvania State University's professional golf management program?

h.   According to the *Encyclopedia of Religion and Ethics*, who was most responsible for starting Sunday schools in England?

i.   What percentage of the United States adult population performed volunteer work in 1989?

j.   According to the 1993 edition of *Current Biography*, what was sportscaster Bob Costas's first professional job?

NOTES

[1] I would like to thank the reference staff of Memorial Library, University of Wisconsin–Madison, for their assistance in providing materials for this section.

Chapter 7

Supporting Your Ideas

Ryan Hoffman decided to give his first classroom speech on the health benefits of drinking large amounts of fresh juice made from a juice extractor such as those advertised on television. Part of his speech ran like this:

"Juicing is a great way to keep your weight down, your energy up, and to get more out of everything you do. Fresh juice contains many more nutrients than store-bought juice, and those nutrients enter your bloodstream almost immediately, producing a great burst of energy. Juicing can conquer the flu, reduce stress, eliminate ulcers, and prevent cancer. It can help you get better grades, be more productive at work, even live to the age of 130, as did Norman Walker, the inventor of juicing. I've had a juicer myself for almost a year, and I've never felt better!"

After the speech, Ryan's listeners were intrigued but skeptical. One of his classmates remarked: "Says who? I've heard about juicing on television, too, but that doesn't make it true. And Ryan's no expert on nutrition. Can anybody prove all that stuff about living longer and preventing cancer?"

Good speeches are not composed of hot air and generalizations. They need strong supporting materials to bolster the speaker's point of view. In Ryan's case, although there has been research published that sustains some of the benefits of juicing, most of the claims about its health value have yet to be verified. So Ryan's listeners were right to be skeptical. Ryan made the mistake of generalizing from his own experience with nothing concrete to support his ideas.

The problem with generalizations is that they do not answer the three questions listeners always mentally ask of a speaker: "What do you mean?" "Why should I believe you?" "So what?" Consider, for example, the following sets of statements:

GENERAL	LESS GENERAL	SPECIFIC
Lots of American women own their own businesses.	Women-owned businesses are becoming more and more important to the American economy.	As many as 7 million American women run their own businesses. Women-owned businesses generate more than $500 billion in annual revenues and employ more workers than all the Fortune 500 companies combined. The U.S. Chamber of Commerce predicts that in the next decade women will own half of all American businesses.[1]

Fiber optics technology is amazing.	Despite their small size, fiber-optic telephone cables can carry many more calls than traditional phone systems.	A typical fiber-optic cable holds a dozen or two plastic-sheathed strands of glass. Including sheath, each strand is the diameter of a tooth-brush bristle. Its calling capa-city, though, is almost un-limited. According to Frank Gratzer, a manager at Bell-core, "you could carry the entire telephone traffic in the United States with one fiber."[2]
Tuberculosis is a deadly disease.	Tuberculosis kills millions of people in the world each year and is a grow-ing health hazard in the United States.	Worldwide, an estimated 1.7 billion people carry the tuber-culosis bacterium. Eight mil-lion of those carriers develop active TB each year, and 3 million die. Since 1985 the disease has grown so fast in the U.S. that TB rates in the poorest sectors of American society now surpass those of the poorest countries on earth.[3]

Which group of statements do you find most interesting? Most convincing? Chances are you will prefer those in the right-hand column. They are sharp and specific, clear and credible—just the sort of thing a speech needs to come alive.

■ SUPPORTING MATERIALS AND CRITICAL THINKING

The skillful use of supporting materials often makes the difference between a poor speech and a good one. It is also closely related to critical thinking. Using supporting materials is not a matter of haphazardly tossing facts and figures into your speech. You must decide which ideas need to be supported given your audience, topic, and specific purpose. You must do research to find mate-rials that will bring your ideas across clearly and creatively. And you must eval-uate your supporting materials to make sure they really do back up your ideas.

As you put your speeches together, you will need to make sure your sup-porting materials are accurate, relevant, and reliable. You will find yourself asking such questions as "Are my examples representative?" "Am I using sta-tistical measures correctly?" "Am I quoting reputable, qualified sources?" As-sessing the supporting materials in your speeches—as well as in the speeches of your classmates—is yet another way in which critical thinking is part of public speaking.

In Chapters 14 and 16, we will look at special uses of supporting materials in informative and persuasive speeches. In this chapter, we focus on the basic kinds of supporting materials—examples, statistics, and testimony—and on general principles for using them effectively and responsibly.

■ EXAMPLES

Across from a small, grassy park dedicated to Greek and Irish immigrants, Joe Cogliano, whose grandparents were Italian, sells mangoes to Hispanic customers from the back of his truck. Children play tag while chattering in Spanish on O'Brien Terrace, part of a housing project built in 1939 for Irish laborers. The pungent odor of Vietnamese fish sauce fills a Southeast Asian restaurant where Giavis' Greek Grocery once thrived for more than 70 years.[4]

These were the opening lines of an article in *Time* magazine about the interaction of cultures in Lowell, Massachusetts. It illustrates a device well known to magazine writers—and speechmakers: Get the audience involved.

See how skillfully this example accomplishes the goal. It begins by focusing attention on a particular person (Joe Cogliano). It then provides details of time and place that set the scene vividly before our eyes. We almost feel ourselves there in Lowell buying mangoes from the back of Cogliano's truck, listening to the sound of children, smelling the Vietnamese fish sauce. We would not be nearly as involved if the article had merely said, "Many cultural groups interact in Lowell on a daily basis." The *example* touches something in us that no generalization can.

Research has shown that vivid, concrete examples have more impact on listeners' beliefs and actions than any other kind of supporting material.[5] Without examples, ideas often seem vague, impersonal, and lifeless. With examples, ideas become specific, personal, and lively. This is nowhere better illustrated than in the Bible, which uses all manner of stories, parables, and anecdotes to make abstract principles clear and compelling.[6] There are several kinds of examples you may want to try in your speeches.

Brief Examples

Brief examples—also called specific instances—may be referred to in passing to illustrate a point. The following excerpt uses a brief example to illustrate the miraculous nature of recent advances in creating artificial limbs for accident victims:

Changes in technology have made it possible for doctors to work wonders that once seemed impossible. *Roger Charter, for example, lost both his feet when they were crushed in a truck accident. Now he has new feet—made of a springy plastic alloy that duplicates a normal arch. Not only can Roger walk normally, but he can run and play sports again!*

A brief example may also be used to introduce a topic:

When archaeologists broke the seal on Tutankhamen's tomb in the autumn of 1922, they uncovered an amazing treasure—a storehouse of ancient Egyptian art of priceless beauty that had lain, untouched and unseen, for more than 3,000 years. Archaeology is a profession of endless drudgery, painstaking research, and the occasional—very rare—marvelous find.

Another way to use brief examples is to pile them one upon the other until you create the desired impression. Here is how the technique might be used to reinforce the point that inadequate safety precautions in school science labs is a serious problem:

Although most of the accidents in school science labs result in nothing more serious than cuts from a broken test tube, some are severe enough to cause permanent disability or even death. Three years ago, Ramsay Bittar was performing a dangerous chemistry experiment when his flask exploded, severing an artery in his neck. By the time paramedics arrived, he had lost enough blood to cause serious brain damage. In another case, a student in a freshman lab received third-degree burns when his hair was accidently ignited with a Bunsen burner. And at Southeastern Massachusetts University, a graduate student died in an explosion after attempting to distill a dangerous chemical.[7]

Extended Examples

Extended examples are often called illustrations, narratives, or anecdotes. They are longer and more detailed than brief examples. By telling a story vividly and dramatically, they pull listeners into the speech. Here is such an example, from a student speech about the astonishing similarities that sometimes exist between identical twins:

After 40 years of separation from his identical twin, James Lewis began his search for his long-lost brother. They had been separated a few weeks after birth and were adopted by different families. Their reunion took place at the home of the other twin—James Springer. Upon meeting, they found that they had more in common than their first names.

Both had married a woman named Betty, been divorced, and remarried a woman named Sally. Both had similar jobs as deputy sheriffs, McDonald's employees, and gas-station attendants. Both liked to build wood furniture in their basement workshops. Both put on 10 pounds as teenagers and lost it later. Both had the same favorite subjects in school, were bad spellers, and suffered from migraine headaches and sleeping problems. All in all, they shared 27 matching characteristics.

This long example captures vividly the many likenesses that often exist between identical twins. The speaker could merely have said, "identical twins are a lot alike," but the story makes the point far more vividly.

Hypothetical Examples

Whether brief or extended, examples can also be either factual or hypothetical. All the examples presented so far are factual; the incidents they refer to really happened. Sometimes, however, speakers will use a hypothetical example—one that describes an imaginary situation. Usually such examples are brief stories that relate a general principle.

Here is how one student used a hypothetical example to illustrate the need to know how to rescue a drowning person:

Imagine yourself lounging by the pool on a hot summer day. The intense sun rays are turning your skin a deep, golden brown. Your only worries are whether your nose or the tops of your feet are burning. Then, suddenly, your friend in the pool gets a cramp and panics. He calls for help, thrashes wildly, gasps for air, and starts to sink. Would you know what to do in this situation? Would you be able to save your friend, or would you just panic along with him?

Even though this situation is hypothetical, it is far from impossible. According to the *World Almanac,* almost 7,000 Americans drowned last year, making it the third leading cause of accidental death in the United States.

This hypothetical example is particularly effective. The speaker creates a realistic scenario, relates it directly to her listeners and gets them involved in the speech. In addition, she uses figures from the *World Almanac* to show that the scenario could really happen to any of her classmates. Whenever you use a hypothetical example, it is a good idea to follow it with statistics or testimony to show that the example is not far-fetched.

Tips for Using Examples

Use Examples to Clarify Your Ideas   You probably use clarifying examples all the time in everyday conversation. If you were explaining to a friend about different body types, you might say, "Look at Professor Shankar. He's a typical ectomorph—tall, thin, and bony." Examples are an excellent way to clarify unfamiliar or complex ideas. This is why so many teachers use examples in the classroom. Examples put abstract ideas into concrete terms that listeners can easily understand.

This principle works exceptionally well in speeches. Suppose you are talking about suspension bridges. You could give a technical description:

The suspension bridge has a roadway suspended by vertical cables attached to two or more main cables. The main cables are hung on two towers and have their ends anchored in concrete or bedrock.

If your audience were made up of people familiar with structural systems, they might be able to visualize what a suspension bridge looks like. But for listeners lacking this background, you might want to add a simple example:

Two well-known suspension bridges are the Golden Gate Bridge in San Francisco and the Brooklyn Bridge in New York.

Because almost everyone has at least seen a picture of the Golden Gate Bridge or the Brooklyn Bridge, using them as examples clarifies your meaning quickly and effectively.

Use Examples to Reinforce Your Ideas   In a speech entitled "Pharmaceutical Roulette," Kelley Melvin, a student at Marshall University, claimed that hundreds of drugs approved by the Food and Drug Administration for use in the United States have not been properly tested for their impact on women. Because most people assume that drugs sanctioned by the FDA are safe, Kelley gave plenty of examples to prove her point. One concerned the acne medication Accutane, which caused over 1,000 birth defects because it was marketed without being tested for its effects on women. Kelley also told the story of Monique Collins, a successful college student who died from the interaction of diet pills and her oral contraceptive. The diet pills caused severe complications in combination with high levels of estrogen, but no one knew this deadly fact before the pills were marketed because they had not been tested with women in mind.[8]

When you use such examples, make sure they are representative—that they do not deal with unusual or exceptional cases. Your listeners are sure to feel betrayed if they suspect you have chosen an atypical example to prove a general point.

Use Examples to Personalize Your Ideas   People are interested in people. As social psychologist Eliot Aronson explains, "Most people are more deeply influenced by one clear, vivid, personal example than by an abundance of statistical data."[9] Whenever you talk to a general audience (such as your speech class), you can include examples that will add human interest to your speech. So far in this section we have seen a number of such examples—the people of Lowell, Massachusetts, accident victim Roger Charter, and so on. The abstract becomes more meaningful when applied to a person. Which of the following would you be more likely to respond to?

There are many hungry families in our community who could benefit from food donations.

Or:

Let me tell you about Arturo. Arturo is four years old. He has big brown eyes and a mop of black hair and an empty belly. In all his four years on this earth, Arturo has never once enjoyed three square meals in a single day.

Try using examples with human interest in your speeches. You will soon discover why accomplished speakers consider them "the very life of the speech."[10]

Make Your Examples Vivid and Richly Textured   The richly textured example supplies everyday details that bring the example to life. Recall the example on page 147 of identical twins James Lewis and James Springer. The speaker provided us with many details about the twins. They were separated a week after birth and reunited forty years later. Despite being apart for so long, both had married a woman named Betty. Both had worked as deputy sheriffs and gas-station attendants. Both had the same favorite subjects in school. Both were bad spellers and suffered from migraine headaches.

How much less compelling the example would have been if the speaker had merely said:

One set of identical twins actually shared more than two dozen personal traits.

Instead, the details let us *see* the astounding similarities between James Lewis and James Springer. Those details are much more likely to stay in our minds than a vague statement about "twins who are a lot alike." Remember, the more vivid your examples—brief or extended—the more impact they are likely to have on your audience.[11]

Practice Delivery to Enhance Your Extended Examples   An extended example is just like a story, and the impact of your story will depend as much on delivery as on content. Many students have discovered this the hard way. After spending much time and energy developing a splendid example, they have seen the example fall flat on the day of the speech because they did not take the extra step to make it vivid and gripping for listeners.

When you use an extended example, think of yourself as a storyteller. Don't race through the example as though you were reading a newspaper, but instead use your voice to get listeners involved. Speak faster here to create a sense of action, slower there to build suspense. Raise your voice in some places, lower it in others. Pause occasionally for dramatic effect.

Most important, maintain eye contact with your audience. The easiest way to ruin a fine example is to read it dully from your notes. As you practice the speech, "talk through" your extended examples without relying on your notes. By the day of your speech, you should be able to deliver your extended examples as naturally as if you were telling a story to a group of friends.

STATISTICS

We live in an age of statistics. Day in and day out we are bombarded with a staggering array of numbers: Billy Joel has sold over 50 million albums; 12 percent of American children under the age of eighteen suffer from some form of psychological illness; France produces almost 2 billion gallons of wine every year; the literacy rate of Iraq is 71 percent; Americans consume more than 700 million pounds of peanut butter annually.

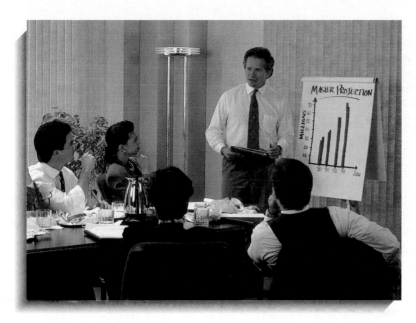

Statistics make us feel more secure in our knowledge. A speech that is supported by statistics is usually more persuasive than an undocumented presentation.

What do all these numbers mean? Most of us would be hard-pressed to say. Yet we feel more secure in our knowledge when we can express it numerically. According to Lord Kelvin, the nineteenth-century physicist, "When you can measure what you are speaking about, and express it in numbers, you know something about it. But when you cannot measure it, when you cannot express it in numbers, your knowledge is . . . meager and unsatisfactory." It is this widely shared belief that makes statistics, when used properly, such an effective way to clarify and support ideas.

Like brief examples, statistics are often cited in passing to clarify or strengthen a speaker's points. The following examples show how three students used statistics in their speeches:

To document the growing problem of homicide among teenagers in the United States: "According to the FBI, more than 2,000 U.S. teenagers will be murdered this year—double the rate of five years ago."

To show the increasing popularity of mountaineering: "The United States Interior Department estimates that 4.1 million Americans currently do some form of mountain climbing—and the number is growing by 100,000 people a year."

To illustrate the disparity between the amount of money the federal government spends on senior citizens and on children: "Figures provided by the U.S. General Accounting Office reveal that for every $1 spent on the needs of children the federal government provides $14 in benefits for elderly Americans."

Statistics can also be used in combination—stacked up to show the magnitude or seriousness of an issue. We find a good instance of this technique in a speech by Richard Lamm, former Governor of Colorado. To help demonstrate his point about the profusion of lawyers and lawsuits in the United States, Lamm cited the following figures:

> There are 279 lawyers per 100,000 people in the United States versus 114 in Great Britain, 77 in West Germany, 29 in France, and 11 in Japan. That means the United States has two and a half times as many lawyers as Great Britain, five times as many as West Germany, and 25 times as many as Japan. With 5 percent of the world's population, we have almost 70 percent of the world's lawyers.[12]

This is a well-supported argument. But what if the speaker had merely said:

> The United States has more lawyers than any other country.

The second statement is neither as clear nor as convincing as the one containing statistics. The statistics make the speaker's claim credible and specific. Of course, the audience didn't remember all the numbers, but that's all right. The purpose of presenting a series of figures is to create an *overall* impact on listeners. What the audience did recall is that an impressive array of statistics supported the speaker's position.

Understanding Statistics

In his classic book *How to Lie with Statistics,* Darrell Huff exploded the notion that numbers don't lie. Strictly speaking, they don't. But they can be easily manipulated and distorted. For example, which of the following statements is true?

a. Enriched white bread is more nutritious than whole-wheat bread because it contains as much or more protein, calcium, niacin, thiamine, and riboflavin.

b. Whole-wheat bread is more nutritious than white bread because it contains seven times the amount of fiber, plus more iron, phosphorus, and potassium.

As you might expect, *both* statements are true. And you might hear either one of them—depending on who is trying to sell you the bread.

One can play with statistics in all kinds of areas. Which of these statements is true?

a. The cheetah, clocked at 70 mph, is the fastest animal in the world.

b. The pronghorn antelope, clocked at 61 mph, is the fastest animal in the world.

The cheetah, right? Not necessarily. It's true the cheetah can go faster, but only for short sprints. The antelope can maintain its high speed over a much greater distance. So which is faster? It depends on what you're measuring. Put in terms of human races, the cheetah would win the hundred-yard dash, but the antelope would win the marathon.

When you are dealing with money, statistics become even trickier. For instance, consider the following facts:

a. In 1947 President Harry Truman earned a salary of $75,000.

b. In 1967 President Lyndon B. Johnson earned a salary of $100,000.

c. In 1987 President Ronald Reagan earned a salary of $200,000.

Which President was paid the most money? It depends. In purely mathematical terms, Reagan was the highest earner. But as we all know, a dollar today does not buy nearly as much as it did when Harry Truman was President. One measure of the inflation rate is the Consumer Price Index, which gauges the value of the dollar in any given year against its purchasing power in 1967. If we apply the Consumer Price Index to the three Presidents' salaries, we can see how much each earned in 1967 dollars:

a. In 1947 President Harry Truman earned a salary of $104,000.

b. In 1967 President Lyndon B. Johnson earned a salary of $100,000.

c. In 1987 President Ronald Reagan earned a salary of $62,000.

In other words, while Reagan had the highest salary, the value of his $200,000 was considerably less than the value of Truman's $75,000.

The point is that there is usually more to statistics than meets the eye.[13] When you track down statistics for your speeches, be sure to evaluate them in light of the following questions.

Are the Statistics Representative?   Say that on your way to class you choose ten students at random and ask them whether they favor or oppose government tax credits for students attending private schools. Say also that six approve of such funding and four do not. Would you then be accurate in claiming that 60 percent of the students on your campus favor spending government money for private schools?

Of course not. Ten students is not a big enough sample. But even if it were, other problems would arise. Do the ten students interviewed accurately reflect your school's proportion of freshmen, sophomores, juniors, and seniors? Do they mirror the proportion of male and female students? Are the various majors accurately represented? What about part-time and full-time students? Students of different cultural and religious backgrounds?

In short, make sure your statistics are representative of what they claim to measure.

Are Statistical Measures Used Correctly?   Here are two groups of numbers:

GROUP A	GROUP B
7,500	5,400
6,300	5,400
5,000	5,000
4,400	2,300
4,400	1,700

Let us apply to each group three basic statistical measures—the mean, the median, and the mode.

The *mean*—popularly called the average—is determined by summing all of the items in a group and dividing by the number of items. The mean for group A is 5,520. For group B it is 3,960.

The *median* is the middle figure in a group once the figures are put in order from highest to lowest. The median for both group A and group B is exactly the same—5,000.

The *mode* is the number that occurs most frequently in a group of numbers. The mode for group A is 4,400. For group B it is 5,400.

Notice the results:

	GROUP A	GROUP B
Mean	5,520	3,960
Median	5,000	5,000
Mode	4,400	5,400

All of these measures have the same goal—to indicate what is typical or characteristic of a certain group of numbers. Yet see how different the results are, depending on which measure you use.

The differences among the various measures can be striking. For instance, the *mean* salary of the top-paid local television news anchor persons throughout the country is $90,400 a year. But most anchors don't earn anywhere near that. The average is highly inflated by the huge salaries (sometimes up to $1 million a year) paid to star anchors at major stations in large media markets such as New York, Los Angeles, and Chicago. In contrast, the *median* salary of top-paid local news anchors is $50,500—not a sum to scoff at, but still $39,900 less than the average salary.[14]

How might a speaker use these different measures? The owner of a television station would probably cite the *mean* ($90,400) to show that news anchors are handsomely compensated for their work. An organization of news anchors might emphasize the *median* ($50,500) to demonstrate that salaries are not nearly as high as the station owner makes them out to be. Both speakers would be telling the truth, but neither would be completely honest unless they made clear the meaning of the statistics.

Are the Statistics from a Reliable Source?   Which is the more reliable estimate of the environmental dangers of toxic waste in a landfill—one from the U.S. Environmental Protection Agency or one compiled by the company that owns the landfill? Easy—the estimate by the EPA, which does not have a vested interest in what the figures look like. What about nutritional ratings for fast foods offered by Consumer's Union (a highly respected nonprofit organization) or by Burger King? That's easy too—Consumer's Union, whose claims are not manipulated by advertising executives.

But now things get tougher. What about the competing statistics offered by groups for and against welfare reform? Or the conflicting numbers tossed out by a school board and the teachers striking against it? In these cases the answer is not so clear, since both sides would present the facts according to their own partisan motives.

As a speaker, you must be aware of possible bias in the use of numbers. Since statistics can be interpreted so many ways and put to so many uses, you should seek figures gathered by objective, nonpartisan sources.

Tips for Using Statistics

Use Statistics to Quantify Your Ideas   The main value of statistics is to give your ideas numerical precision. This can be especially important when you are trying to document the existence of a problem. Examples can bring the problem alive and dramatize it in personal terms. But your listeners may still wonder how many people the problem actually affects. In such a situation, you should turn to statistics. Research has shown that the impact of examples is greatly enhanced when they are followed by statistics that show the examples to be typical.[15]

Suppose you are speaking about the decline in driving skills among elderly motorists. You give an example, you personalize it, you provide many details, as follows:

On June 22 of last year, 77-year-old Pearl Kramm, of Tuscola, Illinois, went to renew her driver's license. She began by backing up over a curb and into a tree. Despite this somewhat inauspicious beginning, she was allowed to continue. She shouldn't have been—because she proceeded to drive straight through the plate-glass window of the Driver Testing Center, killing one person and seriously injuring three others.[16]

Confronted with this example, a listener might think, "Yes, that's very unfortunate, quite tragic, but are there really that many elderly motorists in America who have trouble driving?" Anticipating just such a response, a sharp speaker would include figures to quantify the problem:

According to statistics from the Transportation Research Board, the accident rate for drivers over the age of 65 is second only to that of teenagers. In addition, the National Research Board has found that motorists over the age of 75 are twice as likely to be involved in an accident than the average motorist, while the accident rate for drivers over age 80 is triple that for all other drivers on the road.

Now the audience is much more likely to agree that driver safety among elderly motorists is a serious problem.

Use Statistics Sparingly   As helpful as statistics can be, nothing puts an audience to sleep faster than a speech cluttered with numbers from beginning to end. Insert statistics only when they are needed, and then make sure they are easy to grasp. Even the most attentive listener would have trouble sorting out this barrage of figures:

According to the Department of Health and Human Services, life expectancy at birth in the United States ranks eighteenth among thirty-nine industrialized countries for females, twenty-second for males. For comparison, life expectancy for an American male is 71.5 years; for a Japanese male it is 75.8 years. The United States ranks twenty-second among thirty-nine industrialized countries on infant mortality, with a rate almost twice as great as Japan's. Canada ranks seventh. The per capita health expenditure for the U.S. is currently 40 percent higher than Canada and 127 percent higher than Japan.

Instead of drowning your audience in a sea of statistics, use only those that are most important. For example:

According to the Department of Health and Human Services, people in the United States have one of the lower life expectancies among industrialized nations. We also have one of the highest rates of infant mortality. Yet we spend much more for health care than other countries—40 percent more per person than Canada and 127 percent more than Japan.

This second statement makes the same point as the first statement, but now the ideas emerge more clearly because they are not lost in a torrent of numbers.

Identify the Sources of Your Statistics   As we have seen, figures are easy to manipulate. This is why careful listeners keep an ear out for the sources of a speaker's statistics. One student learned this by experience. In a speech entitled "Logging and the Environment: Fact vs. Fiction," he claimed that although the tall-tree forests of the Pacific Northwest have been hurt by heavy logging in recent decades, American forests as a whole are thriving. Because of environmentally friendly logging practices such as planting more trees than are cut, he said, there are 70 million more acres of forest in the U.S. today than at the end of World War II. This is a startling statistic—especially given the recent concern about logging's impact on the environment. But because the student did not say where he got the figure, most of his classmates were not willing to accept it. They were sure he must be wrong.

As it turned out, the figure was quite reliable. It came from the latest edition of the *Statistical Abstract of the United States,* an annual digest of statistics covering almost every aspect of American life. If the speaker had mentioned this in his speech, he would have been more persuasive.[17]

Explain Your Statistics   Statistics don't speak for themselves. They need to be interpreted and related to your listeners. Notice how effectively one speaker did this:

> Children throughout America dream about growing up to be a professional athlete, but the odds of that dream coming true are extremely slim. To take but one sport, of the 20,000 students who play college basketball in any given year, usually no more than 40 will make it to the National Basketball Association. John Slaughter, President of Occidental College, put these figures in perspective when he stated, "The odds of becoming a brain surgeon are greater than the odds of winning a starting spot on the Boston Celtics."

Explaining what statistics mean is particularly important when you deal with large numbers, since they are hard to visualize. How, for example, can we comprehend the $5 trillion of the U.S. national debt? We could explain that a trillion is a thousand billion and a billion is a thousand million. But that doesn't do much good, since millions and billions are almost as hard to visualize as trillions. Suppose, instead, we translate the huge numbers into terms a listener can relate to. Here is what one speaker came up with:

> How much money is a trillion dollars? Think of it this way. If you had $1 million and spent it at the rate of $1,000 a day, you would run out of money in less than three years. If you had $1 billion and spent it at the rate of $1,000 a day, you would not run out of money for almost three thousand years. And if you had $1 trillion and spent it at the rate of $1,000 a day, you wouldn't run out of money for nearly three million years!

Whenever you use statistics in your speeches, think of how you can make them meaningful to your audience. Rather than simply reciting the fact that, say, the average person in the United States commutes 157,600 miles to work during his or her lifetime, find a way to make your audience *see* how many miles that is. You might say:

> If it seems as if you spend a lot of time going back and forth from your job, it's probably because you do. According to figures compiled by management consultant Jeff Davidson, the average American commutes 157,600 miles to and from work during his or her working life. That's equal to driving six times around the earth.

Or suppose you want to show the high price we all pay because of the glut of liability lawsuits against businesses and manufacturers. You could say,

"According to *Forbes* magazine, U.S. consumers foot the bill for $300 billion of product liability costs each year." This is an alarming statistic, but it is likely to go in one ear and out the other unless you bring it home to your audience. Here's what you might say:

> *Forbes* magazine reports that U.S. consumers pay $300 billion a year on products to cover the manufacturers' liability expenses. This amounts to a staggering $4,000 per household. On a specific basis, product liability costs account for between $15 and $30 of every stepladder we buy, $11.50 of every $12 dose of vaccine we give our children, and over $100 of the cost of a football helmet.[18]

Be creative in thinking of ways to relate your statistics to your audience. This is probably the single most important step you can take to make statistics work in your speeches.

Round Off Complicated Statistics   Mount Everest is 29,028 feet high; the official world land speed record is 622.287 miles per hour; the world's highest waterfall has a total drop of 3,212 feet; the greatest attendance at any boxing match was 135,132 people; the moon is 238,855 miles from Earth.

These are intriguing figures, but they are too complicated to be readily understood by listeners. Unless there is an important reason to give exact numbers, you should round off most statistics. You might say that Mount Everest is 29,000 feet high; the world land speed record is more than 622 miles per hour; the world's highest waterfall has a drop of some 3,200 feet; the greatest attendance at any boxing match was 135,000; and the moon is 239,000 miles from Earth.

Use Visual Aids to Clarify Statistical Trends   Visual aids can save you a lot of time, as well as make your statistics easier to comprehend. Suppose you are discussing the number of major strikes by labor unions in the United States since World War II. You could start by explaining that after the war, during the early 1950s, there were a record number of strikes involving 1,000 or more workers—including the 1950 walkout of 370,000 United Mine Workers that crippled the nation's industries. Then, after the start of Dwight Eisenhower's presidency in 1953, the number of strikes declined fairly steadily until 1964, when they started climbing to a peak of more than 400 in 1968. After a sharp decline in the early 1970s, they jumped again in 1975 to the highest level in two decades. Finally, the number of strikes took a dramatic turn downward during the Reagan years of the 1980s and reached a record low in 1992.

These are interesting statistics, and you could build a good speech around them. But strung together in a few sentences they are hard to digest. Figure 7.1 shows how much more clearly the points can be made with a simple graph. We shall discuss visual aids in detail in Chapter 13. For the moment, keep in mind that they can be helpful in presenting statistical information.

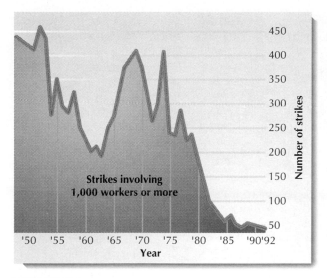

450
400
350
300
250
200
150
100
50

Number of strikes

Strikes involving
1,000 workers or more

'50 '55 '60 '65 '70 '75 '80 '85 '90'92
Year

FIGURE 7.1

Where to Find Statistics

Statistics can be found in any kind of reputable publication—books, magazines, newspapers, scholarly journals, government documents, business reports, and so forth. A world almanac (there are several established versions) can be a treasure house of interesting numbers.

There are also some sources devoted solely to statistics. They include the *Statistical Abstract of the United States* (published annually since 1878) and the *Statistical Yearbook* (put out by the United Nations). These contain statistics on everything from the U.S. economy to world population trends. The *Guinness Book of World Records* offers more esoteric information, such as the weight of the world's largest polished diamond, the internal temperature of the sun, and how many hours of television the average child watches by age eighteen.

You will find these and other handy sources of statistics in the reference room of your library (see Chapter 6). Besides being easy to use, they can be fascinating to look through. This is why the *Guinness Book of World Records* remains a best-seller year after year.

 TESTIMONY

Imagine you are talking with a friend about the classes you plan to take next term. You are not sure whether to sign up for Psychology 230 or Accounting 181. Both are requirements; both meet at the same time of day. Your friend

Citing expert testimony in support of your ideas is an excellent way to bolster your credibility as a speaker. One way to get such testimony is through library research.

says, "I took those classes last year. They're both good, but Professor Hassam was excellent in Psych 230. She's one of the best teachers on campus. If she's teaching the course next term, I'd take it for sure." You check the timetable and find that Professor Hassam is indeed slated for Psychology 230. You sign up for her course.

As this story illustrates, we are often influenced by the testimony of other people when making decisions in everyday life. Much the same thing happens in public speaking. Just as you are likely to be swayed by your friend's recommendation about which class to take, so audiences tend to respect the opinions of people who have special knowledge or experience on the topic at hand. By quoting or paraphrasing such people, you can give your ideas greater strength and impact. The two major kinds of testimony are expert testimony and peer testimony.

Expert Testimony

In most speeches you will probably rely on expert testimony—testimony from people who are acknowledged authorities in their fields. Expert testimony is especially helpful for student speakers because students are seldom recognized as experts on their speech topics. Citing the views of people who are experts is a good way to lend credibility to your speeches. It shows that you are not just mouthing your own opinions, but that your position is supported by people who are knowledgeable about the topic.[19]

Expert testimony is even more important when a topic is controversial or when the audience is skeptical about a speaker's point of view. The following story explains how one student enlisted expert testimony for her speech on the Social Security system:

> As Julia Wang did her research for a speech on America's budget deficit, she became convinced that the present Social Security system should be changed to ensure its long-term stability and to be more equitable for younger taxpayers. Yet Julia was not an expert on the matter. Nor did she have any firsthand experience with the Social Security system. How could she convince her audience to accept her ideas?
>
> Statistics helped, and so did examples. But on such a controversial issue, that was not enough. So to reinforce her credibility, Julia quoted a wide range of experts who agreed with her—Senator Daniel Moynihan of New York; Martin Feldstein, a Harvard economics professor; former U.S. Secretary of Commerce Peter G. Peterson; Illinois Congressman John Porter; Donald Leavens, director of federal budget policy at the U.S. Chamber of Commerce; and Donald Kennedy, former president of Stanford University. By citing the views of these experts—some of whom might be expected to disagree with her point of view—Julia made her speech much more persuasive.

Peer Testimony

Another type of testimony often used in speeches is peer testimony—opinions of people like ourselves; not prominent figures, but ordinary citizens who have firsthand experience on the topic. This kind of testimony is especially valuable because it gives a more personal viewpoint on issues than can be gained from expert testimony. It conveys the feelings, the knowledge, the insight of people who speak with the voice of genuine experience.

For example, if you were speaking about the barriers faced by people with physical disabilities, you would surely include testimony from doctors and other medical authorities. But in this case, the expert testimony would be limited because it cannot communicate what it really means to have a physical disability. To communicate that, you need statements from people who have physical disabilities—such as the following:

> Itzhak Perlman, the world-renowned violinist whose legs are paralyzed, once said: "When you are in a wheelchair, people don't talk to you. Perhaps they think it is contagious, or perhaps they think crippled legs mean a crippled mind. But whatever the reason, they treat you like a thing."

> Paul Langmore, who lost the use of his legs in Vietnam, notes that most people are uncomfortable in the presence of someone who is handicapped. "It's only when they really go out of their way to get to know us," he says, "that they realize we are just as bright, witty, and companionable as they are."

There is no way expert testimony can express these ideas with the same authenticity and emotional impact.

Quoting Versus Paraphrasing

The statements from Itzhak Perlman and Paul Langmore are presented as direct quotations. Testimony can also be presented by paraphrasing. Rather than quoting someone verbatim, you present the gist of that person's ideas in your own words—as did one student in her speech about America's growing water crisis:

> Writing in *Audubon* magazine, Dr. Peter Bourne, president of Global Water, a nonpartisan educational group in Washington, D.C., said most Americans do not yet realize the extent and urgency of the water problem. At the present rate, he says, we are headed for a crisis that will change the way we live in every part of the nation.

When should you use a direct quotation as opposed to paraphrasing? The standard rule of thumb is that quotations are most effective when they are brief, when they convey your meaning better than you can, and when they are particularly eloquent, witty, or compelling. If you find a quotation that fits these criteria, then recite the quotation word for word.

Paraphrasing is better than direct quotation in two situations: (1) when the wording of a quotation is obscure or cumbersome, as is often the case with government documents; (2) when a quotation is longer than two or three sentences. Audiences often tune out partway through lengthy quotations, which tend to interrupt the flow of a speaker's ideas. Since the rest of the speech is in your own words, you should put longer quotations in your own words as well.

Tips for Using Testimony

Quote or Paraphrase Accurately   Accurate quotation involves three things: making sure you do not misquote someone; making sure you do not violate the meaning of statements you paraphrase; making sure you do not quote out of context. Of these, the last is the most subtle—and the most dangerous. By quoting out of context, you can twist someone's remarks so as to prove almost anything. Take movie advertisements. A critic pans a movie with these words:

> This movie is a colossal bore. From beginning to end it is a disaster. What is meant to be brilliant dialogue is about as fascinating as the stuff you clean out of your kitchen drain.

But when the movie is advertised in the newspapers, what appears in huge letters over the critic's name? "COLOSSAL! FROM BEGINNING TO END—BRILLIANT! FASCINATING!"

This is so flagrant as to be humorous. But quoting out of context can have serious consequences. In 1968 Michigan governor George Romney was a leading contender for the Republican presidential nomination until his famous "brainwashing" remark—a remark taken out of context—damaged his campaign beyond repair. Appearing on a Detroit talk show, Romney answered a question about his views on the war in Vietnam this way:

Well, you know, when I came back from Vietnam, I just had the greatest brainwashing that anybody can get when you go over to Vietnam. Not only by the generals, but also by the diplomatic corps over there, and they do a very thorough job. And since returning from Vietnam, I've gone into the history of Vietnam, all the way back into World War II and beyond. And, as a result, I have changed my mind. . . . I no longer believe that it was necessary for us to get involved in South Vietnam to stop communist aggression.

The "brainwashing" line was a throwaway. The main point of Romney's full statement was that he had changed his mind about the need for American military forces in Vietnam. But the day after the telecast, the *New York Times* carried a story with the headline: ROMNEY ASSERTS HE UNDERWENT "BRAINWASHING" ON VIETNAM TRIP. That evening the network news programs showed clips of Romney making his "brainwashing" remark, and the next day it was being quoted in newspapers and shown on television all over the nation—except that it was usually quoted and shown out of context, without the rest of Romney's original statement about his views on the war.

For the next several weeks, Romney tried to clarify his remark and to explain why a man who had been "brainwashed" on Vietnam was competent to be President of the United States. That one remark—taken out of context—helped to destroy Romney's credibility as a presidential candidate.[20]

Clearly, quoting or paraphrasing accurately is an important ethical responsibility for speakers and writers alike.

Use Testimony from Qualified Sources We have all become accustomed to the celebrity testimonial in television and magazine advertising. The professional golfer endorses a particular brand of clubs. The movie star praises a certain hair spray or shampoo. The basketball player plugs a type of athletic shoe. So far, so good. These are the tools of the trade for the people who endorse them.

But what happens when a comedian promotes a credit card? A football announcer represents a chain of hardware stores? A figure skater extols the virtues of a breakfast cereal? Do they know more about these products than you or I? Probably not. They have been paid large sums of money to be photographed with the product in hopes that their popularity will rub off on it.

Being a celebrity or an authority in one area does not make someone competent in other areas. Listeners will find your speeches much more credible if you use testimony from sources qualified *on the subject at hand.* As we have seen, this may include either recognized experts or ordinary citizens with special experience on the speech topic.

Use Testimony from Unbiased Sources   In a speech about the controversial sleeping pill Halcion, which has been blamed for causing side effects such as amnesia, anxiety, delusions, and hostility, a student said:

> Pharmacologist Robert Shaw, director of project management at the Upjohn Company, the Michigan-based manufacturer of Halcion, maintains that it has no more serious side effects than any other sleeping pill when it is used properly. "The vast majority of studies," Shaw says, "back us up on that point."

As you might expect, the student's classmates were not persuaded. After all, what would you expect someone at Upjohn to say—that its product is unsafe and causes psychiatric disorders? One listener reacted this way: "For all I know, the statement by Shaw may be true, but he is hardly an unbiased source. I wish you had cited an impartial expert instead."

Careful listeners are suspicious of opinion from biased or self-interested sources. Be sure to use testimony from credible, competent, objective authorities.

Identify the People You Quote or Paraphrase   The usual way to identify your source is to name the person and sketch her or his qualifications before presenting the testimony. The following excerpt is from a speech on the large number of errors in medical laboratory tests:

> According to *Harvey Klein, a senior scientist at the National Institutes of Health*, the lack of formal training and certification for people working in medical labs is nothing short of scandalous. "In some states," he notes, "a beautician faces more licensing requirements than a medical lab technician."

Had the speaker not identified Harvey Klein, listeners would not have had the foggiest notion who he is or why his opinion should be heeded.

As we saw in Chapter 2, identifying the source of testimony is also an important ethical responsibility. If you use another person's words or ideas without giving credit to that person, you will be guilty of plagiarism. This is true whether you paraphrase the original source or quote it verbatim.

Examples, statistics, and testimony are all helpful devices for the speaker. Depending on your topic, you may want to use some of them, all of them, or none of them. Remember they are tools, and they all serve the same purpose—getting your message across to your listeners.

■ SAMPLE SPEECH WITH COMMENTARY

The following speech illustrates how to work supporting materials into a presentation. As you read, study how the speaker uses a variety of examples, statistics, and quotations to make the ideas clear, credible, and convincing.

SUFFER THE CHILDREN

COMMENTARY

The speaker begins with an extended example to gain attention and interest. The example is specific and detailed. We are told Matthew Garvey's name and age, where he lived, the kind of work he did, and how he was injured. These are the kinds of details that bring examples to life and help get listeners involved in a speech.

The speaker moves smoothly into testimony suggesting that the opening story is representative of a major problem in the U.S. When you use an extended example, it is usually a good idea to precede or follow the example with statistics or testimony showing that the example is not unusual or exceptional.

In her first main point the speaker explores the problem of child labor law violations in the United States. She begins by summarizing the provisions of the law. Notice how clearly she identifies the source of her information.

Statistics in this and the next paragraph back up the speaker's point that violations of child labor laws are widespread in the U.S. Rather than giving the exact number of violations found by Operation Child Watch, the speaker rounds them off, making them easier to grasp and recall.

SPEECH

Matthew Garvey was just 13 years old when he was hired by Quality Car Wash in Laurel, Maryland, to towel dry cars as they came off the line. Not long after he began working, Matthew lost his right leg when it got caught in an industrial machine used to suck the moisture out of the towels. After investigating, the U.S. Department of Labor fined the car wash for illegally hiring a minor and for operating a machine with a broken safety lid.

This is just one of the more tragic examples of what Jeffrey Newman of the National Child Labor Committee calls the crisis of child labor law abuses in the United States. In researching this speech, I discovered that employers from New York to California are breaking the law by hiring children from ages seven to seventeen who often put in long, hard hours in dangerous conditions. Today I would like to show you the extent of the problem and how it jeopardizes the education and safety of millions of young people.

To understand the problem of child labor law violations, we need to begin by looking at the provisions of the law. As explained in the *Congressional Quarterly* of March 14, 1992, the U.S. Fair Labor Standards Act sets a minimum working age of 14. It limits 14-year-olds and 15-year-olds to three hours of work on school days, prohibits them from working after 7 at night, and allows them a total of 18 work hours per week during the school year. The law also restricts employment of children under 18 in dangerous jobs such as construction, meat-cutting, and mining.

Passed in 1938 and amended several times since, the Fair Labor Standards Act was designed to prevent the exploitation of child labor that took place during the nineteenth century. Yet today violations of the law are shockingly widespread. In 1990 a major federal effort called Operation Child Watch uncovered over 39,000 violations of children working for less than minimum wage or for excessive hours. And this is only the tip of the iceberg since most wage and hour infractions are never reported to authorities.

Notice how the speaker identifies the sources of her statistics and integrates those sources deftly into the text. There are many examples of this technique throughout the speech.

The speaker uses a combination of statistics and testimony to support her point about child labor law abuses in the garment industry. The statement from Thomas Gubiak of New York's garment district task force is an example of expert testimony; the closing quotation from Faviola Flores is an instance of peer testimony.

Two brief examples support the speaker's point about child labor law violations in the fast-food and supermarket industries. This is an important point for the speaker to make since a large proportion of minors who hold jobs work in one or the other of these industries. Because the examples deal with large companies such as Burger King and Food Lion, they provide strong evidence to reinforce the speaker's point that violations of the law are widespread.

The speaker begins her second main point—that violations of child labor laws have serious consequences for the education and physical safety of young workers.

Nor do the 39,000 violations discovered by Operation Child Watch include more serious abuses of the law such as exposing children to hazardous working conditions or employing underage children. According to the October 1993 issue of *Scientific American,* there are as many as 676,000 children illegally employed in the United States. All told, says the National Child Labor Committee, as many as 2 million violations of child labor laws take place in the U.S. each year.

Some of the most serious violations occur in garment industry factories known as sweatshops that hire immigrant children at rates well below minimum wage. According to *Scholastic Update,* during the past four years investigators have uncovered major infractions in more than 300 New York City sweatshops alone. Thomas Gubiak, head of the city's garment district task force, says "most of the children in these factories are below 18, some as young as eight." Like Faviola Flores, a 15-year-old Mexican girl in a Manhattan sweatshop, they toil long days in unsafe conditions for as little as $2.50 an hour. "I don't like working here," Flores says, "but I have no choice."

Although the exploitation of child labor has been a problem in the garment trade since the 1800s, it can be found in almost every industry that employs minors, including such traditional businesses as fast-food restaurants and supermarkets. In December 1992 the U.S. Labor Department fined Burger King $500,000—at that time the largest child labor penalty in history—for working 14- and 15-year-olds too long, too late at night, and in prohibited jobs. Less than a year later, in August 1993, the Food Lion supermarket chain broke Burger King's dubious record by paying $16.2 million in civil penalties in a settlement with the U.S. government for hundreds of labor violations, including working teenagers longer hours than legally allowed and letting them operate hazardous machinery such as meat saws and paper-box bailers.

Like other businesses caught breaking child labor laws, Burger King and Food Giant have tried to downplay the seriousness of their offenses. But the growing epidemic of child labor law violations threatens both the education and the physical safety of young workers.

The quotation from Hugh McDaid is a good instance of expert testimony, which the speaker uses well throughout the speech. This quotation, like others in the speech, is short and forceful. There is no reason to use a direct quotation unless it makes the point more clearly and forcefully than you can in your own words.

Here the speaker paraphrases rather than quoting verbatim. Notice that she gives the name of the book she is paraphrasing from and identifies its authors. As we saw in Chapter 2, speakers have an ethical obligation to indicate the sources of paraphrases as well as of quotations.

The examples in this paragraph show specific cases in which teenagers were injured or killed by the violation of child labor laws. The extended example about Michael Hurcone is especially effective. Filled with specific details that make it interesting and credible, it puts the speaker's point in human terms with which the audience can identify.

In this paragraph the speaker presents a series of statistics to prove that the examples in the previous paragraph are not atypical. Here, as elsewhere, the speaker offers statistics from qualified, objective sources, identifies where she found the statistics, and rounds off the numbers. All in all, this speech provides a fine example of how statistics can be used to support a speaker's ideas.

The speaker begins her conclusion by summarizing the two main

The educational consequences are most damaging to illegal underage employees who work instead of attending school. As Hugh McDaid of New York City's garment task force says, illegal underage workers "sacrifice their education and literally commit themselves to a life of working in a sweatshop. They have no future." But even for children who do attend school, too many hours at work can harm their education. In their book *When Teenagers Work,* psychology professors Ellen Greenberger and Laurence Steinberg note that intensive levels of work—especially among youths who take jobs early in high school—tend to produce higher truancy and lower grades. According to Greenberger and Steinberg, one research study after another has found that working more than a very few hours a week has a negative impact on teenagers' academic performance.

Not only do child workers harm their education, but they often endanger their physical safety as well. Recall, for example, the story I told in my introduction about Matthew Garvey, the 13-year-old who lost his leg while working at a car wash. Even more tragic is the case of Michael Hurcone, a 17-year-old Pennsylvania high-school student. While employed at a supermarket, he was working with a bailer—a machine that crushes and binds cardboard boxes and is supposed to be off-limits to minors. Noticing that some material was stuck in the bailer, Michael tried to free up the jam when he got caught in the machine. It crushed his body for 30 minutes before he suffocated.

These are not isolated examples. Although we do not have full statistics on the number of children injured and killed in the workplace, the figures we do have show it is far from uncommon. *Congressional Quarterly* reports that in 1987 and 1988 combined some 128,000 minors were injured while working. According to the National Institute for Occupational Safety and Health, more than 130 children died on the job in 1991. And in 1993 the National Safe Workplace Institute estimated that as many as 300 children are killed and 70,000 injured at work every year—most in accidents involving infractions of child labor laws.

In the light of all this evidence, there can be little doubt that the violation of child labor laws is a wide-points she had made in the body of the speech. She then ends with a dramatic quotation. As we shall see in Chapter 9, this is an effective way to pull a speech together and to reinforce its central idea.

spread problem with serious consequences. The issue is well summarized by U.S. Senator Howard Metzenbaum of Ohio, who stated after congressional hearings on the subject, "I shudder to think that children the same age as my own grandchildren are being robbed of an education, their limbs, and indeed, their lives through illegal child labor."

SUMMARY

Good speeches are not composed of hot air and unfounded assertions. They need strong supporting materials to bolster the speaker's point of view. In fact, the skillful use of supporting materials often makes the difference between a good speech and a poor one. The three basic types of supporting materials are examples, statistics, and testimony.

In the course of a speech you may use brief examples—specific instances referred to in passing—and sometimes you may want to give several brief examples in a row to create a stronger impression. Extended examples—often called illustrations, narratives, or anecdotes—are longer and more detailed. Hypothetical examples describe imaginary situations and can be quite effective for relating ideas to the audience. All three kinds of examples help to clarify ideas, to reinforce ideas, or to personalize ideas. To be most effective, though, they should be vivid and richly textured.

Statistics can be extremely helpful in conveying your message as long as you use them sparingly and explain them so they are meaningful to your audience. Above all, you should understand your statistics and use them fairly. Numbers can easily be manipulated and distorted. Make sure your figures are representative of what they claim to measure, that you use statistical measures correctly, and that you take statistics only from reliable sources.

Testimony is especially helpful for student speakers because students are seldom recognized as experts on their speech topics. Citing the views of people who are experts is a good way to make your ideas more credible. When you include testimony in a speech, you can either quote someone verbatim or paraphrase his or her words. As with statistics, there are guidelines for using testimony. Be sure to quote or paraphrase accurately and to cite qualified, unbiased sources. If the source is not generally known to your audience, be certain to establish that person's credentials.

REVIEW QUESTIONS

After reading this chapter, you should be able to answer the following questions:

1. Why do you need supporting materials in your speeches?

2. What are the three kinds of examples discussed in the chapter? How might you use each kind to support your ideas?

3. What are five tips for using examples in your speeches?

4. Why is it so easy to lie with statistics? What three questions should you ask to judge the reliability of statistics?

5. What are six tips for using statistics in your speeches?

6. What is testimony? Explain the difference between expert testimony and peer testimony.

7. What are four tips for using testimony in your speeches?

APPLICATION EXERCISES

1. Each of the following statements violates at least one of the criteria for effective supporting materials discussed in the chapter. Identify the flaw (or flaws) in each statement.

   a. According to a poll conducted for Hardee's restaurants, most people prefer the taste of Hardee's fried chicken over the taste of Kentucky Fried Chicken.

   b. It's just not true that violence on television has an influence on crimes by young people. All my friends watch television, and none of us has ever committed a violent crime.

   c. According to statistics compiled by the Board of Regents, the median salary for professors at our state university is $44,850. This shows that professors average almost $45,000 a year in salary.

   d. The Department of Health and Human Services reports that single parents now head 25 percent of families with children under age eighteen in the United States. A staggering 54 percent of these families live below the poverty line, compared with 18 percent of all families with children. For families headed by females, the figure is 47 percent compared with 19 percent for families headed by males. By the year 2000, 50 percent of U.S. families may be headed by single parents.

   e. As Kevin Costner said in a recent interview, America must act now to protect its national parks. If we do not take action right away, Costner said, the park system may be permanently damaged.

   f.   A random poll of 265 people taken recently in Washington, D.C., showed that 78 percent of those interviewed opposed term limitations on U.S. Senators and Representatives. Clearly, then, the American people oppose such limitations.

   g.   In the words of one expert, "Genetic screening for job applicants is scientifically unreliable and legally questionable. Not only are the tests highly inaccurate, but they pose a serious threat to a potential employee's right to privacy."

   h.   According to the U.S. Census Bureau, the average annual income of Americans who do not graduate from high school is $5,904. For those with a high-school diploma the average is $12,924 a year. College graduates average $25,392 a year, while people with a master's degree average $33,864.

2. Analyze the speech in the Appendix by Steven Harris ("Family Medical Histories: A Proven Lifesaver," pages 454–456). Identify the main points of the speech and the supporting materials used for each. Evaluate the speaker's use of supporting materials in light of the criteria discussed in this chapter.

NOTES

[1] "The Brick Wall," *Newsweek* (August 24, 1992), 54–56.

[2] James R. Chiles, "Goodbye Telephone, Hello to the New Communications Age," *Smithsonian* (February 22, 1992), 46–51.

[3] "A Deadly Return," *Newsweek* (March 16, 1992), 53–57.

[4] Ann Blackman, "Lowell's Little Acre," *Time* (Fall 1993), 34.

[5] Dean C. Kazoleas, "A Comparison of the Persuasive Effectiveness of Qualitative versus Quantitative Evidence: A Test of Explanatory Hypotheses," *Communication Quarterly,* 41 (1993), 40–50.

[6] For an interesting recent study, see William G. Kirkwood, "Parables as Metaphors and Examples," *Quarterly Journal of Speech,* 71 (1985), 422–440. For a more theoretical discussion, consult Walter R. Fisher, *Human Communication as Narration: Toward a Philosophy of Reason, Value, and Action* (Columbia: University of South Carolina Press, 1989).

[7] Adapted from Susanne Landowski, "Academic Laboratories: Risking Life and Limb for Credit," *Winning Orations, 1988* (Mankato, Minn.: Interstate Oratorical Association, 1988), pp. 64–67.

[8] Kelley Melvin, "Pharmaceutical Roulette," *Winning Orations, 1991* (Mankato, Minn.: Interstate Oratorical Association, 1991), pp. 117–119.

[9] Eliot Aronson, *The Social Animal,* 6th ed. (New York: W.H. Freeman, 1992), p. 91.

[10] James A. Winans, *Speech-Making* (New York: Appleton-Century-Crofts, 1922), p. 141. W. Lance Haynes, "Public Speaking Pedagogy in the Media Age," *Communication Education,* 39 (1990), 100, suggests that examples may be especially valuable in speeches because they fit with the fluid, personal nature of oral experience.

[11] Many of the traits of effective examples in public speaking also apply to the use of examples in other communication settings. For an interesting study, see Mary Helen Brown, "Defining Stories in Organizations: Characteristics and Functions," in James A. Anderson (ed.), *Communication Yearbook 13* (Newbury Park, Calif.: Sage, 1990), pp. 162–190.

[12] Richard D. Lamm, "Lawyers and Lawyering: The Legal System and Its Costs to American Society," *Vital Speeches,* 55 (1989), 207.

[13] For a fascinating study of the use and misuse of statistics, see John Allen Paulos, *Innumeracy: Mathematical Illiteracy and Its Consequences* (New York: Hill and Wang, 1988).

[14] Vernon A. Stone, "TV News Pay Lags Cost of Living; Radio News Directors Gain," *Communicator* (March 1993), 12–14.

[15] John C. Reinard, "The Empirical Study of the Persuasive Effects of Evidence: The Status after Fifty Years of Research," *Human Communication Research,* 15 (1988), 25.

[16] Gregory Solomon, "The Maturing of the American Motorist," *Winning Orations, 1990* (Mankato, Minn.: Interstate Oratorical Association, 1990), pp. 26–27.

[17] For research confirming the preference of listeners for unbiased, objective evidence, see Reinard, "Persuasive Effects of Evidence," 34.

[18] Adpated from Kristine Ockuly, untitled speech in *Winning Orations, 1992* (Mankato, Minn.: Interstate Oratorical Association, 1992), pp. 69–71.

[19] See Daniel J. O'Keefe, *Persuasion: Theory and Research* (Newbury Park, Calif.: Sage, 1990), pp. 135–136.

[20] Theodore White, *The Making of the President, 1968* (New York: Atheneum, 1969), pp. 66–69.

Chapter 8

Organizing the Body of the Speech

ORGANIZATION IS IMPORTANT

MAIN POINTS
Number of Main Points
Strategic Order of Main Points
Tips for Preparing Main Points

SUPPORTING MATERIALS

CONNECTIVES
Transitions
Internal Previews
Internal Summaries
Signposts

I f you thumb through any mail-order catalogue today, you will discover that a large portion of the items for sale are *organizers*—closet organizers, kitchen organizers, office organizers, audio and video equipment organizers. Read enough catalogues, and you must conclude that if something exists, it can be organized.

Why all this quest for organization? Obviously, when the objects you possess are well organized, they serve you better. There's little point in having multiple possessions if you can't find them when you need them. Organization allows you to see what you have and to put your hands immediately on the garment, the tool, the tape, the piece of paper you want without a frenzied search.

Much the same is true of your speeches. If they are well organized, they will serve you better. Organization allows you—and your listeners—to see what ideas you have and to put mental "hands" on the most important ones.

ORGANIZATION IS IMPORTANT

Several years ago a college professor took a well-organized speech and scrambled it by randomly changing the order of its sentences. He then had a speaker deliver the original version to one group of listeners and the scrambled version to another group. After the speeches, he gave a test to see how well each group understood what they had heard. Not surprisingly, the group that heard the original, unscrambled speech scored much higher than the other group.[1]

A few years later, two professors repeated the same experiment at another school. But instead of testing how well the listeners comprehended each speech, they tested to see what effects the speeches had on the listeners' attitudes toward the speakers. They found that people who heard the well-organized speech believed the speaker to be much more competent and trustworthy than did those who heard the scrambled speech.[2]

These are just two of many studies that show the importance of organization in effective speechmaking.[3] They confirm what most of us know from experience. How many times have you listened to someone who rambled aimlessly from one idea to another? You realize how difficult it is to pay attention to the speaker, much less to understand the message. In fact, when students explain what they hope to learn from their speech class, they almost always put "the ability to organize my ideas more effectively" near the top of the list.

This ability is especially vital for speechmaking. Listeners demand coherence. They have little patience with speakers who bounce wildly from idea to idea. Keep in mind that listeners—unlike readers—cannot flip back to a previous page if they have trouble grasping a speaker's ideas. In this respect a speech is much like a movie. Just as a director must be sure viewers can follow the plot of a film from beginning to end, so must a speaker be sure listeners can follow the progression of ideas in a speech from beginning to end.

This requires that speeches be organized *strategically*. They should be put together in particular ways to achieve particular results with particular audiences.

Speech organization is important for other reasons as well. As we saw in Chapter 1, it is closely connected to critical thinking. When you work to organize your speeches, you gain practice in the general skill of establishing clear relationships among your ideas. Many studies have shown that this skill will serve you well throughout your college days and in almost any career you may choose.[4] There is also evidence that using a clear, specific method of speech organization can boost your confidence as a speaker and improve your ability to deliver a message fluently.[5]

The first step in developing a strong sense of speech organization is to gain command of the three basic parts of a speech—introduction, body, and conclusion—and the strategic role of each. In this chapter we deal with the body of the speech. The next chapter will take up the introduction and conclusion.

There are good reasons for talking first about the body of the speech. The body is the longest and most important part. Also, you will usually prepare the body first. It is much easier to create an effective introduction after you know exactly what you will say in the body.

The process of organizing the body of a speech begins when you determine the main points.

MAIN POINTS

The main points are the central features of your speech. You should select them carefully, phrase them precisely, and arrange them strategically. Here are the main points of a student speech about the medical uses of hypnosis:

Specific Purpose: To inform my audience about the major uses of hypnosis.

Central Idea: The major uses of hypnosis today are to control pain in medical surgery, to help people stop smoking, and to help students improve their academic performance.

Main Points:
    I. Hypnosis is used in surgery as an adjunct to chemical anesthesia.
    II. Hypnosis is used to help people stop smoking.
    III. Hypnosis is used to help students improve their academic performance.

These three main points form the skeleton of the body of the speech. If there are three major *uses* of hypnosis for medical purposes, then logically there can be three *main points* in the speech.

How do you choose your main points? Sometimes they will be evident from your specific purpose statement. Suppose your specific purpose is "To inform my audience about the origins, events, and philosophy of the Special Olympics." Obviously, your speech will have three main points. The first will deal with the origins of the Special Olympics, the second with the events of the Special Olympics, the third with the philosophy of the Special Olympics. Written in outline form, the main points might be:

Specific Purpose: To inform my audience about the origins, events, and philosophy of the Special Olympics.

Central Idea: The Special Olympics gives mentally retarded people an opportunity to experience athletic competition.

Main Points:
    I. The Special Olympics was founded in 1968 to promote physical fitness for the mentally retarded.
  II. Held locally every year and internationally every four years, the Special Olympics has sports events similar to those in the Olympic Games.
III. Although medals are awarded, the Special Olympics stresses effort and participation rather than winning.

Even if your main points are not stated expressly in your specific purpose, they may be easy to project from it. Let us say your specific purpose is "To inform my audience of the basic steps in making stained-glass windows." You know each of your main points will correspond to a step in the window-making process. They might look like this in outline form:

Specific Purpose: To inform my audience of the basic steps in making stained-glass windows.

Central Idea: There are four basic steps in making stained-glass windows.

Main Points:
    I. The first step is designing the window.
  II. The second step is cutting the glass to fit the design.
III. The third step is painting the glass.
IV. The fourth step is assembling the window.

You will not always settle on your main points so easily. Often they will emerge as you research the speech and evaluate your findings. Suppose your specific purpose is "To persuade my audience that U.S. Senators and Representatives should not be allowed to hold office for more than twelve years." You know each main point in the speech will present a *reason* why members of Congress should be limited to twelve years in office. But you don't know how many main points there will be or what they will be. As you research and study the topic, you decide there are two major reasons to support your view. Each of these reasons will become a main point in your speech. Written in outline form, they might be:

Specific Purpose: To persuade my audience that U.S. Senators and Representatives should not be allowed to hold office for more than twelve years.

Central Idea:	Limiting the terms of office for U.S. Senators and Representatives will reduce the power of political action committees and make politicians more responsive to the public interest.
Main Points:	I. Limiting the terms of office for U.S. Senators and Representatives will reduce the power of political action committees.
	II. Limiting the terms of office for U.S. Senators and Representatives will make politicians more responsive to the public interest.

You now have two broad areas around which to organize your ideas.

Number of Main Points

You will not have time in your classroom speeches to develop more than four or five main points, and most speeches will contain only two or three. Regardless of how long a speech might run, if you have too many main points, the audience will have trouble sorting them out. When everything is equally important, nothing is important.

Imagine, for example, that you have a particularly lenient professor who gives everyone in the class an A. Your A won't have much value for you. But if only three students in the class get an A and you are one of them, then you stand out from the crowd. That is what you must aim to do in your speeches—to make a few main points stand out and be remembered.

If, when you list your main points, you find you have too many, you may be able to condense them into categories. Here is a set of main points for a speech about lasers:

Specific Purpose:	To inform my audience about the uses of lasers.
Central Idea:	Lasers harness the power of light for a wide range of uses.
Main Points:	I. Laser gravity-wave detectors allow astronomers to "see" deep into space.
	II. Automobile manufacturers use lasers for many purposes in making cars.
	III. Neurosurgeons use lasers to vaporize brain tumors.
	IV. Lasers help create billions of industrial goods every year.
	V. With lasers, scientists can chart the fastest of chemical reactions.
	VI. The telephone industry sends phone calls underseas to Europe with lasers.
	VII. Eye specialists routinely use lasers to "weld" loose retinas back in place.
	VIII. Lasers allow doctors to make early diagnoses of certain kinds of cancer.

You have eight main points—which is too many. But if you look at the list, you see that the eight points fall into three broad categories: lasers in science, lasers in industry, lasers in medicine. You might, therefore, restate your main points this way:

    I.   Lasers have many important uses in science.

    II.   Lasers have become indispensable to industry.

    III.   Lasers are revolutionizing the practice of medicine.

Strategic Order of Main Points

Once you establish your main points, you need to decide in what order you will present them in your speech. This is extremely important, for it will affect both the clarity and the persuasiveness of your ideas.

The most effective order depends on three things—your topic, your purpose, and your audience. Chapters 14 and 15 will deal with special aspects of organizing informative speeches and persuasive speeches. Here let us look briefly at the five basic patterns of organization used most often by public speakers.

Chronological Order   Speeches arranged chronologically follow a time pattern. They may narrate a series of events in the sequence in which they happened. For example:

Specific Purpose: To inform my audience how the Great Wall of China was built.

Central Idea: The Great Wall of China was built in three major stages.

Main Points: I.   Building of the Great Wall began during the Chou dynasty in the fourth century B.C.

              II.   New sections of the Great Wall were added during the Ch'in, Han, and Sui dynasties from 221 B.C. to 618 A.D.

             III.   The Great Wall was completed during the Ming dynasty of 1368–1644.

Chronological order is also used in speeches explaining a process or demonstrating how to do something. For example:

Specific Purpose: To inform my audience of the steps in getting a professional tattoo.

Central Idea: There are four main steps in getting a professional tattoo.

Main Points: I.   First, the skin is shaved and sterilized in the area to be tattooed.

II. Second, the main lines of the tattoo are traced on the skin with a machine called an outliner.

III. Third, colored pigments are applied inside the outline with a machine called a shader.

IV. Fourth, the tattoo is sterilized and bandaged.

As you can see, chronological order is especially useful for informative speeches.

Spatial Order   Speeches arranged in spatial order follow a directional pattern. That is, the main points proceed from top to bottom, left to right, front to back, inside to outside, east to west, or some other route. For example:

Specific Purpose: To inform my audience about the design of the Eiffel Tower.

Central Idea: The Eiffel Tower is divided into three sections.

Main Points:
I. The lowest section of the tower contains the entrance, a gift shop, and a restaurant.
II. The middle section of the tower consists of stairs and elevators that lead to the top.
III. The top section of the tower includes an observation deck with a spectacular view of Paris.

Or:

Specific Purpose: To inform my audience of five major civilizations that existed in different parts of North America centuries before the arrival of Columbus.

Central Idea: Centuries before the arrival of Columbus there were major civilizations in what is today New York, Florida, New Mexico, the Pacific Northwest, and the Mississippi Valley.

Main Points:
I. In New York, the Onondaga were skilled agriculturalists and fierce warriors.
II. In Florida, the Calusa developed one of the most advanced cultures to flourish without agriculture.
III. In New Mexico, the people of Chaco Canyon were sophisticated architectural planners and builders.
IV. In the Pacific Northwest, the Makah were expert mariners and foresters.
V. In the Mississippi Valley, the Cahokia created a complex, prosperous society whose burial mounds are still evident today.

Spatial order, like chronological order, is used most often in informative speeches.

Causal Order   Speeches arranged in causal order organize main points so as to show a cause-effect relationship. When you put your speech in causal order, you have two main points—one dealing with the causes of an event, the other dealing with its effects. Depending on your topic, you can either devote your first main point to the causes and the second to the effects, or you can deal first with the effects and then with the causes.

Suppose your specific purpose is "To persuade my audience that the growing use of aging airplanes by U.S. airline companies is a serious problem." You would begin with the causes of the airline companies' use of aging planes and work toward its effects:

Specific Purpose: To persuade my audience that the growing use of aging airplanes by U.S. airline companies is a serious problem.

Central Idea: The growing use of aging planes by U.S. airline companies threatens the safety of air travel.

Main Points: I.   To meet the demand for air travel, airline companies are keeping more and more old planes in service.
          II.   If this trend continues, it will create serious problems for airline safety.

When the effects you are discussing have already occurred, you may want to reverse the order and talk first about the effects and then about their causes—as in this speech about the Mayan civilization of Central America:

Specific Purpose: To inform my audience about the possible causes for the collapse of Mayan civilization.

Central Idea: The causes for the collapse of Mayan civilization have not yet been fully explained.

Main Points: I.   Mayan civilization flourished for over a thousand years until 900 A.D., when it mysteriously began to disintegrate.
          II.   Scholars have advanced three major explanations for the causes of this disintegration.

Because of its versatility, causal order can be used both for persuasive speeches and informative speeches.

Problem-Solution Order   Speeches arranged in problem-solution order are divided into two main parts. The first shows the existence and seriousness of a problem. The second presents a workable solution to the problem. For example:

Specific Purpose: To persuade my audience that legislation is needed to control the abuses of fraudulent charity fund-raisers.

Central Idea: Fraudulent fund-raising for charities is a serious problem that requires action by government and individuals alike.

The main points of a speech should be strategically organized to communicate the speaker's message. For a speech about the collapse of Mayan civilization, causal order might be highly effective.

Main Points: I.   Fraudulent charity fund-raising has become a widespread national problem.
                 II. The problem can be solved by a combination of government initiative and individual awareness.

Or:

Specific Purpose: To persuade my audience that ignition interlock devices should be required on all automobiles in the United States to help combat the problem of drunk driving.

Central Idea: Drunk driving is a continuing problem that can be reduced by the use of ignition interlock devices that prevent people with excessive blood-alcohol levels from starting their cars.

Main Points: I.   The number of deaths and injuries caused by drunk drivers on U.S. roads is a continuing problem.
                 II. One way to control this problem is by requiring that all automobiles be equipped with ignition interlock devices that prevent people with excessive blood-alcohol levels from starting their cars.

As these examples indicate, problem-solution order is most appropriate for persuasive speeches.

Topical Order Speeches that are not in chronological, spatial, causal, or problem-solution order usually fall into topical order. Topical order results when you divide the speech topic into *subtopics,* each of which becomes a main point in the speech. The main points are not part of a chronological, spatial, causal, or problem-solution sequence, but are simply parts of the whole. If this sound confusing, a few examples should help to make it clearer.

Suppose your specific purpose is "To inform my audience of the major kinds of fireworks." This topic does not lend itself to chronological, spatial, causal, or problem-solution order. Rather, you separate the subject—kinds of fireworks—into its constituent parts, so that each main point deals with a single kind of firework. Your central idea and main points might look like this:

Specific Purpose:	To inform my audience of the major kinds of fireworks.
Central Idea:	The major kinds of fireworks are skyrockets, Roman candles, pinwheels, and lances.
Main Points:	I. Skyrockets explode high in the air, producing the most dramatic effects of all fireworks.
	II. Roman candles shoot out separate groups of sparks and colored flames with a series of booming noises.
	III. Pinwheels throw off sparks and flames as they whirl on the end of a stick.
	IV. Lances are thin, colorful fireworks used in ground displays.

To take another example, let's say your purpose is "To inform my audience about the athletic achievements of Babe Didrikson." Didrikson, who is considered the greatest American female athlete of all time, competed during the 1930s, 1940s, and 1950s. So you could organize your speech chronologically—by discussing Didrikson's exploits during each decade of her career. On the other hand, you could arrange the speech topically—by dividing Didrikson's accomplishments into categories. Then your central idea and main points might be:

Specific Purpose:	To inform my audience about the athletic achievements of Babe Didrikson.
Central Idea:	Babe Didrikson was a world-class athlete in track and field, basketball, and golf.
Main Points:	I. As a track and field athlete, Didrikson set two world records in the Olympic Games.
	II. As a basketball player, Didrikson was twice named to the women's All-America team.
	III. As a professional golfer, Didrikson set a record that still stands by winning seventeen tournaments in a row.

Notice that in both of the above examples the main points subdivide the speech topic logically and consistently. In the first example each main point deals with a single category of fireworks. In the second example each main point isolates one aspect of Didrikson's achievements as an athlete. But suppose your main points look like this:

I. As a track and field athlete, Didrikson set two world records in the Olympic Games.
II. As a basketball player, Didrikson was twice named to the women's All-America team.
III. In the 1940s Didrikson dominated American women's sports.

This would *not* be a good topical order because main point III is inconsistent with the rest of the main points. It deals with a *period* in Didrikson's career, whereas main points I and II deal with *kinds* of athletic events.

All the examples so far refer to informative speeches. But topical order also works for persuasive speeches. Usually the topical subdivisions are the *reasons* why a speaker believes in a certain point of view. Here, for example, are the main points of a speech by NASA official Daniel Goldin on why the United States should expand its program of space exploration:[6]

Specific Purpose: To persuade my audience that the United States should expand its program of space exploration.

Central Idea: The United States should expand its program of space exploration because it will open access to vital natural resources, expand scientific knowledge, and further the search for extraterrestrial life.

Main Points:
I. Space exploration will open access to vital natural resources that are in limited supply on earth.
II. Space exploration will produce scientific knowledge that will benefit life on earth.
III. Space exploration will further the search for extraterrestrial life.

Because it is applicable to almost any subject and to any kind of speech, topical order is used more often than any other method of speech organization.[7]

Tips for Preparing Main Points

Keep Main Points Separate Each main point in a speech should be clearly independent of the other main points. Take care not to lump together what should be separate main points. Compare these two sets of main points for a speech about the process of producing a Broadway play:

INEFFECTIVE	MORE EFFECTIVE
I. The first step is choosing the play.	I. The first step is choosing the play.

INEFFECTIVE	MORE EFFECTIVE
II. The second step is selecting the cast.	II. The second step is selecting the cast.
III. The third step is conducting rehearsals and then performing the play.	III. The third step is conducting the rehearsals.
	IV. The fourth step is performing the play.

The problem with the left-hand list is that point III contains two main points. It should be divided, as shown in the right-hand list.

Try to Use the Same Pattern of Wording for Main Points   Consider the following main points for an informative speech about the benefits of exercise.

INEFFECTIVE	MORE EFFECTIVE
I. Regular exercise increases your endurance.	I. Regular exercise increases your endurance.
II. Your sleeping pattern is improved by regular exercise.	II. Regular exercise improves your sleeping pattern.
III. It is possible to help control your weight by regular exercise.	III. Regular exercise helps control your weight.

The set of main points on the right follows a consistent pattern of wording throughout. Therefore, it is easier to understand and easier to remember than the set on the left.

You will find that it is not always possible to use this kind of parallel wording for your main points. Some speeches just don't lend themselves to such a tidy arrangement. But try to keep the wording parallel when you can, for it is a good way to make your main points stand out from the details surrounding them.

Balance the Amount of Time Devoted to Main Points   Because your main points are so important, you want to be sure they all receive enough emphasis to be clear and convincing. This means allowing sufficient time to develop each main point. Suppose you discover that the proportion of time devoted to your main points is something like this:

I.   85 percent

II.   10 percent

III.   5 percent

A breakdown of this sort indicates one of two things. Either points II and III aren't really *main* points and you have only one main point, or points II and III haven't been given the attention they need. If the latter, you should revise the body of the speech to bring the main points into better balance.

This is not to say that all main points must receive exactly equal emphasis, but only that they should be roughly balanced. For example, either of the following would be fine:

I.	30 percent		I.	20 percent
II.	40 percent		II.	30 percent
III.	30 percent		III.	50 percent

The amount of time spent on each main point depends on the amount and complexity of supporting materials for each point. Supporting materials are, in effect, the "flesh" that fills out the skeleton of your speech.

SUPPORTING MATERIALS

By themselves, main points are only assertions. As we saw in Chapter 7, listeners need supporting materials to accept what a speaker says. When the supporting materials are added, the body of a speech looks like this in outline form:

I. Hypnosis is used in surgery as an adjunct to chemical anesthesia.
   A. Hypnosis reduces both the physical and psychological aspects of pain.
      1. Hypnosis can double a person's pain threshold.
      2. It also reduces the fear that intensifies physical pain.
   B. Hypnosis is most useful in cases when the patient is known to have problems with general anesthesia.
      1. Quotation from Dr. Harold Wain of Walter Reed Army Hospital.
      2. Story of Linda Kuay.
      3. Statistics from *Psychology Today.*
II. Hypnosis is used to help people stop smoking.
   A. Many therapists utilize hypnosis to help people break their addiction to cigarettes.
      1. The U.S. Department of Health and Human Services considers hypnosis a safe and effective means of stopping smoking.
      2. Success rates are as high as 70 percent.
         a. Story of Alex Hamilton.
         b. Quotation from New York psychiatrist Dr. Herbert Spiegel.

    B. Hypnosis does not work for all smokers.
      1. A person must want to stop smoking for hypnosis to work.
      2. A person must also be responsive to hypnotic suggestion.
III. Hypnosis is used to help students improve their academic performance.
    A. Hypnosis enables people to use their minds more effectively.
      1. The conscious mind uses about 10 percent of a person's mental ability.
      2. Hypnosis allows people to tap more of their mental power.
    B. Studies show that hypnosis can help people overcome many obstacles to academic success.
      1. Improves ability to concentrate.
      2. Increases reading speed.
      3. Reduces test anxiety.

In Chapter 7 we discussed the major kinds of supporting materials and how to use them. Here we need stress only the importance of *organizing* your supporting materials so they are directly relevant to the main points they are supposed to support. Misplaced supporting materials are confusing. Here's an example:

    I. There are several reasons why people immigrate to the United States.
      A. Over the years, millions of people have immigrated to the United States.
      B. Many people immigrate in search of economic opportunity.
      C. Others immigrate to attain political freedom.
      D. Still others immigrate to escape religious persecution.

The main point deals with the reasons immigrants come to the United States, as do supporting points B, C, and D. Supporting point A ("Over the years, millions of people have immigrated to the United States") does not. It is out of place and should not be included with this main point.

    If you find such a situation in your own speeches, try to reorganize your supporting points under appropriate main points, like this:

    I. Over the years, millions of people have immigrated to the United States.
      A. Since the American Revolution, an estimated 60 million people have immigrated to the U.S.
      B. Today there are over 20 million Americans who were born in other countries.
   II. There are several reasons why people immigrate to the United States.
      A. Many people immigrate in search of economic opportunity.
      B. Others immigrate to attain political freedom.
      C. Still others immigrate to escape religious persecution.

Now you have two supporting points to back up your "millions of people" point and three supporting points to back up your "reasons" point.

Once you have organized your main points and supporting points, you must give attention to the third element in the body of a speech—connectives.

■ CONNECTIVES

Carla Maggio was speaking to her class about the need for students to vote in state and local elections. She had rehearsed the speech several times, had a well-defined central idea, three sharp main points, and strong evidence to support her position. But when Carla delivered the speech, she said "All right" every time she moved from one thought to the next. All told, she said "All right" ten times in six minutes. After a while, her classmates started counting. By the end of the speech, most had stopped listening. They were too busy waiting for the next "All right." Afterward, Carla said, "I never even thought about saying 'All right.' I guess it just popped out when I didn't know what else to say."

This experience is not unusual. We all have stock phrases that we habitually use to fill the space between thoughts. In casual conversation they are seldom troublesome. But in speechmaking they create a problem—particularly when they call attention to themselves.

What Carla's speech lacked were strong *connectives*—words or phrases that join one thought to another and indicate the relationship between them. Connectives in the body of a speech are like ligaments and tendons in a

When you organize your speeches, make sure to include transitions, internal summaries, and other connectives to help listeners keep track of your ideas.

human body. Without connectives, a speech is disjointed and uncoordinated—much as a person would be without ligaments and tendons to join the bones and hold the organs in place. Four types of speech connectives are transitions, internal previews, internal summaries, and signposts.

Transitions

Transitions are words or phrases that indicate when a speaker has completed one thought and is moving on to another. Technically, transitions state *both* the idea the speaker is leaving and the one she or he is coming up to. In the following examples the transitional phrases are underlined:

<u>In addition to</u> helping people in need, working as a hospital volunteer <u>also</u> provides you with valuable job experience.

Increasing the amount of money spent on education <u>is only one part</u> of the solution. <u>The other part is</u> to ensure that the money is spent wisely.

<u>Now that we have</u> explored the geographical areas of Puerto Rico, <u>let us turn to</u> its political structure.

<u>So much for</u> the present; <u>what about</u> the future?

<u>We have spent a lot of time talking about</u> the problem. <u>It's time now to discuss</u> the solution.

Notice how these phrases remind the listener of the thought just completed, as well as reveal the thought about to be developed.

Internal Previews

Internal previews let the audience know what the speaker will take up next, but they are more detailed than transitions. In effect, an internal preview works just like the preview statement in a speech introduction except that it comes in the body of the speech—usually as the speaker is starting to discuss a main point. For example:

In discussing how women have been neglected by medical research, we will look first at the extent of the problem and second at how it has harmed health care for women in the United States.

After hearing this, the audience knows exactly what to listen for as the speaker develops the "problem" main point.

Internal previews are often combined with transitions. For example:

[*Transition*]: Now that we have seen how serious the problem of faulty credit reports is, let's look at some solutions. [*Internal Preview*]: I will focus on three solutions—instituting tighter government regulation of credit bureaus, holding credit bureaus financially responsible for their errors, and giving individuals easier access to their credit reports.

You will seldom need an internal preview for each main point in your speech, but be sure to use one whenever you think it will help listeners keep track of your ideas.

Internal Summaries

Internal summaries are the reverse of internal previews. Rather than letting listeners know what is coming up next, internal summaries remind listeners of what they have just heard. Such summaries are generally used when a speaker finishes a complicated or particularly important main point or set of main points. Rather than moving immediately to the next point, the speaker takes a moment to summarize the preceding point or points. For example:

In short, palm reading is an ancient art. Developed in China more than five thousand years ago, it was practiced in classical Greece and Rome, flourished during the Middle Ages, survived the Industrial Revolution, and remains popular today in many parts of the world.

I hope I've made clear the benefits of walking as a form of exercise. Unlike running, which often causes as many injuries as it prevents, walking is a gentle but no less effective way to keep in shape. Regular walking at a brisk pace strengthens the heart, increases lung capacity, improves blood circulation, and burns calories—all without the strain on the knees and ankles caused by running.

Such internal summaries are an excellent way to clarify and reinforce ideas. By combining them with transitions, you can also lead your audience smoothly into your next main point:

[*Internal Summary*]: In going back over the effects of exposing the body to extreme cold, we see that the first signs of hypothermia are excessive shivering or numb hands and feet. More serious signs are exhaustion, falling body temperature, dizziness, impaired judgment, slurred speech, heart tremors, and unconsciousness. [*Transition*]: Now that you know the symptoms of hypothermia, I am going to tell you the first-aid measures to take when you see them.

[*Internal Summary*]: Let's pause for a moment to recapitulate what we have found so far. First, we have seen that more than 8 million Latinos and 15 million African Americans live in communities with one or more uncontrolled toxic waste disposal sites. Second, we have seen that most environmental legislation has ignored the needs of minority populations. [*Transition*]: Now we are ready to explore solutions to these problems.

Signposts

Signposts are very brief statements that indicate exactly where you are in the speech. Frequently they are just numbers. Here is how one student used simple numerical signposts to help her audience keep track of the major causes for the continuing problem of famine in Africa:

The first cause of this spreading problem is runaway population growth.

The second cause of continued famine is inefficient agricultural production.

The third cause is recurrent drought in the affected countries.

The final contributing cause for the persistence of famine is mismanagement of available food resources by local bureaucrats.

The signposts are underscored. Notice how they enumerate the introduction of each new point.

Another way to accomplish the same thing is to introduce your main points with a question, as did one student in his speech about mail-order fraud. His first main point dealt with the continuing growth of mail-order fraud. He introduced it this way:

What makes mail-order fraud such a persistent problem? Why do people keep falling for gimmicks that are obviously too good to be true?

His second main point dealt with ways to curb mail-order fraud. He introduced it like this:

How can we solve this problem? Is there a way to protect the rights of legitimate mail-order companies while attacking the fraudulent ones?

Questions are particularly effective as signposts because they invite subliminal answers and thereby get the audience more involved with the speech.

Besides using signposts to indicate where you are in the speech, you can also use them to focus attention on key ideas. You can do this with a simple phrase, as in the following example:

The most important thing to remember about abstract art is that it is always based on forms in the natural world.

The underlined words alert the audience to the fact that an especially significant point is coming up. So do phrases such as these:

Be sure to keep this in mind . . .

This is crucial to understanding the rest of the speech . . .

Above all, you need to know . . .

Let me repeat that last statement . . .

Depending on the needs of your speech, you may want to use two, three, or even all four kinds of connectives in combination. You needn't worry too much about what they are called—whether this one is a signpost and that a transition. In fact, many people lump them all together as "transitions." The important thing is to be aware of their functions. Properly applied, connectives can make your speeches much more unified and coherent.

SUMMARY

Clear organization is vital to speechmaking. Listeners demand coherence. They get only one chance to grasp a speaker's ideas, and they have little patience for speakers who ramble aimlessly from one idea to another. A well-organized speech will enhance your credibility and make it easier for the audience to understand your message.

Speeches should be organized strategically. They should be put together in particular ways to achieve particular results with particular audiences. The first step in organizing speeches is to gain command of the three basic parts of a speech—introduction, body, conclusion—and the strategic role of each. In this chapter we have dealt with the body of the speech.

The process of planning the body of a speech begins when you determine the main points. These are the central features of your speech. You should choose them carefully, phrase them precisely, and organize them strategically. Because listeners cannot keep track of a multitude of main points, most speeches should contain no more than two to five main points. Each main point should focus on a single idea, should be worded clearly, and should receive enough emphasis to be clear and convincing.

You can organize main points in various ways. The strategic order will be determined by your topic, your purpose, and your audience. Chronological order means that your speech follows a time pattern. Speeches arranged in spatial order follow a directional pattern. To put your speech in causal order, you organize main points according to their cause-effect relationship. Topical order results when you divide your main topic into subtopics, each of which covers one aspect of the main topic. For problem-solution order you break the body of your speech into two main parts—the first showing a problem, the second giving a solution.

Supporting materials are the backup ideas for your main points. When organizing supporting materials, make sure they are directly relevant to the main points they are supposed to support.

Once you have organized your main points and supporting materials, you are ready to work out the third element in the body of your speech—connectives. Connectives help tie a speech together. They are words or phrases that join one thought to another and indicate the relationship between them. The four major types of speech connectives are transitions, internal previews, internal summaries, and signposts. Using them effectively will make your speeches more unified and coherent.

REVIEW QUESTIONS

After reading this chapter, you should be able to answer the following questions:

1. Why is it important that speeches be organized clearly and coherently?

2. How many main points will your speeches usually contain? Why is it important to limit the number of main points in your speeches?

3. What are the five basic patterns of organizing main points in a speech? Which are appropriate for informative speeches? Which is used only in persuasive speeches? Which is used most often?

4. What are three tips for preparing your main points?

5. What is the most important thing to remember when organizing supporting materials in the body of your speech?

6. What are the four kinds of speech connectives? What role does each play in a speech?

APPLICATION EXERCISES

1. Identify the organizational method used in each of the following sets of main points.

   I. Cesar Chavez is best known for his efforts to protect the rights of Hispanic farmworkers in California.
   II. Cesar Chavez was also a tireless advocate for Hispanic racial and cultural pride in general.

   I. The outermost section of the ancient Egyptian burial tomb was the entrance passage.
   II. The next section of the Egyptian burial tomb was the antechamber.
   III. The third section of the Egyptian burial tomb was the treasury.
   IV. The innermost section of the Egyptian burial tomb was the burial chamber.

   I. Sickle-cell anemia is a hereditary blood disease caused by abnormal blood cells.
   II. The effects of sickle-cell anemia include liver damage, blindness, paralysis, and early death.

   I. Rodeos began in the Old West as contests of skill among cowboys during cattle roundups.
   II. By 1920 rodeos had become a popular spectator sport for the general public.
   III. Today rodeos combine traditional western events with a circuslike atmosphere and the marketing techniques of big business.

    I. A shortage of trained nurses has become a serious problem at hospitals throughout the United States.

   II. The problem can be solved by offering nurses better salaries and improved working conditions.

2. What organizational method (or methods) might you use to arrange main points for speeches with the following specific purpose statements?

To inform my audience about the major events in the development of the civil rights movement from 1955 to 1970.

To inform my audience of the causes and effects of the erosion of America's seacoasts.

To inform my audience about the educational philosophy of Maria Montessori.

To inform my audience about the geographical regions of the Philippines.

To persuade my audience that our state legislature should enact tougher legislation to deal with the continuing problem of child abuse.

To inform my audience about the major kinds of symbols used in traditional Native American art.

3. Turn to the outline of main points and supporting materials for the speech about hypnosis on pages 185–186. Create appropriate transitions, internal previews, internal summaries, and signposts for the speech.

NOTES

[1] Ernest C. Thompson, "An Experimental Investigation of the Relative Effectiveness of Organizational Structure in Oral Communication," *Southern Speech Journal,* 26 (1960), 59–69.

[2] Harry Sharp, Jr., and Thomas McClung, "Effect of Organization on the Speaker's Ethos," *Speech Monographs,* 33 (1966), 182–183.

[3] See, for example, Margaret Fitch Hauser, "Message Structure, Inference Making, and Recall," in Robert N. Bostrom and Bruce Westley (eds.), *Communication Yearbook 8* (Beverly Hills, Calif.: Sage, 1984), pp. 278–292.

[4] Paul A. Fritz and Richard L. Weaver, II, "Teaching Critical Thinking Skills in the Basic Speaking Course: A Liberal Arts Perspective," *Communication Education,* 35 (1986), 177.

[5] John O. Greene, "Speech Preparation Processes and Verbal Fluency," *Human Communication Research,* 11 (1984), 61–84.

[6] Daniel S. Goldin, "The Light of a New Age: Space Exploration," *Vital Speeches,* 58 (1992), 741–744.

[7] For an interesting recent study on the role of structure in speeches and other public discourses, see Regina M. Hoffman, "Temporal Organization as a Rhetorical Resource," *Southern Communication Journal,* 57 (1992), 194–204.

Chapter 9

Beginning and Ending the Speech

THE INTRODUCTION

Get Attention and Interest
Reveal the Topic
Establish Credibility and Good Will
Preview the Body of the Speech
Sample Introduction with Commentary
Tips for Preparing the Introduction

THE CONCLUSION

Signal the End of the Speech
Reinforce the Central Idea
Sample Conclusion with Commentary
Tips for Preparing the Conclusion

O n the night of October 9, 1986, a conductor stepped up to the podium at Her Majesty's Theatre in London, tapped his baton, raised his arms, and signaled the orchestra to play. Moments later the public first heard the dramatic opening chords of the song "The Phantom of the Opera."

Like most musical stage plays, *Phantom of the Opera* begins with an overture—an orchestral introduction that captures the audience's attention and gives them a preview of the music they are going to hear. Without such an introduction—if the characters simply walked onstage and began singing or speaking—the beginning of the play would seem too abrupt, and the audience would not be suitably "primed" for the entertainment.

Similarly, nearly all musicals end with a finale, when the whole cast is onstage, elements of the dramatic plot are resolved, portions of the principal songs are recalled, and the music is brought to a dramatic climax. If there were no such conclusion, if the actors merely stopped and walked offstage, the audience would be left unsatisfied.

Just as musical plays need appropriate beginnings and endings, so do speeches. The beginning, or introduction, prepares listeners for what is to come. The conclusion ties up the speech and alerts listeners that the speech is going to end. Ideally, it is a satisfying conclusion.

In this chapter we explore the various roles played by an introduction and a conclusion in speechmaking. We also discuss techniques aimed at fulfilling those roles. If you apply these techniques imaginatively, you will take a big step toward elevating your speeches from the ordinary to the splendid.

THE INTRODUCTION

First impressions are important. A poor beginning may so distract or alienate listeners that the speaker can never fully recover. Moreover, getting off on the right foot is vital to a speaker's self-confidence. What could be more encouraging than watching your listeners' faces begin to register interest, attention, and pleasure? The hardest part of any presentation is the beginning. If you get through the opening stages of your speech without blundering, the rest will go much more smoothly. A good introduction, you will find, is an excellent confidence booster.

In most speech situations, there are four objectives you need to accomplish at the outset:

- Get the attention and interest of your audience.

- Reveal the topic of your speech.

- Establish your credibility and good will.

- Preview the body of the speech.

We'll look at each of these objectives in turn.

Get Attention and Interest

"Unless a speaker can interest his audience at once, his effort will be a failure." So said the great lawyer Clarence Darrow. If your topic is not one of extraordinary interest, your listeners are likely to say to themselves, "So what? Who cares?" No matter how famous the speaker or how vital the topic, the speaker can quickly lose an audience if she or he doesn't use the introduction to get their attention and quicken their interest.

Getting the initial attention of your audience is usually easy to do—even before you utter a single word. After you are introduced and step to the lectern, your audience will normally give you their attention. If they don't, merely wait patiently. Look directly at the audience without saying a word. In a few moments all talking and physical commotion will stop. Your listeners will be attentive. You will be ready to start speaking.

Keeping the attention of your audience once you start talking is more difficult. Here are the methods used most often. Employed individually or in combination, they will help get the audience caught up in your speech.

Relate the Topic to the Audience   People pay attention to things that affect them directly. If you can relate the topic to your listeners, they are much more likely to be interested in it.

Suppose, for example, one of your classmates begins her speech like this:

> Today I am going to talk about collecting postcards—a hobby that is both fascinating and financially rewarding. I would like to explain the basic kinds of collectible postcards, why they are so valuable, and how collectors buy and sell their cards.

This is certainly a clear introduction, but it is not one to get you hooked on the speech. Now what if your classmate were to begin her speech this way—as one student actually did:

> It's Saturday morning, and you are helping clean out your grandmother's attic. After working a while, you stumble upon a trunk, open it, and discover inside hundreds of old postcards. Thinking about getting to the football game on time, you start tossing the cards into the trash can. Congratulations! You have just thrown away a year's tuition.

This time the speaker has used just the right bait. Chances are you will be hooked.

Even when you use other interest-arousing lures, you should *always* relate your topic to the audience. At times this will test your ingenuity, but it pays dividends. Here are two excellent examples. The first is from a speech about world hunger. Notice how the speaker gets her classmates to put themselves in the place of someone who is suffering from starvation:

> How many of you barely make it to your first class in the morning? You jump out of bed, shower, dress, and you're out the door—usually without breakfast. By

eleven o'clock, you're concentrating more on the growling of your stomach than on your professor's lecture. As you walk out of class, you say to the person next to you, "I'm starving!"

It's easy for us to use this expression loosely. But imagine yourself being hungry not just for an hour or two before lunch, but all the time. Imagine never having enough to eat—always having that dull, aching feeling in the pit of your stomach, always being weak and undernourished. If you can imagine this, then you have begun to understand the plight of the millions of people in Africa, Asia, and South America who die every year from starvation and hunger-related illnesses.

The second example is from a student speech about dreams. This is how the speaker began his remarks:

You are being chased by an object of unspeakable horror, yet your legs can only move in slow motion. Each step takes unbearably long, and your frantic struggle to run faster is hopeless. Your pursuer gets closer, and your desperation turns to terror. You know you are not going to escape. You can't breathe, and you gulp for air that isn't there. You are completely helpless—eye to eye with death.

Then you wake up, gasping for air, your heart pounding, your face clammy with sweat. It takes a few minutes for you to reorient yourself to reality, for your heart and breathing to slow down. You reassure yourself that it was "just a dream." Soon you drift back to sleep.

By using vivid language to describe something all his classmates had experienced at some time in their lives, the speaker made sure of an attentive audience.

State the Importance of Your Topic   Presumably, you think your speech topic is important. Tell your audience why they should think so, too. Here is how Postmaster General Anthony M. Frank began his speech to the Economic Club of Indianapolis on the future of the U.S. Postal Service:

Thank you for giving me the opportunity to tell you about the United States Postal Service. . . .

We are a huge enterprise—40,000 locations staffed by about 800,000 full- and part-time employees, with income and expenses exceeding $40 billion this year. . . . We faithfully complete an enormous task by delivering 535 million pieces of mail every day, six days a week. We deliver 41 percent of the world's mail volume and we do it faster and at postage rates that are up to 50 percent less expensive than, say, the postal services of Great Britain and Germany.[1]

These are striking statistics. By citing them in the introduction, Frank emphasized the importance of his topic and captured the attention of his audience.

Clearly, this technique is easy to use when discussing social and political issues such as the postal service, poor schools, drug abuse, toxic waste, or drunk driving, but it is appropriate for other kinds of topics as well. Here is how one student handled it in a speech about starting a home aquarium:

It is very hard to cuddle a fish. Fish won't roll over or fetch the morning paper. You won't find them curling up on your lap, chasing a ball of string, or rescuing a child from a burning building.

Yet despite these shortcomings, 250 million tropical fish have found their way into 10 million American homes. Tropical fish make up 50 percent of all live animal sales in the United States, and they have earned a spot next to the all-American dog and the cuddly kitten in the hearts of millions of people. Today I would like to explain how you can start a home aquarium and discover the pleasures of owning tropical fish.

The first paragraph—with its clever opening line—grabs the listener's attention. But it is the second paragraph that keeps the attention. Indeed, whenever you discuss a topic whose importance may not be clear to the audience, you should think about ways to demonstrate its significance in the introduction.

Startle the Audience   One surefire way to arouse interest quickly is to startle your listeners with an arresting or intriguing statement. Everyone in the audience paid close attention after this speaker's introduction:

Take a moment and think of the three women closest to you. Who comes to mind? Your mother? Your sister? Your girlfriend? Your wife? Your best friend? Now guess which one will be sexually assaulted during her lifetime. It's not a pleasant thought, but according to the U.S. Department of Justice, one of every three American women will be sexually assaulted sometime during their life.

Notice the gradual buildup to the speaker's arresting statement, "Now guess which one will be sexually assaulted during her lifetime." This statement startles the audience—especially the men—and drives home at a personal level the problem of sexual assault against women. The effect would have been much less if the speaker had said, "Sexual assault against women is a serious problem."

Sometimes you may want to startle your audience in the very first sentence of your speech. Here is how one student began a speech about the environmental problems created by the 3 billion disposable batteries tossed away in the United States each year:

One day the Energizer bunny will die.[2]

And here is a slightly longer example of the same technique:

Yesterday, millions of dollars in United States currency was burned while a group of people stood and watched. They did nothing to stop the burning—in fact, they encouraged it. They are employees of the United States Mint in Washington, D.C., and they were witnessing the destruction of counterfeit money.

This technique is highly effective and easy to use. Just be sure the startling introduction relates directly to the subject of your speech. The example cited above made a good beginning for an informative speech about counterfeiting. It would not work for a speech about the U.S. banking system. If you choose a strong opening simply for its shock value and then go on to talk about something else, your audience will be confused and possibly annoyed.

Arouse the Curiosity of the Audience   People are curious. One way to draw them into your speech is with a series of statements that progressively whet their curiosity about the subject of the speech. For example:

> It is the most common chronic disease in the United States. Controllable but incurable, it is a symptomless disease. You can have it for years and never know until it kills you. Some 40 million Americans have this disease, and 300,000 will die from it before the year is out. Odds are that five of us in this class have it.
>
> What am I talking about? Not cancer. Not AIDS. Not heart disease. I am talking about hypertension—high blood pressure.

As another example, consider this clever opening from a student informative speech titled "The Licnep":

> The licnep is one of the most common objects on a college campus. First marketed in England in 1564, its core is usually made of graphite and its exterior of cedar. It comes in different strengths and sizes. It can be hard or soft, colored or plain, and its length tends to change throughout its lifetime.
>
> With a little help from us, the licnep has the power to ace a math exam, evaluate our professor, give a message to a loved one, or put our name on the dotted line. Most of us have a licnep in our purse or backpack at this very moment.
>
> What is a licnep? As many of you have no doubt figured out, a "licnep" is pencil spelled backward.

Not only does this student relate the topic directly to his classmates, he gets them further involved by building suspense about what a "licnep" is. Imagine how much less effective his introduction would have been if he had simply said, "Today I am going to talk about pencils." When used appropriately, arousing curiosity is a surefire way to capture and hold your listeners' interest.

Question the Audience   Asking a rhetorical question is another way to get your listeners thinking about your speech. Sometimes a single question will do:

> Do you know how it feels to be the victim of racial discrimination?

> What would you think if you went to a doctor because you were ill and she told you to watch "Seinfeld" as part of your treatment?

> If you had exciting news that you wanted to share with someone, whom would you tell first?

A good introduction will get your speech off to a strong start. To be most effective, it should be delivered smoothly, from a minimum of notes, and with strong eye contact.

In other circumstances you may want to pose a series of questions, each of which draws the audience deeper into the speech. Here is how one student developed this method:

Have you ever spent a sleepless night studying for an exam? Can you remember rushing to finish a term paper because you waited too long to start writing it? Do you often feel overwhelmed by all the things you have to get done at school? At work? At home? If so, you may be the victim of poor time management. Fortunately, there are proven strategies you can follow to use your time more effectively and to keep control of your life.

Like beginning with a startling statement, opening with a question works best when the question is meaningful to the audience and firmly related to the content of the speech. It also works most effectively when you pause for just a moment after each question. This adds dramatic impact and gives the question time to sink in. The audience, of course, will answer mentally—not out loud.

Begin with a Quotation   Another way to arouse the interest of your audience is to start with an attention-getting quotation. You might choose your quotation from the words of a famous speaker or writer, from Shakespeare or Confucius, from the Bible or Talmud, from a poem or song, even from a television show. One student used the last of these to introduce a speech about the role of women in the United States space program:

"Space—the final frontier. These are the voyages of the Starship *Enterprise*. Its five-year mission: To explore new worlds. To seek out new life and new civilizations. To boldly go where no man has gone before."

These well-known words, which opened every episode of the original *Star Trek* television series, captured the spirit of adventure that marked American attitudes toward space exploration during the 1960s and 1970s. They also captured the notion that space exploration was essentially a male activity: "To boldly go where no *man* has gone before."

Today, of course, times have changed. Not only are women central characters in the new *Star Trek* series, but they are playing more and more important roles in the U.S. space program itself. Today I would like to discuss the current status and future prospects of women in the space program.

You need not use a well-known or famous quotation. The following made an effective introduction for a speech about bird watching:

"Even to this day I cannot describe what happened without feeling the excitement of the moment. I glimpsed a flash of color in the thicket. I raised my binoculars to my eyes, and then I saw it—a Bachman's Warbler, one of the rarest birds in all of America. For me, this was the equivalent of a coin collector discovering a rare silver dollar, or of a football player scoring a touchdown in the Super Bowl."

This statement was made by my father. He is just one of the millions of people who have discovered the joys and thrills of bird watching.

A humorous quotation can afford double impact, as in this speech about the need to impose term limitations on members of the U.S. Congress:

Mark Twain once said, "It could probably be shown by facts and figures that there is no distinctly American criminal class except Congress."

By opening with Twain's words, the speaker not only got the audience's attention, she also foreshadowed a central theme of her speech. Notice, too, that all these quotations are relatively short. Opening your speech with a lengthy quotation is a sure way to set your audience yawning.

Tell a Story   We all enjoy stories—especially if they are provocative, amusing, dramatic, or suspenseful. To work well as introductions, they should also be clearly relevant to the main point of the speech. Used in this way, stories are perhaps the most effective way to begin a speech.

Consider, for example, the story one student, an education major, told to open his speech about the ways American teachers are adapting to the cultural diversity of today's school-age population:

On a cloudy winter afternoon, Florann Greenberg, a teacher at P.S. 14 in New York City, noticed that her first-grade class was growing fidgety. One girl, dropping all pretense of work, stared at the snow falling outside the schoolroom windows. Annoyed, Greenberg asked her, "Haven't you seen snow before?" The girl whispered, "No." Her classmates began nodding their heads in agreement.

Then it dawned on Greenberg. Of course these children had never seen snow—almost all were immigrants from Colombia and the Dominican Republic. Immediately Greenberg changed her lesson plan. New topics: What is snow? How is it formed? How do you dress in the snow? What games do you play?

This story, reported in *Time* magazine, illustrates the cultural diversity now found in thousands of school classrooms across the United States and how creative teachers are adjusting to that diversity.

Like many good introductions, this one does a double job—it arouses the interest of the audience and gets listeners emotionally involved in the subject of the speech.

You can also use stories based on your personal experience, or stories with a humorous twist. Here is how one student combined the two in her introduction of an informative speech on the topic of leprosy:

It happened about a week ago. I was in the women's locker room getting ready for my aerobics class. As I changed clothes, I carried on a casual conversation with one of our classmates, Terri. Just as I turned to leave, she asked, "Hey, Kris, how's your leprosy?"

Suddenly the chattering voices that had filled the room were replaced by silent stares. I quickly responded that my *speech* about leprosy was coming along fine. The noise resumed. All was well. And yet, for a single moment, I felt the sense of shame and alienation that has surrounded lepers since Old Testament days.

As you can imagine, such an introduction depends on effective delivery. By using pauses, eye contact, and changes in her tone of voice, this speaker heightened both the humor and the dramatic impact of her words. See if you can do the same in your speech introductions.

The seven methods listed above are the ones used most often by student speakers to gain attention and interest. Other methods include referring to the occasion, inviting audience participation, using audio equipment or visual aids, relating to a previous speaker, and beginning with humor. For any given speech try to choose the method that is most suitable for the topic, the audience, and the occasion.

Reveal the Topic

In the process of gaining attention, be sure to state clearly the topic of your speech. If you do not, your listeners will be confused. And once they are confused, your chances of getting them absorbed in the speech are almost nil. This is a basic point—so basic that it may hardly seem worth mentioning. Yet you would be surprised how many students need to be reminded of it. You may hear speeches in your own class in which the topic is not clear by the end of the introduction. So you will know what to avoid, here is such an introduction, presented in a public speaking class:

> When Roseanne Taos went to the hospital for knee surgery, her biggest concern was how soon she would be able to go skiing again. Tragically, the answer was never. No, Roseanne didn't die, but an overdose of general anesthesia during surgery left her permanently disabled. She will live the rest of her life under custodial supervision. As this example demonstrates, the use of anesthesia can be the most dangerous part of surgery. Today, I would like to discuss this issue with you.

What is the topic of this speech? The potential dangers of anesthesia? No. The need for periodic recertification of anesthesiologists? No. The limits of modern medicine in general? No. This student was speaking about the ancient Chinese practice of acupuncture as an alternative to anesthesia. But he did not make that clear to his audience. Listening to the introduction, they expected him to talk about the hazards of anesthesia.

This student found a dramatic introduction but ignored the fact that it didn't relate properly to his speech. Certainly the story of Roseanne Taos is an excellent attention-getter. But in this case it was wasted. Suppose, instead, the student had begun his speech with a different story:

> The young woman on the operating table at the Institute of Tuberculosis in Beijing, China, is having a diseased lung removed. She has not received any painkilling drugs. Even though she is fully conscious, she experiences no pain and even talks periodically with her surgeons. Her only anesthetic is the array of stainless-steel acupuncture needles in her hands and feet.

This opening would have provided drama and a way to get the listeners' attention, but it also would have related directly to the speech topic.

If you beat around the bush in your introduction, you may lose your listeners. Even if they already know your topic, you should restate it clearly and concisely at some point in the introduction.

Establish Credibility and Good Will

Besides getting attention and revealing the topic, there is a third objective you may need to accomplish in your introduction—establishing your credibility and good will.

Credibility is mostly a matter of being qualified to speak on a given topic—and of being *perceived* as qualified by your listeners. If, for instance, Tom Cruise got up before an audience to speak about nuclear physics, he would have to take drastic steps to establish his credibility on the subject.

Here is how one student established her credibility on the subject of weight lifting without sounding like a braggart:

What is the fastest-growing sport today among American women? If you answered weight lifting, you are absolutely correct. Once seen as an exclusively male activity, weight lifting has crossed the gender barrier—and with good reason. Regardless of whether you are male or female, weight lifting can give you a sense of strength and power, enhance your self-esteem, and make you look and feel better.

I started lifting weights when I was in high school, and I have kept at it for the past eight years. I have also taught weight lifting in several health clubs, and I am a certified instructor through the Aerobics and Fitness Association of America.

Using some of my experience, I would like to explain the basic kinds of weights and how to use them properly.

Whether or not you lift weights, you will probably be more interested in the speech when you realize the speaker knows what she is talking about.

Your credibility need not be based on firsthand knowledge and experience. It can come from reading, from classes, from interviews, from friends—as in these cases:

I have been interested in the history of the civil rights movement for several years, and I have read a number of books and articles about it.

The information I am going to share with you today comes mostly from my biology class and an interview with Reyna Vasquez of the local Audubon Society.

I've learned a great deal about the problems of early childhood education from my mother, who is a teacher in the San Francisco school system.

Whatever the source of your expertise, be sure to let the audience know.

Establishing your good will is a slightly different problem. It is often crucial outside the classroom, where speakers have well-established reputations and may be identified with causes that arouse hostility among listeners. In such a situation, the speaker must try to defuse that hostility right at the start of the speech.

Occasionally you may have to do the same thing in your classroom speeches. Suppose you advocate a highly unpopular position. You will need to make a special effort at the outset to ensure that your classmates will at least consider your point of view. This is how one student tried to minimize his classmates' opposition at the start of a speech in favor of building more nuclear power plants to meet America's energy needs during the next century:

The development of new nuclear power plants in the United States came to a standstill during the 1980s. As *Discover* magazine stated just last month, however, the time has come to look again at the benefits of nuclear power. Unlike fossil fuels, it does not contribute to the greenhouse effect; it does not leave America at the mercy of foreign oil; and, with advances in technology, it is much safer than before.

That is why I am speaking in favor of building more nuclear power plants to meet our future energy needs. I know that most of you oppose nuclear power—I did, too, until I started researching this speech. Today I would like to share with you some of the facts I have found. I know I can't change all your minds. But I do ask you to listen with an open mind and to consider the merit of my arguments.

What reasonable listener could ignore such a sincere, forthright plea?

Preview the Body of the Speech

As we saw in Chapter 3, most people are poor listeners. Even good listeners need all the help they can get in sorting out a speaker's ideas. One way to help your listeners is to tell them in the introduction what they should listen for in the rest of the speech. Here is an excellent example, from a student speech about the potential effects of birth order on personality development:

> Where do you fit in your family structure? Are you at the top of the totem pole, partway down, or at the bottom? And how might your place in the family structure influence who you are? This morning I would like to explore how personality development can be affected by each of the four major patterns of birth order—the only child, the first child followed by younger brothers or sisters, the second or middle child, and the youngest child.

After this introduction, there is no doubt about the speaker's topic, central idea, or main points.

In some types of persuasive speeches, you may not want to reveal your central idea until later in the speech. But even in such a situation you must be sure your audience is not left guessing about the main points they should listen for as the speech unfolds. Nearly always, you should include some preview statement similar to the following:

> Today I will inform you about the basic structure of the knee, some common injuries to the knee, and preventive steps you can take to reduce the chance of injuring your knees.

> This afternoon I want to explain why so many people are upset about the use of Native American names and symbols by college and professional sports teams.

> So let's take a close look at the art of making ceramics. We'll go through the entire process from choosing your clay to producing the final, polished product.

Preview statements such as these serve another purpose as well. Because they usually come at the very end of the introduction, they provide a smooth lead-in to the body of the speech. They signal that the body of the speech is about to begin.

There is one other aspect you may want to cover in previewing your speech. You can use your introduction to give specialized information—definitions or background—that your listeners will need if they are to understand the rest of the speech. Often you can do this very quickly, as in these examples:

"Cryonics" is the science of freezing human organs or body parts in liquid nitrogen to preserve them for later use.

A "triathlon" is a race made up of three different events completed in succession. The events are usually swimming, biking, and running, though canoeing is sometimes substituted for one of these.

In other circumstances, you may have to explain an important term in more detail. Here is how one student handled the problem in a speech about the psychiatric disorder of depression. Knowing that most people use the term "depression" loosely, she took time in her introduction to give a more precise definition:

In popular usage "depression" refers to those brief periods of sadness, grief, or loneliness that everyone goes through from time to time. Thus we might say we are "really depressed" over doing poorly on an exam or over not getting a class we wanted.

In this speech, though, I will use "depression" in its psychiatric sense—a serious mental disorder in which a person suffers long periods of intense sadness and despair. The most common of all mental disorders, depression affects about 10 million to 14 million Americans. People suffering from depression usually feel tired all the time, often break into tears, and lose interest in work, school, social life, and other normal activities. In the most severe cases, depression may lead a person to attempt suicide.

Sample Introduction with Commentary

So far we have seen many excerpts showing how to fulfill the various objectives of an introduction. Now here is a complete introduction from a student speech. The side comments indicate the principles used in developing the introduction.

CANINE COMPANIONS

COMMENTARY	INTRODUCTION
The speaker uses a story to gain attention. This story works particularly well because it is richly detailed and arouses our curiosity about Frances's peculiar behavior.	The doorbell rings. Instantly, Frances jumps up from where she has been sitting, spins around three times, and runs back and forth from the door to the sofa. Next she hops onto the sofa and begins bouncing up and down. Is Frances deranged? No, Frances is a "canine companion," and she has just alerted her deaf owner to the fact that a visitor is at the door.
Now the speaker reveals her topic. She defines what canine compan-	Canine companions are dogs that have been trained to assist people who are hearing-impaired or

ions are and uses statistics to show how many are currently at work. This helps to strengthen the audience's interest.

who have physical disabilities. In addition to answering the door, canine companions perform a wide range of tasks that include locking and unlocking wheelchairs, turning light switches on and off, retrieving books from shelves, even fetching a beer from the refrigerator. According to *Smithsonian* magazine, there are some 3,500 canine companions at work throughout the United States, in addition to the 7,000 "Seeing Eye" dogs that help guide blind people.

The speaker does an excellent job of establishing her credibility and explaining her personal interest in the topic.

I became interested in canine companions two years ago when my older sister, who was paralyzed in a car accident, received a canine companion named Lucky. Since then I have learned about the subject by watching Lucky, by talking with my sister, and by reading a number of articles and pamphlets.

Here the speaker relates the topic directly to her audience and suggests why they should care about it.

As a result of my sister's accident, I have also gained a greater appreciation of the fact that being physically disabled is the one minority we can all join at any time. Due to an accident or serious illness, any of us could one day be in a situation where we—or someone we love—might require the services of a canine companion. So this afternoon I would like to tell you about canine companions—how they are trained and the many benefits they provide for the people they assist.

By previewing the main points of her speech, the speaker lets her audience know what to listen for. She also provides a good lead-in to the body of the speech.

Tips for Preparing the Introduction

1. Keep the introduction relatively brief. Under normal circumstances it should not constitute more than about 10 to 20 percent of your speech.

2. Be on the lookout for possible introductory materials as you do your research. File them with your notes, so they will be handy when you are ready for them.

3. Be creative in devising your introduction. Experiment with two or three different openings and choose the one that seems most likely to get the audience interested in your speech. (Don't hesitate to discard a "great" introduction that doesn't quite fit your speech. You'll think of another great one.)

4. Don't worry about the exact wording of your introduction until you have finished preparing the body of the speech. After you have determined your main points, it will be much easier to make final decisions about how to begin the speech.

5. Work out your introduction in detail. Some teachers recommend that you write it out word for word; others prefer that you outline it. Whichever method you use, practice the introduction over and over until you can deliver it smoothly from a minimum of notes and with strong eye contact. This will get your speech off to a good start and give you a big boost of confidence.

■ THE CONCLUSION

"Great is the art of beginning," said Longfellow, "but greater the art is of ending." Longfellow was thinking of poetry, but his insight is equally applicable to public speaking. Many a speaker has marred an otherwise fine speech by a long-winded, silly, or antagonistic conclusion. Your closing remarks are your last chance to drive home your ideas. Moreover, your final impression will probably linger in your listeners' minds. Thus you need to craft your conclusion with as much care as your introduction.

No matter what kind of speech you are giving, the conclusion has two major functions:

- To let the audience know you are ending the speech.

- To reinforce the audience's understanding of, or commitment to, the central idea.

Let us look at each.

Signal the End of the Speech

It may seem obvious that you should let your audience know you are going to stop soon. However, you will almost certainly hear speeches in your class in which the speaker concludes so abruptly that you are taken by surprise. Even in casual conversation you expect some signal that the talk is coming to an end. You are taken aback when the person you are talking with suddenly walks off without warning. The same is true of speechmaking. Too sudden an ending leaves the audience puzzled and unfulfilled.

How do you let an audience know your speech is ending? One way is through what you say. "In conclusion," "One last thought," "In closing," "My purpose has been," "Let me end by saying"—these are all brief cues that you are getting ready to stop.

You can also let your audience know the end is in sight by your manner of delivery. The conclusion is the climax of a speech. A speaker who has carefully built to a peak of interest and involvement will not need to say anything like "in conclusion." By use of the voice—by its tone, pacing, intonation, and rhythm—a speaker can build the momentum of a speech so there is no doubt when it is over.

The conclusion is a speaker's last chance to drive home his or her ideas. Successful speakers, such as Jesse Jackson, craft their conclusions with great care to leave a strong final impression.

One method of doing this has been likened to a musical crescendo. As in a symphony in which one instrument after another joins in until the entire orchestra is playing, the speech builds in force until it reaches a zenith of power and intensity.[3] (This does *not* mean simply getting louder and louder. It is a combination of many things, including vocal pitch, choice of words, dramatic content, gestures, pauses—and possibly loudness.) A superb example of this method is the memorable conclusion to Martin Luther King's "I Have a Dream" speech:

When we allow freedom to ring—when we let it ring from every village and every hamlet, from every state and every city—we will be able to speed up that day when all of God's children, black men and white men, Jews and Gentiles, Protestants and Catholics, will be able to join hands and sing in the words of the old Negro spiritual, "Free at last! Free at last! Thank God almighty, we are free at last!"[4]

Another effective method might be compared to the dissolve ending of a concert song that evokes deep emotions: "The song seems to fade away while the light on the singer shrinks gradually to a smaller and smaller circle until it lights only the face, then the eyes. Finally, it is a pinpoint, and disappears with the last note of the song."[5] Here is a speech ending that does much the same thing. It is from General Douglas MacArthur's moving farewell to the cadets at West Point in 1962:

In my dreams I hear again the crash of guns, the rattle of musketry, the strange, mournful mutter of the battlefield. But in the evening of my memory always I come back to West Point. Always there echoes and re-echoes: duty, honor, country.

Today marks my final roll call with you. But I want you to know that when I cross the river, my last conscious thoughts will be of the Corps, and the Corps, and the Corps.

I bid you farewell.[6]

The final words fade like the spotlight, bringing the speech to an emotional close.

You may think that you couldn't possibly end a speech with that much pathos—and you'd be right. MacArthur was a masterful speaker addressing a sympathetic audience at an inherently poignant moment. This combination rarely occurs. But that doesn't mean you can't use the dissolve ending effectively. One student employed it with great effect in a speech about visiting his grandparents' family farm as a young boy. During the body of the speech, the student spoke about the sights and sounds of the farm, the love and laughter he shared there as a child. Then, in conclusion, he evoked the images and sentiments of the farm one last time to create a moving dissolve ending:

Now, as with so much of our childhood, the farm is no longer the same. Grandpa is gone. The barn has been rebuilt. The softball sits idly on the shelf. Grandma no longer cooks her huge family dinners. Going to the farm is different without these pleasures. But still the memories remain. I can still see the fields. I can still smell the hay. I can still hear the laughter. I can still feel the love.

Both the crescendo and the dissolve endings must be worked out with great care. Practice until you get the words and the timing just right. The benefits will be well worth your time.

Reinforce the Central Idea

The second major function of a conclusion is to reinforce the audience's understanding of, or commitment to, the central idea. There are many ways to do this. Here are the ones you are most likely to use.

Summarize Your Speech   Restating the main points is the easiest way to end a speech. One student used this technique effectively in her informative speech about color psychology:

As we have seen, color psychology is a fascinating subject that is not yet totally understood by researchers. What I have tried to do, through information from books and articles, is to explain why different colors affect people in certain ways and how this knowledge is being used in advertising, interior decorating, and health care. I hope this will help you understand how seemingly minor things such as the color of our clothes, of our homes, and even of the food we eat can have such an important impact on our daily lives.

The value of a summary is that it explicitly restates the central idea and main points one last time. But as we shall see, there are more imaginative and compelling ways to end a speech. They can be used in combination with a summary or, at times, in place of it.

End with a Quotation   A quotation is one of the most common and effective devices to conclude a speech. Here is a fine example, from a speech on the misuse of television advertisements in political campaigns:

> We cannot ignore the evils of television commercials in which candidates for the highest offices are sold to the voters in thirty-second spots. These ads cheapen the elective process and degrade our political institutions. In the words of historian Arthur Schlesinger, Jr., "You cannot merchandise candidates like soap and hope to preserve a rational democracy."

The closing quotation is particularly good because its urgency is exactly suited to the speech. When you run across a *brief* quotation that so perfectly captures your central idea, keep it in mind as a possible conclusion.

Make a Dramatic Statement   Rather than using a quotation to give your conclusion force and vitality, you may want to devise your own dramatic statement. Some speeches have become famous because of their powerful closing lines. One is Patrick Henry's legendary "Liberty or Death" oration. It takes its name from the final sentences Henry uttered on March 23, 1775, as he exhorted his audience to resist British tyranny:

> Is life so dear, or peace so sweet, as to be purchased at the price of chains and slavery? Forbid it, Almighty God! I know not what course others may take; but as for me, give me liberty, or give me death.[7]

Although your classroom speeches are not likely to become famous, you can still rivet your listeners—as Henry did—with a dramatic concluding statement. What follows is a particularly striking example, from a speech on suicide prevention. Throughout the speech, the student referred to a friend who had tried to commit suicide the previous year. Then, in the conclusion, she said:

> My friend is back in school, participating in activities she never did before—and enjoying it. I'm happy and proud to say she's still fighting for her life and even happier she failed to kill herself. Otherwise, I wouldn't be here today trying to help you. You see, *I* am my "friend," and I'm more than glad to say, I've made it.

As you can imagine, the audience was stunned. The closing lines brought the speech to a dramatic conclusion.

Here is another example of the same technique—this time from a less unusual situation:

It is so easy to label the homeless as "bums" and "bag ladies." It is also easy to see them as people who are just looking for a handout—and often we give it to them and walk away. But as we have seen, most homeless people are not simply looking for a handout—they are reaching for a hand. Don't you think we should extend it to them?

This conclusion works because it takes the listener slightly by surprise and creates a lingering impression in the audience. Here the speaker made it even more effective by pausing for just a moment before the last sentence and by using his voice to give the closing words extra emotional force.

Refer to the Introduction   An excellent way to give your speech psychological unity is to conclude by referring to ideas in the introduction. This is an easy technique to use, and it may give your speech an extra touch of class. Here is how one student used the method in her speech about amnesia:

Introduction: For nearly half a year newspapers all across the country ran her story, complete with her photograph and physical description, in hopes that someone would recognize her. The newspapers described her as a "woman in mid-thirties, five feet seven inches tall, light brown hair, blue-gray eyes, two moles on neck."

That's all they knew about her, because that's all Jane Doe, as she was called, knew about herself. She was found in a park in Florida, lying beneath a tree, unconscious and near starvation. Her belongings were piled neatly beside her. She had not been hurt or molested, but she couldn't tell anyone how she came to be lying under that tree. When asked how she got there or where she had been, Jane Doe repeated over and over, "I don't remember."

Jane drew sympathy from all across the country because she was suffering from a condition we all fear—amnesia.

In the body of her speech the speaker did not mention Jane Doe again. She discussed the types of amnesia, explored their causes, and explained how doctors treat amnesia victims. Then, in her conclusion, she returned to Jane Doe to tie the whole speech together:

Conclusion: Whether amnesia is due to organic or psychological causes, it is a frightening, lonely, frustrating experience. Fortunately, all the publicity about the case of Jane Doe in Florida eventually turned up someone who gave Jane back her true identity. She is Cheryl Ann Tomiczec of Illinois. Family and friends who had lost track of Cheryl years before welcomed her back home, but Cheryl's memory of those intervening years remains murky. Even today, if you asked Cheryl how she ended up under that palm tree in Florida, she would say, "I don't remember."

Summarizing the speech, ending with a quotation, making a dramatic statement, referring to the introduction—all these techniques can be used separately. But you have probably noticed that speakers often combine two or more in their conclusions. Actually, all four techniques can be fused into one—for example, a dramatic quotation that summarizes the central idea while referring to the introduction.

One other concluding technique is making a direct appeal to your audience for action. This applies only to a particular type of persuasive speech, however, and will be discussed in Chapter 15. The four methods covered in this chapter are appropriate for all kinds of speeches and occasions.

Sample Conclusion with Commentary

How do you fit these methods together to make a conclusion? Here is an example, from the same speech about canine companions whose introduction we looked at earlier (pages 207–208).

COMMENTARY	CONCLUSION
The speaker gives an excellent summary of her speech. This is particularly important when you are speaking to inform because it gives you one last chance to make sure the audience remembers your main points.	We have seen, then, that training a canine companion takes a great deal of time and money—up to $10,000 per dog. We have also seen that people who receive the dogs must go through their own training to make sure they and their dog will work as a team. Finally, we have seen the amazing tasks canine companions can perform to help people with physical disabilities enjoy more independent lives.
By referring back to her sister, whom she had mentioned in the introduction, the speaker unifies the entire speech. Her closing quotation reinforces the central idea and ends the speech on a strong note.	It has now been two years since my sister received her canine companion. During that time, Lucky has become her hands, her feet, and her best friend. She says of Lucky, "I don't know what I would do without him. He has given my life new meaning."

Tips for Preparing the Conclusion

1. As with the introduction, keep an eye out for possible concluding materials as you research and develop the speech.

2. Conclude with a bang, not a whimper. Be creative in devising a conclusion that hits the hearts and minds of your audience. Work on several possible endings, and select the one that seems likely to have the greatest impact.

3. Don't be long-winded. The conclusion will normally make up no more than about 5 to 10 percent of your speech. Nothing aggravates audiences more than a speaker who says "In conclusion" and then drones on interminably.

4. Don't leave anything in your conclusion to chance. Work it out in detail, and give yourself plenty of time to practice delivering it. Many students like to write out the conclusion word for word to guarantee it is just right. If you do this, make sure you can present it smoothly, confidently, and with feeling—without relying on your notes or sounding wooden. Make your last impression as forceful and as favorable as you can.

SUMMARY

First impressions are important. So are final impressions. This is why speeches need strong introductions and conclusions.

In most speech situations you need to accomplish four objectives with your introduction—get the attention and interest of the audience, reveal the topic of your speech, establish your credibility and good will, and preview the body of the speech. Gaining attention and interest can be done in several ways. You can show the importance of your topic, especially as it relates to your audience. You can startle or question your audience or arouse their curiosity. You can begin with a quotation or a story.

Be sure to state the topic of your speech clearly in your introduction; otherwise, your audience may be confused and wonder where the speech is going. Establishing credibility means that you tell the audience why you are qualified to speak on the topic at hand; establishing goodwill, although less important for classroom speeches than for speeches outside the classroom, may be necessary if your point of view is unpopular. Previewing the body of the speech helps the audience listen effectively and provides a smooth lead-in to the body of the speech.

The conclusion of a speech is particularly important, because the final impression is often what will stick in your listeners' minds. The conclusion has two major objectives—to let the audience know you are ending the speech, and to reinforce their understanding of, or commitment to, your central idea. Too sudden an ending may leave your audience puzzled; it is always a good idea to alert them that you are finishing. You can do this either by your words or by your manner of delivery.

You can use a number of techniques to reinforce your central idea in the conclusion. They include summarizing the speech, ending with a pertinent quotation, making a dramatic statement, and referring to the introduction. Sometimes you may want to combine two or more of these techniques. Be creative in devising a vivid, forceful conclusion.

REVIEW QUESTIONS

After reading this chapter, you should be able to answer the following questions:

1. What are four objectives of a speech introduction?

2. What are seven methods you can use in the introduction to get the attention and interest of your audience?

3. Why is it important to establish your credibility at the beginning of your speech?

4. What is a preview statement? Why should you nearly always include a preview statement in the introduction of your speech?

5. What are five tips for preparing your introduction?

6. What are the major functions of a speech conclusion?

7. What are two ways you can signal the end of your speech?

8. What are four ways to reinforce the central idea when concluding your speech?

9. What are four tips for preparing your conclusion?

APPLICATION EXERCISES

1. Here are six speech topics. Explain how you might relate each to your classmates in the introduction of a speech.

Social Security	laughter
illiteracy	steroids
soap operas	blood donation

2. Think of a speech topic (preferably one for your next speech in class). Create an introduction for a speech dealing with any aspect of the topic you wish. In your introduction be sure to gain the attention of the audience, to reveal the topic and relate it to the audience, to establish your credibility, and to preview the body of the speech.

3. Using the same topic as in Exercise 2, create a speech conclusion. Be sure to let your audience know the speech is ending, to reinforce the central idea, and to make the conclusion vivid and memorable.

NOTES

[1] Anthony M. Frank, "The U.S. Postal Service: Making Progress," *Vital Speeches,* 56 (1990), 336.

[2] Jeffrey E. Jamison, "Alkali Batteries: Powering Electronics and Polluting the Environment," *Winning Orations, 1991* (Mankato, Minn.: Interstate Oratorical Association, 1991), p. 43.

[3] Dorothy Sarnoff, *Speech Can Change Your Life* (Garden City, N.Y.: Doubleday, 1970), p. 189.

[4] For the full text of King's "I Have a Dream," see the Appendix, pp. 450–462.

[5] Sarnoff, *Speech Can Change Your Life,* p. 190.

[6] Douglas MacArthur, "Farewell to the Cadets," in Richard L. Johannesen, R. R. Allen, and Wil A. Linkugel (eds.), *Contemporary American Speeches,* 7th ed. (Dubuque, Iowa: Kendall/Hunt, 1992), pp. 392–396.

[7] Patrick Henry, "Liberty or Death," in Ronald F. Reid (ed.), *Three Centuries of American Rhetorical Discourse* (Prospect Heights, Ill.: Waveland Press, 1988), pp. 113–116.

Chapter 10

Outlining the Speech

219

T hink what might happen if you tried to build a house without a floor plan or an architect's blueprint. You build the kitchen next to the driveway to make it convenient for carrying in groceries. But the dining room turns up at the other end of the house. When you cook and serve a meal, you have to run with the plates to keep the food from getting cold. You put the bathroom at the head of the stairs to make it accessible to visitors. But the door opens in such a way that the unwary guest is catapulted down the steps. You think it's a wonderful idea to have almost no interior walls. After all, the modern living space is supposed to be free and open. But when the first snowfall comes, your (unsupported) roof collapses.

Plans and blueprints are essential to architecture. So, too, are outlines essential to effective speeches. An outline is like a blueprint for your speech. By outlining, you make sure that related items are together, that ideas flow from one to another, that the structure of your speech will "stand up"—and not collapse.

Probably you will use two kinds of outlines for your speeches—one very detailed, for the planning stage, and one very brief, for the delivery of the speech.

THE PREPARATION OUTLINE

The preparation outline is just what its name implies—an outline that helps you prepare the speech. Writing a preparation outline means actually putting your speech together. It is the stage at which you decide what you will say in the introduction, how you will organize the main points and supporting materials in the body of the speech, and what you will say in the conclusion.

Guidelines for the Preparation Outline

Over the years, a relatively uniform system for preparation outlines has developed. It is explained below and exemplified in the sample outline on pages 225–227. You should check with your teacher to see exactly what format you are to follow.

State the Specific Purpose of Your Speech   The specific purpose statement should be a separate unit that comes before the text of the outline itself. Including the specific purpose with the outline makes it easier to assess how well you have constructed the speech to accomplish your purpose.

Identify the Central Idea   Some teachers prefer that the central idea be given immediately after the purpose statement. Others prefer that it be given and identified in the text of the outline itself. Check to see which your teacher wants.

Label the Introduction, Body, and Conclusion   If you label the parts of your speech, you will be sure that you indeed *have* an introduction and conclusion and have accomplished the essential objectives of each. Usually the names of the speech parts are placed in the middle of the page or in the far left margin. They are technical labels only and are not included in the system of symbolization used to identify main points and supporting materials.

Use a Consistent Pattern of Symbolization and Indentation   In the most common system of outlining, main points are identified by Roman numerals and are indented equally so as to be aligned down the page. Subpoints (components of the main points) are identified by capital letters and are also indented equally so as to be aligned with each other. Beyond this, there may be sub-subpoints and even sub-sub-subpoints. For example:

I. Main point
   A. Subpoint
   B. Subpoint
      1. Sub-subpoint
      2. Sub-subpoint
         a. Sub-sub-subpoint
         b. Sub-sub-subpoint
II. Main point
   A. Subpoint
      1. Sub-subpoint
      2. Sub-subpoint
   B. Subpoint

The clear visual framework of this outline immediately shows the relationships among the ideas of the speech. The most important ideas (main points) are farthest to the left. Less important ideas (subpoints, sub-subpoints, and so on) are progressively farther to the right. This pattern reveals the structure of your entire speech.

Once you have organized the body of your speech (see Chapter 8), you should have identified the main points. You need only flesh out your outline with subpoints and sub-subpoints, as necessary, to support the main points. But suppose, as sometimes happens, you find yourself with a list of statements and are not sure which are main points, which are subpoints, and so forth. Such a list might look like this:

There were 13 people at the Last Supper—Jesus and his 12 disciples.

One of the most common sources of superstition is numbers.

In the United States, 13 is usually omitted in the floor numbering of hotels and skyscrapers.

The number 13 has meant bad luck as long as anyone can remember.

Which statement is the main point? The second statement ("One of the most common sources of superstition is numbers"), which is broader in scope than any of the other statements. This would be one of the main ideas of your speech. The fourth statement is the subpoint; it immediately supports the main point. The other two statements are sub-subpoints; they illustrate the subpoint. Rearranged properly, they look like this:

> I. One of the most common sources of superstition is numbers.
>> A. The number 13 has meant bad luck as long as anyone can remember.
>>> 1. There were 13 people at the Last Supper—Jesus and his 12 disciples.
>>> 2. In the United States, 13 is usually omitted in the floor numbering of hotels and skyscrapers.

Above all, remember that all points at the same level should immediately support the point that is just above and one notch to the left in your outline. If this sounds confusing, think of it as a business organization chart:

> I. President
>> A. Vice president—Operations
>>> 1. Manager—Domestic Operations
>>>> a. Assistant manager—East
>>>> b. Assistant manager—West
>>> 2. Manager—Foreign Operations
>>>> a. Assistant manager—Europe and Asia
>>>> b. Assistant manager—Africa
>>>> c. Assistant manager—Americas
>> B. Vice president—Administration
>>> 1. Manager—Finance
>>> 2. Manager—Personnel

As you can see, every person on this chart reports to the person who is above and one notch to the left—except, of course, the President, who is the "main point."

State Main Points and Subpoints in Full Sentences   Below are two sets of main points and subpoints for the same speech on the life of Martin Luther King.

INEFFECTIVE	MORE EFFECTIVE
I. Montgomery	I. King began his civil rights career in the Montgomery bus boycott of 1955–1956.
II. 1960s	II. King's greatest triumphs came during the early 1960s.

A. Birmingham	A. In 1963 he campaigned against segregation in Birmingham, Alabama.
B. March	B. Later that year he participated in the famous march on Washington, D.C.
1. 200,000	1. More than 200,000 people took part.
2. "Dream"	2. King gave his "I Have a Dream" speech.
C. Prize	C. In 1964 he received the Nobel Peace Prize.
III. Final years	III. King faced great turmoil during his final years.
A. Criticized	A. He was criticized by more militant blacks for being nonviolent.
B. Vietnam	B. He protested against the war in Vietnam.
C. Assassination	C. He was assassinated in Memphis, Tennessee, on April 4, 1968.

The sample at left might serve adequately as a speaking outline, but it is virtually useless as a preparation outline. It gives only vague labels rather than distinct ideas. It does not indicate clearly the content of the main points and subpoints. Nor does it reveal whether the speaker has thought out his or her ideas. But there is no concern about any of these matters with the outline on the right.

In sum, a skimpy preparation outline is of little value. Stating your main points and subpoints in full sentences will ensure that you develop your ideas fully.

Label Transitions, Internal Summaries, and Internal Previews One way to make sure you have strong transitions, internal summaries, and internal previews is to include them in the preparation outline. Usually they are not incorporated into the system of symbolization and indentation, but are labeled separately and inserted in the outline where they will appear in the speech.

Attach a Bibliography You should include with the outline a list of the sources you consulted in preparing the speech. The bibliography will show all the books, magazines, and newspapers you read, as well as any interviews or field research you conducted. You may use any one of a number of bibliographical formats, or your teacher may have a preference. No matter which format you adopt, make sure your statement of sources is clear, accurate, and consistent.

Give Your Speech a Title, If One Is Desired   In the classroom you probably do not need a title for your speech unless your teacher requires one. In some other situations, however, a speech title is necessary—as when the speech is publicized in advance, when the group inviting you to speak requests a title, or when the speech is going to be published. Whatever the reason, if you do decide to use a title, it should (1) be brief; (2) attract the attention of your audience; and (3) encapsulate the main thrust of your speech.

A good title need not have what Madison Avenue would call "sex appeal"—lots of glitter and pizazz. By the same token, there is certainly nothing wrong with a catchy title—as long as it is germane to the speech. Here are two groups of titles. Those on the left are straightforward and descriptive. Those on the right are figurative alternatives to the ones on the left.

GROUP I	GROUP II
Unsafe Drinking Water	Toxins on Tap
Living with Deafness	The Sounds of Silence
Stained-Glass Artwork	A Touch of Glass
The United States Mint	The Buck Starts Here
Gambling Addiction	Against All Odds

Which group do you prefer? Neither is perfect. There are advantages and disadvantages to both. Those in the first group clearly reveal the topic of the speech, but they are not as provocative as those in the second group. Those in the second group are sure to arouse interest, but they do not give as clear an idea of what the speeches are about.

There is one other kind of title you should consider—the question. Phrasing your title as a question can be both descriptive and provocative. Using this method, we can construct a third set of titles combining the virtues of Groups I and II:

GROUP III

Is Your Water Safe to Drink?

Can You See What I'm Saying?

Stained Glass: Is It Just for Churches?

Where Is Making Money a Way of Life?

Do You Really Think You Can Beat the Odds?

Sometimes you will choose a title for your speech very early. At other times you may not find one you like until the last minute. Either way, try to be resourceful about creating titles for your speeches. Experiment with several and choose the one that seems most appropriate.

Sample Preparation Outline with Commentary

The following outline for a six-minute informative speech illustrates the guidelines just discussed.[1] The commentary explains the procedures used in organizing the speech and writing the outline. (Check with your teacher to see if she or he wants you to include a title with your outline.)

INDIA: LAND OF DIVERSITY

Neera Nijhawan

COMMENTARY

Stating your specific purpose and central idea as separate units before the text of the outline makes it easier to judge how well you have constructed the outline to achieve your purpose and to communicate your central idea.

Labeling the introduction marks it as a distinct section that plays a special role in the speech.

Opening with a non-English word helps to get attention.

Here the speaker moves from her attention-getter to reveal the topic of her speech.

Now the speaker establishes her credibility and previews the main points to be discussed in the body of the speech.

Including transitions ensures that the speaker has worked out how to connect one idea to the next. Notice that the transition is not included in the system of symbolization and indentation used for the rest of the speech.

OUTLINE

Specific Purpose: To inform my audience about the diversity of India's geography and languages.

Central Idea: India is a country of great geographical and linguistic diversity.

Introduction

I. "Namaste."
   A. Do you know what I just said?
   B. I greeted you the way I would in India.

II. The same word—"Namaste"—is also used when saying good-bye.
   A. The identical word can have two entirely different meanings.
   B. This is just one example of the diversity of life in India.

III. As a first-generation Indian-American, I have had firsthand experience with Indian life and culture.

IV. Today I would like to give you a glimpse of India's diversity by looking at its geography and languages.

(Transition: Let's start with geography.)

Labeling the body marks it as a distinct part of the speech.

Main point I is phrased as a full sentence. As the outline progresses, notice that the main points are arranged in topical order.

The three subpoints are shown by the capital letters A, B, and C, and are written in complete sentences to ensure that the speaker has thought them out fully.

Points below the level of subpoint are indicated by Arabic numerals and lower-case letters. Often they are not written in full sentences. Check to see what your teacher prefers.

When this speech was presented in class, the speaker used a large map as a visual aid throughout main point I so she could point out the regions of India as she discussed them.

The transition shows how the speaker will move from main point I to main point II.

Main point II, like main point I, is phrased as a full sentence.

Notice the pattern of subordination in this section. Subpoint B announces that there are fourteen

---

Body

I. India is a land of great geographical diversity.

  A. The northernmost part of India consists of the Himalaya mountains.
    1. The highest mountain system in the world, the Himalaya separate India from China.
    2. The Indian Himalaya have many mountains more than 20,000 feet high.

  B. The central part of India consists of the Northern Plains.
    1. About 200 miles wide, the Northern Plains stretch across India from the Arabian Sea on the west to the Bay of Bengal on the east.
    2. Within the Northern Plains, there is considerable diversity.
      a. Fertile farmland.
      b. Major cities such as Delhi and Calcutta.
      c. Great Indian Desert.

  C. The southern part of India consists of the Deccan plateau.
    1. Extending from the edge of the Northern Plains to the southern tip of India, the Deccan plateau is more than 1,200 miles long.
    2. The Deccan plateau includes many geographical features.
      a. Farming and grazing land.
      b. Tropical forests.
      c. Seacoasts.

(Now that you know something about the geographical diversity of India, let's look at its linguistic diversity.)

II. India is a land of great linguistic diversity.

  A. The official language is Hindi.
    1. Spoken by 40 percent of the people.
    2. Opening word of my speech—"Namaste"—is Hindi.

  B. In addition to Hindi, there are fourteen other major languages recognized in the Indian constitution.

major languages besides Hindi recognized in the Indian constitution. Sub-subpoint 1 deals with the distinctiveness of those languages. Because items a and b expand upon the distinctiveness point, they are subordinated to it.

The progressive indentation shows visually the relationships among main points, subpoints, sub-subpoints, etc.

Throughout main point II, the speaker uses well-chosen supporting materials to illustrate India's linguistic diversity in a clear and interesting fashion.

Labeling the conclusion marks it as a distinct part of the speech.

Summarizing the main points is usually standard procedure in an informative speech.

The closing line provides unity by relating back to the introduction.

This is the final bibliography. It lists the sources actually used in writing the speech and is shorter than the preliminary bibliography compiled in the early stages of research. (See Chapter 6 for a discussion of the preliminary bibliography.)

This bibliography follows the format recommended by the *MLA Handbook for Writers of Research Papers.* Check with your instructor to see what format you should use for your bibliography.

---

1. These languages are as distinct from each other as English is from French.
   a. Each has its own grammar and pronunciation.
   b. Some have their own alphabet.
2. Many of these languages have literary traditions that are 2,000 years old.

C. India also has more than 1,000 minor languages and dialects.
   1. These can change entirely from village to village.
   2. This often makes communication very difficult.

D. Most educated Indians also speak English.
   1. Comes from 300 years of British rule.
   2. Spoken by 2 percent of population.
   3. Widely used in colleges and universities.

E. As linguist Kamala Singh has stated, the diversity of India's languages is "unrivaled by any other nation."

Conclusion

I. I hope you can see from India's geography and languages why it is such a diverse—and fascinating—country.

II. Thank you and "Namaste."

Bibliography

Gangult, Sumit. "India: Charting a New Course?" *Current History* December 1993: 426–430.

Gantzer, Hugh, and Gantzer, Colleen. *India.* New York: Prentice-Hall. 1993.

Israel, Samuel, and Grewal, Bikram. *India,* 4th ed. Boston: Houghton Mifflin. 1993.

Krishna, Sumi. *India's Living Languages: The Critical Issues.* New Delhi: Allied Publishers. 1991.

Singh, R.L. *India: A Regional Geography.* Varansi: National Geographic Society of India, 1990.

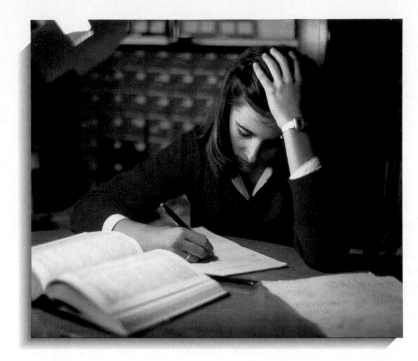

As blueprints are essential to architecture, so outlines are essential to speechmaking. Writing an outline helps ensure that your ideas are fully developed and that the structure of your speech is coherent.

THE SPEAKING OUTLINE

"I was never so excited by public speaking before in my life," wrote one listener in 1820 after listening to Daniel Webster. "Three or four times I thought my temples would burst with the gush of blood. . . . I was beside myself, and am so still."[2]

Such reactions were not unusual among Webster's audiences. He thrilled two generations of Americans with his masterful orations. Incredible as it seems today, he did so while speaking for three, four, even five hours at a time. Equally incredible, he often spoke without using any notes! A reporter once asked how he managed this. "It is my memory," Webster said. "I can prepare a speech, revise and correct it in my memory, then deliver the corrected speech exactly as finished."[3]

Few people have Webster's remarkable powers of memory. Fortunately, it is no longer customary to speak from memory. Today most people speak extemporaneously—which means the speech is thoroughly prepared and carefully practiced in advance, but much of the exact wording is selected while the speech is being delivered (see Chapter 12). Your speeches will probably be of this type. You should know, then, about the speaking outline—the most widely recommended form of notes for extemporaneous speeches.

The aim of a speaking outline is to help you remember what you want to say. In some ways it is a condensed version of your preparation outline. It should contain key words or phrases to jog your memory, as well as essential statistics and quotations that you do not want to risk forgetting. But it should also include material *not* in your preparation outline—especially cues to direct and sharpen your delivery.

Most speakers develop their own variations on the speaking outline. As you acquire more experience, you, too, should feel free to experiment. But for now, you cannot go wrong by following the basic guidelines below and by imitating the sample speaking outline on pages 232–233.

Guidelines for the Speaking Outline

Follow the Visual Framework Used in the Preparation Outline   Your speaking outline should use the same visual framework—the same symbols and the same pattern of indentation—as your preparation outline. This will make it much easier to prepare the speaking outline. More important, it will allow you to see instantly where you are in the speech at any given moment while you are speaking. You will find this a great advantage. As you speak, you will look down at your outline periodically to make sure you are covering the right ideas in the right order. It will be of little help if you have to hunt around to find where you are every time you look down.

Compare the following two versions of a partial speaking outline. They are from an informative speech about the history of feminism in the United States.

INEFFECTIVE	MORE EFFECTIVE
I. 1840–1860	I. 1840–1860
A. World Anti-Slavery Convention	A. World Anti-Slavery Convention
B. Seneca Falls convention	B. Seneca Falls convention
1. Lucretia Mott	1. Lucretia Mott
2. Elizabeth Cady Stanton	2. Elizabeth Cady Stanton
3. Declaration of Sentiments	3. Declaration of Sentiments
II. 1900–1920	II. 1900–1920
A. National American Woman Suffrage Association	A. National American Woman Suffrage Association
1. Founding	1. Founding
2. Objectives	2. Objectives
B. Nineteenth Amendment	B. Nineteenth Amendment
1. Campaign	1. Campaign
2. Ratification	2. Ratification

Novice speakers tend to rely on too many notes when delivering their speeches. Accomplished public speakers often use a minimum of notes, or no notes at all, which helps them communicate more directly with the audience.

The wording of both outlines is exactly the same. But the visual framework of the one on the right makes it easier to take in at a glance and reduces the odds of the speaker losing his or her place.

Make Sure the Outline Is Plainly Legible   You would be surprised how many students try to speak from messy, scribbled notes that would be hard to decipher at leisure, much less under the pressures of a speech situation. Your speaking outline is all but worthless unless it is instantly readable at a distance. When you make your outline, use dark ink and large lettering, leave extra space between lines, provide ample margins, and write or type on one side of the paper only.

Some speakers put their notes on index cards. Most find the 3 × 5 size too cramped and prefer the 4 × 6 or 5 × 8 sizes instead. Other people write their speaking outlines on regular paper. Either practice is fine, as long as your notes are immediately legible to you while you are speaking.

Keep the Outline as Brief as Possible   If your notes are too detailed, you will have difficulty maintaining eye contact with your audience. A detailed outline will tempt you to look at it far too often, as one student discovered:

Mike Spagnola was speaking about the joys of in-line skating. He had prepared the speech thoroughly and practiced it until it was nearly perfect. But when he delivered the speech in class, he referred constantly to his detailed notes. As a result, his delivery was choppy and strained. After the speech, Mike's classmates remarked on how often he had looked at his notes, and he was amazed. "I didn't even know I was doing it," he said. "Most of the time I wasn't even paying attention to the outline. I knew the speech cold."

Many students have had the same experience. Having lots of notes is a psychological security blanket against the possibility that something will go terribly wrong. The feeling seems to be "As long as I have plenty of notes, disaster will not strike." In fact, most beginning speakers use far too many notes. Like Mike, they find they don't need all of them to remember the speech. They also discover that too many notes can actually interfere with good communication.

To guard against having too many notes, keep your speaking outline as brief as possible. It should contain key words or phrases to help you remember major points, subpoints, and connectives. If you are citing statistics, you will probably want to include them in your notes. Unless you are good at memorizing quotations, write them out fully as well. Finally, there may be two, three, or four key ideas whose wording is so important that you want to state them in simple complete sentences. The best rule of thumb is that your notes should be the *minimum* you need to jog your memory and keep you on track. At first you may find it risky to speak from a brief outline, but you will soon become more comfortable with it.

Give Yourself Cues for Delivering the Speech A good speaking outline reminds you not only of *what* you want to say but also of *how* you want to say it. As you practice the speech, you will decide that certain ideas and phrases need special emphasis—that they should be spoken more loudly, softly, slowly, or rapidly than other parts of the speech. You will also determine how you want to pace the speech—how you will control its timing, rhythm, and momentum. But no matter how carefully you work these things out ahead of time, no matter how often you practice, it is easy to forget them once you get up in front of an audience.

The solution is to include in your speaking outline directions for delivering the speech. One way to do this is by underlining or otherwise highlighting key ideas that you want to be sure to emphasize. Then, when you reach them in the outline, you will be reminded to stress them. Another way is to jot down on the outline explicit cues such as "pause," "repeat," "slow down," "louder," and so forth. Both techniques are good aids for beginning speakers, but they are also used by most experienced speakers.

Sample Speaking Outline with Commentary

Below is a sample speaking outline for a six-minute informative talk about the geographical and linguistic diversity of India. By comparing it with the preparation outline for the same speech on pages 225–227, you can see how a detailed preparation outline is transformed into a concise speaking outline.

COMMENTARY

These comments remind the speaker to establish eye contact and not to race through the speech.

The word "pause" reminds the speaker to pause after her opening lines.

Including the main ideas of the introduction helps keep the speaker on track at the start of the speech.

It's usually a good idea to pause briefly before launching into the first main point. This is another way of signaling that you are moving from the introduction to the body.

Most speakers find it helpful to demarcate the body of the speech in the speaking outline as well as in the preparation outline.

Notice how the body of the speech follows the same visual format as the preparation outline. This makes the outline easy to read at a glance.

OUTLINE

Eye Contact !!
Slow Down

I. "Namaste."
   A. Know what I said?
   B. Greeted as if in India.

- Pause -

II. "Namaste" also used when saying good-bye.
   A. Two different meanings.
   B. Example of India's diversity.
III. First-generation Indian-American.
IV. Today—India's diversity in geography and languages.

     (Let's start with geography.)

- Pause -

Body

I. Great geographical diversity.
   A. Himalaya mountains.
     1. Separate India from China.
     2. 20,000 feet high.
   B. Northern Plains.
     1. 200 miles wide.
     2. Diversity of Northern Plains.
       a. Farmland.
       b. Cities: Delhi and Calcutta.
       c. Great Indian Desert.

Throughout the outline key words are used to jog the speaker's memory. Because the final wording of an extemporaneous speech is chosen at the moment of delivery, it will not be exactly the same as that in the preparation outline.

Inserting transitions makes sure the speaker doesn't forget them.

Underlining reminds the speaker to stress key words or ideas.

Quotations are usually written out in full in the speaking outline.

It's usually a good idea to pause before entering the conclusion.

Most speakers label the conclusion in the speaking outline as well as in the preparation outline.

Including the last sentence jogs the speaker's memory and ensures that the speech will end as planned.

C. Deccan plateau.
   1. 1,200 miles long.
   2. Geographical features.
      a. Farming and grazing land.
      b. Tropical forests.
      c. Seacoasts.

(Now you know geographical … look at linguistic.)

II. Great linguistic diversity.
   A. Official language is Hindi.
      1. Spoken by 40 percent.
      2. "Namaste" is Hindi.
   B. 14 other <u>major</u> languages in constitution.
      1. Distinct as English and French.
         a. Grammar and pronunciation.
         b. Alphabet.
      2. Literary traditions—<u>2,000</u> years.
   C. <u>1,000</u> minor languages and dialects.
      1. Change from village to village.
      2. Communication <u>very</u> difficult.
   D. Educated also speak English.
      1. 2 percent.
      2. Colleges and universities.
   E. Kamala Singh: linguistic diversity "unrivaled by any other nation."

—Pause—

Conclusion
I. Hope you see diversity from geography and languages.
II. Thank you and "Namaste."

SUMMARY

Outlines are essential to effective speeches. By outlining, you make sure that related ideas are together, that your thoughts flow from one to another, and that the structure of your speech is coherent. You will probably use two kinds of outlines for your speeches—the detailed preparation outline and the brief speaking outline.

The preparation outline helps you prepare your speech. In this outline you state your specific purpose and central idea, label the introduction, body, and conclusion, and designate transitions, internal summaries, and internal previews. You should identify main points, subpoints, and sub-subpoints by a consistent pattern of symbolization and indentation. It is usually advisable to state at least main points and subpoints in full sentences. Your teacher may require a bibliography with your preparation outline.

The speaking outline consists of brief notes to help you while you deliver the speech. It should contain key words or phrases to jog your memory, as well as essential statistics and quotations. In making up your speaking outline, follow the same visual framework used in your preparation outline. Keep the speaking outline as brief as possible, and be sure it is plainly legible. You can also give yourself cues for delivering the speech—when to speak more softly or more slowly, when to pause, and so forth.

REVIEW QUESTIONS

After reading this chapter, you should be able to answer the following questions:

1. Why is it important to outline your speeches?

2. What is a preparation outline? What are the eight guidelines discussed in the chapter for writing a preparation outline?

3. What is a speaking outline? What are four guidelines for your speaking outline?

APPLICATION EXERCISES

1. In the left-hand column below is a partially blank outline from a speech about sleep deprivation. In the right-hand column, arranged in random order, are the subpoints to fill in the outline. Choose the appropriate subpoint for each blank in the outline.

OUTLINE	SUBPOINTS
I. Most Americans do not get the sleep they need on a regular basis.	Sleep deprivation has been linked to a number of health problems.
A.	The *Times* also blames falling asleep at the wheel for 6,500 U.S. traffic deaths each year.
B.	The typical adult needs about eight hours of sleep each night to function effectively during the day.
1.	Second, it increases the risk of heart disease.
2.	

II. Sleep deprivation is a major cause of traffic accidents and deaths.

   A.

      1.

      2.

   B.

III. Sleep deprivation also contributes to poor personal health.

   A.

   B.

      1.

      2.

      3.

The same study showed that 20 percent of the population gets less than six hours sleep a night.

The statistics linking sleep deprivation to traffic accidents and deaths are alarming.

Yet most Americans consistently get less than eight hours sleep a night.

First, it weakens the immune system.

Sleep deprivation is second only to alcohol as the leading cause of traffic accidents and deaths.

Newsweek reports that "sleep deprivation has become one of the most pervasive health problems facing the U.S."

A Stanford study showed that over half the population gets less than seven hours sleep a night.

Third, it contributes to gastrointestinal illness.

The *Los Angeles Times* reports that drowsiness causes 200,000 auto accidents each year.

2. Following the format used in the sample preparation outline on pages 225–227, outline the sample speech at the end of Chapter 14 ("Dandelions: The Uncommon Weed," pages 329–331). Be sure to include a specific purpose statement, to identify the central idea, to label the introduction, body, and conclusion, to use a consistent pattern of symbolization and indentation, to state the main points and subpoints in full sentences, and to label transitions and internal summaries.

3. From the preparation outline you constructed in Exercise 2, create a speaking outline that you might use in delivering the speech. Follow the guidelines for a speaking outline discussed in this chapter.

NOTES

[1] Reprinted with permission of Neera Nijhawan.
[2] Robert T. Oliver, *History of Public Speaking in America* (Boston: Allyn and Bacon, 1965), p. 143.
[3] *Ibid.,* p. 145.

im·ag·ery \\'im-ij-(ə-)rē\ *n* **1** : the product of imag
: IMAGES; *also* : the art of making images **2** : figurative
3 : mental images; *esp* : the products of imagination
image tube *n* : an electron tube in which incident electro
radiation (as light or infrared) produces a visible ima
fluorescent screen duplicating the original pattern of rad
called also *image converter*
imag·in·able \im-'aj-(ə-)nə-bəl\ *adj* : capable of being
: CONCEIVABLE — **imag·in·able·ness** *n* — **imag·in·ab**
adv
¹imag·i·nal \im-'aj-ən-əl\ *adj* [*imagine* + *-al*] : of or r
imagination, images, or imagery
²ima·gi·nal \im-'ā-gən-əl, -'äg-ən-\ *adj* [NL *imagin-, imag*
relating to the insect imago
imag·i·nary \im-'aj-ə-ner-ē\ *adj* **1** : existing only in im
: lacking factual reality **2** : containing or relating to t
nary unit — **imag·i·nari·ly** \im-aj-ə-'ner-ə-lē\ *adv* —
nari·ness \-'aj-ə-ner-ē-nəs\ *n*
  syn IMAGINARY, FANCIFUL ⟨ONARY, FANTASTIC, CH
  shared meaning element ⟨ d or unbelievable *ant* re
imaginary number *n* ⟨ plex number (as 2 +
imaginary part is not ⟨ called also *imaginary*
imaginary part *n* : ⟨ f a complex number (as *3i*
that has the imag⟨ as a factor
imaginary unit ⟨ sitive square root of minus 1
imag·i·na·tion ⟨ nā-shən\ *n* **1** : the act or
forming a m⟨ of something not present to the
never befo⟨ rceived in reality **2 a** : creative
: ability⟨ and deal with a problem : RESOURC

Chapter 11

Using Language

LANGUAGE IS IMPORTANT

MEANINGS OF WORDS

USING LANGUAGE ACCURATELY

USING LANGUAGE CLEARLY
  Use Familiar Words
  Choose Concrete Words
  Eliminate Clutter

USING LANGUAGE VIVIDLY
  Imagery
  Rhythm

USING LANGUAGE APPROPRIATELY
  Appropriateness to the Occasion
  Appropriateness to the Audience
  Appropriateness to the Topic
  Appropriateness to the Speaker

A NOTE ON NONSEXIST LANGUAGE

H ave you ever played *Pictionary?* The point of the game is to draw words so people watching you can guess them. Some words are easy—"house," "bird," "parachute," and "television," for instance. Even people without any artistic talent can draw these in such a way that observers catch on immediately. But other kinds of words are more challenging. Try drawing "numb," "embarrass," or "dehydrated." The more abstract the word the more difficult it is to represent visually. How would you draw "improvement" or "appropriate"?

This is why language has evolved. Human beings need to communicate at a level far above what can be shown by pictures. But for language to work there must be a common understanding of what words mean. In effect, we've all made a pact that a certain collection of letters and sounds will mean the same thing to everybody. If you say "book," everybody who speaks English will picture something like what you're holding right now. On the other hand, when you don't use words properly, you "break the pact" and communication breaks down. Suppose you say to a friend, "Abby, you're so pedestrian." You may mean she walks a lot; but Abby is likely to get angry because you actually called her boring and ordinary.

LANGUAGE IS IMPORTANT

Good speakers respect language and how it works. How well do you use language? Do you say Shaquille O'Neal plays basketball *good,* when you mean he plays *well?* Do you say *in the eventuality of* when *if* will do? Do you describe a hurricane as a *terrible disaster,* as if there were such a thing as a *good disaster?* Do you litter your speech with such meaningless words as *you know, like, I mean,* and *really?*

If you do these things, you are bound to be less effective as a speaker. And, unfortunately, you are not alone. Much American speech is turning into the linguistic equivalent of junk food. For example:

Advertisement outside a jewelry shop: "Special Offer: Have your ears pierced and get an extra pair to take home!" (Sounds great. Would an extra pair of ears make me a better listener?)

Letter to an insurance company explaining an automobile accident: "The other driver was all over the road. I had to swerve a number of times before I hit him." (So whose fault was the accident, anyway?)

A manual for cafeteria staff at the Pentagon: "It is necessary at all times to maintain an adequate supply of wooden interdental stimulators." (In plain English, "Don't run out of toothpicks.")

Florida State football coach Bobby Bowden after winning a big game: "We've gotten over a major hurdle, but if we put all our eggs in one basket, we're barking up the wrong tree." (It's a good thing Bowden's play calling isn't as mixed up as his metaphors!)

The problem with these statements is not that they violate elitist standards of "good English." People in the United States have always talked casually. Our language has grown with as much vigor and variety as our population. We have borrowed words from other languages. We have coined new words and dropped old ones.[1] The first edition of *Webster's Collegiate Dictionary,* published in 1898, contained about 70,000 words.[2] The tenth edition, published in 1993, has 170,000 words—and these are just the words that are deemed necessary for a college education. One expert has estimated that the English language has as many as 2 million words, with a thousand new ones being added each year.[3]

There is a big difference, however, between the natural growth of a living language and the misuse of that language. To misuse our language is much more than a matter of mere words. Contrary to popular belief, language does not mirror reality. It does not simply describe the world as it is. Instead, language helps create our sense of reality by giving meaning to events. Language is not neutral. The words we use to label an event determine to a great extent how we respond to it.[4]

Consider the continuing public debate over euthanasia. If you see euthanasia as "immoral," as a form of "murder," as "a violation of the doctor's duty to save lives," you will likely oppose efforts to allow it in any form. But if you see euthanasia as "moral," as a way to provide "death with dignity," as "an acceptable alternative to needless pain and suffering" for the terminally ill, you will likely support efforts to permit it in some circumstances.

What separates these two viewpoints? Not the capabilities of modern medicine; not the conditions of terminally ill patients; not even the act of euthanasia itself. All those are the same for both sides. The difference is in the *meaning* given to them by the words that label them. This is why, as one writer has said, a choice of words is also a choice of worlds.[5]

Words are vital to thinking itself. Thought and language are closely linked. We do not get an idea and then come up with words to express it. Rather, we usually think *in* words. How often have you said, "I know what I want to say, but I just don't know how to say it." In fact, if you truly knew what you wanted to say, you probably would be able to say it. On most occasions when we are looking for "just the right word," what we are really looking for is just the right *idea.*[6]

As a speaker, once you get the right idea you must decide how best to *communicate* it to listeners. To do this, you need to be especially conscious of what language can do. Unless you use language accurately and clearly, no one will understand your ideas.

Words are the tools of a speaker's craft. They have special uses, just like the tools of any other profession. Have you ever watched a carpenter at work? The job that would take you or me a couple of hours is done by the carpenter in ten minutes—with the right tools. You can't drive a nail with a screwdriver or turn a screw with a hammer. It is the same with public speaking. You must choose the right words for the job you want to do.

Good speakers are aware of the meanings of words—both their obvious and their subtle meanings. They also know how to use language accurately, clearly, vividly, and appropriately. The balance of this chapter will explore each of these aspects of language use. We will also give special attention to nonsexist language in public speaking.

■ MEANINGS OF WORDS

Words have two kinds of meanings—denotative and connotative. *Denotative* meaning is precise, literal, and objective. It simply describes the object, person, place, idea, or event to which the word refers. One way to think of a word's denotative meaning is as its dictionary definition. For example, denotatively, the noun "school" means "a place, institution, or building where instruction is given."

Connotative meaning is more variable, figurative, and subjective. Put simply, the connotative meaning of a word is what the word suggests or implies. For instance, the connotative meaning of the word "school" includes all the feelings, associations, and emotions that the word touches off in different people. For some people, "school" might connote personal growth, childhood friends, and a special teacher. For others, it might connote frustration, discipline, and boring homework assignments.

Connotative meaning gives words their intensity and emotional power. It arouses in listeners feelings of anger, pity, love, fear, friendship, nostalgia, greed, guilt, and the like. Speakers, like poets, often use connotation to enrich their meaning. For example:

Terrorists neither <u>listen to reason</u> nor <u>engage in reasoning</u> with others. Their aim is to generate <u>fear</u>—<u>to frighten</u> people into <u>submission</u>. They <u>measure success by the magnitude of the fear</u> they generate through <u>brutal, savage</u> acts of violence. Terrorists <u>are prepared</u> to <u>kill to further</u> whatever cause they claim <u>to be pursuing</u>. And the <u>heinousness</u> of <u>these murders</u> is accented by the fact that terrorists <u>murder without passion</u>. They murder with <u>cool deliberation</u> and <u>careful planning</u>. They are <u>utterly amoral</u>.[7]

The underlined words in this passage have powerful connotations that are almost certain to produce a strong emotional revulsion to terrorism.

Here, in contrast, is another version of the same statement—this time using words with a different set of connotations:

Terrorists do not seek to negotiate with their opponents. They seek victory by using political and psychological pressure, including acts of violence that may endanger the lives of some people. To the terrorist, ultimate objectives are more important than the means used to achieve them.

With the exception of "terrorist," the words in this statement are less likely to evoke an intensely negative response than those in the first statement.

Which statement is preferable? That depends on the audience, the occasion, and the speaker's purpose. Do you want to stir up your listeners' emotions, rally them to some cause? Then select words with more intense connotative meanings. Or are you addressing a controversial issue and trying to seem completely impartial? Then stick with words that touch off less intense reactions. Choosing words skillfully for their denotative and connotative meanings is a crucial part of the speaker's craft.

■ USING LANGUAGE ACCURATELY

Using language accurately is as vital to a speaker as using numbers accurately is to an accountant. One student found this out the hard way. In a speech about America's criminal justice system, he referred several times to "criminal *persecution.*" What he meant, of course, was "criminal *prosecution.*" This one error virtually ruined his speech. As one of his classmates said, "How can I believe what you say about our courts when you don't even know the difference between prosecution and persecution?"

Sometimes inaccuracy results from a misguided attempt to be elegant. This happened to the business manager of a magazine.

Mary Jo Hundt had a special fondness for adding "istic" to the end of a word. Addressing the magazine's editorial staff one day, she said, "We are going to streamline our paperwork to make it more *simplistic.* That's the *modernistic* way to do things. With less paperwork, we'll have more time to devote to the magazine, and that will be *impressionistic* to management."

Mary Jo clearly did not realize that "simplistic" doesn't mean simple or easy but instead refers to *over*simplification on shaky grounds. And "modernistic" refers to a particular style of design, not the general condition of being modern. "Impressionistic," of course, has nothing to do with making an impression on someone; it describes a certain type of art or music. But the editorial staff knew all these things, and they were embarrassed for Mary Jo.

The moral of this story is obvious. Don't use a word unless you are sure of its meaning. If you are not sure, look up the word in a dictionary.

Fortunately, such outright blunders are relatively rare among college students. However, we all commit more subtle errors—especially using one word when another will capture our ideas more precisely. Every word has shades of meaning that distinguish it from every other word. As Mark Twain said, "The difference between the right word and the almost right word is the difference between lightning and the lightning bug."

If you look in a thesaurus, you'll find the following words given as synonyms:

partner   friend   ally

colleague   accomplice

All mean roughly the same thing—one person who is associated with another person. But all these words have different shades of meaning. See if you can fill in the best word to complete each of the sentences below:

1. No matter how depressed I get, talking with my best _____ always makes me feel better.

2. No one could have committed this crime alone. The burglar had to have an _____ .

3. England has been a strong _____ of the United States throughout the twentieth century.

4. Legally, each _____ in a business is responsible for any debts incurred by that business.

5. Professor Amali is out of town, so a _____ from her department gave a guest lecture in class today.

The best answers for the five statements are:

1. friend   4. partner

2. accomplice   5. colleague

3. ally

Each of the words is a little different from the others, and each says something special to listeners.

As you prepare your speeches, ask yourself constantly, "What do I *really* want to say? What do I *really* mean?" Choose words that are precise, exact, accurate. When in doubt, consult the dictionary or thesaurus to make sure you have the best words to express your ideas.

If you have serious aspirations as a speaker, you should work out a systematic plan to improve your vocabulary. Years ago Malcolm X, the famous African-American leader, did this by copying the dictionary, word by word! This method is extreme, and few people would take the time for it. A less arduous plan might be to try using one new word every day—and using the word correctly. The purpose of this is not to learn a lot of big words, but to "learn when certain words should be used, . . . to use the proper word at the proper time."[8]

■ USING LANGUAGE CLEARLY

Suppose you are standing on a street corner and you see a careless pedestrian about to step into the path of an oncoming car. Do you say, "It would appear from available empirical evidence as if an unsuspecting person is in danger of being struck and injured by an approaching automotive vehicle?" Of course not. You yell, "Look out!"

As many people have discovered, much to their dismay, it is possible to use language accurately without using it clearly. Here is a well-known story that shows how much trouble can be caused by not communicating clearly. A plumber wrote to a government agency to ask whether there was any harm in using hydrochloric acid to clean out drain pipes. The agency replied:

> The efficacy of hydrochloric acid is indisputable, but the corrosive effect is incompatible with metallic permanence.

The plumber thanked the agency for approving the use of hydrochloric acid. The agency wrote back, saying:

> We cannot assume responsibility for the production of toxic and noxious residue with hydrochloric acid and suggest you use an alternative procedure.

Once more the plumber thanked the agency for its approval. Finally, the agency, alarmed at the prospect of hundreds of ruined drain pipes, called in another scientist. He wrote:

> Don't use hydrochloric acid. It eats holes in the pipes!

Remember, people are different. What makes perfect sense to some may be gobbledegook to others. You cannot assume that what is clear to you is clear to your audience. This is particularly true in speechmaking. Listeners, unlike readers, cannot turn to a dictionary or reread an author's words to discover their meaning. A speaker's meaning must be *immediately* comprehensible; it must be so clear there is virtually no chance of misunderstanding. You can ensure this by using familiar words, by choosing concrete words over abstract words, and by eliminating verbal clutter.

Use Familiar Words

It may seem obvious that familiar words are better than unfamiliar ones. But you would be amazed at how many speakers persist in bombarding listeners with complicated words—usually out of the mistaken belief that such words sound impressive. In truth, filling a speech with long, multisyllabic words only marks the speaker as stuffy and pretentious. Worse, it usually destroys

Words are the tools of a speaker's craft. Well-known speakers, such as Ann Richards, sharpen their word skills over many years of trial, error, and practice.

understanding. One of the greatest barriers to clear speech is using big, bloated words where short, sharp ones will do the job better.[9]

Here, for example, are two passages expressing much the same idea. Which is easier to understand?

Is this a genuine affirmation that the utterances you anticipate communicating during the time period immediately succeeding the present shall be entirely veracious and devoid of deception, complete in all pertinent minutiae and particularities, and absent of all misleading obfuscation or superfluous and undocumentable specificities, on the authority of your allegiance and fidelity to the supreme deity?

Or,

Do you swear that the testimony you are about to give shall be the truth, the whole truth, and nothing but the truth, so help you God?

The second passage is the standard oath taken by a witness before testifying in a court of law. It consists of short, simple, familiar words that are easy to comprehend. Its meaning comes across without forcing you to perform complex mental gymnastics. The first passage says essentially the same thing as the second, but is full of stuffy, ostentatious words that make its meaning almost impossible to decipher.

When speaking about technical subjects, you may not be able to avoid unfamiliar words. If this happens, keep the technical terms to a minimum and define clearly those your audience may not understand. If you work at it, you will almost always be able to translate even the most specialized topic into clear, familiar language.

Here, for instance, are three passages explaining the devastating effects of a pregnant woman's drinking on her unborn child. The first passage is in medical jargon, and it defies comprehension by ordinary listeners:

Alcohol consumption by the pregnant woman seriously influences the intra-uterine milieu and therefore contributes to the morbidity and mortality of children born to these mothers. In regard to the pathophysiology of this syndrome, genetic polymorphism of enzymes for ethanol metabolism may alter fetal susceptibility. There may also be poor microsomal or mitochondrial function or decreased ATP activity.

Even an educated person without a medical background would have trouble with "pathophysiology" and "polymorphism" and "mitochondrial," much less be able to put them all together.

The second passage represents an attempt to adapt to a nonmedical audience. It is in more familiar language but retains enough obscure words to be difficult:

The deleterious effects of alcohol on the unborn child are very serious. When a pregnant mother consumes alcohol, the ethanol in the bloodstream easily crosses the placenta from mother to child and invades the amniotic fluid. This can produce a number of abnormal birth syndromes, including central-nervous-system dysfunctions, growth deficiencies, a cluster of facial aberrations, and variable major and minor malformations.

Well-informed listeners could probably figure out "deleterious effects," "central-nervous-system dysfunctions," and "facial aberrations." But these terms don't create a sharp mental image of what the speaker is trying to say. We still need to go one step further away from medical jargon toward ordinary language.

So we come to the third passage, which is utterly clear. It is from a speech by Annmarie Mungo, a student at Eastern Michigan University, and shows what can be done with work, imagination, and a healthy respect for everyday words:

When the expectant mother drinks, alcohol is absorbed into her bloodstream and distributed throughout her entire body. After a few beers or a couple of martinis, she begins to feel tipsy and decides to sober up. She grabs a cup of coffee, two aspirin, and takes a little nap. After a while she'll be fine.

But while she sleeps, the fetus is surrounded by the same alcoholic content as its mother had. After being drowned in alcohol, the fetus begins to feel the effect. But it can't sober up. It can't grab a cup of coffee. It can't grab a couple of aspirin. For the fetus's liver, the key organ in removing alcohol from the blood, is just not developed. The fetus is literally pickled in alcohol.[10]

This kind of plain talk is what listeners want. You cannot go wrong by following the advice of Winston Churchill to speak in "short, homely words of common usage." If you think big words (or a lot of words) are needed to impress listeners, bear in mind that the Gettysburg Address—considered the finest speech in the English language—contains 271 words, of which 251 have only one or two syllables.[11]

Choose Concrete Words

Concrete words refer to tangible objects—people, places, and things. They differ from abstract words, which refer to general concepts, qualities, or attributes. "Carrot," "pencil," "nose," and "door" are concrete words. "Humility," "science," "progress," and "philosophy" are abstract words.

Of course, few words are completely abstract or concrete. Abstractness and concreteness are relative. "Apple pie" is concrete, but the phrase also has abstract values of patriotism and conventional morals. Usually, the more specific a word, the more concrete it is. Let us say you are talking about tennis. Here are several words and phrases you might use:

physical activity	abstract/general
sports	
tennis	
professional tennis	
Steffi Graf	concrete/specific

As you move down the list, the words become less abstract and more concrete. You begin with a general concept (physical activity), descend to one type of activity (sports), to a particular sport (tennis), to a division of that sport (professional tennis), to one specific professional tennis player (Steffi Graf).

The more abstract a word, the more ambiguous it will be. Although abstract words are necessary to express certain kinds of ideas, they are much easier to misinterpret than are concrete words. Also, concrete words are much more likely to claim your listeners' attention. Suppose you make a speech about fire ants, which have long plagued the South and are now attacking western states. Here are two ways you could approach the subject—one featuring abstract words, the other concrete words:

ABSTRACT WORDS:

Fire ants have been a problem ever since they came to the United States from South America. They have spread across the South and now threaten various parts of the West as well. This is a serious problem because fire ants are highly aggressive. There have even been human casualties from fire ant stings.

CONCRETE WORDS:

Since fire ants arrived here from South America sometime before World War II, they have spread like a biblical plague across eleven states from Florida to Texas. Now they are invading New Mexico, Arizona, and California. Fire ants attack in swarms and they will climb any foot that is left in the wrong spot for a few seconds. They have even turned up indoors, in clothes hampers, beds, and closets. Fortunately, fewer than 1 percent of people who are stung have to see a doctor, but toddlers who have fallen on fire ant mounds have sometimes died from stings, as have highly allergic adults.[12]

Notice how much more persuasive the second version is. A speech dominated by concrete words will almost always be clearer, more interesting, and easier to recall than one dominated by abstract words.

Eliminate Clutter

Cluttered speech has become a national epidemic. Whatever happened to such simple words as "before," "if," and "now"? When last seen they were being routed by their cluttered counterparts—"prior to," "in the eventuality of," and "at this point in time." By the same token, why can't weather forecasters say "It's raining," instead of saying "It appears as if we are currently experiencing precipitation activity"? And why can't politicians say "We have a crisis," instead of saying "We are facing a difficult crisis situation that will be troublesome to successfully resolve"?

This type of clutter is deadly to clear, compelling speech. It forces listeners to hack through a tangle of words to discover the meaning. When you make a speech, keep your language lean and lively. Beware of using several words where one or two will do. Avoid flabby phrases. Let your ideas emerge sharply and firmly. Above all, watch out for redundant adjectives and adverbs. Inexperienced speakers (and writers) tend to string together two or three synonymous adjectives, such as "a learned and educated person," or "a hot, steamy, torrid day."

Here is part of a student speech that has been revised to eliminate clutter:

Sitting Bull was one of the most important ~~and significant of all~~ Native American leaders. He was born in ~~the year of~~ 1831 near Grand River, in ~~an area that is~~ *present-day* ~~now part of the state of~~ South Dakota. A fearless ~~and courageous~~ warrior, he ~~ended~~ *was* ~~up being~~ elected chief of the Hunkpapa Sioux in 1867. In the following years, he also attracted a large ~~and numerous~~ following among the ~~tribes of the~~ Cheyenne and Arapaho. He is best known ~~to people in this~~ *today* ~~day and age~~ for his ~~instrumental~~ role in ~~helping to lead the defeat of~~ *defeating* General Custer at the Battle of Little Bighorn in 1876. Although eventually ~~required against his will~~ *forced* to live ~~his life~~ on the Standing Rock Reservation in South Dakota, he never surrendered ~~to anyone~~ his dignity or his ~~personal~~ devotion to the Sioux way of life.

Notice how much cleaner and easier to follow the revised version is. No longer are the speaker's ideas hidden in a thicket of wasted words.

This kind of pruning is easy once you get the knack of it. The hardest part—and it is often very hard—is recognizing clutter for what it is and then forcing yourself to throw away the unnecessary words. Watch for clutter when you write your speech outlines. Be prepared to revise the outline until your ideas emerge as clearly and crisply as possible. As with revising an essay or a term paper, this will take extra time. But if you keep at it, you will become a much more effective speaker—and writer.

You can also help eliminate clutter by practicing your speeches with one or more reliable friends. Ask your friends to keep an ear out not just for flabby phrases but for verbal fillers such as "you know," "like," and "really." (If you are a habitual "like"-er, you will find this exasperating at first, but try to stay with it. You will discover that people listen to you much more seriously when you conquer this verbal tic.)

After your friends have helped you trim the clutter, practice delivering the speech again. At first you may feel awkward and unnatural because you are forcing yourself to break old habits. But if you practice regularly and concentrate on trimming your speeches of wasted words, you will gradually develop a new habit of speaking naturally without all that clutter. This will not only make you a better public speaker, but it will help you present ideas more effectively in meetings, conversations, and group discussions.

■ USING LANGUAGE VIVIDLY

Just as you can be accurate without being clear, so you can be both accurate and clear without being interesting. Here, for example, is how Martin Luther King *might have* phrased part of his great "I Have a Dream" speech:

> Turning back is something we cannot do. We must continue to work against police brutality, segregated housing, disfranchisement, and alienation. Only when these problems are solved will we be satisfied.

Here is what King *actually* said:

> We cannot turn back. There are those who ask the devotees of civil rights, "When will you be satisfied?" We can never be satisfied as long as the Negro is the victim of the unspeakable horrors of police brutality. We can never be satisfied as long as our bodies, heavy with the fatigue of travel, cannot gain lodging in the motels of the highways and the hotels of the cities. . . . We cannot be satisfied as long as a Negro in Mississippi cannot vote and a Negro in New York believes he has nothing for which to vote. No, no, we are not satisfied, and we will not be satisfied until justice rolls down like waters and righteousness like a mighty stream.[13]

Much more stirring, isn't it? If you want to move people with your speeches, use moving language. Dull, dreary words make for dull, dreary speeches. Bring your speeches to life by using vivid, animated language. Although there are several ways to do this, here are two of the most important—imagery and rhythm.

Imagery

One sign of a good novelist is the ability to create word pictures that get you totally involved with a story. These word pictures let you "see" the haunted house, or "feel" the bite of the snow against your face, or "hear" the birds chirping on a warm spring morning, or "smell" the bacon cooking over an open campfire, or "taste" the hot enchiladas at a Mexican restaurant.

Speakers can use imagery in much the same way to make their ideas come alive. Three ways to generate imagery are by using concrete words, simile, and metaphor.

Concrete Words   As we saw earlier in this chapter, choosing concrete words over abstract words is one way to enhance the clarity of your speeches (pages 246–247). Concrete words are also the key to effective imagery. Consider the following description of the 1994 Los Angeles earthquake:

Inside the houses, families slept. A few people here and there were rising from their beds, drinking coffee, taking their first steps toward another normal day. But January 17, 1994, was not to be a normal day for the people of Los Angeles.

The earthquake that struck Los Angeles at 4:31 a.m. reached up from deep inside the earth to grab the city and shake it from its slumber. Drivers on their way to work felt their cars weaving on roads that were suddenly in motion. Other residents, awake but still at home, saw their walls and ceilings crumble around them. But for most people it was a matter of waking to a nightmare of darkness and destruction. For almost a minute, while the earth rumbled, they waited and prayed.

When the tremor finally stopped, no fearsome silence followed. The wail of sirens, the shatter of breaking glass, the cries of hurt and frightened people filled the early morning air. The day had begun for the people of Los Angeles—a day they would never forget.

Cirete words call up mental impressions of sights, sounds, touch, smell, and taste. In the speech just quoted, we do not merely learn that Los Angeles experienced a devastating earthquake. We visualize the earthquake reaching up "from deep inside the earth" to terrorize the city and its people. We see the walls and ceilings crumbling, the drivers losing control of their cars. We hear the wail of sirens, the sound of breaking glass, the cries of the injured. The concrete words create images of sights and sounds, feelings and emotions that pull us irresistibly into the speech.

Simile   Another way to create imagery is through the use of simile. Simile is an explicit comparison between things that are essentially different yet have something in common. It always contains the words "like" or "as." Here are examples from student speeches:

Walking into my grandparent's home when I was a child was like being wrapped in a giant security blanket.

Air pollution is eating away at the monuments in Washington, D.C., like a giant Alka-Seltzer tablet.

These are bright, fresh similes that clarify and vitalize ideas. Some similes, however, have become stale through overuse. Here are a few:

fresh as a daisy	hungry as a bear
fit as a fiddle	busy as a bee
strong as an ox	big as a mountain
stubborn as a mule	happy as a lark
blind as a bat	light as a feather

Such clichés are fine in everyday conversation, but you should avoid them in speechmaking. Otherwise, you are likely to be "dull as dishwater" and to find your audience "sleeping like a log"!

Metaphor   You can also use metaphor to create imagery in your speeches. Metaphor is an implicit comparison between things that are essentially different yet have something in common. Unlike simile, metaphor does not contain the words "like" or "as." For example:

I talk about gasoline prices and interest rates because they have always been the twin engines that drive my business. (Lee Iacocca)

America's cities are the windows through which the world looks at American society. (Henry Cisneros)

These are both brief metaphors. Sometimes, however, a speaker will develop a longer metaphor. Here is an excellent example from Elizabeth Cady Stanton's classic speech "The Solitude of Self":

No matter how much women prefer to lean, to be protected and supported, nor how much men desire to have them do so, they must make the voyage of life alone, and for safety in an emergency they must know something of the laws of navigation. To guide our own craft, we must be captain, pilot, engineer; with compass and chart to stand at the wheel; to watch the wind and waves and know when to take in the sail, and to read the signs in the firmament over all.[14]

As you can see, metaphor is an excellent way to turn a phrase. Sometimes, however, metaphors get out of control. The result is a *mixed metaphor,* in which two or more incongruous comparisons are run together—often with comic results. Here, for example, is what one speaker (a U.S. Senator, no less!) said about a proposal to change the current method of funding Social Security:

This thing could sprout wings and become an irresistible political juggernaut that will thunder through the halls of Congress like a locomotive.

The speaker began by saying that the plan could "sprout wings." Having done so, he then needed to make the plan behave like a bird (not an airplane, because airplanes do not "sprout" wings). Instead, he turned it into a juggernaut, which the *Random House Dictionary* defines as a "large, overpowering, destructive force or object." It's hard to imagine a juggernaut with wings. Still, the speaker could have recovered a bit by having the juggernaut act like a winged creature. So what did he do? He had it "thunder through the halls of Congress like a locomotive"!

Needless to say, such a metaphor does more harm than good. When used effectively, however, metaphor—like simile—is an excellent way to bring color to a speech, to make abstract ideas concrete, to clarify the unknown, and to express feelings and emotions.

Rhythm

Language has a rhythm created by the choice and arrangement of words. Sometimes the appeal of a statement depends almost entirely on its rhythm—as in this children's verse:

> Pease porridge hot,
>   Pease porridge cold,
> Pease porridge in the pot,
>   Nine days old.

There is little meaning here. The appeal comes from the combination of sounds, which gives the passage an almost musical cadence.[15]

Speakers, like poets, sometimes seek to exploit the rhythm of language. By catching up their listeners in an arresting string of sounds, speakers can enhance the impact of their words—and therefore of their ideas.[16] Winston Churchill was a master at this. Here is a passage from one of his famous speeches during World War II. To emphasize its cadence, the passage has been printed as if it were poetry rather than prose:

> We shall not flag or fail.
>   We shall go on to the end.
> Even though large tracts of Europe
>   and many old and famous states
> May fall into the grip of the Gestapo
>   and all the odious apparatus of Nazi rule,
> We shall fight with growing confidence
>   and strength in the air.
> We shall defend our island
>   whatever the cost may be.

> We shall fight on the beaches.
> We shall fight on the landing grounds.
> We shall fight in the fields
>   and in the streets.
> We shall fight in the hills.
> We shall never surrender.

The impact of the passage was heightened by Churchill's superb delivery; but even by themselves the words take on an emphatic rhythm that reinforces the message. You can see why John Kennedy said later that Churchill "mobilized the English language and sent it into battle."

A speech, however, is not a poem. You should never emphasize sound and rhythm at the expense of meaning. And you may never have paid much conscious attention to the rhythm and flow of language. But you can develop an ear for vocal rhythms by study and practice. What's more, you can easily begin now to use four basic stylistic devices employed by Churchill and other fine speakers to enhance the rhythm of their prose.

Parallelism   The first device is parallelism—the similar arrangement of a pair or series of related words, phrases, or sentences. For example:

> *Rich and poor, intelligent and ignorant, wise and foolish, virtuous and vicious, man and woman*—it is ever the same, each soul must depend wholly on itself. (Elizabeth Cady Stanton)

> The denial of human rights *anywhere is a threat to* human rights *everywhere.* Injustice *anywhere is a threat to* justice *everywhere.* (Jesse Jackson)

The effects of parallelism are perhaps best illustrated by seeing what happens when it is absent. For instance, compare this statement:

> I speak as a Republican. I speak as a woman. I speak as a United States Senator. I speak as an American. (Margaret Chase Smith)

with this one:

> I speak as a Republican. I speak as a woman. I speak as a United States Senator. And I am also addressing you as an American.

The first statement is clear, consistent, and compelling. The second is not. By violating the principle of parallel structure, its final sentence ("And I am also addressing you as an American") destroys the progression begun by the preceding three sentences ("I speak as a Republican. I speak as a woman. I speak as a United States Senator"). It thereby turns a strong, lucid, harmonious statement into one that is fuzzy and jarring.

Repetition   The second device you can use to lend rhythm to your speeches is repetition. This means repeating the same word or set of words at the beginning or end of successive clauses or sentences. For example:

We left America safe, *we left America* secure, *we left America* free—*still a* beacon of hope to mankind, *still a* light unto the nations. (Ronald Reagan)

We are a people in a quandary about the present. *We are a people* in search of our future. *We are a people* in search of a national community. (Barbara Jordan)

As you can see, repetition inevitably results in parallelism. In addition to building a strong cadence, it also unifies a sequence of ideas, emphasizes an idea by stating it more than once, and helps to create a strong emotional effect.

Alliteration   The third device you can use to enhance the rhythm of your speeches is alliteration. The most common method of alliteration is repeating the initial consonant sound of close or adjoining words. For example:

We should not *d*emean our *d*emocracy with the politics of *d*istraction, *d*enial, and *d*espair. (Al Gore)

In a nation founded on the promise of human dignity, our *c*olleges, our *c*ommunities, our *c*ountry should challenge hatred wherever we find it. (Hillary Rodham Clinton)

By highlighting the sounds of words, alliteration catches the attention of listeners and can make ideas easier to remember. Used sparingly, it is a marvelous way to spruce up your speeches. Used to excess, however, it can be laughable and draw too much attention, so that listeners get more involved in listening for the next alliteration than in absorbing the content of the speech.

Antithesis   Finally, you might try using antithesis—the juxtaposition of contrasting ideas, usually in parallel structure. For example:

Ask not what your country can do for you; ask what you can do for your country. (John F. Kennedy)

Your success as a family, our success as a society, depends not on what happens at the White House, but on what happens inside your house. (Barbara Bush)

Antithesis has long been a favorite device of accomplished speakers. Because it nearly always produces a neatly turned phrase, it is a fine way to give your speeches a special touch of class.

You may be thinking that imagery and rhythm are fine for famous people, but are too fancy for ordinary speeches like yours. This is not true. Imagery and rhythm are easy to use and can enliven even the most routine of speeches. As an example, take a look at the following excerpt from a student speech about Mother Teresa, the nun who received the Nobel Peace Prize for her work among the poor people of Calcutta, India:

Faced with the same position, could we survive? Could we survive the stench and stink of the wretched Calcutta shanty towns? Mother Teresa survives.

Could we survive the sickness and disease which slowly rot these poor people to the skin and bones of half-existence? Mother Teresa survives.

Could we survive the cries of hunger which squeal, then groan, then stop—eternally extinguished? Mother Teresa survives.

Could we survive the sight of emaciated bodies, thin shrouds of skin stretched tightly over brittle, bulging bones? Mother Teresa survives—because she touches the sick, she touches the homeless, she touches the underclothed and undernourished, she touches the helpless and the hopeless and the dying.

This is vivid, moving language. The imagery is sharp and poignant, the rhythm strong and insistent. Think of how you can do similar things to enliven your own speeches.

■ USING LANGUAGE APPROPRIATELY

Here is part of a famous oration given by John Hancock in 1774, during the American Revolution. Speaking of the British soldiers who killed five Americans in the Boston massacre, Hancock exclaimed:

Ye dark designing knaves, ye murderers, parricides! How dare you tread upon the earth, which has drank in the blood of slaughtered innocents shed by your wicked hands? How dare you breathe that air which wafted to the ear of heaven the groans of those who fell a sacrifice to your accursed ambition? . . . Tell me, ye bloody butchers, ye villains high and low, ye wretches . . . do you not feel the goads and stings of conscious guilt pierce through your savage bosoms?[17]

This is certainly vivid language—and Hancock's audience loved it. But can you imagine speaking the same way today? In addition to being accurate, clear, and vivid, language should also be appropriate—to the occasion, to the audience, to the topic, and to the speaker.

Appropriateness to the Occasion

Language that is appropriate for some occasions may not be appropriate for others. "There is a time for dialect, a place for slang, an occasion for literary form. What is correct on the sports page is out of place on the op-ed page; what is with-it on the street may well be without it in the classroom."[18] As a simple example, a coach might address the football team as "you guys" (or worse!), whereas the speaker in a more formal situation would begin with "distinguished guests." Try reversing these two situations, and see how ridiculous it becomes. It's only common sense to adjust your language to different occasions.

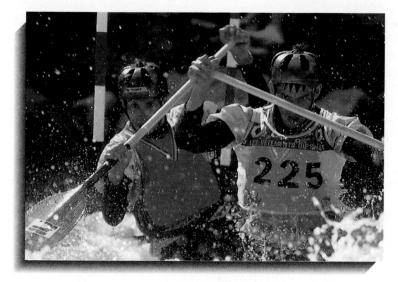

Language needs to be appropriate to a speaker's topic, as well as to the audience and occasion. A speech on canoe racing, for example, would probably use more action-oriented words than a speech about theories of psychology.

Appropriateness to the Audience

Appropriateness also depends on the audience. If you keep this in mind, it will help you greatly when dealing with technical or scientific topics. When addressing an audience of physicians, you might use the word "paratosis" to refer to a viral disease marked by the swelling of the parotid glands. Your audience would know just what you meant. But when talking to a nonmedical audience, such as your classmates, a word like "paratosis" would not be appropriate. The appropriate word in this case would be "mumps."

You should be especially careful to avoid language that might offend your audience. If you were a stand-up comedian, off-color humor or profanity might be appropriate in a night-club routine, but most listeners would find it offensive in a formal public speech. Remember, speakers are expected to elevate and polish their language when addressing an audience.

They are also expected to avoid name-calling and other forms of abusive language. As we saw in Chapter 2, such language is ethically suspect because it demeans the basic human worth of the people it is directed against. In addition, most listeners take offense at statements that denounce people on the basis of their religious beliefs or ethnic heritage. If you include such statements in your speeches, you will not only violate an important ethical responsibility, you will almost surely alienate a good portion of your audience. (You will also have problems with appropriateness if you pepper your speeches with sexist language. This has become such an important issue for speakers that we discuss it in detail later in this chapter.)

Of course, you cannot always be sure of how listeners will respond to what you say. As a general rule, bend over backward to avoid language that may confuse or offend your listeners. When it comes to appropriateness, you will seldom go wrong by erring on the side of caution. (Put simply, "erring on the side of caution" means "when in doubt—don't.")

Appropriateness to the Topic

Language should also be appropriate to the topic. You would not use metaphor, antithesis, and alliteration when explaining how to change a bicycle tire or how to perform routine maintenance on a car. But you might use all three in a speech celebrating the genius of Leonardo da Vinci or honoring the American soldiers who served in the Persian Gulf War. The first two topics call for straightforward description and explanation. The latter two call for special language skills to evoke emotion, admiration, and appreciation.

Appropriateness to the Speaker

No matter what the occasion, audience, or topic, language should also be appropriate to the speaker. Imagine the effect if Al Gore tried to adopt the religious imagery and rhythmical cadence of Jesse Jackson. The results would be comical. Every public speaker develops her or his own language style. Ann Richards and Mario Cuomo seek to create striking phrases through imagery, antithesis, and metaphor. Elizabeth Dole and Colin Powell seldom use such devices. Yet all four are among the most successful speakers in America.

"Terrific," you may be thinking. "I have my own style too. I feel more comfortable using abstract words, slang, and technical jargon. That's just me. It's *my* way of speaking." But to say language should be appropriate to the speaker does not justify ignoring the other needs for appropriateness. There is a difference between one's everyday personal style and one's *developed* style as a public speaker. Richards, Powell, and other accomplished speakers have developed their speaking styles over many years of trial, error, and practice. They have *worked* at using language effectively.

You can do the same if you become language-conscious. Analyze your strengths and weaknesses. Read and listen to the speeches of people like Richards, Powell, Churchill, and King. Study their techniques for achieving accuracy, clarity, and vividness, and try to adapt those techniques to your own speeches. But do not try to "become" someone else when you speak. Learn from other speakers, blend what you learn into your own language style, and seek to become the best possible you.

■ A NOTE ON NONSEXIST LANGUAGE

"Above all it is language that separates man from the other creatures."

"When a soldier goes to war, he should have the best possible equipment."

"The major responsibility of a school teacher is to make sure her students learn reading, writing, and arithmetic."

Thirty years ago, most people in the United States who heard these statements in a speech would not have given them a second thought. Today the same statements would raise more than a few eyebrows—and perhaps tempers—in almost any audience. Here's why:

It's not just "man" but all people who are separated from the other creatures by the use of language. To use "man" as a generic word for all people leaves out half of humanity. You can test this by rewording the original statement as follows: "Above all it is language that separates woman from the other creatures."

Soldiers in the U.S. military include women as well as men. To say, "When a soldier goes to war, *he* should have the best possible equipment," ignores the existence of female soldiers. It also can be interpreted as meaning that only male soldiers should go to war with the finest equipment—hardly a comforting thought to female soldiers or their loved ones!

It may be the major job of an elementary-school teacher to teach reading, writing, and arithmetic, but the third statement ignores the fact that not all elementary-school teachers are female. The statement stereotypes this occupational group as being suitable only for women, in the same way that the second statement stereotypes all soldiers as men.

For centuries, English has been a male-dominated language with countless words and phrases that favor men and convey stereotyped, misleading, or demeaning views of women.[19] Today that is changing—not as fast, perhaps, as some people might like, and doubtless too fast for other people—but changing nonetheless. If current trends continue, thirty years from now the statements at the beginning of this section will seem as outdated as bloomers and corsets.

Whatever your feelings about these trends, avoiding sexist language is important as a matter of accuracy in speechmaking. To speak as if all soldiers (or doctors, or lawyers, or firefighters) are men is incorrect—just as it is erroneous to speak as if all elementary-school teachers (or secretaries, or nurses, or flight attendants) are women. Being accurate in such matters is no less important than being accurate in other aspects of your language.

As we saw in Chapter 5, avoiding sexist language is also a vital part of audience adaptation. Even if you do not care about sexist language yourself, you can be sure that almost any audience you address will contain people—men and women alike—who do care and who will be upset if you use it in your speech. In this respect, as in others, an effective speaker must adjust to the values and expectations of the audience.

When editors, linguists, and others first proposed nonsexist alternatives to traditional words and phrases, some people reacted with shock and indignation. You cannot change the language, they said, without destroying its beauty and purity. But the English language has been changing for centuries—just as it will continue to change in the future. Today a number of nonsexist usages have become so widely accepted that no aspiring speaker (or writer) can afford to ignore them. Let us look at four of these usages.

Avoid the Generic "He"

Ineffective: Each time a surgeon walks into the operating room, *he* risks being sued for malpractice.

More Effective: Each time a surgeon walks into the operating room, *she or he* risks being sued for malpractice.

Often, a more graceful way to solve this problem is to pluralize. For example:

More Effective: Whenever surgeons walk into the operating room, *they* risk being sued for malpractice.

Avoid the Use of "Man" When Referring to Both Men and Women

Ineffective: If a large comet struck the earth, it could destroy all of mankind.

More Effective: If a large comet struck the earth, it could destroy all human life.

Ineffective: No matter how popular cats have become, the dog is still man's best friend.

More Effective: No matter how popular cats have become, the dog is still a person's best friend.

Avoid Stereotyping Jobs and Social Roles by Gender

Ineffective: Being a small businessman in the current economic climate is not easy.

More Effective: Being a small businessperson in the current economic climate is not easy.

Sometimes you can solve this problem with a simple twist in sentence construction. For example:

More Effective: Owning a small business is not easy in the current economic climate.

Avoid Unnecessary or Patronizing Gender Labels

Ineffective: Sandra Day O'Connor is an outstanding lady judge.

More Effective: Sandra Day O'Connor is an outstanding judge.

Ineffective: When I phoned the registrar's office this morning, a male receptionist told me to call back during the afternoon.

More Effective: When I phoned the registrar's office this morning, the recep-
                         tionist told me to call back during the afternoon.

Like many other aspects of modern life, questions of sexist and nonsexist language can sometimes be confusing. Although "steward" and "stew-
ardess" gave way long ago to "flight attendant," most people—including those
who bestow the Academy Awards—continue to distinguish between "actor"
and "actress."[20] Is this logical? Hardly—and it could change any time. If you do
a lot of public speaking (or writing), you should consider purchasing a guide-
book to nonsexist language. Two of the most helpful are the *Handbook of Non-
Sexist Writing,* by Casey Miller and Kate Swift, and the *Bias-Free Word Finder,*
by Rosalie Maggio.

SUMMARY

Of all human creations, language may be the most remarkable. Through language we share experiences, formulate values, exchange ideas, transmit
knowledge, and sustain culture. Indeed, language is vital to thinking itself.
Contrary to popular belief, language does not simply mirror reality, but helps
create our sense of reality by giving meaning to events.

Good speakers have respect for language and how it works. Words are
the tools of a speaker's craft. They have special uses, just like the tools of any
other profession. As a speaker, you should be aware of the meanings of words
and know how to use language accurately, clearly, vividly, and appropriately.

Words have two kinds of meanings—denotative and connotative. Denotative meaning is precise, literal, and objective. One way to think of a word's
denotative meaning is as its dictionary definition. Connotative meaning is
more variable, figurative, and subjective. It is whatever the word suggests or
implies. Connotative meaning includes all the feelings, associations, and emotions that a word touches off in different people.

Using language accurately is as vital to a speaker as using numbers accurately is to an accountant. Never use a word unless you are sure of its
meaning. If you are not sure, look up the word in a dictionary. As you prepare
your speeches, ask yourself constantly, "What do I *really* want to say? What do
I *really* mean?" Choose words that are precise and accurate.

Using language clearly allows listeners to grasp your meaning immediately. You can assure this by using familiar words that are known to the average person and require no specialized background; by choosing concrete
words in preference to more abstract ones; and by eliminating verbal clutter.

Using language vividly helps bring your speech to life. One way to make
your language more vivid is through imagery, or the creation of word pictures. You can develop imagery by using concrete language, simile, and
metaphor. Simile is an *explicit* comparison between things that are essentially
different yet have something in common; it always contains the words "like"
or "as." Metaphor is an *implicit* comparison between things that are different
yet have something in common; it does not contain the words "like" or "as."

Another way to make your speeches vivid is by exploiting the rhythm of language. Four devices for creating rhythm are parallelism, repetition, alliteration, and antithesis. Parallelism is the similar arrangement of a pair or series of related words, phrases, or sentences. Repetition is the use of the same word or set of words at the beginning or end of successive clauses or sentences. Alliteration comes from repeating the initial consonant sounds of close or adjoining words. Antithesis is the juxtaposition of contrasting ideas, usually in parallel structure.

Using language appropriately means adapting to the particular occasion, audience, and topic at hand. It also means developing your own language style instead of trying to copy someone else's. If your language is appropriate in all respects, your speech is much more likely to succeed.

You will also be more likely to succeed if you do not pepper your speech with sexist language. Although the topic of sexist language is complex and controversial, a number of nonsexist usages are so widely accepted that no aspiring speaker can afford to ignore them. They include avoiding the generic "he," dropping the use of "man" when referring to both men and women, refraining from stereotyping jobs and social roles by gender, and discarding unnecessary or patronizing gender labels.

REVIEW QUESTIONS

After reading this chapter, you should be able to answer the following questions:

1. How does language help to shape our sense of reality?

2. What is the difference between denotative and connotative meaning? How might you use each to convey your message most effectively?

3. What are the four criteria for using language effectively in your speeches?

4. What are the two aspects of accurate language you should pay attention to in preparing your speeches?

5. What are three things you should do to use language clearly in your speeches?

6. What are two ways to bring your speeches to life with vivid, animated language?

7. What does it mean to say you should use language appropriately in your speeches?

8. Why is sexist language a problem for public speakers? What are four nonsexist language usages which have become so widely accepted that no speaker can afford to ignore them?

APPLICATION EXERCISES

1. Arrange each of the sequences below in order, from the most abstract word to the most concrete word.

    a.   housing complex, building, dining room, structure, apartment

    b.   *Mona Lisa,* art, painting, creative activity, portrait

    c.   Communication Department, university, educational institution, Stanford, school

    d.   automobile, vehicle, Ferrari, transportation, sports car

2. In each of the following sentences, select the most appropriate word to complete the statement.

    a.   subsidy, award, contribution, present

    Tanya received a special _____ from the city for her heroism in saving a drowning child.

    According to *USA Today,* a tie is the most popular _____ for a man's birthday.

    Many farmers get a government _____ for not planting certain crops.

    Einstein's theory of relativity was a major _____ to the development of modern physics.

    b.   fact, evidence, proof, data

    To get a refund, a customer must provide _____ of purchase.

    The statistical _____ show that more and more college students are working their way through school.

    It is a scientific _____ that the earth revolves around the sun.

    In the jury's mind, the _____ clearly showed that the defendant was guilty.

3. Rewrite each of the following sentences using clear, familiar words.

    a.   Some students were not cognizant of the fact that the professor made a modification in the assignment subsequent to the last class meeting.

    b.   My employment objective is to attain a position of maximum financial reward.

    c.   All professors at this school are expected to achieve high standards of excellence in their instructional duties.

    d.   The burglar evaded security personnel and is no longer on the premises.

    e.   In the eventuality of a fire, it is imperative that all persons evacuate the building without undue delay.

4. Each of the statements below uses one or more of the following stylistic devices—metaphor, simile, parallelism, repetition, alliteration, antithesis. Identify the device (or devices) used in each statement.

   a. "It will be up to you who are graduating today to take from Harvard not just knowledge, but wisdom; not just intelligence, but humanity; not just a drive for self-fulfillment, but a sense of service and a taste for hard work." (Colin Powell)

   b. "The vice presidency is the sand trap of American politics. It's near the prize, and designed to be limiting." (Howard Fineman)

   c. "For too long American leadership has waffled and wiggled and wavered." (Bill Bradley)

   d. "America is not like a blanket—one piece of unbroken cloth, the same color, the same texture, the same size. America is more like a quilt—many patches, many sizes, and woven and held together by a common thread." (Jesse Jackson)

5. Analyze Martin Luther King's "I Have a Dream" (Appendix, pages 450–454). Identify the methods King uses to make his language clear, vivid, and appropriate. Look particularly at King's use of familiar words, concrete words, imagery, and rhythm.

NOTES

[1] For two excellent and highly readable studies of changes in the English language, see Bill Bryson. *The Mother Tongue: English and How It Got That Way* (New York: Morrow, 1990); Kenneth Cmiel, *Democratic Eloquence: The Fight over Popular Speech in Nineteenth-Century America* (New York: Morrow, 1990).

[2] Raymond Gozzi, Jr., *New Words and a Changing American Culture* (Columbia, S.C.: University of South Carolina Press, 1990), p. 97.

[3] Richard Lederer, *The Miracle of Language* (New York: Simon and Schuster, 1991), p. 32.

[4] See, for example, John McCrone, *The Ape That Spoke: Language and the Evolution of the Human Mind* (New York: Morrow, 1991).

[5] James R. Andrews, *A Choice of Worlds: The Practice and Criticism of Public Discourse* (New York: Harper & Row, 1973).

[6] This has been understood for many years by teachers of rhetoric. See the comment of Hugh Blair, in his *Lectures on Rhetoric and Belles Lettres* (London: W. Strahan, 1783), I, 245: "We may rest assured, that whenever we express ourselves ill, there is, besides the mismanagement of language, for the most part, some mistake in conceiving the subject. Embarrassed, obscure, and feeble sentences are generally, if not always, the result of embarrassed, obscure, and feeble thought. Thought and language react upon each other mutually. . . . He that is learning to arrange his sentences with accuracy and order is learning, at the same time, to think with accuracy and order."

[7] Adapted from Clarence M. Kelly, quoted in Robert C. Jeffrey and Owen Peterson, *Speech: A Basic Text,* 3rd ed. (New York: Harper & Row, 1988), pp. 386–387.

[8] Quoted in Edward P. J. Corbett, *Classical Rhetoric for the Modern Student* (New York: Oxford University Press, 1990), p. 418.

[9] Dorothy Sarnoff, *Speech Can Change Your Life* (Garden City, N.Y.: Doubleday, 1970), p. 71.

[10] Annmarie Mungo, "A Child Is Born," *Winning Orations, 1980* (Mankato, Minn: Interstate Oratorical Association, 1980), pp. 49–50.

[11] These numbers are based on the text of the Gettysburg Address in Roy P. Basler (ed.), *The Collected Works of Abraham Lincoln* (New Brunswick, N.J.: Rutgers University Press, 1953), VII, 23.

[12] Adapted from Richard Conniff, "You Never Know What the Fire Ant Is Going to Do Next," *Smithsonian* (July 1990), p. 49.

[13] For the full text of King's speech, see the Appendix, pages 450–454.

[14] Elizabeth Cady Stanton, "The Solitude of Self," in Karlyn Kohrs Campbell (ed.), *Man Cannot Speak for Her: Key Texts of the Early Feminists* (New York: Praeger, 1989), p. 374.

[15] Lawrence Perrine, *Sound and Sense: An Introduction to Poetry,* 8th ed. (Fort Worth, Tex.: Harcourt Brace Jovanovich, 1992), p. 191.

[16] For an interesting discussion of rhythm in speechmaking, see Jerry Tarver, "Words in Time: Some Reflections on the Language of Speech," *Vital Speeches,* 54 (1988), 410–412.

[17] In James Andrews and David Zarefsky (eds.), *American Voices: Significant Speeches in American History, 1640–1945* (New York: Longman, 1989), pp. 44–45.

[18] William Safire, *On Language* (New York: Times Books, 1980), p. xiv.

[19] There are many excellent writings on this subject. A classic work, recently updated, is Casey Miller and Kate Swift, *Words and Women: New Language in New Times* (New York, 1991). For a communication-oriented perspective, see Diana K. Ivy and Phil Backlund, *Exploring GenderSpeak: Personal Effectiveness in Gender Communication* (New York: McGraw-Hill, 1994), pp. 67–102.

[20] Frederick Crews, Sandra Schor, and Michael Hennessy, *The Borzoi Handbook for Writers,* 3rd ed. (New York: McGraw-Hill, 1993), p. 185.

Chapter 12

Delivery

WHAT IS GOOD DELIVERY?

METHODS OF DELIVERY
Reading from a Manuscript
Reciting from Memory
Speaking Impromptu
Speaking Extemporaneously

THE SPEAKER'S VOICE
Volume
Pitch
Rate
Pauses
Vocal Variety
Pronunciation
Articulation
Dialect

NONVERBAL COMMUNICATION
Personal Appearance
Bodily Action
Gestures
Eye Contact

PRACTICING DELIVERY

I f you were to tape-record one of David Letterman's comedy routines, memorize it word for word, and stand up before your friends to recite it, would you get the same response Letterman does? Not very likely. And why not? Because you would not *deliver* the jokes as Letterman does. Of course, the jokes are basically funny. But David Letterman brings something extra to the jokes—his manner of presentation, his vocal inflections, his perfectly timed pauses, his facial expressions, his gestures. All these are part of an expert delivery. It would take you years of practice—as it took Letterman—to duplicate his results.

No one expects your speech class to transform you into a multimillion-dollar talk-show host. Still, this example demonstrates how important delivery can be to any public speaking situation. Even a mediocre speech will be more effective if it is presented well, whereas a wonderfully written speech can be ruined by poor delivery.

This does not mean dazzling delivery will turn a mindless string of nonsense into a triumphant oration. You cannot make a good speech without having something to say. But having something to say is not enough. You must also know *how* to say it.

WHAT IS GOOD DELIVERY?

Wendell Phillips was a leader in the movement to abolish slavery in the United States during the 1800s. Some people considered him the greatest speaker of his time. The following story suggests one reason why:

Shortly before the Civil War an Andover student, learning that Phillips was to lecture in Boston, made a twenty-two mile pilgrimage on foot to hear him. At first the trip seemed hardly worthwhile, for the student discovered that Phillips was not an orator in the grand manner, but spoke in an almost conversational style. He stood on the platform, one hand lightly resting on a table, talked for what seemed to be about twenty minutes, concluded, and sat down. When the student looked at his watch, he found to his astonishment that he had been listening for an hour and a half![1]

Good delivery does not call attention to itself. It conveys the speaker's ideas clearly, interestingly, and without distracting the audience. If you mumble your words, shuffle your feet, gaze out the window, or talk in a monotone, you will not get your message across. Nor will you be effective if you show off, strike a dramatic pose, or shout in ringing tones. Most audiences prefer delivery that combines a certain degree of formality with the best attributes of good conversation—directness, spontaneity, animation, vocal and facial expressiveness, and a lively sense of communication.[2]

When you begin speaking in public, you will probably have many questions about delivery: "Should I be strong and aggressive or low-key?" "Where should I stand?" "How should I gesture?" "How should I handle my notes?"

"How fast should I speak? "When should I pause?" "Where should I look?" "What do I do if I make a mistake?"

There are no hard-and-fast answers to these questions. Speech delivery is an art, not a science. What works for one speaker may fail for another. And what succeeds with today's audience may not with tomorrow's. You cannot become a skilled speaker just by following a set of rules in a textbook. In the long run, there is no substitute for experience. But take heart! A textbook *can* give you basic pointers to get you started in the right direction.

When you plan your first speech (or second or third), you should concentrate on such basics as speaking intelligibly, avoiding distracting mannerisms, and establishing eye contact with your listeners. Once you get these elements under control and begin to feel fairly comfortable in front of an audience, you can work on polishing your delivery to enhance the impact of your ideas. Eventually, you may find yourself able to control the timing, rhythm, and momentum of a speech as skillfully as a conductor controls an orchestra.

■ METHODS OF DELIVERY

There are four basic methods of delivering a speech: (1) reading verbatim from a manuscript; (2) reciting a memorized text; (3) speaking impromptu; and (4) speaking extemporaneously. Let us look at each.

Reading from a Manuscript

Certain speeches *must* be delivered word for word, according to a meticulously prepared manuscript. Examples include a Pope's religious proclamations, an engineer's report to a professional meeting, or a President's message to Congress. In such situations, absolute accuracy is essential. Every word of the speech will be analyzed by the press, by colleagues, perhaps by enemies. In the case of the President, a misstated phrase could cause an international incident.

Timing may also be a factor in manuscript speeches. Much of today's political campaigning is done on radio and television. If the candidate buys a one-minute spot and pays a great deal of money for it, that one minute of speech must be just right.

Although it looks easy, delivering a speech from a manuscript requires great skill. Some people do it well. Their words "come alive as if coined on the spot."[3] Others seem to ruin it every time. Instead of sounding vibrant and conversational, they come across as wooden and artificial. They falter over words, pause in the wrong places, read too quickly or too slowly, speak in a monotone, and march through the speech without even glancing at their audience. In short, they come across as *reading to* their listeners, rather than *talking with* them.

If you are in a situation where you must speak from a manuscript, do your best to avoid these problems. Practice aloud to make sure the speech sounds natural. Work on establishing eye contact with your listeners. Be certain the final manuscript is legible at a glance. Above all, reach out to your audience with the same directness and sincerity that you would if speaking extemporaneously.[4]

Reciting from Memory

Among the feats of the legendary orators, none leaves us more in awe than their practice of presenting even the longest and most complex speeches entirely from memory. Nowadays it is no longer customary to memorize any but the shortest of speeches—toasts, congratulatory remarks, acceptance speeches, introductions, and the like. If you are giving a speech of this kind and want to memorize it, by all means do so. However, be sure to memorize it so thoroughly that you will be able to concentrate on communicating with the audience, not on trying to remember the words. Speakers who gaze at the ceiling or stare out the window trying to recall what they have memorized are no better off than those who read dully from a manuscript.

Speaking Impromptu

An impromptu speech is delivered without any immediate preparation whatever. Few people choose to speak impromptu, but sometimes it cannot be avoided. In fact, many of the speeches you give in life will be impromptu. You might be called on suddenly to "say a few words" or, in the course of a class discussion, business meeting, or committee report, want to respond to a previous speaker.[5]

When such situations arise, don't panic. No one expects you to deliver a perfect speech on the spur of the moment. If you are in a meeting or discussion, pay close attention to what the other speakers say. Take notes of major points with which you agree or disagree. In the process, you will automatically begin to formulate what you will say when it is your turn to speak.

Whenever you are responding to a previous speaker, try to present your speech in four simple steps: First, state the point you are answering. Second, state the point you wish to make. Third, support your point with appropriate statistics, examples, or testimony. Fourth, summarize your point. This four-step method will help you organize your thoughts quickly and clearly.

If time allows, sketch a quick outline of your remarks on a piece of paper before you rise to speak. Use the same method of jotting down key words and phrases followed in a more formal speaking outline (see Chapter 10). This will help you remember what you want to say and will keep you from rambling.

In many cases, you will be able to speak informally without rising from your chair. But if the situation calls for you to speak from a lectern, walk to it calmly, take a deep breath or two (not a visible gasp), establish eye contact with your audience, and begin speaking. No matter how nervous you are inside, do your best to look calm and assured on the outside.

Once you begin speaking, maintain strong eye contact with the audience. If you are prone to talking rapidly when you are nervous, concentrate on speaking at a slower pace. Help the audience keep track of your ideas with signposts such as "My first point is . . . ; second, we can see that . . . ; in conclusion, I would like to say. . . ." If you have had time to prepare notes, stick to what you have written. By stating your points clearly and concisely, you will come across as organized and confident.

Whether you realize it or not, you have given thousands of impromptu "speeches" in daily conversation—as when you informed a new student how to register for classes, or explained to your boss why you were late for work, or answered questions in a job interview, or tried to persuade your roommate to lend you ten dollars until next week. There is no reason to fall apart when you are asked to speak impromptu in a more formal situation. If you keep cool, organize your thoughts, and limit yourself to a few remarks, you should do just fine.

As with other kinds of public speaking, the best way to become a better impromptu speaker is to practice. If you are assigned an impromptu speech in class, do your best to follow the guidelines discussed here. You can also practice impromptu speaking on your own. Simply choose a topic on which you are already well informed, and give a one- or two-minute impromptu talk on some aspect of that topic. Any topic will do—no matter how serious or frivolous it may be. Nor do you need an audience—you can speak to an empty room. Better yet, you can speak to a tape recorder and play the speech back to see how you sound. The purpose is to gain experience in pulling your ideas together quickly and stating them succinctly. Over the years, many people have found this an effective way to improve their skills of impromptu speaking.

Speaking Extemporaneously

In popular usage, "extemporaneous" means the same as "impromptu." But technically the two are different. Unlike an impromptu speech, which is totally off the cuff, an extemporaneous speech is carefully prepared and practiced in advance. In presenting the speech, the extemporaneous speaker uses only a set of brief notes or a speaking outline to jog the memory (see Chapter 10). The exact wording is chosen at the moment of delivery.

This is not as hard as it sounds. Once you have your outline (or notes) and know what topics you are going to cover and in what order, you can begin to practice the speech. Every time you run through it, the wording will be slightly different. As you practice the speech over and over, the best way to present each part will emerge and stick in your mind.

The extemporaneous method has several advantages. It gives more precise control over thought and language than does impromptu speaking; it of-

Extemporaneous speeches are fully prepared ahead of time, but the exact words are chosen at the moment of delivery. This allows for stronger eye contact and more natural gestures than does reading from a manuscript.

fers greater spontaneity and directness than does speaking from memory or from a full manuscript; and it is adaptable to a wide range of situations. It also encourages the conversational quality audiences look for in speech delivery. "Conversational quality" means that no matter how many times a speech has been rehearsed, it still *sounds* spontaneous to the audience. When you speak extemporaneously—and have prepared properly—you have full control over your ideas, yet you are not tied to a manuscript. You are free to establish strong eye contact, to gesture naturally, and to concentrate on talking *with* the audience rather than declaiming *to* them.

Most experienced speakers prefer the extemporaneous method, and most teachers emphasize it. At the end of this chapter, we'll look at a step-by-step program for practicing your extemporaneous delivery.

THE SPEAKER'S VOICE

What kind of voice do you have? Is it rich and resonant like James Earl Jones's? Soft and alluring like Michelle Pfeiffer's? Thin and nasal like Dana Carvey's? Deep and raspy like Whoopi Goldberg's? Harsh and irritating like Roseanne Arnold's?

Whatever the characteristics of your voice, you can be sure it is unique. Because no two people are exactly the same physically, no two people have identical voices. This is why voiceprints are sometimes used in criminal trials as guides to personal identity. The human voice is produced by a complex series of steps that starts with the exhalation of air from the lungs. (Try talking intelligibly while inhaling and see what happens.) As air is exhaled, it passes through the larynx (or voice box), where it is vibrated to generate sound. This sound is then amplified and modified as it resonates through the throat, mouth, and nasal passages. Finally, the resonated sound is shaped into specific vowel and consonant sounds by the movement of the tongue, lips, teeth, and roof of the mouth. The resulting sounds are combined to form words and sentences.

The voice produced by this physical process will greatly affect the success of your speeches. A golden voice is certainly an asset, but you can manage without. Some of the most famous speakers in history had undistinguished voices. Abraham Lincoln had a harsh and penetrating voice; Winston Churchill suffered from a slight lisp and an awkward stammer; Will Rogers spoke with a nasal twang. Like them, you can overcome natural disadvantages and use your voice to the best effect. If you speak too softly to be heard, constantly stumble over words, spit out your ideas at machine-gun speed, or plod along as if you were reading a grocery list, your speeches will fail. Lincoln, Churchill, and Rogers learned to *control* their voices. You can do the same thing.

The aspects of voice you should work to control are volume, pitch, rate, pauses, variety, pronunciation, articulation, and dialect.

Volume

At one time a powerful voice was all but essential for an orator. Today, electronic amplification allows even the most feeble of speakers to be heard in any setting. But in the classroom you will speak without a microphone. When you do, be sure to adjust your voice to the acoustics of the room, the size of the audience, and the level of background noise. If you speak too loudly, your listeners will think you boorish. If you speak too softly, they will not understand you. Remember that your own voice always sounds louder to you than to a listener. Soon after beginning your speech, glance at the people farthest away from you. If they look puzzled, are leaning forward in their seats, or are otherwise straining to hear, you need to talk louder.

Pitch

Pitch is the highness or lowness of the speaker's voice. The faster sound waves vibrate, the higher their pitch; the slower they vibrate, the lower their pitch. Pitch distinguishes the sound produced by the keys at one end of a piano from that produced by the keys at the other end.

In speech, pitch can affect the meaning of words or sounds. Pitch is what makes the difference between the "Aha!" triumphantly exclaimed by Sherlock Holmes upon discovering a seemingly decisive clue and the "Aha" he mutters when he learns the clue is not decisive after all. If you were to read the preceding sentence aloud, your voice would probably go up in pitch on the first "Aha" and down in pitch on the second.

Changes in pitch are known as *inflections*. They give your voice luster, warmth, and vitality. It is the inflection of your voice that reveals whether you are asking a question or making a statement; whether you are being sincere or sarcastic. Your inflections can also make you sound happy or sad, angry or pleased, dynamic or listless, tense or relaxed, interested or bored.

In ordinary conversation we instinctively use inflections to convey meaning and emotion. People who do not are said to speak in a *monotone*—a trait whose only known benefit is to cure insomnia in one's listeners. Few people speak in an absolute monotone, with no variation whatever in pitch, but many fall into repetitious pitch patterns that are just as hypnotic as a monotone. You can guard against this problem by tape-recording your speeches as you practice them. If all your sentences end on the same inflection—either upward or downward—work on varying your pitch patterns to fit the meaning of your words. As with breaking any other habit, this may seem awkward at first, but it is guaranteed to make you a better speaker.[6]

Rate

Rate refers to the speed at which a person speaks. People in the U.S. usually speak at a rate between 120 and 150 words per minute, but there is no uniform rate for effective speechmaking. Daniel Webster spoke at roughly 90 words per minute, Franklin Roosevelt at 110, John Kennedy at 180. Martin Luther King opened his "I Have a Dream" speech at a pace of 92 words per minute and finished it at 145. The best rate of speech depends on several things—the vocal attributes of the speaker, the mood he or she is trying to create, the composition of the audience, and the nature of the occasion.

For example, if you wanted to convey the excitement of the Indianapolis 500 car race, you would probably speak rather quickly, but a slower rate would be more appropriate to describe the serenity of the Alaskan wilderness. A fast rate helps to create feelings of happiness, fear, anger, and surprise, while a slow rate is better for expressing sadness or disgust. A slower tempo is called for when you explain complex information, a faster tempo when the information is already familiar to the audience. Finally, research suggests that in most situations listeners will find a speaker with a somewhat faster rate than normal to be more competent and more persuasive than a speaker with a slower rate.[7]

Two obvious faults to avoid are speaking so slowly that your listeners get bored or so quickly that they lose track of your ideas. Novice speakers are particularly prone to racing through their speeches at a frantic rate. Fortunately, once a speaker begins to work on it, this is usually an easy habit to break, as is the less common one of crawling through one's speech at a snail's pace.

The key in both cases is becoming aware of the problem and concentrating on solving it. Use a tape recorder to check how fast you speak. Pay special attention to rate when practicing your speech. Finally, be sure to include reminders about delivery on your speaking outline, so you won't forget to make the adjustments when you give your speech in class.

Pauses

Learning when and how to pause is a major challenge for most beginning speakers. Even a moment of silence can seem like an eternity. As you gain more poise and confidence, however, you will discover how useful the pause can be. It can signal the end of a thought unit, give an idea time to sink in, and lend dramatic impact to a statement. "The right word may be effective," said Mark Twain, "but no word was ever as effective as a rightly timed pause."[8]

As Twain knew, the crucial factor is timing. "For one audience," he cautioned, "the pause will be short, for another a little longer, for another a shade longer still." Looking back on his own career as a speaker, he recalled: "When the pause was right the effect was sure; when the pause was wrong . . . the laughter was only mild, never a crash."[9]

Developing a keen sense of timing is partly a matter of common sense, partly a matter of experience. You will not always get your pauses just right at first, but keep trying. Listen to accomplished speakers to see how they use pauses to modulate the rate and rhythm of their messages. Work on pauses when you practice your speeches.

When you do pause, make sure you pause at the end of thought units and not in the middle. Otherwise, you may distract listeners from your ideas. Most important, do not fill the silence with "uh," "er," or "um." These *vocalized pauses,* as they are called, are always annoying, and they can be devastating. Not only do they create negative perceptions about a speaker's intelligence, but they often make a speaker appear deceptive.[10]

Vocal Variety

Just as variety is the spice of life, so is it the spice of public speaking. A flat, listless, unchanging voice is just as deadly to speechmaking as a flat, listless, unchanging routine is to daily life.

Try reading this limerick aloud:

> I sat next to the Duchess at tea.
> It was just as I feared it would be:
>> Her rumblings abdominal
>> Were simply abominable
> And everyone thought it was me!

Now recite this passage from James Joyce's "All Day I Hear the Noise of Waters":

> The grey winds, the cold winds are blowing
>> Where I go.
> I hear the noise of many waters
>> Far below.
> All day, all night, I hear them flowing
>> To and fro.[11]

Certainly you did not utter both passages the same way. You instinctively varied the rate, pitch, volume, and pauses to distinguish the light-hearted limerick from the solemn melancholy of Joyce's poem. When a giving a speech, you should modulate your voice in just this way to communicate your ideas and feelings.

How can you develop a lively, expressive voice? Above all, by approaching every speech as an opportunity to share with your listeners ideas that are important to you. Your sense of conviction and your desire to communicate will help give your voice the same spark it has in spontaneous conversation.

Diagnose your present speaking voice to decide which aspects need improvement. Tape-record your speeches to hear how they sound. Try them out on members of your family, a friend, or a roommate. Check with your teacher for suggestions. Practice the vocal variety exercise at the end of this chapter. Vocal variety is a natural feature of ordinary conversation. There is no reason why it should not be as natural a feature of your speeches.[12]

Pronunciation

We all mispronounce words now and again. Here, for example, are six words with which you are probably familiar. Say each one aloud:

genuine	err
arctic	nuclear
theater	February

Very likely you made a mistake on at least one, for they are among the most frequently mispronounced words in the English language. Let's see:

WORD	COMMON ERROR	CORRECT PRONUNCIATION
genuine	gen-u-wine	gen-u-win
arctic	ar-tic	arc-tic
theater	thee-até-er	theé-a-ter
err	air	ur
nuclear	nu-cu-lar	nu-cle-ar
February	Feb-u-ary	Feb-ru-ary

Every word leads a triple life: it is read, written, and spoken. Most people recognize and understand many more words in reading than they use in ordinary writing, and about three times as many as occur in spontaneous speech.[13] This is why we occasionally stumble when speaking words that are part of our reading or writing vocabularies. At other times, we may mispronounce the most commonplace words out of habit.

The problem is that we usually don't *know* when we are mispronouncing a word; otherwise we would say it correctly. If we are lucky, we learn the right pronunciation by hearing someone else say the word properly or by having someone gently correct us in private. If we are unlucky, we mispronounce the word in front of a roomful of people, who may raise their eyebrows, groan, or laugh. Even experienced speakers sometimes fall into this trap. In reporting about a recent presidential election, a local TV news anchor referred several times to the number of votes needed to capture a majority in the e-lec-tor-e-al college. When he had finished, his coanchor said (on the air!), "And it also takes 270 votes to win a majority in the e-lec-tor-al college." The first announcer tried to shrug it off, but he was noticeably embarrassed.

All of this argues for practicing your speech in front of as many trusted friends and relatives as you can corner. If you have any doubts about the proper pronunciation of certain words, be sure to check a dictionary.

Articulation

Articulation and pronunciation are not identical. Sloppy articulation is the failure to form particular speech sounds crisply and distinctly. It is one of several causes of mispronunciation; but not all errors in pronunciation stem from poor articulation.[14] You can articulate a word sharply and still mispronounce it. For example, if you say the "s" in "Illinois" or the "p" in "pneumonia," you are making a mistake in pronunciation, regardless of how precisely you articulate the sounds.

Errors in articulation can be caused by a cleft palate, by an overly large tongue, by a misaligned jaw, even by a poorly fitted dental plate or braces on the teeth. Serious problems require the aid of a certified speech therapist. But most of the time poor articulation is caused by laziness—by failing to manipulate the lips, tongue, jaw, and soft palate so as to produce speech sounds clearly and precisely. Whether or not people in the U.S. have "the worst articulation in the Western world,"[15] as one scholar claims, many of us are unquestionably sloppy speakers. We habitually chop, slur, and mumble our words, rather than enunciating them plainly.

Among college students, poor articulation is more common than ignorance of correct pronunciation. We know that "let me" is not "lemme," that "going to" is not "gonna," that "did you" is not "didja," yet we persist in articulating these words improperly. Here are some other common errors in articulation you should work to avoid:

WORD	MISARTICULATION
ought to	otta
didn't	dint
for	fur
don't know	dunno

have to	hafta
them	em
want to	wanna
will you	wilya

If you have sloppy articulation, work on identifying and eliminating your most common errors. Practice the articulation exercise at the end of this chapter. Like other bad habits, careless articulation can be broken only by persistent effort—but the results are well worth it. Not only will your speeches be more intelligible, but employers will be more likely to hire you, to place you in positions of responsibility, and to promote you. As Shakespeare advised, "Mend your speech a little, lest it may mar your fortunes."

Dialect

Most languages have dialects, each with a distinctive accent, grammar, and vocabulary. Dialects are usually based on regional or ethnic speech patterns. The United States has four major regional dialects—Eastern, New England, Southern, and General American. These dialects affect the way people talk in different parts of the country. In New York people may get "idears" about "dee-ah" friends. In Alabama parents tell their children to stop "squinching" their eyes while watching television and to go clean up their rooms "rat" now. In Utah people praise the "lard" and put the "lord" in the refrigerator.[16]

There are also a number of well-established ethnic dialects in the United States, including Black English, Jewish English, Hispanic English, and Cajun English.[17] In recent years we have also seen the emergence of newer dialects such as Haitian English and Cuban English. As the United States becomes more diverse culturally, it is also becoming more diverse linguistically.

Over the years linguists have done a great deal of research on dialects. They have concluded that no dialect is inherently better or worse than another. There is no such thing as a right or wrong dialect. Dialects are not linguistic badges of superiority or inferiority. They are usually shaped by our regional or ethnic background, and every dialect is "right" for the community of people who use it.

When is dialect appropriate in public speaking? The answer depends above all on the composition of your audience. Heavy use of any dialect—regional or ethnic—can be troublesome for a speaker when the audience does not share that dialect. In such a situation, the dialect may cause listeners to make negative judgments about the speaker's personality, intelligence, and competence.[18] This is why professional speakers have been known to invest large amounts of time (and money) to master the General American dialect used by most television news broadcasters. This dialect has become so widely accepted throughout the United States that it is suitable for almost any audience.

Does this mean you must talk like a television news broadcaster if you want to be successful in your speeches? Not at all. Regional or ethnic dialects do not pose a problem as long as the audience is familiar with them and finds them appropriate to the occasion. When speaking in the North, for example, a southern politician will probably avoid heavy use of regional dialect. But when addressing audiences in the South, the same politician may intentionally include regional dialect as a way of creating common ground with his or her listeners.

Although not strictly speaking a matter of dialect, the proficiency of non-native speakers of English often arises in the speech classroom. Fortunately, teachers and students alike usually go out of their way to be helpful and encouraging with international students and others for whom English is not the primary language. Over the years many non-native speakers of English have found speech class a supportive environment in which to improve their proficiency in spoken English.

Sometimes a speaker may be able to overcome a lower proficiency level by discussing it in her or his speech. Consider the experience of Myung Yi, an international student from Hong Kong. In a speech on human rights abuses in China, a subject about which she felt deeply, Myung included the following statement as part of her introduction:

I know my English is not yet perfect. I know at times it may be hard for some of you to understand me. But I ask you to listen carefully because my message is important. We may speak different languages, but we should all be concerned about the violations of democracy and human rights by the Chinese government.

By dealing head-on with the rough edges in her spoken English, Myung turned a potential barrier to communication into a positive factor that enhanced her credibility and generated sympathy for her position.[19]

NONVERBAL COMMUNICATION

Imagine you are at a party. During the evening you form impressions about the people around you. Tyrone seems relaxed and even-tempered, Nicole tense and irritable. Jolanda seems open and straightforward, Amy hostile and evasive. Amin seems happy to see you; Seth definitely is not.

How do you reach these conclusions? To a surprising extent, you reach them not on the basis of what people say with words, but because of what they say *nonverbally*—with their posture, gestures, eyes, and facial expressions. Suppose you are sitting next to Amin, and he says, "This is a great party. I'm really glad to be here with you." However, his body is turned slightly away from you, and he keeps looking at someone across the room. Despite what he says, you know he is *not* glad to be there with you.

Much the same thing happens in speechmaking. Here is the story of one student's first two classroom speeches and the effect created by his nonverbal actions on each occasion:

> Sean O'Connor's first speech did not go very well. Even though he had chosen an interesting topic, researched the speech with care, and practiced it faithfully, he did not take into account the importance of nonverbal communication. When the time came for him to speak, a stricken look crossed his face. He got up from his chair like a condemned man and plodded to the lectern as though going to the guillotine. His vocal delivery was good enough, but all the while his hands were living a life of their own. They fidgeted with his notes, played with the buttons of his shirt, and drummed on the lectern. Throughout the speech Sean kept his head down, and he looked at his watch repeatedly. Regardless of what his *words* were saying, his *body* was saying, "I don't want to be here!"
>
> Finally it was over. Sean rushed to his seat and collapsed into it, looking enormously relieved. Needless to say, his speech was not a great success.
>
> Fortunately, when Sean's problem with nonverbal communication was pointed out to him, he worked hard to correct it. His next speech was quite a different story. This time he got up from his chair and strode to the lectern confidently. He kept his hands under control and concentrated on making eye contact with his listeners. This was truly an achievement, because Sean was just as nervous as the first time. However, he found that the more he made himself *look* confident, the more confident he became. After the speech his classmates were enthusiastic. "Great speech," they said. "You really seemed to care about the subject, and you brought this caring to the audience."
>
> In fact, the wording of Sean's second speech wasn't much better than that of the first. It was his nonverbal signals that made all the difference. From the time he left his seat until he returned, his actions said, "I am confident and in control of the situation. I have something worthwhile to say, and I want you to think so too."

Posture, facial expression, gestures, eye contact—all affect the way listeners respond to a speaker. How we use these and other body motions to communicate is the subject of a fascinating area of study called kinesics. One of its founders, Ray Birdwhistell, estimates that more than 700,000 possible physical signals can be sent through bodily movement.[20] Studies have shown that in some situations these signals account for much of the meaning communicated by speakers. Research has also confirmed what the Greek historian Herodotus observed more than 2,400 years ago: "People trust their ears less than their eyes." When a speaker's body language is inconsistent with his or her words, listeners tend to believe the body language rather than the words.[21]

Here are the major aspects of nonverbal communication that will affect the outcome of your speeches.

Personal Appearance

If you were Madonna, you could show up to make an Academy Award presentation speech wearing a bizarre creation that left little to the imagination.

If you were Albert Einstein, you could show up to address an international science conference wearing wrinkled trousers, a sweater, and tennis shoes. While the members of your audience would certainly comment on your attire, your reputation would not be harmed. In fact, it might be enhanced. You would be one of the few, the very few, who live outside the rules, who are expected to be unusual.

Now imagine what would happen if the president of a corporation showed up to address a stockholders' meeting attired like Madonna, or if the President of the United States spoke on national television wearing wrinkled clothes and tennis shoes. Both presidents would soon be looking for work. Barring the occasional eccentric, every speaker is expected by her or his audience to exhibit a personal appearance in keeping with the occasion of the speech.

The President of the United States can be photographed in golfing clothes or hiking clothes for a quick weekend interview at Camp David, but that same president will don a conservative suit and tie to address a joint session of Congress. Similarly, a business executive speaking at a winter sales conference in Acapulco would probably wear slacks and a casual shirt or blouse because a business suit, in this atmosphere, would seem much too formal. But back home in San Francisco, Chicago, or New York, the same executive will be immaculately dressed in a well-tailored suit.

A number of studies have confirmed that personal appearance plays an important role in speechmaking.[22] Listeners always see you before they hear you. Just as you adapt your language to the audience and the occasion, so should you dress and groom appropriately. Although the force of your speech can sometimes overcome a poor impression created by personal appearance, the odds are against it. (In a survey of top business executives, 84 percent revealed that their companies do not hire people who appear at job interviews improperly attired.)[23] Regardless of the speaking situation, you should try to evoke a favorable first impression—an impression that is likely to make listeners more receptive to what you say.

Bodily Action

Novice speakers are often unsure about what to do with their bodies while giving a speech. Some pace nonstop back and forth across the podium, fearing that if they stop, they will forget everything. Others are perpetual-motion machines, constantly shifting their weight from one foot to the other, bobbing their shoulders, fidgeting with their notes, or jingling coins in their pockets. Still others turn into statues, standing rigid and expressionless from beginning to end.

Such quirks usually stem from nervousness. If you are prone to distracting mannerisms, your teacher will identify them so you can work on controlling them in later speeches. With a little concentration, these mannerisms should disappear as you become more comfortable speaking in front of an audience.

As important as how you act during the speech is what you do just *before* you begin and *after* you finish. As you rise to speak, try to appear calm, poised, and confident, despite the butterflies in your stomach. When you reach the lectern, don't lean on it, and don't rush into your speech. Give yourself time to get set. Arrange your notes just the way you want them. Stand quietly as you wait to make sure the audience is paying attention. Establish eye contact with your listeners. Then—and only then—should you start to talk.

When you reach the end of your speech, maintain eye contact for a few moments after you stop talking. This will give your closing line time to sink in. Unless you are staying at the lectern to answer questions, collect your notes and return to your seat. As you do so, maintain your cool, collected demeanor. Whatever you do, don't start to gather your notes before you have finished talking; and don't cap off your speech with a huge sigh of relief or some remark like "Whew! Am I glad that's over!"

All of this advice is common sense; yet you would be surprised how many people need it. When practicing your speeches, spend a little time rehearsing how you will behave at the beginning and at the end. It is probably one of the easiest—and one of the most effective—things you can do to improve your image with an audience.

Gestures

Few aspects of delivery seem to cause students more anguish than deciding what to do with their hands. "Should I clasp them behind my back? Let them hang at my sides? Put them in my pockets? Rest them on the lectern? And what about gesturing? When should I do that—and how?" Even people who normally use their hands expressively in everyday conversation seem to regard them as awkward appendages when speaking before an audience.

Over the years, more nonsense has been written about gesturing than about any other aspect of speech delivery. Adroit gestures *can* add to the impact of a speech; but there is nothing to the popular notion that public speakers must have a vast repertoire of graceful gestures. Some accomplished speakers gesture frequently; others hardly at all. The primary rule is this: Whatever gestures you make should not draw attention to themselves and distract from your message. They should *appear* natural and spontaneous, help to clarify or reinforce your ideas, and be suited to the audience and occasion.

At this stage of your speaking career, you have many more important things to concentrate on than how to gesture. Gesturing tends to work itself out as you acquire experience and confidence. In the meantime, make sure your hands do not upstage your ideas. Avoid flailing them about, wringing them together, cracking your knuckles, or toying with your rings. Once you have eliminated these distractions, forget about your hands. Think about communicating with your listeners, and your gestures will probably take care of themselves—just as they do in conversation.[24]

Eye Contact

The eyeball itself expresses no emotion. Yet by manipulating the eyeball and the areas of the face around it—especially the upper eyelids and the eyebrow—we are able to convey an intricate array of nonverbal messages. So revealing are these messages that we think of the eyes as "the windows of the soul." We look to them to help gauge the truthfulness, intelligence, attitudes, and feelings of a speaker.

Like many aspects of communication, eye contact is influenced by cultural background. When engaged in conversation, Arabs, Latin Americans, and Southern Europeans tend to look directly at the person with whom they are talking. People from Asian countries and parts of Africa tend to engage in less eye contact. In Kenya a discussion between a woman and her son-in-law may well be conducted with each person turning her or his back to the other![25]

When it comes to public speaking, there appears to be fairly wide agreement across cultures on the importance of some degree of eye contact. In most circumstances, one of the quickest ways to establish a communicative bond with your listeners is to look at them personally and pleasantly. Avoiding their gaze is one of the surest ways to lose them. There is a great deal of research to show that speakers in the United States who refuse to establish eye contact are perceived as tentative or ill at ease and may be seen as insincere or dishonest.[26] It is no wonder, then, that teachers urge students to look at the audience 80 to 90 percent of the time they are talking.

You may find this disconcerting at first. But after one or two speeches, you should be able to meet the gaze of your audience fairly comfortably. As

In most situations, establishing a strong sense of eye contact is an excellent way to enhance the communicative bond between a speaker and the audience.

you look at your listeners, be alert for their reactions. Can they hear you? Do they understand you? Are they awake? Your eyes will help you answer these questions.

It isn't enough just to look at your listeners; *how* you look at them also counts. A blank stare is almost as bad as no eye contact at all. So is a fierce, hostile glower or a series of frightened, bewildered glances. Also beware of the tendency to gaze intently at one part of the audience while ignoring the rest. In speech class some students look only at the section of the room where the teacher is sitting. Others avoid looking anywhere near the teacher and focus on one or two sympathetic friends. You should try to establish eye contact with your whole audience.

When addressing a small group (such as your class), you can usually look briefly from one person to another. For a larger group, you will probably scan the audience rather than trying to engage the eyes of each person individually. No matter what the size of your audience, you want your eyes to convey confidence, sincerity, and conviction. They should say, "I am pleased to be able to talk with you. I believe deeply in what I am saying, and I want you to believe in it too."[27]

PRACTICING DELIVERY

Popular wisdom promises that practice makes perfect. This is true, but only if we practice properly. No matter how long and hard you practice playing the piano, you will never make beautiful music if you don't know the difference between a sharp and a flat. By the same token, you will do little to improve your speech delivery unless you practice the right things in the right ways. Here is a five-step method that has worked well for many students:

1. Go through your preparation outline *aloud* to check how what you have written translates into spoken discourse. Is it too long? Too short? Are the main points clear when you speak them? Are the supporting materials distinct, convincing, interesting? Do the introduction and conclusion come across well? As you answer these questions, revise the speech as needed.

2. Prepare your speaking outline. In doing so, be sure to follow the guidelines discussed in Chapter 10. Use the same visual framework as in the preparation outline. Make sure the speaking outline is easy to read at a glance. Keep the outline as brief as possible. Give yourself cues on the outline for delivering the speech.

3. Practice the speech aloud several times using only the speaking outline. Be sure to "talk through" all examples and to recite in full all quotations and statistics. If your speech includes visual aids, use them as you practice. The first couple of times you will probably forget something or make a mistake, but don't worry about that. Keep going and complete the speech as well as you can. Concentrate on gaining control of the *ideas;* don't try to learn the speech word for word. After a few tries you should be able to get through the speech extemporaneously with surprising ease.

4. Now begin to polish and refine your delivery. Practice the speech in front of a mirror to check for eye contact and distracting mannerisms. Tape-record the speech to gauge volume, pitch, rate, pauses, and vocal variety. Most important, try it out on friends, roommates, family members—anyone who will listen and give you an honest appraisal. Don't be shy about asking. Most people love to give their opinion about something. Since your speech is designed for people rather than for mirrors or tape recorders, you need to find out ahead of time how it goes over with people.

5. Finally, give your speech a dress rehearsal under conditions as close as possible to those you will face in class. Some students like to try the speech a couple of times in an empty classroom the day before the speech is due. No matter where you hold your last practice session, you should leave it feeling confident and looking forward to speaking in your class.

If this or any practice method is to work, you must start early. Don't wait until the day of your speech, or even the night before, to begin working on delivery. A single practice session—no matter how long—is rarely enough. Allow yourself *at least* a couple of days, preferably more, to gain command of the speech and its presentation. No matter how brilliant your preparation outline, what counts is how the speech comes across when you deliver it. Give yourself plenty of time to make sure it comes across well.

SUMMARY

The impact of a speech is strongly affected by how the speech is delivered. You cannot make a good speech without having something to say. But having something to say is not enough. You must also know *how* to say it.

Good delivery does not call attention to itself. It conveys the speaker's ideas clearly, interestingly, and without distracting the audience. In your earliest speeches you should concentrate on speaking intelligibly, avoiding distracting mannerisms, and establishing eye contact with your listeners. Once you get these elements under control, you can work on refining your delivery so it adds to the impact of your ideas.

There are four basic methods of delivering a speech: reading verbatim from a manuscript, reciting a memorized text, speaking impromptu, and speaking extemporaneously. The last of these—speaking extemporaneously—is the method you probably will use for classroom speeches and for most speeches outside the classroom. When speaking extemporaneously, you will have only a brief set of notes or a speaking outline. You will choose the exact wording of your speech at the moment of delivery.

A primary factor in delivery is the speaker's voice. In using your voice effectively you should work to control your volume, pitch, rate, pauses, vocal variety, pronunciation, articulation, and dialect. Volume is the relative loudness of your voice, and pitch is the relative highness or lowness. Rate refers to the speed at which you talk. Pauses, when carefully timed, can add great impact to your speech, but you should avoid vocalized pauses ("er," "um," and the like). Vocal variety refers to changes in volume, pitch, rate, and pauses, and is crucial to making your voice lively and animated. Most of us speak casually in everyday conversation, but for public speaking you should be sure to pronounce words correctly and to articulate them distinctly. You should also avoid heavy use of dialect in situations where the audience does not share the dialect or will find it inappropriate to the occasion.

Nonverbal communication is another vital factor in delivery. Posture, personal appearance, facial expression, bodily movement, gestures, and eye contact all affect the way listeners respond to speakers. You can do little to change your face or body, but you can dress and groom appropriately for the situation at hand. You can also learn to control gestures and bodily movements so they enhance your message, rather than distract from it. Making eye contact with listeners is the quickest way to establish a communicative bond with them.

You should practice all these aspects of delivery along with the words of your speech. Start your practice sessions early, so you will have plenty of time to gain command of the speech and its presentation.

REVIEW QUESTIONS

After reading this chapter, you should be able to answer the following questions:

1. What is good speech delivery? Why is good delivery important to successful speaking?

2. What are the four methods of speech delivery?

3. Why is every person's voice unique?

4. What are the eight aspects of voice usage you should concentrate on in your speeches?

5. Why is nonverbal communication important to a public speaker?

6. What are the four aspects of nonverbal communication you should concentrate on in your speeches?

7. What are the five steps you should follow in practicing your speech delivery?

APPLICATION EXERCISES

1. Radio and television announcers must have outstanding articulation. One way they develop it is by practicing tongue twisters. Try these. Start by say-

ing them slowly and firmly so that each sound is clearly formed. Gradually increase to your normal rate of speech.

a. Which wily wizard wished wicked wishes for Willy?

b. The sixth sick Sheik's sheep is sick.

c. Fetch me the finest french-fried freshest fish that Finney fries.

d. Shy Sarah saw six Swiss wrist watches.

e. One year we had a Christmas brunch with Merry Christmas mush to munch. But I don't think you'd care for such. We didn't like to munch mush much.

2. An excellent way to improve your vocal variety is to read aloud selections from poetry that require emphasis and feeling. Choose one of your favorite poems that falls into this category, or else find one by leafing through a poetry anthology. Practice reading the selection aloud. As you read, use your voice to make the poem come alive. Vary your volume, rate, and pitch. Find the appropriate places for pauses. Underline the key words or phrases you think should be stressed. Modulate your tone of voice; use inflections for emphasis and meaning.

     For this to work, you must overcome your fear of sounding affected or "dramatic." Most beginning speakers do better if they exaggerate changes in volume, rate, pitch, and expression. This will make you more aware of the many ways you can use your voice to express a wide range of moods and meanings. Besides, what sounds overly "dramatic" to you usually does not sound that way to an audience. By adding luster, warmth, and enthusiasm to your voice, you will go a long way toward capturing and keeping the interest of your listeners.

     If possible, practice reading the selection into a tape recorder. Listen to the playback. If you are not satisfied with what you hear, practice the selection some more and record it again.

3. Watch a ten-minute segment of a television drama with the sound turned off. What do the characters say with their dress, gestures, facial expressions, and the like? Do the same with a television comedy. How do the nonverbal messages in the two shows differ? Be prepared to report your observations in class.

4. Attend a speech on campus. You may choose either a presentation by a guest speaker from outside the college or a class session by a professor who has a reputation as a good lecturer. Prepare a brief report on the speaker's vocal and nonverbal communication.

     In your report, first analyze the speaker's volume, pitch, rate, pauses, vocal variety, pronunciation, and articulation. Then evaluate the speaker's personal appearance, bodily action, gestures, and eye contact. Explain how the speaker's delivery added to or detracted from what the speaker said. Finally, note at least two techniques of delivery used by the speaker that you might want to try in your next speech.

NOTES

[1] Irving Bartlett, *Wendell Phillips: Boston Brahmin* (Boston: Beacon Press, 1961), p. 192.

[2] See, for example, Valerie Manusov, "Perceiving Nonverbal Messages: Effects of Immediacy and Encoded Intent on Receiver Judgments," *Western Journal of Speech Communication,* 55 (1991), 235–253; Miles L. Patterson, Mary E. Churchill, Gary K. Burger, and Jack L. Powell, "Verbal and Nonverbal Modality Effects on Impressions of Political Candidates: Analysis from the 1984 Presidential Debates," *Communication Monographs,* 59 (1992), 231–242.

[3] A. Craig Baird, *Rhetoric: A Philosophical Inquiry* (New York: Ronald Press, 1965), p. 207.

[4] Two excellent guides to speaking from a manuscript are James C. Humes, *Talk Your Way to the Top* (New York: McGraw-Hill, 1980), pp. 125–135; Jack Valenti, *Speak Up with Confidence: How to Prepare, Learn, and Deliver Effective Speeches* (New York: Morrow, 1982), pp. 23–36.

[5] In a recent survey, alumni at five colleges and universities ranked impromptu speaking to be the most important mode of speech delivery in business situations. See John R. Johnson and Nancy Szczupakiewicz, "The Public Speaking Course: Is It Preparing Students with Work-Related Skills?" *Communication Education,* 36 (1987), 131–137.

[6] For research on the tie between effective pitch patterns and successful speaking, see David B. Buller and Judee K. Burgoon, "The Effects of Vocalics and Nonverbal Sensitivity on Compliance: A Replication and Extension," *Human Communication Research,* 13 (1986), 126–144.

[7] See, for example, David B. Buller, Beth A. LePoire, R. Kelly Aune, and Sylvie V. Eloy, "Social Perceptions as Mediators of the Effect of Speech Rate Similarity on Compliance," *Human Communication Research,* 19 (1992), 286–311.

[8] Mark Twain, *Mark Twain's Speeches* (New York: Harper and Brothers, 1923), p. xv.

[9] Mark Twain, *Autobiography,* ed. Charles Neider (New York: Harper & Row, 1959), pp. 181–182.

[10] This is confirmed by a large number of research studies. For a recent reiteration of the point, see John O. Greene, Tamara L. McDaniel, Kathryn Buksa, and Susan M. Ravizza, "Cognitive Processes in the Production of Multiple-Goal Messages: The Evidence from the Temporal Characteristics of Speech," *Western Journal of Communication,* 57 (1993), 65–86.

[11] James Joyce, "Chamber Music," stanza XXXV, from *The Portable James Joyce,* ed. Harry Levin (New York: Viking, 1946–1947).

[12] For research on the importance of vocal variety to effective speechmaking, see Judee K. Burgoon, Thomas Birk, and Michael Pfau, "Nonverbal Behaviors, Persuasion, and Credibility," *Human Communication Research,* 17 (1990), 140–169.

[13] Dorothy Sarnoff, *Speech Can Change Your Life* (Garden City, N.Y.: Doubleday, 1970), p. 73.

[14] The relationship between articulation and pronunciation is a matter of some dispute among experts and is far from clear in many books. I would like to thank Professor Raymond D. Kent of the Department of Communicative Disorders, University of Wisconsin, Madison, for helping me to sort out the distinctions.

[15] William Norwood Brigance, *Speech: Its Techniques and Disciplines in a Free Society* (New York: Appleton-Century-Crofts, 1961), p. 349.

[16] The most authoritative guide to regional dialects in the United States is Frederic G. Cassidy and Joan H. Hall (eds.), *Dictionary of American Regional English* (Cam-

bridge, Mass.: Harvard University Press). The first two volumes of this work were published in 1985 and 1991, respectively. Three more volumes are in preparation.

[17] See Tom McArthur (ed.), *The Oxford Companion to the English Language* (New York: Oxford University Press, 1992).

[18] For a brief summary of research on this topic, see Mark L. Knapp and Judith A. Hall, *Nonverbal Communication in Human Interaction,* 3rd ed. (Fort Worth, Tex.: Holt, Rinehart and Winston, 1992), pp. 337–339.

[19] For a more detailed guide on how to use your voice effectively, consult Jeffrey C. Hahner, Martin A. Sokoloff, and Sandra L. Salisch, *Speaking Clearly: Improving Voice and Diction,* 4th ed. (New York: McGraw-Hill, 1993).

[20] Ray L. Birdwhistell, *Introduction to Kinesics* (Louisville, Ky.: University of Louisville Press, 1952).

[21] See, for example, James B. Stiff and Gerald R. Miller, "'Come to Think of It . . .': Interrogative Probes, Deceptive Communication, and Deception Detection," *Human Communication Research,* 12 (1986), 339–357.

[22] See Richard M. Perloff, *The Dynamics of Persuasion* (Hillsdale, N.J.: Erlbaum, 1993), pp. 149–152.

[23] John T. Malloy, *Dress for Success* (New York: Warner, 1975), p. 36.

[24] For an excellent recent study of gesture and its role in communication, see Jurgen Streek, "Gesture as Communication I: Its Coordination with Gaze and Speech," *Communication Monographs,* 60 (1993), 275–299.

[25] Knapp and Hall, *Nonverbal Communication,* pp. 310–311.

[26] Judee K. Burgoon, Deborah A. Coker, and Ray A. Coker, "Communicative Effects of Gaze Behavior: A Test of Two Contrasting Explanations," *Human Communication Research,* 12 (1986), 495–524.

[27] For fuller discussion of the various dimensions of nonverbal communication, see Judee K. Burgoon, David B. Buller, and W. Gill Woodall, *Nonverbal Communication: The Unspoken Dialogue* (New York: HarperCollins, 1990); Joseph DeVito and Michael L. Hecht (eds.), *The Nonverbal Communication Reader* (Prospect Heights, Ill.: Waveland, 1990).

Chapter 13

Using Visual Aids

ADVANTAGES OF VISUAL AIDS

KINDS OF VISUAL AIDS
Objects
Models
Photographs
Drawings
Graphs
Charts
Slides and Videotapes
Computer-Generated Graphics
Transparencies
The Speaker

TIPS FOR USING VISUAL AIDS
Avoid Using the Chalkboard for Visual Aids
Prepare Visual Aids in Advance
Make Sure Visual Aids Are Large Enough
Display Visual Aids Where Listeners Can See Them
Avoid Passing Visual Aids Among the Audience
Display Visual Aids Only While Discussing Them
Talk to Your Audience, Not to Your Visual Aid
Explain Visual Aids Clearly and Concisely
Practice with Your Visual Aids

J oan Blake is a nutritionist with Medical Care Affiliates in Boston. An excellent public speaker, she is often hired by corporations to talk with employees about how to improve their health by good eating habits. On this particular day she is speaking to a group in Sudbury, Massachusetts, about reducing the amount of fat in their diets.

To illustrate her point, she pulls out five brightly colored wooden sticks. "If I were to puree fish in a food processor, then pour the mixture into a test tube, this is what it would look like," she says, holding up a stick painted in three colors. "The blue is water, the red is protein, and the yellow—well, watch out for the yellow. That's fat." The "fish stick" she is holding up has a fair amount of red, lots of blue, and only a thin band of yellow.

Blake then holds up a second stick with slightly more yellow. "This is chicken," she says. "See why nutritionists recommend fish and poultry?"

A third stick follows. "Here's lean hamburger," Blake says. "What's happening?" It's obvious that the yellow portion of the stick is much larger than with the sticks representing fish and chicken. "You sure that's lean?" someone asks, aghast.

Blake brandishes another stick, a full third of it yellow. She pauses for effect. "Pork chop." The audience begins to groan, but she cuts them off. "Ready? Here comes steak!"—and she lifts a stick, half yellow. "Oh, my God, say you're kidding," comes the response.[1]

As the old saying tells us, one picture is worth a thousand words. People find a speaker's message more interesting, grasp it more easily, and retain it longer when it is presented visually as well as verbally. Can you picture the amount of fat in chicken, fish, and steak? You could if you had watched Joan Blake use her colored sticks to illustrate those amounts. This dramatic visual evidence brought home Joan's point more forcefully than any recitation of facts and figures could have done. "After they see those colored sticks," Joan says of her listeners, "they think twice about steaks."

ADVANTAGES OF VISUAL AIDS

Visual aids offer several advantages. The primary advantage is *clarity.* If you are discussing an object, you can make your message clearer by showing the object or some representation of it. If you are citing statistics, showing how something works, or demonstrating a technique, a visual aid will make your information more vivid to your audience. After all, we live in a visual age. Television and movies have conditioned us to expect a visual image. By using visual aids in your speeches, you often will make it easier for listeners to understand exactly what you are trying to communicate.

Another advantage of visual aids is *interest.* The interest generated by visual images is so strong that visual aids are now used routinely in many areas, not just speechmaking. A generation or so ago, most college textbooks were rather dry—page after page of words. Today they are enlivened with photographs, drawings, and other visual aids that both clarify the material and make it more interesting. Encyclopedias have blossomed with photographs and maps; even dictionaries contain small drawings to highlight word definitions. You can do the same thing with your speeches.

Still another advantage of visual aids is *retention.* Visual images often stay with us longer than verbal ones. The audience who heard Joan Blake's speech about nutrition may not remember exactly how much fat is in the American diet. But they will probably remember the colored sticks showing the amount of fat in chicken, fish, and steak. And perhaps they will remember those sticks the next time they have to decide what to order in a restaurant or what to buy in a supermarket. We've all heard that words can "go in one ear and out the other." Visual images tend to last.

In fact, when used well, visual aids can enhance almost *every* aspect of a speech. One recent study showed that an average speaker who uses visual aids will come across as better prepared, more credible, and more professional than a dynamic speaker who does not use visual aids. According to the same study, visual aids can increase the persuasiveness of a speech by over 40 percent.[2]

For all these reasons, you will find visual aids of great value in your speeches. In this chapter we shall concentrate primarily on visual aids suitable for classroom speeches. However, the principles outlined here are true for all circumstances. For speeches outside the classroom—in business or community situations, for instance—you may use sophisticated, professionally prepared visual aids such as flip charts, overhead slides, or film clips. In these situations you should have no difficulty applying the general suggestions given here.

Let us look first at the kinds of visual aids you are likely to use, and then at some tips for using them effectively.

KINDS OF VISUAL AIDS

Objects

Tracy Collins is an avid downhill skier. When it came time for her informative speech, she chose as her specific purpose "To inform my audience how to choose the right ski equipment." On the day of her speech, she brought to class a pair of skis, boots, bindings, and ski clothing. It was then easy for her to explain exactly what to look for in each item.

By *showing* her classmates the equipment rather than just telling them about it, Tracy presented her ideas much more effectively than she could have by using words alone. She also made her speech more interesting to nonskiers. As one of her classmates said afterward, "I don't ski, but I found your speech fascinating. Using the skis and other equipment as visual aids really helped get me involved. Now I have a little better idea of what my friends who ski are talking about. Without the visual aids I would have been lost."

As in Tracy's speech, bringing the object of your talk to class can be an excellent way to clarify your ideas and give them dramatic impact. If you talk about guitars, why not bring one to class to show your listeners? If you plan to explain the different kinds of tennis racquets, what could be better than showing a sample of each kind? Or suppose you want to inform your audience about the Japanese art of doll making? You could bring several dolls to class and explain to your classmates how they were made.

In certain situations you might use living objects as visual aids. This worked well for a high-school wrestling coach who returned to college to take a night class in public speaking. Not surprisingly, the coach gave one of his speeches about wrestling. On the night of his speech he brought along two of his high-school students, who demonstrated each of the basic holds as the coach discussed them.

Many objects, however, cannot be used effectively in classroom speeches. Some are too big to be hauled into a classroom. Others are too small to be seen clearly by the audience. Still others may not be available to you. If you were speaking about a rare suit of armor in the local museum, you could, theoretically, transport it to class, but it is most unlikely that the museum would let you borrow it. You would have to look for another kind of visual aid.

Models

If the item you want to discuss is too large, too small, or unavailable, you may be able to work with a model. One kind is a small-scale model of a large object. A speaker used such a model to help explain the events connected with the sinking of the ocean liner *Titanic.* Another speaker brought to class a scaled-down model of a hang glider to demonstrate the equipment and techniques of hang gliding.

Like other kinds of visual aids, models help make a speaker's message clearer, more interesting, and easier to retain.

A second kind of model is a large-scale representation of a small object. Science teachers use such models to help students visualize minuscule structures like molecules. A good example of this type of model came in a speech about watches. Since the workings of a real watch would be too small for everyone to see, the speaker brought a large-scale model showing the interior mechanisms of a Swiss-movement watch.

Finally, models can be life-size. To demonstrate the techniques of cardiopulmonary resuscitation, one speaker borrowed a life-size dummy of a human torso from the Red Cross. Another speaker, an anthropology major, illustrated his speech with a full-scale model of a human skull, to show how archaeologists use bone fragments to reconstruct the forms of early humans.

Photographs

In the absence of an object or a model, you may be able to use photographs. A well-known instance of such use came in speeches at the United Nations in 1990 by refugees from Kuwait after it was invaded by Iraq. They showed dramatic enlargements of photographs smuggled out of Kuwait to prove the brutality and torture inflicted on the populace by Iraqi troops.

Photographs will not work in a speech, however, unless you have access to oversize enlargements. Normal-size photos are not big enough to be seen clearly without being passed around—which only diverts the audience from what you are saying. The same is true of photographs in a book. Even oversize books are too small to be seen clearly by all members of an audience.

How can you get large-scale photos for use in a speech? One student, who had his own darkroom, showed 2- × 3-foot enlargements to demonstrate the differences between professional and amateur photography. A second student used large art posters to illustrate her points in a speech about the famous painter Vincent van Gogh. Yet another speaker used enlargements produced by a color copier to show the spectacular markings of various species of saltwater tropical fish. The enlargements were 18 × 24 inches, and the speaker mounted them on white poster board to make them easier to see.

There is yet another option. Copy services can now convert photographs (or slides) into transparencies that can be used with an overhead projector. The projector enlarges the image and displays it on a screen, where it can be seen clearly even by large audiences. If you have photographs that are essential to your speech, you might want to explore this option. The cost is fairly minimal, and the results can be dramatic.

Drawings

Diagrams, sketches, and other kinds of drawings are superb alternatives to photographs. They are inexpensive to make. Moreover, since they are drawn specifically for one speech, they can be designed to illustrate your points exactly. This more than compensates for what they may lack in realism.

For example, Figure 13.1 is a drawing used by a student in a speech about Navajo sandpainting. The student wanted to show his audience what sandpainting looks like and to explain its symbolism and religious significance. As you can imagine, it would have been almost impossible for him to do so without some kind of visual aid.

FIGURE 13.1

Figure 13.2 shows a drawing used in a speech about the kinds of problems faced by people who suffer from dyslexia. This aid was particularly effective because it allowed the speaker to translate complex ideas into visual terms the audience could grasp almost immediately.

Maps are another kind of drawing that is easy to prepare. You can trace the basic outlines from an atlas and then enlarge the scale to make your visual aid. Figure 13.3 is a map used in a speech about the Central American country of Costa Rica. The map places Costa Rica in relation to its neighbors, Panama

This si wɦat a qerson with dγslexia mihgt ƨe wɦem reding this ƨentnce.

FIGURE 13.2

and Nicaragua, shows the major regions of the country (the Caribbean Low-lands, the Central Highlands, and the Pacific Coastal Strip), and identifies the location of its capital (San José). Each site on the map illustrated a different point in the speech.

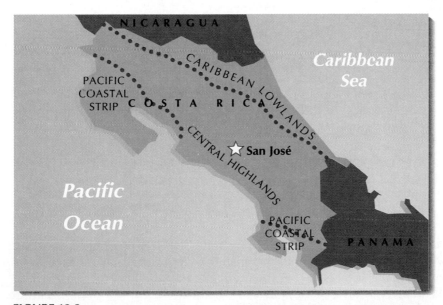

FIGURE 13.3

Graphs

Graphs are a good way to simplify and clarify statistics. Audiences often have trouble grasping a complex series of numbers. You can ease their difficulty by using graphs to show statistical trends and patterns.

The most common type is the *line graph*. Figure 13.4 shows such a graph, used in a speech about the American movie industry. The speaker explained the graph by saying:

As you can see from this graph based on figures in *Newsweek* magazine, the video revolution has had a major impact on the American movie industry. From 1981 to 1994, the percent of movie industry revenues generated by box office receipts declined dramatically—from 61 percent to 22 percent. At the same time, the percent of movie industry revenues generated by videocassettes and films shown on television almost doubled—from 39 percent in 1981 to 78 percent in 1994.

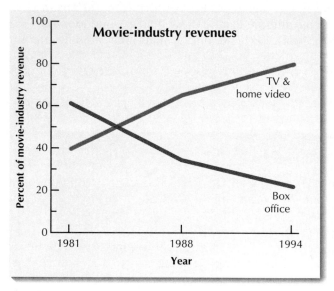

FIGURE 13.4

The *pie graph* is best suited for illustrating simple distribution patterns. You will see such a graph in your newspaper each year to show the division of the national budget. Figure 13.5 shows how one speaker used a pie graph to help listeners visualize changes in marital status among working women in the past century. The graph on the left shows the percent of working women who were single, married, and widowed or divorced in 1890. The graph on the right shows percentages for the same groups in 1990.

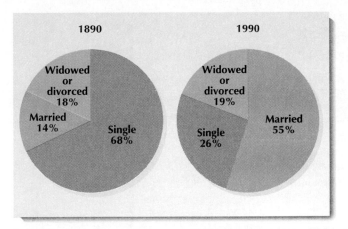

FIGURE 13.5

These pie graphs helped the speaker make three points: (1) The percent of working women who are widowed or divorced has remained relatively stable since 1890; (2) the percent of working women who are single has declined greatly during the past century; (3) the percent of married women has more than tripled, to the point that they are now far and away the largest group of working women in the United States.

Other distributions easily shown by a pie graph might include the proportional breakdown of the world's major religions; the ratio of registered Democrats, Republicans, and Independents; the nutritional constituents of a particular food; or the amount of money spent annually on admission tickets to various professional sports.

Because a pie graph is used to dramatize relationships among the parts of a whole, you should keep the number of different segments in the graph as small as possible. A pie graph should ideally have from two to five segments; under no circumstances should it have more than eight.

The *bar graph* is a particularly good way to show comparisons between two or more items. It also has the advantage of being easy to understand, even by people who have no background in reading graphs. Figure 13.6 (next page) is an example of a bar graph from a speech entitled "The Politics of Race in America." It shows visually the relative standing of whites and blacks with respect to median household income, infant mortality, unemployment, and college education. By using a bar graph, the speaker made her points much more vividly than if she had just cited the numbers orally.

Charts

Charts are particularly useful for summarizing large blocks of information. One student, in a speech about noise pollution, used a chart to summarize the

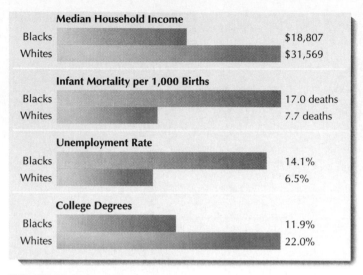

FIGURE 13.6

sound levels of everyday noises and to indicate their potential danger for hearing loss (Figure 13.7). These are too many categories to be presented effectively in a bar graph. By listing them on a chart, the speaker made it much easier for listeners to keep the information straight.

Notice, when you look at the chart, how the speaker used color to emphasize the different levels. He put sounds that are definitely harmful to hearing in red, sounds that may cause hearing loss in blue, and sounds that are loud but safe in green. This reinforced the speaker's ideas and, at the same time, made his chart easier to read.

IMPACT ON HEARING	DECIBEL LEVEL	TYPE OF NOISE
Harmful	140	Firecracker
to	130	Jackhammer
Hearing	120	Jet Engine
Risk	110	Rock Concert
Hearing	100	Chain Saw
Loss	90	Motorcycle
Loud	80	Alarm Clock
but	70	Busy Traffic
Safe	60	Air Conditioner

FIGURE 13.7

EMERGENCY TREATMENT FOR POISONOUS SNAKEBITES

1. TIE A CONSTRICTING BAND 2 TO 4 INCHES ABOVE THE WOUND.

2. CLEAN THE WOUND WITH ALCOHOL.

3. MAKE TWO SHALLOW VERTICAL INCISIONS AT THE PUNCTURE POINTS.

4. DRAW THE VENOM FROM THE WOUND.

5. WASH THE AREA THOROUGHLY WITH SOAP AND WATER.

6. APPLY COLD COMPRESSES.

FIGURE 13.8

Charts are also valuable for presenting the steps of a process. One speaker used several charts in a speech about survival techniques in the wilderness, including one outlining the steps in emergency treatment of snakebites (Figure 13.8).

You can also use charts to present information your audience may want to write down. In a speech about consumer protection organizations, for example, a student might use a chart to let the audience know exactly where to write or phone for consumer services.

Slides and Videotapes

Slides and videotapes can be extremely effective as visual aids. If you are talking about the principles of architecture, what could be better than showing slides of buildings that demonstrate those principles? Or suppose you are explaining the advertising techniques used in television commercials. Your best visual aid would be a videotape with excerpts from various commercials showing those techniques in action. The detail, immediacy, and vividness of slides and videotapes are hard to match. This is why they are found so often in business speeches and other kinds of professional presentations.

When used with care, slides and videotapes can also be employed in classroom speeches. Until a few years ago, the only way to present slides was with a slide projector that required a darkened room and was often difficult to coordinate with a speaker's words. Today slides can be converted into full-color transparencies that can be shown in a lighted room with an overhead projector. This makes it much easier to integrate slides with the rest of a speech. The conversion process is not overly expensive and can be done quickly by most major copy services.

Using videotape in a classroom speech can be complicated. It requires cumbersome equipment, distracts attention from the speaker, and may do more harm than good if used carelessly. If you decide to employ videotape in one of your speeches, practice with the monitor and playback equipment so you can use it flawlessly during the speech. When using a videotape that you have put together from several sources, make sure the editing is clean and expert. As with any other kind of visual aid, videotapes are only effective when they are carefully prepared and skillfully integrated into the speech.

Computer-Generated Graphics

If you own a personal computer or have access to a computer center on campus, you may be able to create computer-generated graphics for your speeches. Depending on the kind of software you use, these graphics can include anything from simple diagrams to sophisticated charts and graphs such as shown in Figure 13.9.

Computer-generated graphics allow you to have dramatic, professional-looking visual aids regardless of your artistic talent. Creating the graphic, however, is only the first step in making it suitable for use in a speech. When used in classroom speeches, computer-generated graphics are usually presented on transparencies that can be shown with an overhead projector.

If you have access to an inkjet or laser printer, you may be able to print your graphic directly on a transparency. If you use a dot matrix printer, you will probably have to print your graphic on a regular sheet of paper. Because this will be too small for your audience to see from a distance, you should take the graphic to a copy service, which will convert it to a transparency. The cost is minimal, and the conversion process works with both color and black-and-white originals.

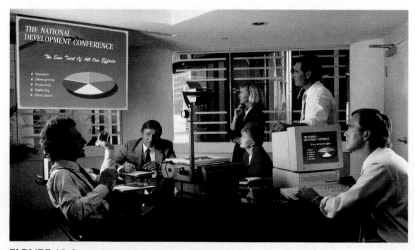

Computer-generated graphics can be used to create striking charts, graphs, and diagrams. As with other types of visual aids, they need to be explained clearly and concisely to be most effective.

FIGURE 13.9

Transparencies

Several times in this chapter we have mentioned the possibility of converting photographs, slides, and computer-generated graphics to transparencies, which can be shown with an overhead projector. You can also use transparencies to present drawings, graphs, and charts. Transparencies are inexpensive, easy to create, and produce a strong visual image. This is why they are one of the most widely used methods of presenting visual aids.

Transparencies are made of clear acetate and are the same size as a regular sheet of paper. You can use them to create visual aids in one of two ways. The first is to draw or write directly on the transparency with a special felt-tipped pen. The second is to take a photograph, drawing, graph, or chart to a copy service, where you can have it copied onto a transparency. This is no more work—and little more expense—than xeroxing from one sheet of paper to another.

Despite their many advantages, transparencies can present pitfalls for the unwary. Unless you are a very experienced speaker, trying to write or draw on a transparency while you are speaking is an almost certain recipe for disaster. Prepare your transparencies well in advance and make sure any writing is large enough to be seen from the back of the room. A good rule of thumb is that all numbers and letters—whether typed or handwritten—should be at least one-quarter inch high (about three times as large as the print on this page).

In addition, check your overhead projector ahead of time to make sure it is working and that you know how to operate it. Better yet, arrange to practice with the projector when you rehearse the speech. This will help ensure that your transparencies are well coordinated with the rest of your presentation.

The Speaker

Sometimes you can use your own body as a visual aid—by showing how to perform sign language for the deaf, by demonstrating the skills of modern dance, by doing magic tricks, and so forth. One student gave an informative speech on the art of mime. Throughout the speech she illustrated her points by performing mime routines. In addition to clarifying her ideas, this kept her classmates deeply engrossed in the speech. Many students have also found that doing some kind of demonstration reduces their nervousness during a speech by providing an outlet for their extra adrenaline.

Doing a demonstration well requires special practice to coordinate your actions with your words and to control the timing of your speech. Be especially cautious when attempting to demonstrate a process that takes longer to complete than the time allocated for your speech. If you plan to show a long process, you might borrow the techniques of television cooks. They work through most of the steps in making a perfect enchilada, but they have a second, finished enchilada ready to show you at the last minute.

TIPS FOR USING VISUAL AIDS

Avoid Using the Chalkboard for Visual Aids

At first thought, using the chalkboard in your classroom to present visual aids seems like a splendid idea. Usually, however, it is not. You have too much to do during a speech to worry about drawing or writing legibly on the board. Many students have marred an otherwise fine speech by turning their backs on the audience to use the chalkboard. Even if your visual aid is put on the chalkboard ahead of time, it seldom is as vivid or as neat as one composed on poster board, on a flip chart, or on a transparency.

There are, however, some speaking situations in which use of the chalkboard is essential. A teacher giving a lecture or a coach explaining a new play will write on the board while speaking. If you ever need to do this, make sure your writing is clear and large enough for all to read.

Prepare Visual Aids in Advance

No matter what visual aids you plan to use, prepare them well ahead of time. This has two advantages. First, it means you can make your visual aid at leisure, while you are not so nervous that you can barely draw a straight line or write legibly. You will have the time and resources to devise a creative, attractive visual aid that will truly enhance your speech. Audiences respond much more favorably to speakers who have obviously put a great deal of thought and effort into their visual aids.

Second, preparing your visual aids well ahead of time means you can use them while practicing your speech. Visual aids are effective only if they are integrated smoothly with the rest of the speech. If you lose your place, drop your aids, or otherwise stumble around when presenting them, you will distract your audience and shatter your concentration. You can avoid such disasters by preparing your visual aids far enough in advance.

Make Sure Visual Aids Are Large Enough

A visual aid is useless if nobody can see it. This is another of those points that would seem so obvious as to need no comment. But as many speakers have discovered, it is one thing to nod your head in agreement and another to prepare a visual aid properly. Beginning speakers in particular tend to use visual aids that are too small.

When you choose or make a visual aid, keep in mind the size of your classroom. Be sure the aid is big enough to be seen easily by everyone in the room. If you make a diagram, a chart, or a graph, guard against the tendency to write and draw too small. You probably will need a piece of poster board at least 2 × 3 feet in size. Use dark ink and an extrawide marker, so that what- ever you write or draw can be seen from the back of the room. Any lettering should be at least 2 to 3 inches tall. As you prepare the aid, check its visibility by getting as far away from it as your most distant listener will be sitting. If you have trouble making out the words or drawings, your audience will too. By making sure your visual aid is large enough, you will avoid having to introduce it with the lame comment, "I know some of you can't see this, but. . . ."

Display Visual Aids Where Listeners Can See Them

Check the classroom ahead of time to decide exactly where you will display your visual aid. Keep in mind that inexpensive poster board is too flimsy to stand by itself in front of a lectern or on the edge of a chalkboard. Unless you use heavyweight poster board or unless your classroom has an easel, you will need to hang your charts, graphs, and drawings in some fashion. Decide in ad- vance what will work best, and on the day of the speech bring your own tape or thumbtacks in case nothing is available in the classroom.

Once you have set up the aid in the best location, don't undo all your preparation by standing where your audience can't see the aid without wrenching their necks. Stand to one side of the aid, and point with the arm nearest it. If possible, use a pencil, a ruler, or some other pointer. This will allow you to stand farther away from the visual aid, thereby reducing the like- lihood that you will obstruct the view of people sitting on the same side of the room as you are standing.

Avoid Passing Visual Aids Among the Audience

Once visual aids get into the hands of your listeners, you are in trouble. At least three people will be paying more attention to the aid than to you—the person who has just had it, the person who has it now, and the person waiting to get it next.[3] By the time the visual aid moves on, all three may have lost track of what you are saying.

Nor do you solve this problem by preparing a handout for every member of the audience. There is no guarantee they will pay attention to it only when you want them to. In fact, they are likely to spend a good part of the speech looking over the handout at their own pace, rather than listening to you. Al- though handouts can be valuable, they usually just create competition for be- ginning speakers.

Every once in a while, of course, you will want listeners to have copies of some material to take home. When such a situation arises, keep the copies until after you've finished talking and can distribute them without creating a distraction. Keeping control of your visual aids is essential to keeping control of your speech.

Display Visual Aids Only While Discussing Them

Just as circulating visual aids distracts attention, so does displaying them throughout a speech. Whenever an aid is visible, at least some people will spend their time looking at it rather than listening to you.

If you are using an object or a model, keep it out of sight until you are ready to discuss it. When you finish your discussion, place the object or model back out of sight. The same is true of charts, graphs, or drawings prepared on poster board. If you are using an easel, put a blank sheet of poster board in front of the sheet with the visual aid. When the time comes, remove the blank sheet to show the aid. When you are finished with the aid, remove it from the easel or cover it back up with a blank piece of poster board so it will not divert the attention of your listeners.

Talk to Your Audience, Not to Your Visual Aid

When explaining a visual aid, it is easy to break eye contact with your audience and speak to the aid. Of course, your listeners are looking primarily at the aid, and you will need to glance at it periodically as you talk. But if you keep your eyes fixed on your visual aid, you may lose your audience. By keeping eye contact with your listeners, you will also pick up feedback about how the visual aid and your explanation of it are coming across.

Explain Visual Aids Clearly and Concisely

Visual aids don't explain themselves. Like statistics, they need to be translated and related to the audience. Figure 13.10, for example, is an excellent diagram, but do you know what it means? You do if you are a photography buff. You will see at once that it shows the different lens openings of a 35-milli-

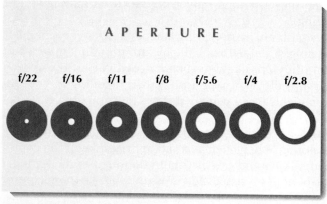

FIGURE 13.10

meter camera. But if you are not versed in photography, you will have no idea what the different numbers and circles mean until they are explained to you.

Beginning speakers often rush over their visual aids without explaining them clearly and concisely. A visual aid can be of enormous benefit—but only if the viewer knows what to look for and why. Be sure to adapt your visual aid to your audience. Don't just say "As you can see . . ." and then pass quickly over the aid. Tell listeners what the aid means. Describe its major features. Spell out the meaning of charts and graphs. Interpret statistics and percentages. Remember, a visual aid is only as useful as the explanation that goes with it.

Practice with Your Visual Aids

Mention has been made several times in this chapter of the need to practice with visual aids, but the point bears repeating. You do not want to suffer through an experience like the one that follows:

This is the story of a young man who was a brilliant designer and a good inventor, but who failed to realize that to complete his work he had to be able to explain it and to convince his supervisors that his invention was a worthwhile investment.

He had designed a machine that used several new and patentable ideas. The stage was set for him not only to show off his invention but to show himself to the managers, who would help him shape his ideas and give him additional opportunities. This was the part of the test he flunked.

He knew who his audience would be. He had been told to compose his talk thoughtfully, to prepare slides and other visual aids, and to practice in the conference room, using its rather complex lectern and public address system. At the lectern he could control the lights, show his slides in any sequence he chose, and have his choice of microphones and other visual and speaking aids.

Unfortunately, although he had done a brilliant job on the engineering project, he neglected to plan his presentation with similar care. His worst mistake was not practicing with the equipment he was now called on to operate. When he dimmed the lights, he could not read his text. When the first slide came on, it was not his but belonged to a former speaker. When the first correct slide was reached, the type was too small for anyone but the people in the first row to see. He could not turn on the light arrow indicator to point out the line he was talking about, so he walked away from the lectern to point things out directly on the screen. But he left the microphone behind, so people in the back rows could neither see nor hear.

When a picture of his machine appeared, he was too close to see the critical parts. Since he could not read his text because of the darkness, he lost track of what he was supposed to say. Reaching for a steel-tipped pointer because he could not operate the optical one, he managed to punch a hole through the screen.

In desperation, he abandoned the slides, turned up the lights, and in utter consternation raced through the rest of his talk so fast and with such poor enunciation that he was almost completely unintelligible. Finally, in embarrassment both for himself and for the audience, he sat down.[4]

This sounds like a routine from *Saturday Night Live,* but it is a true story. What makes the story especially sad is that it didn't have to happen. With some effort, thought, and preparation, the young inventor could have made a success of his presentation instead of turning it into a fiasco.

You can avoid following in his footsteps if you practice with the visual aids you have chosen. Rehearse with your equipment to be sure you can set up the visual aid with a minimum of fuss. Run through the entire speech several times, practicing the handling of the aids, the gestures you will make, the timing of each move. If necessary, practice removing the visual aid when you are finished with it. In using visual aids, as in other aspects of speechmaking, there is no substitute for the Boy Scout motto—"Be prepared."

SUMMARY

Visual aids can be of great help to you as a speaker. Listeners find a speaker's message more interesting, grasp it more easily, and retain it longer when it is presented visually as well as verbally.

There are many kinds of visual aids. Most obvious is the object about which you are speaking or a model of it. Photographs can be useful if generous-size enlargements are available; but for classroom speeches, drawings may be more practical. One kind of drawing—a map—is especially useful for a speech topic involving physical terrain. Graphs can illustrate any subject dealing with numbers, while charts can help you summarize large blocks of information. Although slides and videotapes can be effective as visual aids, they need to be used with caution in classroom speeches. Much the same is true of computer-generated graphics, which are usually best displayed with an overhead projector. Finally, you can act as your own visual aid by performing actions that demonstrate processes or ideas.

No matter what kind of visual aid you choose, it will be effective only if you prepare it carefully and present it skillfully. Try to avoid writing or drawing visual aids on the chalkboard. Work them up in advance, and make sure they are large enough to be seen easily by all your listeners. It is usually not advisable to pass visual aids among your audience. Instead, display each visual aid only while you are talking about it, and be sure to display it where everyone can see it without straining. When presenting a visual aid, maintain eye contact with your listeners. Talk to the audience, not to the aid, and explain the aid clearly and concisely. Above all, practice with your visual aids, so they fit into your speech smoothly and expertly.

REVIEW QUESTIONS

After reading this chapter, you should be able to answer the following questions:

1. What are the three major advantages of using visual aids in your speeches?

2. What are the kinds of visual aids you might use?

3. What tips for using visual aids are given in the chapter?

APPLICATION EXERCISES

1. Watch a "how to" type of television program (a cooking or gardening show, for example) or the weather portion of a local newscast. Notice how the speaker uses visual aids to help communicate the message. What kinds of visual aids are used? How do they enhance the clarity, interest, and retainability of the speaker's message? What would the speaker have to do to communicate the message effectively without visual aids?

2. Consider how you might use visual aids to explain each of the following:

   a. How to perform the Heimlich maneuver to help a choking victim.
   b. The location of the five boroughs of New York City.
   c. The proportion of the electorate that votes in major national elections in the United States, France, Germany, England, and Japan, respectively.
   d. Where to write for information about student loans.
   e. The wing patterns of various species of butterflies
   f. The increase in the amount of money spent by Americans on health care since 1965.
   g. How to change a bicycle tire.
   h. The basic equipment and techniques of rock climbing.

3. Plan to use visual aids in at least one of your classroom speeches. Be creative in devising your aids, and be sure to follow the guidelines discussed in the chapter for using them. After the speech, analyze how effectively you employed your visual aids, what you learned about the use of visual aids from your experience, and what changes you would make in using visual aids if you were to deliver the speech again.

NOTES

[1] Patricia Long, "The Way to a Worker's Heart," *Hippocrates* (January–February 1989), pp. 52–59.

[2] Douglas R. Vogel, Gary W. Dickson, and John A. Lehman, *Persuasion and the Role of Visual Presentation Support: The UM/3M Study* (Minneapolis: University of Minnesota School of Management, 1986).

[3] Bert E. Bradley, *Fundamentals of Speech Communication: The Credibility of Ideas*, 6th ed. (Dubuque, Iowa: W.C. Brown, 1991), p. 280.

[4] Adapted from Eric A. Walker, "About the 'Death' of an Engineer," *Centre Daily Times*, April 25, 1972.

Chapter 14

Speaking to Inform

Mitsue Yamada is the sales manager for a company that sells business equipment such as computers, copiers, and fax machines. She began that particular workday by meeting with her sales force to discuss the company's new line of copiers. She pointed out the special features of each machine, demonstrated how the machines worked, and answered questions about them.

Later that morning, Mitsue had a long talk with the head of the company's technical division. "Can you show me," she asked, "how to use the new graphics software we got in last week? I know we have some clients who will be interested in it." Mitsue then took notes as the head of the technical division went through the graphics program step by step. Mitsue also asked questions along the way to make sure she understood exactly how the program worked.

In the afternoon, Mitsue met with the president and vice president of the company to go over the previous quarter's sales results. She reviewed the sales curve, assessed the performance of each sales representative, and then laid out her ideas for a new marketing strategy to increase copier sales in the next quarter. Afterward, the president complimented Mitsue for giving such a clear presentation. "Anyone who can communicate that well," the president said, "is going to go a long way in this company."

Mitsue doesn't consider herself a "public speaker," but much of her job involves absorbing and communicating information clearly and effectively. Although Mitsue is just one businessperson, her experience is not unusual. In a recent survey, graduates from five U.S. colleges were asked to rank the speech skills most important to their jobs. They rated informative speaking number one.[1] In another survey, 62 percent of the respondents said they used informative speaking "almost constantly."[2]

Nor are people in business the only ones who rely on informative speaking. What kinds of people make informative speeches? The city manager explaining next year's budget. The architect reviewing plans for a new building. The military officer briefing subordinates. The union leader informing members about details of a new contract. The church worker outlining plans for a fund drive. The teacher in a classroom. There are endless situations in which people need to inform others. Competence in this form of communication will prove most valuable to you throughout your life.

One of your first classroom assignments probably will be to deliver an informative speech in which you will act as a lecturer or teacher. You may describe an object, show how something works, report on an event, explain a concept. Your aim will be to convey knowledge and understanding—not to advocate a cause. Your speech will be judged in light of three general criteria:

Is the information communicated *accurately?*

Is the information communicated *clearly?*

Is the information made *meaningful* and *interesting* to the audience?

In this chapter, we shall look at four types of informative speeches and the basic principles of informative speaking. Along the way, we shall apply various general principles discussed in previous chapters.

◼ TYPES OF INFORMATIVE SPEECHES: ANALYSIS AND ORGANIZATION

There are many ways to classify informative speeches. Here we focus on the four kinds of informative speeches you are most likely to give in your speech class: (1) speeches about objects; (2) speeches about processes; (3) speeches about events; and (4) speeches about concepts. These are not hard-and-fast categories, but they provide an effective method of analyzing and organizing informative speeches.

Speeches About Objects

As the word is used here, "objects" include anything that is visible, tangible, and stable in form. Objects may have moving parts or be alive; they may include places, structures, animals, even people. Here are examples of subjects for speeches about objects:

Nelson Mandela	subways
Grand Canyon	in-line skates
the human eye	Sitting Bull
sharks	notebook computers
comic strips	U.S. Army

You will not have time to tell your classmates everything about any of these subjects. Instead, you will choose a specific purpose that focuses on one aspect of your subject. Working from the topics presented above, the following are examples of good specific purpose statements for informative speeches about objects:

To inform my audience about the role of female soldiers in the Vietnam war.

To inform my audience about the anatomy of the human eye.

To inform my audience about the geological features of the Grand Canyon.

To inform my audience about the social functions of comic strips.

To inform my audience what to look for when buying a notebook computer.

Notice how precise these statements are. As we saw in Chapter 4, you should select a specific purpose that is not too broad to achieve in the allotted time. "To inform my audience about notebook computers" is far too general for a classroom speech. "To inform my audience what to look for when buying a notebook computer" is more exact and is a purpose you could reasonably hope to achieve in a brief talk.

If your specific purpose is to explain the history or evolution of your subject, you will put your speech in *chronological* order. For example:

Specific Purpose:	To inform my audience about the major achievements of Frederick Douglass.
Central Idea:	Although born in slavery, Frederick Douglass became one of the greatest African Americans in history.

Main Points:

   I.   Douglass spent the first twenty years of his life as a slave in Maryland.

  II.   After escaping to the North, Douglass became a leader in the abolitionist movement to end slavery.

 III.   During the Civil War, Douglass helped to establish black regiments in the Union Army.

 IV.   After the war, Douglass was a tireless champion of equal rights for his race.

If your specific purpose is to describe the main features of your subject, you may organize your speech in *spatial* order:

Specific Purpose:	To inform my audience about the major land regions in Spain.
Central Idea:	There are five major land regions in Spain.

Main Points:

   I.   The Northern Mountains extend across northernmost Spain from the Atlantic Ocean to the Coastal Plains.

  II.   The Ebro Basin consists of broad plains that extend along the Ebro River in northeastern Spain.

 III.   The Coastal Plains stretch along Spain's entire east coast.

 IV.   The Guadalquivir Basin is a dry but extremely fertile region in southern Spain.

  V.   The Mesata is a huge plateau that covers central Spain.

As often as not, you will find that speeches about objects fall into *topical* order. Here is an example:

Specific Purpose:	To inform my audience about the major alternative-fuel cars now being developed.
Central Idea:	The major alternative-fuel cars now being developed are powered by electricity, natural gas, methanol, or hydrogen.

Main Points:

   I.   One kind of alternative-fuel car is powered by electricity.

  II.   A second kind of alternative-fuel car is powered by natural gas.

III. A third kind of alternative-fuel car is powered by methanol.

IV. A fourth kind of alternative-fuel car is powered by hydrogen.

No matter which of these organizational methods you use—chronological, spatial, or topical—be sure to follow the guidelines discussed in Chapter 8: (1) limit your speech to between two and five main points; (2) keep main points separate; (3) try to use the same pattern of wording for all main points; (4) balance the amount of time devoted to each main point.

Speeches About Processes

A process is a systematic series of actions that leads to a specific result or product. Speeches about processes explain how something is made, how something is done, or how something works. Here are examples of good specific purpose statements for speeches about processes:

To inform my audience how hurricanes develop.

To inform my audience how to write an effective job résumé.

To inform my audience how to save people from drowning.

To inform my audience how oriental rugs are made.

To inform my audience how fiber-optics technology works.

As these examples suggest, there are two kinds of informative speeches about processes. One kind explains a process so listeners will *understand* it better. Your goal in this kind of speech is to have your audience know the steps of the process and how they relate to one another. If your specific purpose is "To inform my audience how a nuclear bomb works," you will explain the basic steps in making a bomb and how they result in a nuclear explosion. You will not instruct your listeners how they can *make* a nuclear bomb.

A second kind of speech explains a process so listeners will be better able to *perform* the process themselves. Your goal in this kind of speech is to have the audience learn a particular skill. Suppose your specific purpose is "To inform my audience how to take pictures like a professional photographer." You will present the basic techniques of professional photography and show your listeners how they can utilize those techniques. You want the audience to be able to *use* the techniques as a result of your speech.

Both kinds of speeches about processes may require visual aids. At the very least, you should prepare a chart outlining the steps or techniques of your process. In some cases you will need to demonstrate the steps or techniques by performing them in front of your audience. One student did sleight-of-hand magic tricks to show the techniques behind them. Another acted out the basic methods of mime. Yet another executed elementary karate maneuvers. In each case, the demonstration not only clarified the speaker's process, but captivated the audience as well. (If you are using visual aids of any kind, be sure to review Chapter 13 before your speech.)

When informing about a process, you will usually arrange your speech in *chronological* order, explaining the process step by step from beginning to end. For example:

Specific Purpose: To inform my audience how a batik fabric is printed.

Central Idea: There are four basic steps in printing a batik fabric—designing, applying the wax, dyeing, and removing the wax.

Main Points:
I. The design is first sketched on paper.
II. A wax resist is applied to the fabric wherever you don't want the dye to penetrate.
III. The fabric is then dipped in the dye.
IV. When the fabric has dried, the wax resist is removed.

Sometimes, rather than leading your audience through a process step by step, you will focus on the major principles or techniques involved in performing the process. Then you will organize your speech in *topical* order. Each main point will deal with a separate principle or technique. For example:

Specific Purpose: To inform my audience of the common methods used by stage magicians to perform their tricks.

Central Idea: Stage magicians use two common methods to perform their tricks—mechanical devices and sleight of hand.

Main Points:
I. Many magic tricks rely on mechanical devices that may require little skill by the magician.
II. Other magic tricks depend on the magician's skill in fooling people by sleight-of-hand manipulation.

Concise organization is especially important in speeches about processes. You must make sure each step in the process is clear and easy to follow. If your process has more than four or five steps, group the steps into units so as to limit the number of main points. Otherwise, you will have too many main points for listeners to grasp and recall. For example, in a speech explaining how to set up a home aquarium, a student presented the following main points:

I. First you must choose the size of your tank.
II. Then you must determine the shape of your tank.
III. You must also decide how much you can afford to pay for a tank.
IV. Once you have the tank, you need a filter system.
V. A heater is also absolutely necessary.
VI. You must also get an air pump.

   VII.   Once this is done, you need to choose gravel for the tank.

  VIII.   You will also need plants.

    IX.   Other decorations will round out the effects of your aquarium.

     X.   Now you are ready to add the fish.

    XI.   Freshwater fish are the most common.

   XII.   Saltwater fish are more expensive and require special care.

Not surprisingly, this was too much for the audience to follow. The speaker should have organized the points something like this:

    I.   The first step in establishing a home aquarium is choosing a tank.
       A.   The size of the tank is important.
       B.   The shape of the tank is important.
       C.   The cost of the tank is important.

   II.   The second step in establishing a home aquarium is equipping the tank.
       A.   You will need a filter system.
       B.   You will need a heater.
       C.   You will need an air pump.
       D.   You will need gravel.
       E.   You will need plants.
       F.   You may also want other decorations.

  III.   The third step in establishing a home aquarium is adding the fish.
       A.   Freshwater fish are the most common for home aquariums.
       B.   Saltwater fish are more expensive and require special care.

As you can see, the subpoints cover the same territory as that originally covered by the twelve main points. But three main points are much easier to understand and remember than twelve.

Speeches About Events

The *Random House Dictionary* defines an event as "anything that happens or is regarded as happening." By this definition, the following are examples of suitable subjects for informative speeches about events:

Holocaust	mountain climbing
civil rights movement	Olympic Games
modern dance	job interviews
Cinco de Mayo	therapeutic massage
Gulf War syndrome	Battle of Little Big Horn

As usual, you will need to narrow your focus and pick a specific purpose you can accomplish in a short speech. Here are examples of good specific purpose statements for informative speeches about events:

To inform my audience about the equipment used in mountain climbing.

To inform my audience of the festivities at Mexico's Cinco de Mayo celebration.

To inform my audience what happened at the Battle of Little Big Horn.

To inform my audience about the techniques of therapeutic massage.

To inform my audience about the development of the modern Olympic Games.

As you can see, there are many ways to discuss events. If your specific purpose is to recount the history of an event, you will organize your speech in *chronological* order, relating the incidents one after another in the order they occurred. For example:

Specific Purpose: To inform my audience about the history of the disability-rights movement.

Central Idea: The disability-rights movement has made major strides during the past thirty years.

Main Points:
  I.   The disability-rights movement began in Berkeley, California, during the mid-1960s.
  II.   The movement achieved its first major victory in 1973 with passage of the federal Rehabilitation Act.
  III.   The movement reached another milestone in 1990 when Congress approved the Americans with Disabilities Act.
  IV.   Today the movement is spreading to countries beyond the United States.

Instead of recounting the history of an event, you might take a more analytical approach and explain its causes and/or effects. In such a case, you will organize your speech in *causal* order. Let's say your specific purpose is "To inform my audience why so many lives were lost when the 'unsinkable' ocean liner *Titanic* sank." Working from cause to effect, your outline might look like this:

Specific Purpose: To inform my audience why so many lives were lost when the "unsinkable" ocean liner *Titanic* sank.

Central Idea: Inability to remove the passengers and crew from the doomed *Titanic* caused the death of more than two-thirds of those on board.

Main Points:
  I.   There were two major causes for the great loss of life when the *Titanic* went down.
    A.   The *Titanic* carried insufficient lifeboats for the number of people on board.
    B.   On the ship *Californian,* which was nearby, the radio operator had shut down the radio and gone to sleep.

II.   The effects of these two situations were disastrous.
    A.   When all usable lifeboats had been filled, more than 1,500 people remained on board the *Titanic.*
    B.   The *Californian,* unaware of the distress signal, steamed on while the *Titanic* went to the bottom.

There are other ways to deal with an event besides telling what happened or why it happened. Indeed, you can approach an event from almost any angle or combination of angles—features, origins, implications, benefits, future developments, and so forth. In such cases, you will put your speech together in *topical* order. And you should make sure your main points subdivide the subject logically and consistently. For instance:

Specific Purpose: To inform my audience about the four traditional events in women's gymnastics.

Central Idea: The four traditional events in women's gymnastics are floor exercise, vault, balance beam, and uneven parallel bars.

Main Points:
    I.   The floor exercise combines dancing, acrobatics, and tumbling.
    II.   The vault features explosive strength and dramatic midair maneuvers.
    III.   The balance beam requires precise routines and perfect coordination.
    IV.   The uneven parallel bars demand great strength, flexibility, and agility.

Speeches About Concepts

Concepts include beliefs, theories, ideas, principles, and the like. They are more abstract than objects, processes, or events. The following are some examples of subjects for speeches about concepts:

Confucianism	chaos theory
philosophies of education	principles of feminism
original intent doctrine	Afrocentrism
concepts of science	theories of psychology
religious beliefs	Keynesian economics

Taking a few of these general subjects, here are some good specific purpose statements for speeches about concepts:

To inform my audience about the basic principles of Afrocentrism.

To inform my audience about the doctrine of original intent in constitutional interpretation.

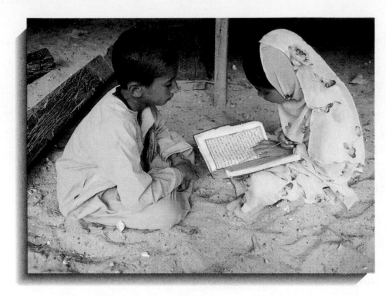

Informative speeches can be given about objects, processes, concepts, or events. A speech about the history of Islam, for example, would treat its topic as an event, while a speech about the beliefs of Islam would deal with its subject as a concept.

To inform my audience about the different philosophies of education in Japan and the United States.

To inform my audience about the concept of patriarchy in feminist thought.

To inform my audience about the principles of chaos theory.

Speeches about concepts are usually organized in *topical* order. One common approach is to enumerate the main features or aspects of your concept. For example:

Specific Purpose: To inform my audience about the basic principles of Afrocentrism.

Central Idea: The basic principles of Afrocentrism have a theoretical and a practical dimension.

Main Points: I.   The theoretical dimension of Afrocentrism looks at historical and social events from an African rather than a European perspective.

II.   The practical dimension of Afrocentrism calls for reforming the school curriculum to fit the needs and cultural experiences of African-American children.

A more complex approach is to define the concept you are dealing with, identify its major elements, and illustrate it with specific examples. An excellent instance of this came in a student speech about the religion of Islam:

Specific Purpose: To inform my audience of the basic principles of Islam.

Central Idea: The beliefs of Islam can be traced to the prophet Muhammad, are written in the Koran, and have produced a number of sects.

Main Points:
  I. Islam was founded by the prophet Muhammad in the early 600s.
  II. The teachings of Islam are written in the Koran, the holy book of Islam.
  III. Today Islam is divided into a number of sects, the largest of which are the Sunnites and the Shiites.

Yet another approach is to explain competing schools of thought about the same subject. For example:

Specific Purpose: To inform my audience of the arguments for and against bilingual education in the United States.

Central Idea: Supporters and opponents of bilingual education both have legitimate arguments that center on the welfare of the student.

Main Points:
  I. Supporters of bilingual education maintain that non-English-speaking students learn more effectively if they are taught primarily in their native language.
  II. Opponents of bilingual education maintain that teaching non-English-speaking students primarily in their native language harms their long-term chances for educational and economic success.

As you can see from these examples, speeches about concepts are often more complex than other kinds of informative speeches. Concepts are abstract and can be very hard to explain to someone who is learning about them for the first time. When explaining concepts, pay special attention to avoiding technical language, to defining terms clearly, and to using examples and comparisons to illustrate the concepts and make them understandable to your listeners.

The lines dividing speeches about objects, processes, events, and concepts are not absolute. Some subjects could fit into more than one category, depending on how you develop the speech. You could treat the Declaration of Independence as an object—by explaining its history and its role in the American Revolution. Or you could deal with the meaning of the Declaration, in which case you would be speaking about a concept—an idea bound up with freedom and democracy.

To take another example, a speech about the destruction of ancient Pompeii by the eruption of Mount Vesuvius would probably deal with its subject as an event, but a speech on what causes volcanoes to erupt would most likely treat its subject as a process. The important step is to decide how you will handle your subject—as an object, a process, an event, or a concept. Once you do that, you can develop the speech accordingly.

One final word about organizing your informative speech: Regardless of which method of organization you use, be sure to give your listeners plenty of help in sorting out facts and ideas during the speech. One way is by using enough transitions, internal previews, internal summaries, and signposts (see Chapter 8). Another way is to follow the old maxim: "Tell 'em what you're going to say; say it; then tell 'em what you've said." In other words, preview the main points of your speech in the introduction, and summarize them in the conclusion. This will make your speech not only easier to understand but also easier to remember.

GUIDELINES FOR INFORMATIVE SPEAKING

All the previous chapters of this book relate to the principles of informative speaking. Choosing a topic and specific purpose, analyzing the audience, gathering materials, choosing supporting details, organizing the speech, using words to communicate meaning, delivering the speech—all of these must be done effectively if your informative speech is to be a success. Here we shall emphasize five points to help you avoid the mistakes that plague many informative speakers.

Don't Overestimate What the Audience Knows

In a speech about meteorology, a student said, "If modern methods of weather forecasting had existed in 1900, the Galveston hurricane disaster would never have taken place." Then he was off to other matters, leaving his listeners to puzzle over what the Galveston hurricane was, when it happened, and what kind of destruction it wreaked.

The speaker assumed the audience already knew these things. But his classmates were not experts on meteorology or on American history. Even those who had heard of the hurricane had only a fuzzy notion of it. Some were not even sure about the location of Galveston. Only the speaker knew that the hurricane, which killed more than 6,000 people when it unexpectedly struck Galveston, Texas, on September 8, 1900, is still the deadliest natural disaster in American history.

As many speakers have discovered, it is easy to overestimate the audience's stock of information. In most informative speeches, your listeners will only be vaguely knowledgeable (at best) about the details of your topic. (Otherwise, there would not be much need for an informative speech!) Therefore, you must lead your listeners step by step, without any shortcuts. You cannot *assume* they will know what you mean. Rather, you must be *sure* to explain everything so thoroughly that they cannot help but understand. As you work on your speech, always consider whether it will be clear to someone who is hearing about the topic for the first time.

Suppose you are talking about the protective tariff. Although many of your classmates might have heard of the protective tariff, you cannot assume they have a firm grasp of it. So you should start by telling them what it is. How will you tell them? Here's one way:

> A protective tariff is a form of customs duty. It is a tax on imported goods, but it differs from other taxes in that its primary purpose is not financial but economic—not to increase a nation's revenue but to protect its domestic industry from foreign competition.

To someone who knows a lot about business and commerce this is perfectly clear. But someone who does not will probably get lost along the way. The tone of the statement is that of a speaker reviewing information already familiar to the audience—not of a speaker introducing new information.

Here, in contrast, is another explanation of protective tariffs:

> What is a protective tariff? Let me explain with an example.
>
> Suppose you make shoes. So does a business in Taiwan. But that business can sell its shoes here cheaper than you can. As a result, you are going bankrupt.
>
> So you appeal to the government for help. The government sets up a tariff to protect you from being ruined by the cheap foreign shoes. This means that the government puts a tariff—a tax—on every shoe that comes into the United States for sale from Taiwan. If the tariff is high enough, the shoes from Taiwan will now be more expensive than yours.
>
> Your business has been protected by the tariff. Hence the name, protective tariff.[3]

This statement is clear and simple. Its tone is that of a teacher unraveling a new subject.

Is it too simple? Will your classmates feel you are talking down to them? Almost certainly not. Many students hesitate to speak simply because they are afraid they will sound simpleminded. They think they need big words and complicated sentences to sound intelligent. But nothing could be further from the truth. The test of a good speaker is to communicate even the most complex ideas clearly and simply. Anyone can go to a book and find a learned-sounding definition of a protective tariff like the first one above. But to say in plain English what a protective tariff is—that takes hard work and creative thinking.

Also, remember that readers can study a printed passage again and again until they extract its meaning, but listeners don't have that luxury. They must understand what you say in the time it takes you to say it. The more you assume they know about the topic, the greater your chances of being misunderstood.

If you have circulated a questionnaire among your listeners before the speech, you should have a good idea of their knowledge about the topic. If not, you will usually do better to aim for the low end of the knowledge spectrum. Some experts recommend preparing a speech as if the audience had never heard of the subject. That may be a bit extreme, but it is one way to make sure you define every special term, clarify every idea, illustrate every concept, and support every conclusion.[4] You cannot go wrong by following the news reporters' code: "Never *over*estimate the information of your audience; never *under*estimate the intelligence of your audience."

Relate the Subject Directly to the Audience

The British dramatist Oscar Wilde arrived at his club after the disastrous opening-night performance of his new play.

"Oscar, how did your play go?" asked a friend.

"Oh," Wilde quipped, "the play was a great success, but the audience was a failure."

Speakers have been known to give much the same answer in saving face after a dismal informative speech. "Oh," they say, "the speech was fine, but the audience just wasn't interested." And they are at least partly right—the audience *wasn't* interested. Then was the speech fine? Not by any objective standard. A speech is measured by its impact on a particular audience. There is no such thing as a fine speech that puts people to sleep. It is the speaker's job to get listeners interested—and to keep them interested.

Informative speakers have one big hurdle to overcome. They must recognize that what is fascinating to them may not be fascinating to everybody. A mathematician, for example, might be truly enthralled by a perfect equation, but most people wouldn't want to hear about it. Once you have chosen a topic that could possibly be interesting to your listeners, you should take special steps to relate it to them. You should tie it in with their interests and concerns.

Start in the introduction. Instead of saying,

I want to talk with you about stress.

You could say,

Do you get butterflies in your stomach when you have to give a speech? Can you feel your blood pressure rising when you have an argument with your spouse or your roommate? Are you worried sick about finishing the paper you've been putting off all week? If so, you have experienced the symptoms of stress.

Get your audience involved right at the beginning. Let them know why your message is important to them. Don't assume they will figure it out for themselves. Don't leave it to chance. Tell them. (If you are having trouble with this, recheck the sample introduction on pages 207–208.)

The principles of informative speaking are applicable in a wide range of situations, formal and informal alike. Knowing those principles will help you whenever you need to convey knowledge and understanding.

Don't stop with the introduction. Whenever you can, put your listeners into the body of the speech. After all, nothing interests people more than themselves. Don't just rattle off statistics and concepts as if you were reciting a shopping list. Find ways to talk about your topic in terms of your listeners. Bring your material home to them. Get it as close to them as possible.

Here's an example. Let's say you are explaining how people can discover whether they are "secret southpaws"—that is, people who are naturally left-handed but who have grown up preferring the right hand because they were taught to use it as a child. You have plenty of facts and could recite them like this:

According to *Science* magazine, half of all people who are naturally left-handed assume they are right-handed because that is the hand they use to eat, to write, and to play sports. But how can it be determined whether one is a natural southpaw? According to Abram Blau, author of *The Master Hand,* there are a number of simple tests. For one thing, most natural left-handers can write spontaneously backwards or upside down with the left hand. For another, when left-handers clasp their hands in front of themselves, they usually place the left thumb on top. In contrast, when left-handers grab a broom, they normally place their left hand below the right. Finally, when using the right hand, natural left-handers will draw a circle clockwise, while natural right-handers will draw it counterclockwise. People who give a left-handed response on three or more of these tests may well be secret southpaws.[5]

This is fascinating information, but it is not made fascinating to the audience. Let's try again:

Just because *you* use *your* right hand to eat, to write, and to play sports, *you* may assume *you* are naturally right-handed. But, says *Science* magazine, half of all people who are naturally left-handed grow up using their right hands. How can *you* tell if *you* are a natural lefty? Dr. Abram Blau, author of *The Master Hand,* gives some tests *you* can try.

First, on a sheet of paper see if *you* can write backwards or upside down with *your* left hand. If *you* are left-handed, *you* can probably do this spontaneously, without practice or training. Second, clasp *your* hands in front of *you;* whichever thumb *you* place on top usually indicates *your* dominant hand. Third, grab hold of a broomstick. Odds are *you* will place *your* dominant hand on the bottom. Finally, draw a circle on a piece of paper with *your* right hand. If *you* draw it counterclockwise, *you* are probably a natural right-hander. But if *you* draw it clockwise, *you* are very likely a natural lefty.

If *you* test left-handed on three of these tests, there is a good chance *you* are a secret southpaw.

Look at all the "you's" and "your's." The facts are the same, but now they are pointed directly at the audience. This is the kind of thing that gets listeners to sit up and pay attention.

Don't Be Too Technical

What does it mean to say an informative speech is too technical? It may mean the subject matter is too specialized for the audience. Any subject can be popularized—but only up to a point. The important thing for a speaker to know is what can be explained to an ordinary audience and what cannot.

Say your subject is stereo amplifiers. It's no trick to demonstrate how to operate an amplifier (how to turn it on and off, adjust the volume, set the tone and balance controls). It's also relatively easy to explain what an amplifier does (it boosts the sound received from a radio, disc player, or tape deck). But to give a full scientific account of how an amplifier works—that is another matter. It cannot be done in any reasonable time unless the audience knows the principles of audio technology. You would be better off not even trying. The material is just too technical to be understood by a general audience.

Even when the subject matter is not technical, the language used to explain it may be. Every activity has its jargon. This is true of golf (bogey, wedge, match play); of chemistry (colloid, glycogen, heavy water); of photography (aperture, f-stop, depth of field); of ballet (arabesque, jeté, pas de deux). If you are talking to a group of specialists, you can use technical words and be understood. But you must do all you can to avoid technical words when informing a general audience such as your speech class.

You may find this hard to do at first. Many people are so addicted to the lingo of their subject that they have trouble escaping it. As you give more speeches, though, you will become increasingly adept at expressing your ideas in everyday, nontechnical language.

Here, for instance, are two statements explaining the symptoms of Alzheimer's disease. The first is heavily laden with medical jargon and would have little impact on ordinary listeners:

Alzheimer's disease is a degenerative brain disorder whose initial symptoms are short-term memory loss and impaired concentration. As the disease progresses, its manifestations include dysfunctions of speech, personality, muscle coordination, and mental processes. Eventually, the victim may become incontinent and totally incapacitated. The duration of the disease is variable.

The second statement is perfectly understandable. It shows how technical information can be made clear to the average person:

Of all the diseases which strike people in old age, Alzheimer's may be the cruelest, for it kills its victims twice. First it kills the mind. The simplest tasks—tying a shoe, cooking a hamburger, making a bed—become impossible because the victim can no longer remember how to do them. Names, dates, places—the mental scrapbook of an entire life—fade away like an aging photograph. In the most tragic cases, people with Alzheimer's forget their own names and can no longer recognize their own children.
Then the body dies. No longer able to walk or to control bodily functions, the victim lies curled in a fetal position, gradually sinking into a coma and then death. Most Alzheimer's victims live for six to eight years after the disease begins, although some suffer for as long as twenty years.[6]

Much clearer, isn't it? The only specialized word in the whole passage is "Alzheimer's." The language is straightforward, the ideas easy to grasp. This is what you should strive for in your informative speeches.

Avoid Abstractions

"My task," said the novelist Joseph Conrad, "is, before all, to make you see." And make the reader see is just what Conrad did. Witness this passage, in which Conrad describes the aftermath of an explosion on shipboard:

The first person I saw was Mahon, with eyes like saucers, his mouth open, and the long white hair standing straight on end round his head like a silver halo. He was just about to go down when the sight of the main deck stirring, heaving up, and changing into splinters before his eyes, petrified him on the top step. I stared at him in unbelief, and he stared at me with a queer kind of shocked curiosity. I did not know that I had no hair, no eyebrows, no eyelashes, that my young mustache was burnt off, that my face was black, one cheek laid open, my nose cut, and my chin bleeding.[7]

A speech is not a novel. Still, too many abstractions are tedious—whether in a novel or in a speech. Many informative speeches would be vastly improved by the novelist's bent for color, specificity, and detail.

One way to avoid abstractions is through *description*. When we think of description, we usually think of external events such as the explosion described by Conrad. But description is also used to communicate internal feelings. Here is how one student tried to convey to his audience the sensations he experienced when he first began sky diving:

As we wait for the plane to climb to the jump altitude of 12,000 feet, my mind races with a frenzied jumble of thoughts: "Okay, this is the moment you've been waiting for. It's going to be great. Am I really going to jump out of an airplane from 12,000 feet? What if something goes wrong? Can I still back out? Come on now, don't worry. It'll be fine."

Even if we have not been sky diving, we have all had the same kinds of emotions on similar occasions. So what happened next?

Now it is time to jump. My palms are sweating and my heart is pounding so hard I think it may burst. "Get ready," yells the instructor. As I jump into the blue, I wonder, "What am I doing here?"

Yes—and then what?

The blast of air resistance blows me backward like a leaf at the mercy of an autumn wind. In about ten seconds my body levels out and accelerates to a speed of 120 miles an hour. The air supports my body like an invisible flying carpet. There is no sound except for the wind rushing around my face. The earth appears soft and green, rivers look like strips of silver, and in every direction the scenery forms a panoramic landscape. Any fears or doubts I had are gone in the exhilaration of free flight. Every nerve in my body is alive with sensation; yet I am overcome by a peaceful feeling and the sense that I am at one with the sky.

As we listen to the speaker, we are almost up there with him, sharing his thoughts, feeling his heart pound, joining his exhilaration as he floats effortlessly through the sky. The vivid description lends reality to the speech and draws us further in.

Another way to escape abstractions is with *comparisons* that put your subject in concrete, familiar terms. Do you want to convey what would happen if a comet or large asteroid struck the earth? You could say this:

If a comet or large asteroid struck the earth, the impact would be devastating.

True, but "the impact would be devastating" is vague and abstract. It does not communicate your meaning clearly and concretely. Now suppose you add this:

To give you an idea how devastating the impact would be, it would be like all the nuclear bombs in the world going off at one spot.

Now you have made the abstract specific and given us a sharp new slant on things.

Like comparison, *contrast* can put an idea into concrete terms. Suppose you want to make the point that a person's chances of winning a state lottery are extremely low. You could say, "The odds, for example, of winning a state lottery are an astronomical 7 million to 1." The word "astronomical" suggests that you consider 7 million to 1 long odds, but long in comparison to what? One speaker offered this contrast:

> The odds of picking the correct six-digit sequence in a typical state lottery are more than 7 million to 1. In contrast, the odds of getting hit by lightning are only 2 million to 1. The chances of being dealt a royal flush in a poker game are 650,000 to 1. The odds of dying in an automobile accident are about 6,000 to 1. In other words, the odds are much stronger that you will get hit by lightning or be killed in a car crash than that you will win the jackpot in a state lottery.

Now an abstract fact has been put into meaningful perspective. See if you can do something similar in your informative speech.

Personalize Your Ideas

Listeners want to be entertained as they are being enlightened.[8] Nothing takes the edge off an informative speech more than an unbroken string of facts and figures. And nothing enlivens a speech more than personal illustrations. Remember, people are interested in people. They react to stories, not statistics. Whenever possible, you should try to *personalize* your ideas and dramatize them in human terms.

Let's say you are talking about Gulf War syndrome, the name given to recurring ailments which have struck thousands of U.S. soldiers who served in the Persian Gulf War. You would surely note that these ailments include skin rashes, memory loss, insomnia, joint pains, fevers, chest pains, and chronic fatigue. You would also note that there is great debate about the causes of Gulf War syndrome. Some researchers trace it to a condition called multiple chemical sensitivity. Others think it may come from chemical or biological weapons used by Iraq. Still others blame an anti-chemical weapons vaccine given to 400,000 U.S. soldiers before the war.

But these are dry facts and figures. If you really want to get your audience involved, you will weave in some examples of people who have suffered from Gulf War syndrome. You might do as one student did and tell the story of Troy Albuck, of Barrington, Illinois:

> As a U.S. Army platoon leader in the Persian Gulf War, Troy Albuck thought nothing of doing 200 push-ups a day or leading his troops on eight-mile runs through the desert. But a year after returning home from the war, he began losing his health. The cause, he believes, is Gulf War syndrome.

The trouble started with spots on his shins, which soon spread to other parts of his body. Then his eyes swelled shut and his lips bloated until the skin split. When his skin cleared up, his joints started hurting. Today, at age 26, Albuck feels like an arthritic codger. "I have to . . . unfold myself in the morning from how I slept," he says, "and I can't run at all. Literally a block and I'm done."

One speaker, discussing the differences between primary-school education in Japan and the United States, found an ingenious way to personalize his subject. He created a "fictional, yet typical, Japanese child—Ruriko," and led his audience through a day in Ruriko's life. Here is an excerpt:

Ruriko awakens at 6:30 a.m. By 7:30 she has put on her neat, plaid-skirted school uniform, eaten her breakfast of rice and fish, picked up the beautifully arranged box lunch made by her mother, and departed for her school in central Yokohama. Ruriko is ten years old.

Classes continue, with only a break for lunch, until early afternoon. Then Ruriko's mother picks her up and takes her to a gymnastics lesson. (Tomorrow it will be a music lesson, the next day calligraphy, the day after that swimming.) As soon as the lesson is over, Ruriko and her mother jump on the train and hurry to the next scheduled appointment. It is time for *juko,* the special "cram school" many Japanese children attend to improve their chances of gaining admission to private school. For three hours at *juko* Ruriko is tutored in science and math.

Ruriko and her mother board the train again and return home, where they enjoy a hasty supper. Then Ruriko settles down to her homework. Around 11:00 p.m. her mother brings her a snack of noodles and tea to keep up her energy for study. Shortly after 1:00 a.m. Ruriko goes to bed. Another day in the life of an ambitious Japanese schoolchild has ended.

This speaker could simply have listed facts about the Japanese system of primary education as though he were reciting from an encyclopedia. Instead he chose a better method—inventing "Ruriko"—to bring the topic to life. No matter what your subject, you can almost always find a way to express it in personal terms.

SAMPLE SPEECH WITH COMMENTARY

The following classroom speech provides an excellent example of how to apply the guidelines for informative speaking discussed in this chapter.[9] As you study the speech, notice how the speaker takes what could be a dry topic and makes it interesting. Pay special attention to how crisply the speech is organized, how the speaker uses well-chosen supporting materials to bring her topic to life, and how she clarifies her ideas with concrete language and vivid description.

DANDELIONS: THE UNCOMMON WEED

Susan R. Hirsch

SPEECH

What starts out yellow and ends up as a fluffy white ball? If I told you it was *Taraxacum Officinale*, would that ring a bell? What if I told you it was of the family *Compositae*—would that excite your senses?

If you haven't figured it out by now, the subject of which I am speaking is none other than the common, ordinary dandelion. Yes, those bright, yellow flowers which we all, as kids, eagerly snapped off the stems while chanting the words, "Mama had a baby and its head popped off!" I'm sure all of us remember having blown the fluffy white tufts into the air above.

Although we have these pleasant memories from our childhoods, most homeowners consider the dandelion as the most irritating and troublesome of all the weeds—partly because their deep root system makes them almost impossible to get rid of. However, from a botany class, I learned that the dandelion, in reality, is a very useful plant. From further research, I discovered that the dandelion has both wide medical and culinary uses. Today, I will explain these uses to you. We'll start by looking at the dandelion's medicinal value.

The scientific name of the dandelion, *Taraxacum Officinale*, testifies to its value as a medicine. According to Edward Spencer, in his book *All About Dandelions*, *Taraxacum* refers to medical properties of a plant found in Persia. *Officinale*, the species name, when given to any plant, indicates that it is used by druggists and pharmacists.

Throughout history, dandelions have been used to help cure various medical ailments. Dandelions were reportedly used by the ancient Egyptians to treat kidney and stomach disorders. The dandelion's many cures were recorded by Arabian physicians in the tenth century. And in sixteenth-century England, dandelion waters were used in the treatment of illness among the nobility.

COMMENTARY

Beginning with a question is a fine way to capture attention and interest. In this case, the questions work particularly well because they arouse curiosity about the subject of the speech.

Now the speaker reveals her subject and relates it directly to her audience.

In this paragraph the speaker states her central idea, establishes her credibility, and previews the main points to be discussed in the body of the speech. An explicit preview statement at the end of the introduction is especially important in speaking to inform.

Now the speaker moves into her first main point. When she delivered the speech in class, she used a visual aid so her audience could see the spelling of *Taraxacum Officinale*.

The historical details in this paragraph add variety, color, and interest.

The speaker explains the medical value of dandelions clearly and straightforwardly. Because she is not an expert on dandelions, she is careful to identify the sources of her information.

Today, scientists know as a fact that the dandelion has great medicinal value. According to Mea Allan, in her book *Weeds,* the plant contains chemicals that stimulate blood circulation, the liver, digestive organs, and especially the kidneys and bladder—which has gained the dandelion fame as a so-called "potty herb." Audrey Hatfield, in her book *How to Enjoy Your Weeds,* says that a tea made from dandelion roots or leaves is helpful in relieving many conditions. It helps relieve liver and lung disorders, and it helps treat anemia. In addition, it serves as a mild laxative and is helpful in aiding digestion. Hatfield also suggests that dandelion tea is highly effective in cases of eczema, scurvy, and similar skin conditions. So valuable is the dandelion in treating medical ailments that 100,000 pounds are imported into the United States each year for this purpose.

This paragraph begins with a transition into the second main point. As in the first main point, the speaker uses historical information to underscore the importance of dandelions. Notice also how she explains Passover, just in case some of her listeners are not familiar with it.

If you have no interest in using dandelions for your health, you can still find them of use in the kitchen. Historically, dandelions have been used as food for thousands of years. According to an article in *National Wildlife* magazine, they were among the original bitter herbs of Passover, a Jewish holiday which commemorates the Hebrews' liberation from slavery in Egypt. The English have been using dandelions in salads since the Middle Ages. And currently, many ethnic groups in the United States—such as Greeks, Poles, French, Italians, and even the Amish—all eat dandelions.

The speaker illustrates the culinary uses of dandelions with a variety of interesting facts that she discovered through her library research. This speech is a fine model of how well-chosen supporting materials can bring an ordinary topic to life.

All parts of the dandelion can be utilized to make a variety of delicious foods. Its bitter leaves, if picked before the yellow flowers appear, can be added to a salad. The leaves are usually mixed with other vegetables to vary their flavor. The dandelion's roots may be roasted in an oven, then ground and used as a caffeine-free coffee substitute. The golden yellow flowers can be steeped in water and then used to produce a delicious wine. And the entire dandelion plant may be used to make beer.

A transition at the beginning of this paragraph gets the speaker into her next subpoint. The quotation from Peter Gail convincingly demonstrates the nutritional value of dandelions. Notice how the speaker identifies Professor Gail before giving his testimony.

In addition to being tasty, dandelions are extremely nutritious. According to Peter Gail, a professor of economic botany at Cleveland State University, "the dandelion's nutrient qualities read almost like a One-A-Day vitamin." Dandelion greens have 50 percent more vitamin C than tomatoes, twice as much protein as eggplant, and double the fiber of asparagus. They have as much iron as spinach and more potassium than bananas.

The story of Vineland, New Jersey, "Dandelion Capital of the World," is entertaining as well as informative. Its details about the size of Vineland's dandelion crop, the price per pound of dandelions, and the seven-course dandelion dinner dramatize the speaker's point. Imagine how much less effective the speech would have been if the speaker had merely said, "Dandelions are very important to people in Vineland, New Jersey." The extended example brings the speaker's ideas to life and gives them human interest.

All of this may sound strange to you, but not to the people of Vineland, New Jersey, the official Dandelion Capital of the World. In Vineland, the dandelion has grown from being a $68,000 crop in 1977 to almost half a million dollar crop today. At the beginning of the season, dandelions sell for as much as $1.25 a pound. Most of Vineland's dandelion crop ends up in restaurants and markets in Baltimore, Philadelphia, and New York City.

Every March the town hosts its annual seven-course dandelion dinner. The menu consists of dandelion soup, dandelion salad, dandelion sausage, dandelions and vegetables, dandelion beef roulette, dandelion sweet cup, and dandelion wine. Tickets for the dinner sell for $25 apiece, with people coming from as far away as Ohio. Former Vineland mayor Patrick Fiorilli has humorously summed up Vineland's position in the dandelion world: "In your yard, you go out and pull the dandelions out of the grass. Our farmers pull the grass out of the dandelions."

The quotation from former mayor Fiorilli is a perfect ending for the body of the speech.

The conclusion is short and to the point. The phrase "As we have seen," cues listeners that the speech is nearing an end. The speaker then summarizes her main points and restates her central idea—that, despite its negative reputation, the dandelion is a very useful plant.

As we have seen, then, the dandelion is a greatly misunderstood plant. Despite its reputation as an irritating weed, in reality it is a very useful plant. Having various medical and culinary uses, the dandelion stands as one of the most underrated and least appreciated plants in the world. Hopefully, in the future, more people will come to recognize the usefulness of the dandelion, thereby reestablishing this "common" weed as a truly uncommon plant.

SUMMARY

Speaking to inform occurs in a wide range of everyday situations. Yet it is a difficult task that requires more skill than you might think. Improving your ability to convey knowledge effectively will be most valuable to you throughout your life.

Informative speeches may be grouped into four categories—speeches about objects, speeches about processes, speeches about events, and speeches about concepts. These categories are not absolute, but they are helpful in analyzing and organizing informative speeches.

Objects, as defined here, include places, structures, animals, even people. Speeches about objects usually are organized in chronological, spatial, or topical order. A process is a series of actions that work together to produce a final result. Speeches about processes explain how something is made, how something is done, or how something works. Clear organization is especially important in speeches about processes because listeners must be able to follow each step in the process. The most common types of organization for speeches about processes are chronological and topical.

An event is anything that happens or is regarded as happening. You can approach an event from almost any angle. You might explain its origins, causes, effects, implications, major features, and so on. Usually speeches about events are arranged in chronological, causal, or topical order. Concepts include beliefs, theories, ideas, and principles. Speeches about concepts are often more complex than other kinds of informative speeches, and they typically follow a topical pattern of organization.

No matter what the subject of your informative speech, be careful not to overestimate what your audience knows about it. In most classroom speeches your listeners will be no more than slightly familiar with your topic. Therefore, you cannot assume they will know what you mean. Explain everything so thoroughly they cannot help but understand. Avoid being too technical. Make sure your ideas and your language are fully comprehensible to someone who has no specialized knowledge about the topic.

Equally important, recognize that what is fascinating to you may not be fascinating to everybody. It is your job to make your informative speech interesting and meaningful to your audience. Find ways to talk about the topic in terms of your listeners. Avoid too many abstractions. Use description, comparison, and contrast to make your audience *see* what you are talking about. Finally, try to personalize your ideas. No matter what your subject, you can almost always find a way to dramatize it in human terms.

REVIEW QUESTIONS

After reading this chapter, you should be able to answer the following questions:

1. What are the four types of informative speeches discussed in the chapter? Give an example of a good specific purpose statement for each type.

2. Why must informative speakers be careful not to overestimate what the audience knows about the topic? What can you do to make sure your ideas don't pass over the heads of your listeners?

3. What should you do as an informative speaker to relate your topic directly to the audience?

4. What two things should you watch out for in making sure your speech is not overly technical?

5. What are three methods you can use to avoid abstractions in your informative speech?

6. What does it mean to say that informative speakers should personalize their ideas?

APPLICATION EXERCISES

1. Below is a list of subjects for informative speeches. Your task is twofold: (1) Select four of the topics and prepare a specific purpose statement for an informative speech about each of the four. Make sure that your four specific purpose statements include at least one that deals with its topic as an object, one that deals with its topic as a process, one that deals with its topic as an event, and one that deals with its topic as a concept. (2) Explain what method of organization you would most likely use in structuring a speech about each of your specific purpose statements.

computers	sports
animals	music
science	cultural customs
education	technology
television	hobbies

2. Analyze the speech in the Appendix by Kyle Knoeck, "The Hidden World of Perfumes," pages 444–447). Identify the specific purpose, central idea, main points, and method of organization. Evaluate the speech in light of the guidelines for informative speaking discussed in this chapter.

NOTES

[1] John R. Johnson and Nancy Szczupakiewicz, "The Public Speaking Course: Is It Preparing Students with Work-Related Public Speaking Skills?" *Communication Education,* 36 (1987), 131–137.

[2] Andrew D. Wolvin and Diana Corley, "The Technical Speech Communication Course: A View from the Field," *Association for Communication Administration Bulletin,* 49 (1984), 83–91.

[3] Adapted from Rudolf Flesch, *The Art of Readable Writing* (New York: Harper & Row, 1949), p. 82.

[4] James J. Welsh, *The Speech Writing Guide* (New York: Wiley, 1968), p. 51.

[5] Adapted from a speech by Kenda Creasy Dean. Used with permission.

[6] Adapted from Brenda Gerlach, "The Thickening Fog," *Winning Orations, 1985* (Mankato, Minn.: Interstate Oratorical Association, 1985), p. 73.

[7] Joseph Conrad, "Youth: A Narrative," in *Typhoon and Other Tales of the Sea* (New York: Dodd, Mead, 1963), p. 256.

[8] James Humes, *Roles Speakers Play* (New York: Harper & Row, 1976), p. 25.

[9] Reprinted with permission of Susan R. Hirsch. This speech is also available on the videotape supplement to *The Art of Public Speaking.*

Chapter 15

Speaking to Persuade

Ramon Trujillo began that particular school day by stopping at the library to return an overdue book. "Look," he explained to the librarian, "I know this book was due last week, but I was sick with the flu and couldn't even get out of bed. Do I still have to pay the fine? I can get you a note from my doctor if you need one." The librarian hemmed and hawed. Then he said, "Okay. You don't have a record of any other fines. Just this once."

With a sigh of relief, Ramon went on to his morning classes. At noon he was dashing across campus when a friend stopped him. "How about some lunch?" she asked. "I really can't," replied Ramon. "I have to stand at the table and get signatures on the petition against higher tuition. I'll see you later, though."

During the afternoon, Ramon had a free period, and he used the time to meet with his history professor. "The reason I wanted to see you," he began, "is . . . well . . . I think I deserved a better grade on my last exam. I know you don't like to change grades, but I went back and reviewed all my notes on the World War II question, and I really think I got everything you were looking for." The professor agreed to look at Ramon's exam. "Well," she said when she was finished, "it certainly looks good to me. I'm going to raise your grade from a B-plus to an A-minus."

At dinner that evening, Ramon asked his roommate to loan him $20 until the end of the month. "You know," he said, "it was my Mom's birthday last week. In addition to getting a present for her, I had to buy the last book for my biology class. But I'm working some extra hours next weekend at the pizza place, and I'll be able to pay you back without any problem." After checking to make sure he had enough money, Ramon's roommate said, "Sure. After all, what are friends for?"

If you asked Ramon how he spent his day, he might say, "I returned a book to the library, I went to classes, I worked the petition table, I talked with my history professor, I ate dinner with my roommate." In fact, he spent a large part of his day *persuading*—persuading people to do things that they were reluctant to do or that had not occurred to them. Most of us do a certain amount of persuading every day, although we may not realize it or call it that. Public speaking to persuade is essentially an extension of this. It involves trying to convert a whole group, not just an individual, to your point of view on a particular subject.

Although persuasion has been studied for the past 2,000 years, it is still the subject of lively debate among scholars. There are a number of respected theories about how persuasion works, a variety of scientific models of the persuasive process, even a wide range of competing definitions of persuasion.[1]

For our purpose it is enough to know that when you speak to persuade, you act as an advocate. Your job is to change listeners' minds—to get them to agree with you and, perhaps, to act on that belief. Your goal may be to defend an idea, to refute an opponent, to sell a program, or to inspire people to action. Because persuasive speakers must communicate information clearly and concisely, you will need all the skills you used in speaking to inform. But you will also need new skills—skills that take you from giving information to affecting your listeners' beliefs or actions.

As with other kinds of public speaking, you will be more effective in persuasion if you approach it systematically. Let us begin by looking at some of the psychological principles involved in the persuasive process.

▌ THE PSYCHOLOGY OF PERSUASION

Persuasion is a psychological process. It always occurs in a situation where two or more points of view exist. The speaker believes irradiating fresh meats and vegetables poses a danger to human health, but many listeners do not. The speaker considers euthanasia to be murder, but some in the audience think it is justified in certain circumstances. The speaker wants everyone in the audience to sign up immediately to learn CPR, but most listeners are inclined to procrastinate and will do it "someday." The different points of view may be completely opposed, or they may simply be different in degree. Whichever the case, there must be a disagreement, or else there would be no need for persuasion.

The Challenge of Persuasive Speaking

Of all the kinds of public speaking, persuasion is the most complex and the most challenging. Your objective is more ambitious than in speaking to inform, and audience analysis and adaptation become much more demanding. In some persuasive speeches you will deal with controversial topics that touch on your listeners' most basic attitudes, values, and beliefs. This will increase your listeners' resistance to persuasion and make your task that much more difficult.

It is much easier, for example, to explain the history of capital punishment than to persuade an audience either that capital punishment should be abolished or that it should be reinstituted in every state. In the persuasive speech you must contend not only with your audience's knowledge of capital punishment but also with their attitudes toward crime and justice, their beliefs about whether capital punishment deters people from committing violent crimes, and their values about the taking of human life. Lines of argument that work with one part of the audience may fail with—or even upset—another part. What seems perfectly logical to some listeners may seem wildly irrational to others. No matter how expert you are on the topic, no matter how skillfully you prepare the speech, no matter how captivating your delivery—some listeners will not agree with you.

But this does not mean persuasion is impossible. It does mean you should enter a persuasive speaking situation with a realistic sense of what you can accomplish. You cannot expect a group of die-hard Democrats to become Republicans or a steak lover to turn vegetarian as a result of one speech. If listeners are not strongly committed one way or another on your topic, you can realistically hope your speech will move at least some of them toward your side. If listeners are strongly opposed to your viewpoint, you can consider your speech a success if it leads even a few to reexamine their views.

How successful you are in any particular persuasive speech will depend above all on how well you tailor your message to the values, attitudes, and beliefs of your audience. Persuasion is a strategic activity. Just as a businesswoman or a military commander plots a strategy to gain a big sale or to be victorious in battle, so a persuasive speaker must have a strategy to win the audience to her or his side. In Chapter 5 we considered the general principles of audience analysis and adaptation. Here we need to emphasize two additional principles that are crucial to the psychology of persuasion. The first deals with how listeners process and respond to persuasive messages. The second pertains to the target audience for persuasive speeches.

How Listeners Process Persuasive Messages

We often think of persuasion as something a speaker does "to" an audience.[2] In fact, as a great deal of research shows, persuasion is something a speaker does *with* an audience. Although audiences in the United States seldom interrupt a speaker while she or he is talking, they do not just sit passively and soak in everything the speaker has to say.

Instead, they often engage in a mental give-and-take with the speaker. While they listen, they actively assess the speaker's credibility, delivery, supporting materials, language, reasoning, and emotional appeals. They may respond positively at one point, negatively at another. At times they may argue, inside their own minds, with the speaker. This mental give-and-take is especially vigorous when listeners are highly involved with the topic of the speech and believe it has a direct bearing on their lives.[3]

In a sense, the psychological interaction between a speaker and audience during a persuasive speech is similar to what happens vocally during a conversation—as in this example:

TANYA: I think the government should clamp down on pornography. In addition to being morally offensive, it degrades women and promotes aggressive acts against them.

RASHEED: I agree pornography's a real problem, but I'm not sure the government has a right to censor it. What about free speech? Isn't pornography protected under the First Amendment?

TANYA: I'm all in favor of free speech—especially when it comes to politics. But pornography is not what the Founders had in mind with the Bill of Rights.

RASHEED: What the Founders had in mind is not the issue. The point is that the First Amendment guarantees freedom of speech. If we ban pornography, we would open the door to banning other forms of expression as well.

TANYA: Not necessarily. We already outlaw some kinds of speech because they are dangerous to the community—such as threatening the life of the President or shouting "Fire!" in a crowded building. Why is banning pornography any different?

Much the same kind of interaction might occur during a persuasive speech except that the listener—in this case, Rasheed—would respond to himself rather than out loud.

What does this mean to you as a speaker? It means you must think of your persuasive speech as a kind of mental dialogue with your audience. Most important, you must anticipate possible objections the audience will raise to your point of view and then answer those objections in your speech. You cannot convert skeptical listeners unless you deal directly with the reasons for their skepticism.

As you prepare your persuasive speech, put yourself in the place of your audience and imagine how they will respond. For this to work, you must be as tough on your speech as your audience will be. Every place they will raise a question, answer it. Every place they will have a criticism, answer it. Every place they will see a hole in your argument, fill it. Leave nothing to chance.[4]

The Target Audience

Unfortunately, no matter how carefully you plot your speech, you will seldom be able to persuade all your listeners. Some will be so opposed to your views that you have absolutely no chance of changing their minds. Others will already agree with you, so there is no need to persuade them. Like most audiences, yours will probably contain some listeners who are hostile to your position, some who favor it, some who are undecided, and some who just don't care. You would like to make your speech equally appealing to everyone, but this is rarely possible. Most often you will have a particular *part* of the whole audience that you want to reach with your speech. That part is called the target audience.

Concentrating on a target audience does not mean you should ignore or insult the rest of your listeners. You must always keep in mind the ideas and feelings of your entire audience. But no matter how noble your intentions or how hard you try, you can't persuade all the people all the time. It only makes sense, then, to decide which portion of the audience you *most* want to reach.

Advertising gives us an effective model. Successful commercials are aimed at particular segments of the market, and their appeals are picked to fit the target audience. Banks have found that modern-looking advertisements don't draw as many deposits as old-fashioned ones. Why? Because older people have more money to deposit. Soft-drink commercials, on the other hand, are meant to hook young people. So they feature teenagers, play their kind of music, and echo their values. Beer commercials? They focus on men who portray the strong, masculine, hearty qualities of male blue-collar workers. The reason? Blue-collar men drink the most beer.[5]

For your classroom speeches, you don't have the sophisticated research capability of a large advertising agency. But as we saw in Chapter 5, you can use observation, interviews, and questionnaires to find out where your classmates stand on your speech topic. This is your equivalent of market research. From it you can identify your target audience and the issues you will have to discuss to be convincing. Once you know where your target audience stands, you can tailor your speech to fit their values and concerns—aim at the target, so to speak.

Here, for example, is how one student, Amy Shapiro, determined her

Effective persuasive speakers adjust their remarks to reach their target audience. Here Jack Kemp addresses a committee of the U.S. Congress. His speech would probably have a different tone if he were addressing an audience on a college campus.

target audience for a persuasive speech urging her classmates to pass on the gift of life by signing organ-donor cards.

> There are 22 students in my audience. My audience-analysis questionnaires show that 3 are opposed to donating their organs under any circumstances. I cannot persuade them no matter what I say. My questionnaires also show that 4 have already signed organ-donor cards. I don't need to persuade them. The other 15 students could be persuaded if they knew more about the need for organ donors and about how the process works. They are my target audience.

Not only did Amy pinpoint her target audience, she also knew from her audience-analysis questionnaires the issues she would have to discuss to be convincing:

> The members of my target audience break down this way: 7 give "fear of being pronounced dead prematurely" as their main reason for not signing organ cards; 5 are concerned about their body being "cut up or disfigured"; and 3 cite religious reasons for their opposition. The questionnaires also show that 10 of the 15 don't fully understand the need for organ donors.

With all this information, Amy was able to put together a first-rate speech that focused specifically on her classmates' attitudes and beliefs about signing organ-donor cards. In the speech, she showed the need for organ donations by explaining that there are thousands of people whose only hope for life is to receive a heart, liver, or kidney transplant. She also took care to answer her classmates' fears and objections. She showed that there are strict safeguards to prevent doctors from pulling the plug prematurely to make a heart or liver available for transplant surgery, that donated organs are removed as carefully as if the doctor were operating on a live patient, and that almost all religious leaders approve of organ donation as a way to help save lives. As a result, she was able to convince several of her classmates to sign organ-donor cards.

In the next chapter, we will discuss the methods you can use to hit the target in your persuasive speeches. In the rest of this chapter, we focus on the three major kinds of persuasive speeches and how to organize them most effectively. We will look first at speeches on questions of fact, then at speeches on questions of value, and finally at speeches on questions of policy.

◼ PERSUASIVE SPEECHES ON QUESTIONS OF FACT

What Are Questions of Fact?

What college basketball team has won the most games since 1985? Who was the first African American to sit on the U.S. Supreme Court? How far is it from New York to London? These questions of fact can be answered absolutely. You can look up the answers in a reference book, and no reasonable person would dispute them. The answers are either right or wrong.

But many questions of fact cannot be answered absolutely. There *is* a true answer, but we don't have enough information to know what it is. Some questions like this involve prediction: Will the economy be better or worse next year? Who will win the Super Bowl this season? Will another major earthquake strike California before the year 2000?

Other questions deal with issues on which the facts are murky or inconclusive. What caused the extinction of the dinosaurs? Is sexual orientation genetically determined? How harmful is radon to human health? Who wrote the plays attributed to William Shakespeare? No one knows the final answers to these questions, but that doesn't stop people from speculating about them or from trying to convince other people that they have the best possible answers.

Analyzing Questions of Fact

In some ways, a persuasive speech on a question of fact is similar to an informative speech. But the two kinds of speeches take place in different kinds of situations and for different purposes. The situation for an informative speech is *nonpartisan*. The speaker acts as a lecturer or a teacher. The aim is to give information as impartially as possible, not to argue for a particular point of view. On the other hand, the situation for a persuasive speech on a question of fact is *partisan*. The speaker acts as an advocate. His or her aim is not to be impartial but to present one view of the facts as persuasively as possible. The speaker may mention competing views of the facts, but only to refute them.

As an example of this, consider the assassination of John Kennedy. After more than thirty years, there is still much public debate about what really happened in Dallas on November 22, 1963. Did Lee Harvey Oswald act alone, or was he part of a conspiracy? How many shots were fired at President Kennedy and from what locations? If there was a conspiracy, who was involved in it? The informative speaker would merely recite the known facts on both sides of these questions without drawing a conclusion about which side is correct. The persuasive speaker, however, would draw a conclusion from the known facts and try to convert listeners to his or her point of view.

If there were no possibility of dispute on questions of fact, there would be no need for courtroom trials. In a criminal trial there is usually at least one known fact—a crime has been committed. But did the defendant commit the crime? And if so, for what reason? The prosecuting attorney will try to persuade the jury that the defendant is guilty. The defense attorney will try to persuade the jury that the defendant is innocent. It will be up to the jury to decide which view of the facts is more persuasive.[6]

Organizing Speeches on Questions of Fact

Persuasive speeches on questions of fact are usually organized *topically*. Suppose, for example, you want to convince your classmates that long-term exposure to the electromagnetic fields emitted by power lines and many everyday items such as electric blankets, video display terminals, and microwave ovens can cause serious health problems. You will put your speech together so that each main point presents a *reason* why someone should agree with you:

Specific Purpose: To persuade my audience that long-term exposure to electromagnetic fields can cause serious health problems.

Central Idea: There is increasing evidence that long-term exposure to electromagnetic fields can cause serious health problems.

Main Points:
   I. Laboratory research on cell cultures suggests that electromagnetic fields may promote cancer by interfering with cell growth and the immune system.
  II. Case studies have connected a number of health problems with exposure to electromagnetic fields.
III. A growing number of scientists have expressed concern about the health effects of long-term exposure to electromagnetic fields.

Or suppose you try to persuade your classmates that standardized achievement tests are culturally biased against racial and ethnic minorities. Your specific purpose, central idea, and main points might be:

Specific Purpose: To persuade my audience that standardized achievement tests are culturally biased against racial and ethnic minorities.

Central Idea: The vocabulary, the questions, and the situation of standardized achievement tests all work to lower the scores of children from ethnic and racial minorities.

Main Points:	I.	The vocabulary used in standardized achievement tests is often unfamiliar to children from racial and ethnic minorities.
	II.	The questions asked in standardized achievement tests are frequently based on white, middle-class values and experiences.
	III.	The testing situation for standardized achievement tests may also hinder the performance of minority children.

Occasionally you might arrange a persuasive speech on a question of fact *spatially.* For example:

| *Specific Purpose:* | To persuade my audience that poaching of wild animals is a serious international problem. |
| *Central Idea:* | Poaching—or illegal hunting of wildlife—is threatening the survival of animal species throughout the world. |

Main Points:	I.	In Africa poaching has claimed thousands of leopards, cheetahs, rhinoceroses, and elephants.
	II.	In Asia poaching has all but eliminated Bengal tigers, snow leopards, and musk deer.
	III.	In South America poaching has driven jaguars and swamp deer to the brink of extinction.
	IV.	In North America poaching has drastically reduced the number of bald eagles, grizzly bears, timber wolves, and giant otters.

Notice that in all these examples the speaker's purpose is limited to persuading the audience to accept a particular view of the facts. Sometimes, however, the dispute that gives rise to a persuasive speech will go beyond a question of fact and will turn on a question of value.

■ PERSUASIVE SPEECHES ON QUESTIONS OF VALUE

What Are Questions of Value?

Who is the best NFL quarterback of all time? Is fetal-tissue research morally justifiable? What are the ethical responsibilities of journalists? Such questions not only involve matters of fact, but they also demand *value judgments*—judgments based on a person's own beliefs about what is right or wrong, good or bad, moral or immoral, proper or improper, fair or unfair.

Take the issue of euthanasia. It can be discussed on a purely factual level by asking questions such as, "How long can a person showing no brain activity be sustained on life-support systems?" Or, "How much does it cost to maintain such a person in a hospital or nursing home for one month?" Or, "Are there any countries in which euthanasia is practiced legally?" These are factual questions. The answers you reach are independent of your belief about the morality of euthanasia.

But suppose you ask, "Is it morally justifiable to remove life-support systems from a living body?" Or, "Is it acceptable to burden a family with the cost of maintaining life support when there is no hope for the patient's recovery?" Now you are dealing with questions of value. How you answer will depend not only on your factual knowledge about euthanasia, but also on your moral values.[7]

Analyzing Questions of Value

Contrary to what many people think, questions of value are not simply matters of personal opinion or whim. If you say, "I enjoy bicycle riding," you do not have to give a reason why you enjoy it. You are making a statement about your personal taste—not about the value of biking as a sport or a form of transportation. Even if bicycle riding were the most unpleasant activity ever invented, it could still be one of your favorites.

On the other hand, if you say, "Bicycle riding is the ideal form of land transportation," you are no longer making a statement about your personal enjoyment of biking. Now you are making a statement about a question of value. Whether bicycling is the ideal form of land transportation does not depend on your own likes and dislikes. To defend the statement, you cannot say, "Bicycle riding is the ideal form of land transportation because I like it."

Instead, you must *justify* your claim. The first step is to define what you mean by an "ideal form of land transportation." Do you mean a mode of transportation that gets people where they want to go as fast as possible? That is relatively inexpensive? That is fun? Nonpolluting? Beneficial for the user? In other words, you must establish your *standards* for an "ideal form of land transportation." Then you can show how bicycle riding measures up against those standards.

Whenever you give a speech on a question of value, be sure to give special thought to the standards for your value judgment.

Organizing Speeches on Questions of Value

Persuasive speeches on questions of value are almost always organized *topically*. The most common approach is to devote your first main point to establishing the standards for your value judgment and your second main point to applying those standards to the subject of your speech.

Think back for a moment to the speech about bicycle riding as the ideal form of land transportation. If you organized this speech in topical order, your first main point would identify the standards for an ideal form of land transportation. Your second main point would show how biking measures up against those standards. Here is how your specific purpose, central idea, and main points might look:

Specific Purpose: To persuade my audience that bicycle riding is the ideal form of land transportation.

Central Idea: Bicycle riding is the ideal form of land transportation because it is faster than walking or running, does not exploit animals or people, is nonpolluting, and promotes the health of the rider.

Main Points:
    I. An ideal form of land transportation should meet four major standards.
        A. It should be faster than running or walking.
        B. It should not exploit animals or people.
        C. It should be nonpolluting.
        D. It should be beneficial for the person who uses it.
   II. Bicycle riding meets all these standards for an ideal form of land transportation.
        A. Bicycle riding is faster than walking or running.
        B. Bicycle riding does not exploit the labor of animals or other people.
        C. Bicycle riding is not a source of air, land, water, or noise pollution.
        D. Bicycle riding is extremely beneficial for the health of the rider.

When you speak on a question of value, you do not always have to devote your first main point to setting forth the standards for your value judgment and the second to applying those standards to the topic of the speech. But you must make sure to justify your judgment against *some* identifiable standards. In the following example, notice how the speaker devotes her first main point to judging capital punishment against moral standards and her second main point to judging it against legal standards:

Specific Purpose: To persuade my audience that capital punishment is morally and legally wrong.

Central Idea: Capital punishment violates both the Bible and the U.S. Constitution.

Main Points:
    I. Capital punishment violates the biblical commandment "Thou shalt not kill."
   II. Capital punishment violates the constitutional ban on "cruel and unusual punishment."

As you can see, speeches on questions of value may have strong implications for our actions. A person who is persuaded that capital punishment is morally and legally wrong is more likely to support legislation abolishing the death penalty. But speeches on questions of value do not argue directly for or against particular courses of action. They do not urge listeners to *do* anything.

Once you go beyond arguing right or wrong to arguing that something should or should not be done, you move from a question of value to a question of policy.

PERSUASIVE SPEECHES ON QUESTIONS OF POLICY

What Are Questions of Policy?

Questions of policy arise daily in almost everything we do. At home we debate what to do during spring vacation, whether to buy a new compact-disc player, which movie to see on the weekend. At work we discuss whether to go on strike, what strategy to use in selling a product, how to improve communication between management and employees. As citizens we ponder whether to vote for or against a political candidate, what to do about abortion, how to reduce the federal budget deficit.

All these are questions of policy because they deal with specific courses of action. Questions of policy inevitably involve questions of fact. (How can we decide whether to vote for a candidate unless we know the facts of her or his stand on the issues?) They may also involve questions of value. (The policy you favor on abortion will be affected by whether you think abortion is moral or immoral.) But questions of policy *always* go beyond questions of fact or value to decide whether something should or should not be done.

When put formally, questions of policy usually include the word "should," as in these examples:

> What steps should-be taken to protect people's right to privacy in the information age?

> How should the United States deal with the growing problem of gun use by teenagers?

> Should sports teams be required to change names and mascots that are demeaning to Native Americans?

> What measures should be taken to improve the quality of public education in the United States?

> Should Washington, D.C., be granted statehood?

Types of Speeches on Questions of Policy

When you speak on a question of policy, your goal may be either to gain passive agreement or to motivate immediate action from your listeners. Deciding which goal you want to achieve is crucial, for it will affect almost every aspect of your speech.

Speeches to Gain Passive Agreement   If your goal is passive agreement, you will try to get your audience to agree with you that a certain policy is desirable, but you will not necessarily encourage the audience to do anything to enact the policy. For example, suppose you want to persuade people that the United States should abolish the electoral college and elect the President by direct popular vote. If you seek passive agreement, you will try to get your audience to concur that the President should be chosen directly by the people rather than by the electoral college. But you will not urge the audience to take any action right now to help change presidential election procedures.

Here are some specific purpose statements for policy speeches that seek passive agreement:

> To persuade my audience that the United States should institute a national sales tax to help balance the federal budget.

> To persuade my audience that there should be tougher enforcement of child-support payments when the parents become separated or divorced.

> To persuade my audience that the federal government should institute a ban on all advertising for cigarettes and other tobacco products.

> To persuade my audience that college scholarship athletes should receive a $200 monthly stipend for personal expenses.

> To persuade my audience that businesses should not be allowed to use genetic testing to screen prospective employees.

In each of these cases, the speaker's aim is to affect the thinking of listeners—to convince them that the speaker's policy is necessary and practical. The speaker is not trying to get listeners to take action in support of the policy.

Speeches to Gain Immediate Action   When your goal is immediate action, you want to do more than get your listeners to nod their heads in agreement. You want to motivate them to action. Beyond convincing them that your cause is sound, you will try to rouse them to take action right away—to sign a petition for abolishing the electoral college, to campaign for lower tuition, to begin a regular exercise program, to contribute to a fund drive, to vote for a political candidate, to donate time to the Special Olympics, and so forth.

Here are some examples of specific purpose statements for policy speeches that seek immediate action:

> To persuade my audience to volunteer as literacy tutors.

> To persuade my audience to participate in intramural athletics.

> To persuade my audience to vote in the next presidential election.

> To persuade my audience to give blood through the Red Cross.

> To persuade my audience to sign a petition for longer library hours.

Some experts say you should seek action from your audience whenever possible. Although it is much easier to evoke passive agreement than to elicit action, the listener is not making much of a commitment by thinking, "Sure, I agree with you." Within a day or two that same listener may forget entirely about your speech—and about her or his agreement with it.

Action, however, reinforces belief. There is a great deal of research showing that if you can persuade a listener to take some kind of action—even if it is no more than signing a petition, putting a bumper sticker on a car, or attending a meeting to learn about the sorority system—you have gained a more serious commitment. Once a listener acts in behalf of a speaker's position, no matter if the action is minor, she or he is more likely to remain committed to the speaker's position and to take future action in support of it.[8]

When you call for action in a persuasive speech, you should make your recommendations as specific as possible. Don't just urge listeners to "do something." Tell them exactly what to do and how to do it. If you want them to donate blood to the Red Cross, tell them where to go, how to get there, what will happen after they arrive, and how long the whole procedure will take. After the speech give everyone a brochure from the Red Cross to reinforce your message. The more specific your instructions, the more likely your call to action will succeed.[9]

Analyzing Questions of Policy

Regardless of whether your aim is to elicit passive agreement or to gain immediate action, you will face three basic issues whenever you discuss a question of policy—need, plan, and practicality.

Need   There is no point in arguing for a policy unless you can show a need for it:

Is there a need for more student parking on campus?

Is there a need for a system of standardized national tests for high-school graduation?

Is there a need for a balanced budget amendment to the U.S. Constitution?

Your first step is to convince listeners there is a problem with things as they are. No doubt you have heard the old saying, "If it ain't broke, don't fix it." People are not inclined to adopt a new policy unless they are convinced the old one is not working. This is why the burden of proof always rests with the speaker who advocates change. If you are speaking in favor of a new policy, you must prove to your listeners' satisfaction that there is a serious problem with existing policy, that the problem will only get worse with time, and that action must be taken now to solve the problem. (Of course, you may be defending present policy, in which case you will argue that there is *no* need to change—that things are already working as well as can be expected.)

Plan   The second basic issue of policy speeches is plan. Once you have shown that a problem exists, you must explain your plan for solving it.

> What can we do to get more student parking on campus?

> What subjects should be covered in a system of national education testing, and who will create the tests?

> What specific provisions should be part of a balanced budget amendment to the U.S. Constitution?

Answering such questions is especially important if you call for a new policy. It's easy to complain about problems; the real challenge is to develop solutions.

In most classroom speeches, you will not have time to describe your plan in detail, but you should at least identify its major features. For example, if you advocate new measures to protect personal privacy against electronic data gathering in our high-tech society, you might follow the lead of some proponents and urge the creation of strict controls over the collection, storage, and sharing of personal information by all businesses and government agencies. When explaining your plan, you might draw upon European countries such as England, France, Germany, and Sweden, all of which have curbs on the electronic storage of personal information. But whatever your plan, be sure to explain any aspects of it that might seriously affect your audience's willingness to accept it.

Practicality   The third basic issue of policy speeches is practicality. Once you have presented a plan, you must show that it will work. Will it solve the problem? Or will it create new and more serious problems?

> You could provide more student parking by building a multilevel parking ramp on campus, but the cost would require a sharp increase in tuition.

> National testing for all high-school students would create uniform educational standards throughout the United States, but there is no guarantee it would produce better teaching and learning.

> A balanced budget amendment to the U.S. Constitution would help eliminate deficit spending, but it might also reduce the government's ability to respond to short-term financial crises.

These are significant concerns. Whenever you advocate a new policy, you must be prepared to show it is workable. No matter how serious a problem may be, listeners usually want some assurance that a speaker's plan will actually solve the problem.[10] One way to provide this assurance is to cite expert testimony in support of your policy. An even better way is to show that a plan similar to yours has been successfully implemented elsewhere. For example, if you support giving the President of the United States line-item veto power, you might point to the fact that the governors of 43 states have used the line-item veto for years to help balance their budgets.

If you oppose a shift in policy, one of your major arguments will be that the change is impractical—that it will create more problems than it can solve. Many parents and educators, for instance, say that imposing standardized national tests for high-school graduation will destroy the autonomy of local school districts and result in federal control of classrooms in every part of the nation. Other opponents say that such tests will discriminate against late bloomers, racial and ethnic minorities, and other children with special needs. If listeners accept these arguments, they will probably decide that a policy requiring standardized national tests for high-school graduation should not be adopted.

How much of your speech should you devote to need, to plan, and to practicality? The answer depends on your topic and your audience. If your audience is not aware of the dangers posed by privacy-invading technology in government and business, you will have to give much of your time to need before covering plan and practicality. On the other hand, if your listeners already know about the problems of the federal budget deficit, you can remind them quickly of need and then devote most of your speech to plan and practicality.

Or suppose you advocate a ban on smoking in local restaurants. Most people agree that secondhand smoke is a serious health problem, but many are concerned that restaurants will lose customers if smoking is prohibited.

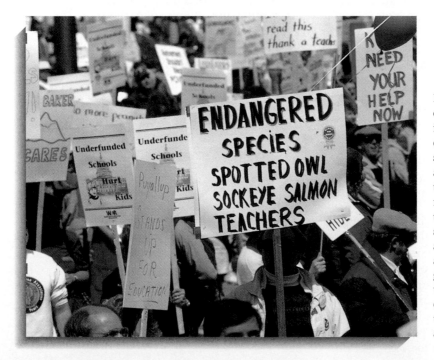

Persuasive speeches on questions of policy are given whenever people debate specific courses of action. To be effective, such speeches need to deal with the three basic issues of need, plan, and practicality. The amount of attention given to each issue will vary depending on the speaker's topic, purpose, and audience.

Therefore, you should devote a large part of your speech to practicality—to showing that smoke-free laws have already been passed in a number of cities without causing a decline in restaurant business.[11]

Organizing Speeches on Questions of Policy

Effective organization is crucial when you seek to persuade listeners on a question of policy. Although any of the basic patterns of organization explained in Chapter 8 can be used when discussing a question of policy, there are four special patterns that are especially useful for policy speeches. They are problem-solution order, problem-cause-solution order, comparative advantages order, and Monroe's motivated sequence.

Problem-Solution Order   If you advocate a change in policy, your main points often will fall naturally into problem-solution order. In the first main point you demonstrate the need for a new policy by showing the extent and seriousness of the problem. In the second main point you explain your plan for solving the problem and show its practicality. For example:[12]

Specific Purpose: To persuade my audience that urgent action is needed to deal with the environmental problems created by disposable batteries.

Central Idea: Solving the environmental dangers created by disposable batteries requires action by business, government, and individual citizens.

Main Points: I.   Disposable batteries have become one of America's most serious environmental dangers.
  A.   Disposable batteries are composed of three highly toxic elements—cadmium, mercury, and lead.
  B.   After the batteries are thrown away, these toxic elements escape into the environment, polluting the air and groundwater.
  II.   The problem can be solved by business, government, and individual action.
  A.   Business should continue its efforts to develop new kinds of batteries.
  B.   Government should require recycling of disposable batteries.
  C.   Individuals should use rechargeable batteries instead of disposable batteries.

You can use the problem-solution format just as easily to organize a speech opposing a change in policy. In such a speech your job is to defend the current system and to attack your opponents' proposed policy. Thus in the first main point you might argue that there is *not* a need for change. In the second main point you might show that even if there were a serious problem, the suggested new policy would *not* solve it and would create serious problems of its own. For example:

Specific Purpose: To persuade my audience that the government should not pass laws limiting the amount of money spent in political campaigns.

Central Idea: Limiting the amount of money spent in political campaigns is neither necessary nor practical.

Main Points:
 I. Campaign spending limits are not necessary.
  A. The amount of money spent by a candidate is not the decisive factor in most elections.
  B. Almost all of the rise in campaign spending since 1980 is due either to inflation or to the high cost of television advertising.
 II. Besides being unnecessary, campaign spending limits are highly impractical.
  A. National campaign spending limits cannot adjust to the diverse needs of candidates in different parts of the country.
  B. Campaign spending limits hurt a challenger's odds of unseating an incumbent officeholder.

Problem-Cause-Solution Order For a variation on problem-solution order, you might arrange your speech in problem-cause-solution order. This produces a speech with three main points—the first identifying a problem, the second analyzing the causes of the problem, and the third presenting a solution to the problem. For instance:[12]

Specific Purpose: To persuade my audience that colleges and universities should take stronger action to control campus crime.

Central Idea: Campus crime is a serious problem that requires action by security officials, school administrators, and students alike.

Main Points:
 I. Violent crime on college campuses is a serious problem.
  A. Recent studies show an alarming increase in reported cases of robbery and physical assault on college campuses all across the U.S.
  B. The problem is worse than statistics reveal because many campus crimes are not reported to law-enforcement authorities.
 II. There are three major causes specific to college life for the growth of campus crime.
  A. Campus security officials are often unqualified and poorly trained.

    B. College administrators have not given priority to programs for preventing campus crime.

    C. Students often do not take sufficient precautions to protect themselves and their possessions.

  III. An effective solution must deal with all three major causes of the problem.

    A. Schools must upgrade the quality and training of campus security officials.

    B. College administrators must develop programs to help prevent campus crime from occurring.

    C. Students must be more cautious in protecting themselves and their possessions.

Some teachers prefer this method of organization because it requires a speaker to identify the causes of the problem. This in turn makes it easier to check whether the proposed solution will get at the causes of the problem, rather than merely controlling its symptoms.

Comparative Advantages Order When your audience already agrees that a problem exists, you can devote your speech to comparing the advantages and disadvantages of competing solutions. In such a situation, you might put your speech in comparative advantages order. Rather than dwelling on the problem, you would devote each main point to explaining why your solution is preferable to other proposed solutions.

Suppose you want to convince your audience that the U.S. space program should shift its emphasis from highly glamorous staffed flights such as the space shuttle to unstaffed scientific missions that gather information about other planets and the nature of the solar system. Using comparative advantages order, you would compare unstaffed scientific missions with staffed space flights and show why the former would be a better choice. Your specific purpose, central idea, and main points might look like this:

Specific Purpose: To persuade my audience that the U.S. space program should put greater priority on unstaffed scientific missions that gather information about the planets and the solar system.

Central Idea: Unstaffed scientific missions are less costly and more beneficial than staffed space flights.

Main Points: I. Unstaffed scientific missions are far less costly than staffed space flights.

       II. Unstaffed scientific missions provide many more practical benefits than staffed space flights.

Monroe's Motivated Sequence Developed in the 1930s by Alan Monroe, a professor of speech at Purdue University, the motivated sequence is tailor-made for policy speeches that seek immediate action. The sequence has five steps that follow the psychology of persuasion:[14]

1. *Attention.* First you gain the attention of your audience. You do this in the introduction by using one or more of the methods described in Chapter 9—relating to the audience, showing the importance of the topic, making a startling statement, arousing curiosity or suspense, posing a question, telling a dramatic story, or using visual aids.

2. *Need.* Having captured the interest of your audience, you next make them feel a need for change. You show there is a serious problem with the existing situation. It is important to state the need clearly and to illustrate it with strong supporting materials—statistics, examples, and testimony—that relate directly to the audience's values or vital interests. By the end of this step, listeners should be so concerned about the problem that they are psychologically primed to hear your solution.

3. *Satisfaction.* Having aroused a sense of need, you satisfy it by providing a solution to the problem. You present your plan and show how it will work. Be sure to offer enough details about the plan to give listeners a clear understanding of it.

4. *Visualization.* Having given your plan, you intensify desire for it by visualizing its benefits. The key to this step is using vivid imagery to show your listeners how *they* will profit from your policy. Make them *see* how much better conditions will be once your plan is adopted.

5. *Action.* Once the audience is convinced your policy is beneficial, you are ready to call for action. Say exactly what you want the audience to do—and how to do it. Give them the address to write to. Tell them where they should go to join the Young Republicans. Show them how to sign up for counseling. Then conclude with a final stirring appeal that reinforces their commitment to act.

Many students prefer the motivated sequence because it is more detailed than problem-solution order. It follows the process of human thinking and leads the listener step by step to the desired action. One indication of its effectiveness is that it is widely used by people who make their living by persuasion—especially advertisers. The next time you watch television, pay close attention to the commercials. You will find that many of them follow the motivated sequence, as in this example:

Attention: It is late in the day. We see a business conference room. A project manager and several others are gathered around a table. Some are sitting; others are standing. They are putting the final touches on the company's bid for an important contract. Tightly framed close-ups and quick snatches of conversation heighten the sense of tension and drama.

Need: "This is great work," says an associate seated to the manager's left. "I don't see how the competition can beat it." "They can't,"

Persuasive speeches on questions of policy require careful organization to move listeners to the speaker's point of view. Speeches that seek immediate action from the audience can often be arranged according to a special five-step method known as Monroe's motivated sequence.

the manager replies. "Now we have to get it to the coast by tomorrow morning. If we don't, we're all in trouble."

Satisfaction: The manager and her associate exchange knowing looks. "U.S. Express," they say in unison, nodding their heads in agreement. The announcer, in voice-over, tells us: "U.S. Express guarantees overnight delivery—without fail."

Visualization: We see the business conference room the next day. The manager is listening to the speaker phone. "Your bid arrived this morning," the voice on the phone announces. "You really put all the pieces together. The competition couldn't come close." The manager and her colleagues smile in satisfaction. One person raises his right arm in a signal of triumph.

Action: The audience is urged to rely on U.S. Express whenever shipments have to arrive overnight.

Try using the motivated sequence when you want to spur listeners to action. You should find it easy and effective, as did one student who used it in a speech urging classmates to work for passage of a local tenants' rights bill. Here are the highlights of his speech:

Attention: Have you ever had cockroaches running through the cupboards in your apartment? Have you sweltered in the heat because the air conditioning didn't work? Or shivered in the cold because the furnace was broken? Or waited months for the security deposit you never got back even though you left your apartment as clean as when you moved in?

Need: Throughout this city students and other apartment tenants are being victimized by unresponsive and unethical landlords. Just last year more than 200 complaints were filed with the city housing department, but no action has been taken against the landlords.

Satisfaction: These problems could be solved by passing a strong tenants' rights bill that defines the rights of tenants, specifies the obligations of landlords, and imposes strict penalties for violators.

Visualization: Such bills have worked in a number of college communities across the nation. If one were passed here, you would no longer have to worry about substandard sanitary or safety conditions in your apartment. Your landlord could not violate the terms of your lease or steal your security deposit.

Action: A tenants' rights bill has been proposed to the city council. You can help get it passed by signing the petition I will pass around after my speech. I also urge you to help by circulating petitions among your friends and by turning out to support the bill when it is debated in the city council next week. If we all work together, we can get this bill through the council.

Monroe's motivated sequence is entirely compatible with the standard method of speech outlining discussed in Chapter 10. The following outline shows how one speaker incorporated the sequence into a speech supporting legislation to protect the personal privacy of Americans against electronic data gathering. In its full form, the outline included supporting materials for all the subpoints in the body of the speech.

Specific Purpose: To persuade my audience that the United States should act now to protect its citizens against electronic invasions of their personal privacy.

Central Idea: The loss of personal privacy in our electronic society is a serious problem that requires decisive action.

INTRODUCTION

Attention:
I. Would you let a perfect stranger examine your medical files, peek at your personal finances, eavesdrop on your phone calls, or invade other aspects of your private life?
II. Yet all of these are happening as a result of privacy-invading technology by businesses and government agencies.
III. The erosion of personal privacy has become one of the most serious problems facing Americans in our high-tech, electronic age.
IV. Today I would like to explain the extent of this problem and encourage you to support a solution to it.

BODY

Need: I.   The use of electronic data gathering by business and government poses a serious threat to personal privacy.
                   A. Businesses and government agencies have compiled massive amounts of information on the personal lives of most Americans.
                   B. There are few laws protecting Americans against the gathering or misuse of personal information by businesses and government agencies.

Satisfaction: II. The problem could be greatly reduced by the passage of federal privacy laws.
                   A. These laws should impose strict controls on the collection of personal information by businesses and government agencies.
                   B. These laws should also include stiff penalties on anyone who uses personal information for unauthorized purposes.

Visualization: III. Similar laws have worked in other countries and can work in the United States.
                   A. The practicality of privacy laws has been demonstrated by their success in almost all the countries of Western Europe.
                   B. If the U.S. had such laws, you would once again have control over your medical files, financial records, and other kinds of personal information.

CONCLUSION

Action: I.   So I urge you to support privacy legislation by signing the petition I am passing around to be sent to our state's U.S. Senators and Representatives.
                   II. As Congressman Jack Fields has stated, "This is not a Democratic or Republican issue. . . . Privacy is a basic human right."

Try using the motivated sequence when you seek immediate action from your listeners. Over the years it has worked for countless speakers—and it can work for you as well.

▮ SAMPLE SPEECH WITH COMMENTARY

The following persuasive speech was presented in a public speaking class at the University of Wisconsin.[15] It deals with a question of policy and provides an excellent example of problem-solution structure.

As you read the speech, notice how the speaker deals with the issues of need, plan, and practicality. Notice also how she anticipates the potential objections of her audience and answers those objections at various stages of the speech. Finally, observe how clear and uncluttered the speech is. There are few wasted words, and the ideas progress cleanly and crisply.

THE PROBLEM WITH PENNIES

Susan Ingraham

COMMENTARY

SPEECH

The opening quotations capture attention with their clever variations on traditional sayings about pennies.

The contrast between the three traditional sayings quoted here and the variations on those sayings presented in paragraph 1 provides a witty way for the speaker to lead into revealing her topic and stating her central idea. The final sentence of this paragraph—"It's time to let this dinosaur of our economy go extinct"—is especially effective.

The speaker begins this paragraph with three questions that most listeners have in their minds at this stage of the speech. By stating that she changed her mind about these questions as a result of her research, the speaker suggests that listeners should change their minds too.

The speaker starts the body of her speech by stating her first main point—that pennies cause problems for individuals, for businesses, and for the nation as a whole. Her repeated use of "you" throughout this paragraph relates the topic to the audience and helps draw them further into the speech.

"A nickel for your thoughts." "A nickel saved is a nickel earned." "Nickels from heaven."

Okay, maybe these phrases don't have quite the same ring as the original sayings—"A penny for your thoughts," "A penny saved is a penny earned," and "Pennies from heaven." But it's a fact of our nation's economic life that the penny is becoming obsolete. Inflation over the past few decades has been the death of penny candy, penny arcades, and penny bubble gum. The fact is that pennies don't buy much of anything any more. The age of the penny is over. It's time to let this dinosaur of our economy go extinct.

Sure, most of you say, pennies can be annoying. But why do we have to get rid of them? Why must we change something that's worked for so long? And what would we do without pennies? I had the same questions when I started work on this speech. But as a result of my research, I'm convinced that the continued use of pennies is a costly problem and that we can get along just fine without them. Today, I hope to convince you of the same thing.

The place to begin is by noting that pennies cause problems for individuals, for businesses, and for the nation as a whole. Many Americans consider pennies a useless annoyance. According to my class survey, about two-thirds of you find pennies bothersome. They take up space and add weight to your pockets, wallets, and purses. They get in the way when you're trying to find other coins. They slow down checkout lines when you have to search for exact change. And most of the time when you really need coins—for copy machines, pay phones, vending machines, and video games—you can't use pennies anyway.

The speaker uses statistics and an example to support her claim that many people don't use pennies. The story from Noel Gunther works well because it is richly textured and recounts a situation with which many college students can identify.

In fact, many people *don't* use pennies. A survey by the U.S. Mint showed that only half of the 12,000 people questioned use pennies on a daily basis. Most of the other half collect pennies around the house, waiting until they have enough to cash in at the bank. It can be a long wait. In a *Los Angeles Times* article, writer Noel Gunther explained that during his last two years in college, he and his roommate saved all their pennies so they could throw a "Pennies from Heaven" party for graduation. They filled six jars with what looked like a fortune. The day before graduation, they emptied the jars and counted out $21.56—barely enough to buy beverages!

The statistics in this paragraph are presented clearly and come from credible sources. Although most listeners were skeptical at the start of this speech about the need to abolish pennies, the strength of the speaker's evidence won most of them over by the end.

Pennies are a nuisance for the business community as well as for individuals. The National Association of Convenience Stores estimates that an average of two seconds is spent handling pennies during each of its members' 10 billion annual cash transactions. That comes out to a total of 5.5 million hours spent handling pennies—at an annual cost of $22 million. According to *Fortune* magazine, some banks charge up to 30 cents for every dollar's worth of pennies they process. This makes it very costly for some businesses to accept pennies.

In this and the next paragraph, the speaker presents a combination of statistics and testimony to demonstrate the problems created for the nation as a whole by keeping pennies in circulation.

Keeping pennies in circulation also costs the nation as a whole. Every year the Treasury Department takes about 7 billion pennies out of circulation because they are bent or worn out. According to the Treasury Department, several billion more pennies go into mayonnaise jars, coffee cans, piggy banks, and dresser drawers. Or they are simply thrown away. In the survey mentioned earlier in my speech, the U.S. Mint reported that 6 percent of American adults simply jettison their pennies with the trash!

The evidence in this paragraph is particularly strong and builds cumulatively to the statement, based on testimony from U.S. Treasury officials, that "it costs our society considerably more than a penny to transact a penny's worth of business."

To keep an adequate supply of pennies in circulation, the U.S. Mint creates approximately 12 billion new pennies each year. The cost of manufacturing these new pennies is .66 of a cent apiece, which adds up to almost $80 million a year. As Treasury officials told *U.S. News & World Report,* when you add on storage and handling expenses, it costs our society considerably more than a penny to transact a penny's worth of business.

A transition bridging the first and second main points helps listeners keep track of where the speaker is in the speech.

Now the speaker moves into her second main point, in which she presents a solution to the problems caused by pennies. The solution has four steps, each of which is explained clearly and concisely so listeners will understand exactly what the speaker is proposing.

By demonstrating how her plan will work, the speaker answers the potential objections of her audience to the plan. Notice how much less effective the speech would have been if the speaker had failed to explain the procedures by which purchases and sales taxes will be rounded off to the nearest nickel.

The speaker reaches the final step in her plan, which calls for the total elimination of pennies from the economy.

Having presented her plan, the speaker now shows its practicality. In this paragraph, she argues that pennies can be eliminated from the U.S. economy today as easily as half-cent coins were eliminated during the nineteenth century.

Here the speaker reinforces the practicality of her plan by relating it to the everyday experiences of her audience. Dealing with questions of practicality is especially im-

You can now see the magnitude of the problem with pennies. Fortunately, it is a problem that can be easily solved.

The solution I recommend is similar to a plan supported by the Coin Coalition, a group working to eliminate pennies from our economy. The plan has four basic steps. First, the federal government should legalize and standardize the rounding off of all purchases to the nearest nickel. This rounding off should take place after all items in a given transaction are totaled but before the sales tax is added. Because the number of purchases rounded up would roughly equal the number rounded down, this would not cause any increased cost to consumers.

Second, the sales tax should also be rounded off to the nearest nickel. Both the customer and the state would stand an equal chance of gaining or losing a maximum of two cents on each purchase. In essence, this is no different from what you do when you file your income taxes—except that in computing your income taxes, you round everything off to the nearest dollar.

Because the first two steps of this plan will eliminate the need for pennies, the third step is for the U.S. Mint to stop making new pennies. As we have seen, this will save the taxpayers some $80 million a year in minting costs alone.

The fourth step of this plan is for people to cash in the pennies already in circulation, thereby removing pennies entirely from the money supply.

I admit that it may be hard to imagine a world without pennies, but there is plenty of evidence that this plan will work. James Benfield, Executive Director of the Coin Coalition, notes that when the U.S. stopped minting half-cent coins in 1857, a similar procedure of rounding off purchases and phasing out the coins worked extremely well. None of us miss the half-cent, and in a few years none of us will miss the penny.

Whether we realize it or not, many of us already round off some of our purchases to the nearest nickel. Think for a moment of the "Take a Penny, Leave a Penny" containers next to the cash registers at local portant in a speech such as this in which listeners are likely to be skeptical about the speaker's plan.

The speaker begins her conclusion by summarizing her main points.

The closing sentence of the speech is especially effective. By echoing the introduction in tone as well as content, it gives the speech a strong sense of closure and reinforces the speaker's point that eliminating pennies from the economy can be easily accomplished.

convenience stores. Every time you take a few pennies from the box to pay for your purchase or leave a few pennies from your change, you are actually rounding off the amount you pay to the nearest nickel.

In conclusion, pennies create problems for individuals, for businesses, and for the nation as a whole. The time and money currently wasted in using and minting pennies could be put to more productive ends. By rounding off purchases and sales taxes to the nearest nickel, by ending production of new pennies, and by letting old pennies drop out of use, the problems created by pennies could be eliminated without upsetting the economy. And just as we have gotten used to life without penny candy, penny arcades, and penny bubble gum, so I think, given time, we will also get used to the phrase "a nickel saved is a nickel earned."

SUMMARY

Of all the kinds of public speaking, persuasion is the most complex and the most challenging. When you speak to persuade, you act as an advocate. Your job is to sell a program, to defend an idea, to refute an opponent, or to inspire people to action.

How successful you are in any particular persuasive speech will depend above all on how well you tailor your message to the values, attitudes, and beliefs of your audience. Careful listeners do not sit passively and soak in everything a speaker has to say. While they listen, they actively assess the speaker's credibility, supporting materials, language, reasoning, and emotional appeals. You should think of your speech as a kind of mental dialogue with your audience. Most important, you need to identify your target audience, anticipate the possible objections they will raise to your point of view, and answer those objections in your speech. You cannot convert skeptical listeners unless you deal directly with the reasons for their skepticism.

Persuasive speeches may center on questions of fact, questions of value, or questions of policy. Some questions of fact can be answered absolutely. Others cannot—either because the facts are murky or because there is not enough information available to us. When giving a persuasive speech about a question of fact, your role is akin to that of a lawyer in a courtroom trial. You will try to get your listeners to accept your view of the facts.

Questions of value go beyond the immediate facts to involve a person's beliefs about what is right or wrong, good or bad, moral or immoral, ethical or unethical. When speaking about a question of value, you must justify your opinion by establishing standards for your value judgment. Although questions of value often have strong implications for our actions, speeches on questions of value do not argue directly for or against particular courses of action.

Once you go beyond arguing right or wrong to urging that something should or should not be done, you move to a question of policy. When you speak on a question of policy, your goal may be to evoke passive agreement or to spark immediate action. In either case, you will face three basic issues— need, plan, and practicality. How much of your speech you devote to each issue will depend on your topic and your audience.

There are several options for organizing speeches on questions of policy. If you advocate a change in policy, your main points will often fall naturally into problem-solution order or into problem-cause-solution order. If your audience already agrees that a problem exists, you may be able to use comparative advantages order. Whenever you seek immediate action from listeners, you should consider a more specialized organizational pattern known as Monroe's motivated sequence, whose five steps are based on the psychology of persuasion.

REVIEW QUESTIONS

After reading this chapter, you should be able to answer the following questions:

1. What is the difference between an informative speech and a persuasive speech? Why is speaking to persuade more challenging than speaking to inform?

2. What does it mean to say that audiences engage in a mental dialogue with the speaker as they listen to a speech? What implications does this mental give-and-take hold for effective persuasive speaking?

3. What is the target audience for a persuasive speech?

4. What are questions of fact? How does a persuasive speech on a question of fact differ from an informative speech? Give an example of a specific purpose statement for a persuasive speech on a question of fact.

5. What are questions of value? Give an example of a specific purpose statement for a persuasive speech on a question of value.

6. What are questions of policy? Give an example of a specific purpose statement for a persuasive speech on a question of policy.

7. Explain the difference between passive agreement and immediate action as goals for persuasive speeches on questions of policy.

8. What are the three basic issues you must deal with when discussing a question of policy? What will determine the amount of attention you give to each of these issues in any particular speech?

9. What four methods of organization are used most often in persuasive speeches on questions of policy?

10. What are the five steps of Monroe's motivated sequence? Why is the motivated sequence especially useful in speeches that seek immediate action from listeners?

APPLICATION EXERCISES

1. Look back at the story of Ramon Trujillo at the beginning of this chapter (page 336). Like Ramon, most people do a certain amount of persuading every day in normal conversation. Keep a journal of your communication activities for an entire day, making special note of all instances in which you tried to persuade someone else to your point of view. Choose one of those instances and prepare a brief analysis of it.

   In your analysis, answer the following questions: (1) Who was the audience for your persuasive effort? (2) What was the "specific purpose" and "central idea" of your persuasive message? (3) Did you rehearse your persuasive message ahead of time, or did it arise spontaneously from the situation? (4) Were you successful in achieving your "specific purpose"? (5) If you faced the same situation again, what strategic changes would you make in your persuasive effort?

2. Below are four specific purposes for persuasive speeches. In each case explain whether the speech associated with it concerns a question of fact, a question of value, or a question of policy. Then rewrite the specific purpose statement to make it appropriate for a speech about one of the other two kinds of questions. For instance, if the original purpose statement is about a question of policy, write a new specific purpose statement that deals with the same topic as either a question of fact or a question of value.

   EXAMPLE:

   Original statement: To persuade my audience that it is unfair for judges to favor natural parents over adoptive parents in child custody disputes. (question of value)

   Rewritten statement: To persuade my audience that the courts should establish clear guidelines for settling disputes between adoptive parents and natural parents in child custody cases. (question of policy)

   a. To persuade my audience to donate time as a community volunteer.

   b. To persuade my audience that violence on television is a major cause of violent behavior in society.

   c. To persuade my audience that a national sales tax should be adopted to help balance the federal budget.

   d. To persuade my audience that it is unethical for businesses to use genetic testing in screening potential employees.

3. Choose a topic for a persuasive speech on a question of policy. Create two specific purpose statements about that topic—one for a speech to gain passive agreement, another for a speech to motivate immediate action. Once you have the specific purpose statements, explain how the speech seeking immediate action would differ in structure and persuasive appeals from the speech seeking passive agreement.

4. Analyze the sample speech with commentary at the end of this chapter ("The Problem with Pennies," pages 358–360). Because this is a speech on a question of policy, pay special attention to how the speaker deals with the three basic issues of need, plan, and practicality. Does the speaker present a convincing case that a serious problem exists? Does she offer a clear plan to solve the problem? Does she demonstrate that the plan is practical?

5. Select a television commercial that is organized according to Monroe's motivated sequence. Prepare a brief analysis in which you (a) identify the target audience for the commercial and (b) describe each step in the motivated sequence as it appears in the commercial.

NOTES

[1] On the difficulty of defining persuasion, see Richard M. Perloff, *The Dynamics of Persuasion* (Hillsdale, N.J.: Lawrence Erlbaum, 1993), pp. 10–16; Deirdre D. Johnston, *The Art and Science of Persuasion* (Dubuque, Iowa: W.C. Brown, 1994), pp. 2–27.

[2] Kathleen Kelley Reardon, *Persuasion in Practice* (Newbury Park, Calif.: Sage, 1991), p. 3.

[3] Readers familiar with recent research in communication will recognize that this paragraph reflects cognitive processing theories of persuasion—especially Petty and Cacioppo's Elaboration Likelihood Model. For a full presentation of their model, see Richard E. Petty and John T. Cacioppo, "The Elaboration Likelihood Model of Persuasion," in Leonard T. Berkowitz (ed.), *Advances in Experimental and Social Psychology*, Vol. 19 (New York: Academic Press, 1986), pp. 123–205. For an excellent overview, see Alice H. Eagly and Shelly Chaiken, *The Psychology of Attitudes* (Fort Worth, Tex.: Harcourt Brace Jovanovich, 1993), pp. 305–325.

[4] There is a great deal of research confirming the need for persuasive speakers to answer potential objections to their arguments. See, for example, Mike Allen, "Meta-Analysis Comparing the Persuasiveness of One-Sided and Two-Sided Messages," *Western Journal of Speech Communication*, 55 (1991), 390–404.

[5] Alec Benn, *The 27 Most Common Mistakes in Advertising* (New York: American Management Association, 1978), pp. 84–85.

[6] See David L. Vancil, *Rhetoric and Argumentation* (Boston: Allyn and Bacon, 1993), pp. 26–30, for further discussion of questions of fact.

[7] For fuller discussion of the relationship between questions of value and questions of fact, see Vancil, *Rhetoric and Argumentation*, pp. 30–32; Ronald Lee and Karen King Lee, *Arguing Persuasively* (New York: Longman, 1989), pp. 50–52.

[8] See, for example, James Price Dillard, "Self-Inference and Foot-in-the-Door Technique," *Human Communication Research*, 16 (1990), 422–447.

[9] Daniel J. O'Keefe, *Persuasion: Theory and Research* (Newbury Park, Calif.: Sage, 1990), pp. 159–161.

[10] Kim Witte, "Putting the Fear Back into Fear Appeals: The Extended Parallel Process Model," *Communication Monographs,* 59 (1992), 329–349.

[11] For more detail on strategies to deal with the issues of need, plan, and practicality, see Ruth Anne Clark, *Persuasive Messages* (New York: Harper & Row, 1984), pp. 119–185.

[12] Based on Jeffrey E. Jamison, "Alkali Batteries: Powering Electronics and Polluting the Environment," *Winning Orations, 1991* (Mankato, Minn.: Interstate Oratorical Association, 1991), pp. 43–46.

[13] Based on Jenelle C. Martin, "Campus Safety: The Forgotten Priority," *Winning Orations, 1989* (Mankato, Minn.: Interstate Oratorical Association, 1989), pp. 14–16.

[14] Bruce E. Gronbeck, Raymie E. McKerrow, Douglas Ehninger, and Alan H. Monroe, *Principles and Types of Speech Communication,* 11th ed. (Glenview, Ill.: Scott, Foresman, 1990), pp. 180–203.

[15] Reprinted with permission of Susan Ingraham.

Chapter 16

Methods of Persuasion

R oger Dawson has a secret. With this secret, Dawson promises, you can get exactly what you want from almost anyone. You can develop "an aura of personal charisma that will have people respect you, understand you, and gladly agree with you." You can acquire "a new power that's so important to you, you'll wonder how you ever got along without it!"

What is Roger Dawson's secret? He calls it the "Secret of Power Persuasion." This secret is so valuable that America's biggest corporations pay Dawson $10,000 a day to share it with them. So valuable that the Book-of-the-Month Club chose Dawson's book *Secrets of Power Persuasion* as one of its offerings. So valuable that thousands of people have purchased Dawson's *Secrets of Power Persuasion* audio cassette.[1]

Can Dawson really give people "magical persuasion techniques" that will transform their lives? Probably not. Persuasion is too complicated for that. Yet, as the popularity of Dawson's book, tape, and business seminars shows, there is a perpetual fascination with the strategies and tactics of effective persuasion.

What makes a speaker persuasive? Why do listeners accept one speaker's views and reject those of another speaker? How can a speaker motivate listeners to act in support of a cause, a campaign, or a candidate? People have been trying to answer these questions for thousands of years—from the ancient Greek philosopher Aristotle to modern-day communication researchers.[2] Although many answers have been given, we can say that listeners will be persuaded by a speaker for one or more of four reasons:

Because they perceive the speaker as having high *credibility*

Because they are won over by the speaker's *evidence*

Because they are convinced by the speaker's *reasoning*

Because their *emotions* are touched by the speaker's ideas or language

In this chapter we will look at each of these. We will not discover any magical secrets that will make you an irresistible persuasive speaker. Persuasion is a complex activity that cannot be reduced to snappy formulas or simple techniques. But if you learn the principles discussed in this chapter and apply them astutely, you will greatly increase your odds of winning the minds and hearts of your listeners.

■ BUILDING CREDIBILITY

Here are two sets of imaginary statements. Which one of each pair would you be more likely to believe?

"The U.S. judicial system needs major changes to deal with the increased number of court cases." (Sandra Day O'Connor)

"The U.S. judicial system is working fine and does not need any major changes at this time." (Steven Spielberg)

"American movies during the late 1990s will feature more family-oriented adventure films." (Steven Spielberg)

"The family-oriented adventure film is no longer an important form of moviemaking." (Sandra Day O'Connor)

Most likely you chose the first in each pair of statements. If so, you were probably influenced by your perception of the speaker. You are more likely to respect the judgment of O'Connor, U.S. Supreme Court justice, when she speaks about the judicial system, and to respect the judgment of Spielberg, director of such films as *Schindler's List, E.T., Jurassic Park,* and *Raiders of the Lost Ark,* when he speaks about trends in the movie industry. Some teachers call this factor *source credibility.* Others refer to it as *ethos,* the name given by Aristotle.

Factors of Credibility

Over the years researchers have given much time to studying credibility and its effect on speechmaking.[3] They have discovered that many things affect a speaker's credibility, including sociability, dynamism, physical attractiveness, and perceived similarity between speaker and audience. Above all, though, a speaker's credibility is affected by two factors:

- *Competence*—how an audience regards a speaker's intelligence, expertise, and knowledge of the subject.

- *Character*—how an audience regards a speaker's sincerity, trustworthiness, and concern for the well-being of the audience.[4]

The more favorably listeners view a speaker's competence and character, the more likely they are to accept what the speaker says. No doubt you are familiar with this from your own experience. Suppose you take a course in economics. The course is taught by a distinguished professor who has published widely in all the prestigious journals, who sits on a major international commission, and who has won several awards for outstanding research. In class, you hang on this professor's every word. One day the professor is absent; a colleague of hers from the Economics Department—fully qualified but not as well known—comes to lecture in the professor's place. Possibly the fill-in instructor gives the same lecture the distinguished professor would have given, but you do not pay nearly as close attention. The other instructor does not have as high credibility as the professor.

It is important to remember that credibility is an attitude. It exists not in the speaker, but in the mind of the audience. A speaker may have high credibility for one audience and low credibility for another. A speaker may also have high credibility on one topic and low credibility on another. Looking back to our imaginary statements, most people would more readily believe Steven Spielberg speaking about moviemaking than Steven Spielberg speaking about the judicial system.

Types of Credibility

Not only can a speaker's credibility vary from audience to audience and topic to topic, but it can also change during the course of a speech—so much so that we can identify three types of credibility:

- *Initial credibility*—the credibility of the speaker before she or he starts to speak.

- *Derived credibility*—the credibility of the speaker produced by everything she or he says and does during the speech itself.

- *Terminal credibility*—the credibility of the speaker at the end of the speech.[5]

All three are dynamic. High initial credibility is a great advantage for any speaker, but it can be destroyed during a speech, resulting in low terminal credibility. The reverse can also occur. A speaker with low initial credibility may enhance her or his credibility during the speech and end up with high terminal credibility, as in the following example:

Daniel Tsang, the public-relations officer for a cable television firm, was scheduled to address a local citizens' group. His topic was "The Future of Cable Television."

Like many cable television companies, this one had a poor service record and a history of rapid price increases for consumers. Moreover, it was not unusual for the cable transmission to be interrupted for several hours at a stretch, leaving people without any programs at all to watch. When viewers called to complain, they either received a busy signal or were put on hold for so long that they finally hung up. Yet the company had raised its rates by 25 percent in the past two years! In the face of all this, Daniel stood up to address his audience.

As you might expect, Daniel had low initial credibility. No one believed the cable company would ever do anything right. But Daniel realized this and was prepared. He knew changes had been made in the company, and he came armed with facts to show that steps were being taken to improve service. The operating manager had been fired and a replacement brought in. New equipment was being installed to improve the quality of reception. The company was adding three new stations to its cable lineup. And it pledged not to raise prices for two years.

All through his speech Daniel took the approach, "We know we have not done a good job in the past, and we are working to do a better job in the future." By the time he had finished, much of the audience believed him. He had achieved high terminal credibility.

In classroom speeches, you will not face the same problems with credibility as do controversial public figures. Nonetheless, credibility is important in *every* speaking situation, no matter who the participants are or where it takes place. In every speech you give you will have some degree of initial credibility, which will always be strengthened or weakened by your message and how you deliver it. And your terminal credibility from one speech will affect your initial credibility for the next one. If your classmates see you as sincere and competent, they will be much more receptive to your ideas.

Enhancing Your Credibility

How can you build your credibility in your speeches? At one level, the answer is frustratingly general. Since everything you say and do in a speech will affect your credibility, you should say and do *everything* in a way that will make you appear capable and trustworthy. Good organization will improve your credibility. So will appropriate, clear, vivid language. So will fluent, dynamic delivery. So will strong evidence and cogent reasoning. In other words—give a brilliant speech and you will achieve high credibility!

The advice is sound, but not all that helpful. There are, however, some specific, proven ways you can boost your credibility while speaking. They include explaining your competence, establishing common ground with the audience, and speaking with genuine conviction.

Explain Your Competence   One way to enhance your credibility is to advertise your expertise on the speech topic. Did you investigate the topic thoroughly? Then say so. Do you have experience that gives you special knowledge or insight? Again, say so.

Here is how two students revealed their qualifications. The first stressed his study and research:

I never knew much about UFOs until I did a research project on them in my high school science class. Since then, I have read quite a bit about them, including the latest reports of the highly respected Center for UFO Studies in Evanston, Illinois. As a result, I have decided that the evidence strongly suggests that Earth has been—and continues to be—visited by spaceships from other planets.

The second student emphasized her background and personal experience:

Most of us have no idea what it means to be poor and hungry. But before returning to school last year, I spent eight years as a volunteer at local assistance centers. During those years I worked in every part of the city and with every kind of person, from struggling welfare mothers to hardened street people. I cannot begin to tell you everything I have seen—how poverty destroys people's souls and how hunger drives them to desperation. But on the basis of what I can tell you, I hope you will agree with me that government help for the poor and the needy must be increased.

In both of these cases, the speakers greatly increased their persuasiveness by establishing their credibility.[6]

Establish Common Ground with Your Audience   Another way to bolster your credibility is to establish common ground with your audience. You do not persuade listeners by assaulting their values and rejecting their opinions. This only antagonizes people. It puts them on the defensive and makes them resist your ideas. As the old saying goes, "You catch more flies with honey than with vinegar." The same is true of persuasion. Show respect for your listeners. You can make your speech more appealing by identifying your ideas with those of your audience—by showing how your point of view is consistent with what they believe.[7]

Creating common ground is especially important at the start of a persuasive speech. Begin by identifying with your listeners. Show that you share their values, attitudes, and experiences. Get them nodding their heads in agreement, and they will be much more receptive to your ultimate proposal. Here is how a businesswoman from Massachusetts, hoping to sell her product to an audience of people in Colorado, began her persuasive speech:

I have never been in Colorado before, but I really looked forward to making this trip. A lot of my ancestors left Massachusetts and came to Colorado nearly 150 years ago. Sometimes I have wondered why they did it. They came in covered wagons, carrying all their possessions, and many of them died on the journey. The ones who got through raised their houses and raised their families. Now that I've seen Colorado, I understand why they tried so hard!

The audience laughed and applauded, and the speaker was off to a good start.

This method of establishing common ground is used often in speeches outside the classroom. Now look at a different approach, used in a classroom speech favoring a tuition increase at the speaker's school—a very unpopular point of view with his classmates. He began by saying:

As we all know, there are many differences among the people in this class. But regardless of our age, major, background, or goals, we all have one thing in common—we are all concerned about the quality of education at this school. And that quality is clearly in danger. Because of budget reductions, faculty salaries have fallen below those at comparable schools, library purchases have been cut back, and more and more students are being crowded out of classes they need to take. Whether we like it or not, we have a problem—a problem that affects each of us. Today I would like to discuss this problem and whether it can be solved by an increase in tuition.

By stressing common perceptions of the problem, the student hoped to get off on the right foot with his audience. Once that was done, he moved gradually to his more controversial ideas.

Deliver Your Speeches Fluently, Expressively, and with Conviction   There is a great deal of research to show that a speaker's credibility is strongly affected by his or her delivery. Moderately fast speakers, for example, are usually seen as more intelligent and confident than slower speakers. So too are speakers who use vocal variety to communicate their ideas in a lively, animated way. On the other hand, speakers who consistently lose their place, hesitate frequently, or pepper their talk with vocalized pauses such as "uh," "er," and "um" are seen as significantly less competent than speakers who are more poised and dynamic.[8]

All of this argues for practicing your persuasive speech fully ahead of time so you can deliver it fluently and expressively. In addition to being better prepared, you will take a major step toward enhancing your credibility. (Be sure to review Chapter 12 if you have questions about speech delivery.)

Speaking techniques aside, the most important way to strengthen your credibility is to deliver your speeches with genuine conviction. President Harry Truman once said that in speaking, "sincerity, honesty, and a straightforward manner are more important than special talent or polish." If you wish to convince others, you must first convince yourself. If you want others to believe and care about your ideas, you must believe and care about them yourself. Let your audience know you are in earnest—that your speech is not just a classroom exercise. Your spirit, your enthusiasm, your conviction will carry over to your listeners.

■ USING EVIDENCE

Evidence consists of supporting materials—examples, statistics, testimony— used to prove or disprove something. As we saw in Chapter 7, most people are skeptical. They are suspicious of unsupported generalizations. They want speakers to justify their claims. If you hope to be persuasive, you must support your views with evidence. Whenever you say something that is open to question, you should give evidence to prove you are right.

Evidence is particularly important in classroom speeches because few students are recognized as experts on their speech topics. Research has shown that speakers with very high initial credibility do not need to use as much evidence as do speakers with lower credibility. For most speakers, though, strong evidence is absolutely necessary. It can enhance your credibility, increase both the immediate and long-term persuasiveness of your message, and help "inoculate" listeners against counterpersuasion.[9]

Evidence is also crucial whenever your target audience opposes your point of view. As we saw in Chapter 15, listeners in such a situation will not only be skeptical of your ideas, they will challenge them at every step of the speech. They will mentally argue with you—asking questions, raising objections, and creating counterarguments to "answer" what you say. The success of your speech will depend partly on how well you anticipate these internal responses and give evidence to refute them.[10]

You may want to review Chapter 7, which shows how to use supporting materials. The following case study illustrates how they work as evidence in a persuasive speech.

Persuasive speeches need strong evidence to convince skeptical listeners. Evidence is especially crucial for student speakers because they are not recognized as experts on their speech topics. Finding the best evidence takes hard digging and resourceful research, but it is well worth the effort.

How Evidence Works: A Case Study

Let's say one of your classmates is talking about the harmful effects of repeated exposure to loud music and other noises. Instead of just telling you what she thinks, the speaker offers you strong evidence to prove her point. As you read the case study, notice how the speaker carries on a mental dialogue with her listeners. At each juncture she imagines what they might be thinking, anticipates their questions and objections, and gives evidence to answer the questions and resolve the objections.

She begins this way:

As college students we are exposed to loud music and other noise all the time. We go to parties, clubs, and concerts where the volume is so loud we have to shout so the person next to us can hear what we are saying. We play our personal stereos so high they can be heard halfway across the room. And we seldom give it a second thought. But we should, because excessive noise can have a serious impact on our health and well-being.

How do you react? If you already know about the problems caused by noise pollution, you probably nod your head in agreement. But what if you don't know? Or don't agree? If you enjoy rock concerts and listening to your personal stereo at high volumes, you probably don't *want* to hear anything bad about it. Certainly you will not be persuaded by the general statement that exposure to loud music and other noises can have "a serious impact on our health and well-being." Mentally you say to the speaker, "How do you know? Can you prove it?"

Anticipating just such a response, the speaker gives evidence to support her point:

The American Medical Association reports that 28 million Americans suffer from serious hearing loss, and that 10 million of those cases are caused by too much exposure to loud noise.

"That's unfortunate," you may think. "But everyone loses some hearing as they grow old. Why should I be concerned about it now?" The speaker answers:

According to *Health* magazine, more and more victims of noise-induced deafness are adolescents and even younger children. Dr. James Snow, director of the National Institute on Deafness, reports that noise-induced hearing loss can begin as early as ten years of age. Audiologist Dean Garsetcki, head of the hearing-impairment program at Northwestern University, says, "we've got 21-year-olds walking around with hearing-loss patterns of people 40 years their senior."

"These are impressive facts," you say to yourself. "Luckily, I haven't noticed any problems with my hearing. When I do, I'll just be careful until it gets better." Keeping one step ahead of you, the speaker continues:

The problem with hearing loss is that it creeps up on you. *Sierra* magazine notes that today's heavy-metal fans won't notice the effects of their hearing loss for another fifteen years. And then it will be too late.

"What do you mean, too late?" you ask mentally. The speaker tells you:

Unlike some physical conditions, hearing loss is irreversible. Loud noise damages the microscopic hairs in the inner ear that transmit sound to the auditory nerve. Once damaged, those hairs can never recover and can never be repaired.

"I didn't know that," you say to yourself. "Is there anything else?"

One last point. Repeated exposure to loud music and other noise does more than damage your hearing. The latest issue of *Prevention* magazine reports that excessive noise has been linked to such problems as stress, high blood pressure, chronic headaches, fatigue, learning disorders, even heart disease. It's easy to see why Jill Lipoti, chief of Rutgers University's Noise Technical Assistance Center, warns that "noise affects more people than any other pollutant."

Now are you convinced? Chances are you will at least think about the possible consequences the next time you are set to pump up the volume on your stereo. Maybe you will use earplugs when you sit in front of the speakers at a rock concert. You may even begin to reassess your whole attitude toward the problem of noise pollution. Why? Because the speaker did not just spout her opinions as if they were common knowledge, but instead supported each of her claims with evidence. You should try to do the same in your persuasive speeches.

Tips for Using Evidence

Any of the supporting materials discussed in Chapter 7—examples, statistics, testimony—can work as evidence in a persuasive speech. As we saw in that chapter, there are guidelines for using each kind of supporting material regardless of the kind of speech you are giving. Here we need to look at four special tips for using evidence in a persuasive speech.

Use Specific Evidence   No matter what kind of evidence you employ—statistics, examples, or testimony—it will be more persuasive if you state it in specific rather than general terms.[11] In the speech about noise pollution, for instance, the speaker did not say, "Lots of people suffer from hearing loss." That would have left the audience wondering how many "lots" amounts to. By saying, "28 million Americans suffer from serious hearing loss," the speaker made her point much more effectively. She also enhanced her credibility by showing she had a firm grasp of the facts.

Use Novel Evidence   Evidence is more likely to be persuasive if it is new to the audience. You will gain little by citing facts and figures that are already well known to your listeners. If those facts and figures have not persuaded your listeners already, they will not do so now. You must go beyond what the audience already knows and present striking new evidence that will get them to say, "Hmmm, I didn't know *that*. Maybe I should rethink the issue." Finding such evidence is not always easy. It usually requires hard digging and resourceful research, but the rewards can be well worth the effort.[12]

Use Evidence from Credible Sources   There is a good deal of research to show that listeners find evidence from competent, credible sources more persuasive than evidence from less qualified sources.[13] Above all, listeners are suspicious of evidence from sources that appear to be biased or self-interested. In assessing the current state of airline safety, for example, they are more likely to be persuaded by testimony from impartial aviation experts than by statements from the president of American Airlines. In judging the conflict between a corporation and the union striking against it, they will usually be leery of statistics offered by either side. If you wish to be persuasive—especially to careful listeners—you should rely on evidence from objective, nonpartisan sources.

Make Clear the Point of Your Evidence   When speaking to persuade, you use evidence to prove a point. Yet you would be surprised how many novice speakers present their evidence without making clear the point it is supposed to prove. A number of studies have shown that you cannot count on listeners to draw, on their own, the conclusion you want them to reach.[14] When using evidence, be sure listeners understand the point you are trying to make.

Suppose, for example, you recite the following evidence about the growth of America's coyote population:

Despite being hunted and trapped relentlessly for over 100 years, coyotes now live in every state of the Union except Hawaii. According to *Smithsonian* magazine, Mississippi has more than 200,000 coyotes, Massachusetts and Pennsylvania both have several thousand, and there is even a good-sized coyote population in the northern suburbs of New York City.

What is the point of this evidence? That efforts to control America's coyote population should be expanded because there are too many coyotes? Or that programs to control America's coyote population are futile and should be stopped? On the basis of the evidence, a listener could draw either conclusion. To help prevent this from happening, you should be sure to state the conclusion you want the audience to draw.

REASONING

The story is told about Hack Wilson, a hard-hitting outfielder for the Brooklyn Dodgers baseball team in the 1930s.[15] Wilson was a great player, but he had a fondness for the good life. His drinking exploits were legendary. He was known to spend the entire night on the town, stagger into the team's hotel at the break of dawn, grab a couple of hours' sleep, and get to the ballpark just in time for the afternoon game.

This greatly distressed Max Carey, Wilson's manager. At the next team meeting, Carey spent much time explaining the evils of drink. To prove his point, he stood beside a table on which he had placed two glasses and a plate of live angleworms. One glass was filled with water, the other with gin—Wilson's favorite beverage. With a flourish Carey dropped a worm into the glass of water. It wriggled happily. Next Carey plunged the same worm into the gin. It promptly stiffened and expired.

A murmur ran through the room, and some players were obviously impressed. But not Wilson. He didn't even seem interested. Carey waited a little, hoping for some delayed reaction from his wayward slugger. When none came, he prodded, "Do you follow my reasoning, Wilson?"

"Sure, skipper," answered Wilson. "It proves that if you drink gin you'll never get worms!"

What does this story prove? No matter how strong your evidence, you will not be very persuasive unless listeners grasp your reasoning. You should know, therefore, how to reason clearly and persuasively.

Many people think of reasoning as an esoteric subject of interest only to philosophers, but in fact we all use reasoning every day in practical life. Reasoning is simply the process of drawing a conclusion based on evidence. Sometimes we reason well—as when we conclude that ice particles forming on the trees may mean the roads will be slippery. Other times we reason less effectively—as when we conclude that spilling salt will bring bad luck. Most superstitions are actually no more than instances of faulty reasoning.[16]

As we saw in Chapter 1, reasoning is an important component of critical thinking, and it permeates all areas of our lives. We are bombarded daily with persuasive messages ranging from television commercials to political appeals. Sometimes the reasoning in those messages is sound, but often it is faulty—as when we are told that drinking Pepsi will make us more youthful or that using an IBM personal computer will turn the drudgery of writing a term paper into an effortless pleasure. Unless you know how to reason clearly, you may be easy prey for unscrupulous advertisers and glib politicians.

Reasoning in public speaking is basically an extension of reasoning in other aspects of life. As a public speaker you have two major concerns with respect to reasoning. First, you must make sure your own reasoning is sound. Second, you must try to get listeners to agree with your reasoning. Let us look, then, at four basic methods of reasoning and how to use them in your speeches.

Reasoning from Specific Instances

When you reason from specific instances, you progress from a number of particular facts to a general conclusion.[17] For example:

Fact 1:   My physical education course last term was easy.

Fact 2:   My roommate's physical education course was easy.

Fact 3:   My brother's physical education course was easy.

Conclusion: Physical education courses are easy.

As this example suggests, we use reasoning from specific instances daily, although we probably don't realize it. Think for a moment of all the general conclusions that arise in conversation: Politicians are corrupt. Professors are bookish. Dorm food is awful. Accounting courses are hard. Republicans are conservative. Marines are tough. Where do such conclusions come from? They come from observing particular politicians, professors, Republicans, marines, accounting courses, and so on.

The same thing happens in public speaking. The speaker who concludes that America's drinking water is becoming unsafe because several cities have had major outbreaks of waterborne diseases in recent years is reasoning from specific instances. So is the speaker who argues that female politicians are becoming more popular with voters because women have won several major elections. And so is the speaker who argues that racial tension is growing on college campuses because there have been a number of racial incidents at schools across the country.

Such conclusions are never foolproof. No matter how many specific instances you give (and you can give only a few in a speech), it is always possible that an exception exists. Throughout the ages people observed countless white swans in Europe without seeing any of a different color. It seemed an undeniable fact that all swans were white. Then in the nineteenth century, blacks swans were discovered in Australia![18]

Guidelines for Reasoning from Specific Instances   When you reason from specific instances, you should follow a few basic guidelines.

First, avoid generalizing too hastily. Beware of the tendency to jump to conclusions on the basis of insufficient evidence. Make sure your sample of specific instances is large enough to justify your conclusion. Also make sure the instances you present are fair, unbiased, and representative. (Are three physical education courses *enough* to conclude that physical education courses in general are easy? Are the three courses *typical* of most physical education courses?)

Second, be careful with your wording. If your evidence does not justify a sweeping conclusion, qualify your argument. Suppose you are talking about the crisis in America's national park system brought on by overuse and commercial development. You document the problem by discussing a number of specific instances—Yosemite, Yellowstone, the Everglades. Then you draw your conclusion. You might say:

> As we have seen, America's national park system is serving almost 400 million people a year, with the result that some parks are being overcome by traffic, pollution, and garbage. We have also seen that more and more parks are being exploited for mining, logging, and other forms of commercial development. It certainly seems fair, then, to conclude that new measures are needed to ensure that the beauty, serenity, and biological diversity of America's national parks are preserved for future generations as well as for our own.

This is not as dramatic as saying, "America's national parks are on the brink of destruction," but it is more accurate and will be more persuasive to careful listeners.

Third, reinforce your argument with statistics or testimony. Since you can never give enough specific instances in a speech to make your conclusion irrefutable, you should supplement them with testimony or statistics demonstrating that the instances are in fact representative. If you were talking about the safety problems caused by businesses that violate child-labor laws, you could say:

> The violation of child-labor laws often exposes teenagers to dangerous working conditions. Matthew Garvey of Laurel, Maryland, lost his leg at the age of thirteen working in a car wash. Jesse Colson, age seventeen, of Plainfield, Indiana, died in a

car crash while making a pizza delivery. Rosalia Ybarra, fifteen, of Los Angeles, was permanently scarred when she was splashed in the face with hot grease during her shift at a fast-food restaurant.

The specific examples help make the conclusion persuasive, but a listener could easily dismiss them as sensational and atypical. To prevent this from happening, you might go on to say:

Although these examples are dramatic, they are representative of what is happening around the country. According to *Time* magazine, a report by the Government Accounting Office shows that during the past two years 48 minors were reported killed and 128,000 injured in work-related accidents. Congressman Tom Lantos, chair of the House Employment and Housing Subcommittee, summarized the problem when he stated, "Thousands of youngsters are jeopardizing their education, health and safety by working too many hours, too late at night, and in dangerous, prohibited occupations."

With this backup material, not even a skeptical listener could reject your examples as isolated.

When you reason from specific instances in a speech, you can either state your conclusion and then give the specific instances upon which it is based or give the specific instances and then draw your conclusion. Look back at the example about national parks. In that example, the speaker first gives three facts and then draws a conclusion ("It certainly seems fair, then, to conclude that new measures are needed to ensure that the beauty, serenity, and biological diversity of America's national parks are preserved for future generations as well as for our own").

Now look again at the example just given about child-labor laws. In this example the conclusion—"The violation of child-labor laws often exposes teenagers to dangerous working conditions"—is stated first, followed by three specific instances. It doesn't matter which order you use as long as your facts support your conclusion.

Reasoning from Principle

Reasoning from principle is the opposite of reasoning from specific instances. It moves from the general to the specific.[19] When you reason from principle, you progress from a general principle to a specific conclusion. We are all familiar with this kind of reasoning from statements such as the following:

    a. All people are mortal.

    b. Socrates is a person.

    c. Therefore, Socrates is mortal.

This is a classic example of reasoning from principle. You begin with a general statement ("All people are mortal"), move to a minor premise

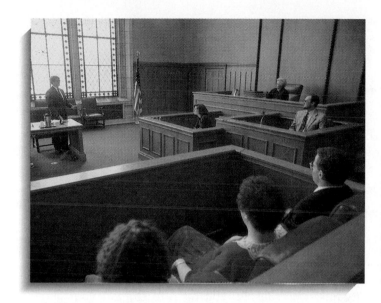

Reasoning is an important part of persuasive speaking. In a criminal trial, for example, neither the prosecution nor the defense are likely to sway the jury unless their reasoning about who committed the crime is clear and convincing.

("Socrates is a person"), and end with a specific conclusion ("Socrates is mortal").

Speakers often use reasoning from principle when trying to persuade an audience. One of the clearest examples from American history is Susan B. Anthony's famous speech "Is It a Crime for U.S. Citizens to Vote?" Delivered on numerous occasions in 1872 and 1873, at a time when women were legally barred from voting, Anthony's speech reasoned along the following lines:

a. The United States Constitution guarantees all U.S. citizens the right to vote.

b. Women are U.S. citizens.

c. Therefore, the United States Constitution guarantees women the right to vote.

This, too, is an instance of reasoning from principle. It progresses from a general principle ("The United States Constitution guarantees all U.S. citizens the right to vote") through a minor premise ("Women are U.S. citizens") to a conclusion ("Therefore, the United States Constitution guarantees women the right to vote").[20]

Guidelines for Reasoning from Principle   When you use reasoning from principle in a speech, pay special attention to your general principle. Will listeners accept it without evidence? If not, give evidence to support it before moving to your minor premise. You may also need to support your minor premise with evidence. When both the general principle and the minor premise are soundly based, your audience will be much more likely to accept your conclusion.

Suppose, for example, you plan to speak about excessive salt in the American diet. You begin by formulating a specific purpose:

Specific Purpose: To persuade my audience to limit their consumption of fast foods, canned goods, and frozen foods because of their excessive salt content.

Next, you decide to use reasoning from principle to help persuade your audience. Your argument looks like this:

a. Excessive consumption of salt is unhealthy.

b. Fast foods, canned goods, and frozen foods contain excessive amounts of salt.

c. Therefore, excessive consumption of fast foods, canned goods, and frozen foods is unhealthy.

To make the argument persuasive, you have to support your general principle: "Excessive consumption of salt is unhealthy." You cite medical evidence and research studies. Part of your speech might go like this:

High salt intake has been linked with hypertension, or high blood pressure, which is a major cause of heart disease, kidney disease, and stroke. In northern Japan, where the typical diet contains enormous amounts of sodium, hypertension is the major cause of death. But among people who eat very little salt, such as the preliterate tribes of New Guinea, hypertension and hypertension-related deaths are virtually unknown.

Having supported your general principle, you now go on to bolster your minor premise: "Fast foods, canned goods, and frozen foods contain excessive amounts of salt." Your evidence includes the following:

The human body needs only 230 milligrams of sodium per day to function efficiently. But many fast foods, canned goods, and frozen foods deliver several times that amount in a single serving. One McDonald's Big Mac has 1,510 milligrams of sodium—nearly seven times the daily requirement. One serving of canned tomato soup has 1,050 milligrams of sodium—nearly five times the daily requirement. One frozen turkey dinner has 2,567 milligrams of sodium—*eleven* times the daily requirement. No wonder we have a salt overload!

Now you have lined up your ammunition very effectively. You have supported your general principle and your minor premise. You can feel confident in going on to your conclusion:

Therefore, excessive consumption of fast foods, canned goods, and frozen foods is unhealthy.

And you can expect your audience to take you seriously. When used properly, reasoning from principle is highly persuasive.

Causal Reasoning

There is a patch of ice on the sidewalk. You slip, fall, and break your arm. You reason as follows: "*Because* that patch of ice was there, I fell and broke my arm." This is an example of causal reasoning, in which someone tries to establish the relationship between causes and effects. In this example the causal reasoning is pretty straightforward. You can test it in reverse: "If the patch of ice *hadn't* been there, I wouldn't have fallen and broken my arm."

As with reasoning from specific instances, we use causal reasoning daily. Something happens and we ask what caused it to happen. We want to know the causes of violent crime, of the football team's latest defeat, of our roommate's peculiar habits. We also wonder about effects. We speculate about the consequences of television violence on young children, of the star quarterback's leg injury, of telling our roommate that a change is needed.

Guidelines for Causal Reasoning   As any scientist (or detective) will tell you, causal reasoning can be a tricky business. The relationship between causes and effects is not always as clear as it seems. There are two common errors to avoid when using causal reasoning.

The first is the fallacy of false cause. This fallacy is often known by its Latin name *post hoc, ergo propter hoc,* which means "after this, therefore because of this." In other words, the fact that one event happens after another does not mean that the first is the cause of the second. The closeness in time of the two events may be entirely coincidental. If a black cat crosses your path and five minutes later you fall and break your arm, you needn't blame it on the poor cat.

One student in speech class argued that the cold war that existed between the Western democracies and the communist nations of Eastern Europe until the demolishing of the Berlin Wall in 1989 was caused by the United States' decision to drop the atomic bomb at Hiroshima and Nagasaki at the end of World War II. His reasoning? Hiroshima and Nagasaki were bombed in August 1945. The cold war began a few months later. Therefore, the beginning of the cold war was caused by the bombing of Hiroshima and Nagasaki. The student's classmates were not persuaded. They pointed out that just because the cold war started after the bombing of Hiroshima and Nagasaki, this does not prove that it was *caused* by the bombing; the cold war would have broken out even if the United States had not dropped atomic bombs on Japan.

A second pitfall when using causal reasoning is assuming that events have only one cause. We all tend to oversimplify events by attributing them to single, isolated causes. In fact, though, most events have several causes. What, for example, causes the election of a presidential candidate? Unhappiness with the incumbent? A good media campaign? Economic conditions? Desire for a change? World affairs? Support of the party regulars? A clever makeup job for a television debate? A solid, intelligent party platform? *All* of these factors—and others—affect the outcome of a presidential election. When you use causal reasoning, be wary of the temptation to attribute complex events to single causes.

You cannot escape causal reasoning. All of us use it daily, and you are almost certain to use it when speaking to persuade—especially if you deal with a question of fact or policy.

Analogical Reasoning

What do these statements have in common?

If you're good at racquetball, you'll be great at Ping-Pong.

In Great Britain the general election campaign for Prime Minister lasts less than three weeks. Surely we can do the same with the U.S. presidential election.

Both statements use reasoning from analogy. By comparing two similar cases, they infer that what is true for one must be true for the other. The first speaker reasons that because a person is good at playing racquetball, he or she should also be good at playing Ping-Pong. The second speaker reasons that because the British can elect a Prime Minister with less than three weeks of campaigning, the United States should be able to do the same when electing a President.

Guidelines for Analogical Reasoning   The most important question in assessing analogical reasoning is whether the two cases being compared are essentially alike. If they are essentially alike, the analogy is valid. If they are not essentially alike, the analogy is invalid.

Look back, for example, to the analogies at the start of this section. Is playing racquetball the same as playing Ping-Pong? Not really. To be sure, both involve hitting the ball with a racquet or a paddle. But racquetball uses a stringed racquet and a rubber ball. Ping-Pong uses a solid paddle and a smaller, lighter, celluloid ball. Racquetball is played by hitting the ball against the walls or ceiling of an enclosed court. Ping-Pong is played by hitting the ball back and forth over a net stretched across a table. Skill at one is no guarantee of skill at the other. The analogy is not valid.

What about the second analogy? That depends on how much alike the British and American political systems are. Are the countries similar in size and diversity? Is it possible for candidates in both countries to canvass the entire land in less than three weeks? Do both countries have nationwide primaries before the general election? Are the two electorates equally informed about political issues? Does the party system operate the same in both countries? In other words, are the factors that allow Great Britain to conduct campaigns for Prime Minister in less than three weeks also present in the United States? If so, the analogy is valid. If not, the analogy is invalid.

Reasoning from analogy is used most often in persuasive speeches on questions of policy. When arguing for a new policy, you should find out whether a similar policy has been tried somewhere else. You may be able to claim that your policy will work because it has worked in like circumstances elsewhere. Here is how one student used reasoning from analogy to support her claim that controlling handguns will reduce violent crime in the United States:

> Will my policy work? The experience of foreign countries suggests it will. In England, guns are tightly regulated; even the police are unarmed, and the murder rate is trivial by American standards. In Japan, the ownership of weapons is severely restricted and handguns are completely prohibited. Japan is an almost gun-free country, and its crime rate is even lower than England's. On the basis of these comparisons, we can conclude that restricting the ownership of guns will control the crime and murder rates in America.

By the same token, if you argue against a change in policy, you should check whether the proposed policy—or something like it—has been implemented elsewhere. Here, too, you may be able to support your case by reasoning from analogy—as did one student who opposed gun control:

> Advocates of gun control point to foreign countries to prove their case. They often cite England, which has strict gun-control laws and little violent crime. But the key to low personal violence in England—and other foreign countries—is not gun-control laws but the generally peaceful character of the people. For example, Switzerland has a militia system; 600,000 assault rifles each with two magazines of ammunition are sitting at this moment in Swiss homes. Yet Switzerland's murder rate is only 15 percent of ours. In other words, cultural factors are much more important than gun control when it comes to violent crime.

As these examples illustrate, argument from analogy can be used on both sides of an issue. You are more likely to persuade your audience if the analogy truly shows a parallel situation.[21]

■ APPEALING TO EMOTIONS

When Carol Moseley-Braun of Illinois took her oath of office on January 20, 1993, she became the only African-American member of the United States Senate. A few months later, in one of her first speeches as a Senator, she gave a memorable address opposing a bill that would have given the United Daughters of the Confederacy a design patent on the Confederate flag used by the southern states during the U.S. Civil War.

Speaking with great emotion, Moseley-Braun called the flag a symbol of slavery that "would keep us slipping back into the darkness of division, into the snake pit of racial hatred, of racial antagonism." Approving the design patent, she said, would force millions of African Americans "to suffer the indignity of being reminded time and time again that at one point in this country's history we were human chattel. We were property. We could be traded, bought, and sold. . . . It is an outrage. It is an insult."

The speech was highly persuasive and brought Moseley-Braun accolades from Republicans and Democrats alike. Reversing its previous position, the Senate followed Moseley-Braun's lead and defeated the design patent by a 75-25 margin. Afterward most listeners attributed the success of her speech to its emotional power. One Senator called it "the most powerful, moving statement I have heard on the floor of the Senate."

Effective persuasion often requires emotional appeal. As the Roman rhetorician Quintilian stated, "It is feeling and force of imagination that make us eloquent."[22] By adding "feeling" and the "force of imagination" to her logical arguments, Carol Moseley-Braun produced a compelling address. Although your words may never change the course of national policy, you too can use emotional appeal to bring your persuasive speeches home to your listeners.

What Are Emotional Appeals?

Emotional appeals—sometimes called *motivational appeals*—are intended to make listeners feel sad, angry, guilty, afraid, happy, proud, sympathetic, reverent, or the like. These are often appropriate reactions when the question is one of value or policy. Few people are moved to change their attitudes or take action when they are complacent or bored. As George Campbell wrote in his *Philosophy of Rhetoric,* "When persuasion is the end, passion also must be engaged."[23]

Below is a list of some of the emotions evoked most often by public speakers. Following each emotion are a few examples of subjects that might stir that emotion:

- *fear*—of serious illness, of natural disasters, of sexual assault, of unsafe aviation standards, of personal rejection, of economic hardship

- *compassion*—for the physically disabled, for battered women, for neglected animals, for the unemployed, for starving children in Africa, for victims of AIDS

- *pride*—in one's country, in one's family, in one's school, in one's ethnic heritage, in one's personal accomplishments

- *anger*—at the actions of political terrorists, at members of Congress who abuse the public trust, at landlords who exploit student tenants, at businesses who sell unsafe products, at vandals and thieves

While strong evidence and sound reasoning are vital to persuasion, emotional appeals often make a speaker's ideas come alive for an audience. To be most effective, emotional appeals need to be delivered with conviction and sincerity.

- *shame*—about not helping people less fortunate than ourselves, about not considering the rights of others, about not doing one's best

- *reverence* for an admired person, for traditions and institutions, for one's deity

Obviously this list is not complete. There are many other emotions and many other subjects that might stir them. However, this brief sample should give you an idea of the kinds of emotional appeals you might use to enhance the message of your persuasive speech.[24]

Generating Emotional Appeal

Use Emotional Language   As we saw in Chapter 11, one way to generate emotional appeal is to use emotion-laden words. If you want to move your listeners, use moving language. Here, for instance, is part of the conclusion from a student speech about the challenges and rewards of working as a community volunteer with young children:

The promise of America sparkles in the eyes of every child. Their dreams are the glittering dreams of America. When those dreams are dashed, when innocent hopes are betrayed, so are the dreams and hopes of the entire nation. It is our duty—

to me, it is a <u>sacred duty</u>—to give <u>all children</u> the chance to <u>learn and grow</u>, to share <u>equally</u> in the <u>American dream</u> of <u>freedom, justice, and opportunity</u>.

The underlined words and phrases have strong emotional power. By using them, the speaker hopes to produce an emotional response.

There can be a problem with this, however. Packing too many emotionally charged words into one part of a speech can call attention to itself and undermine its impact. When a sudden barrage of passionate language is inconsistent with the rest of the speech, it may strike the audience as ludicrous—obviously not the desired effect. Remember, the emotion rests in your audience, not in your words. Even the coldest facts can touch off an emotional response if they strike the right chords in a listener.

Develop Vivid Examples   Often a better approach than relying on emotionally charged language is to let your emotional appeal grow naturally out of the content of your speech. The most effective way to do this is with vivid, richly textured examples that personalize your ideas and help pull listeners into the speech emotionally.

Here is how one speaker used a vivid example for emotional appeal. The subject was illegal trapping of wild animals. The audience was a group of citizens and the village board in a semirural town. The speaker was a representative of the Humane Society. Here is what she might have said, stripping the content of emotional impact:

> Trapping of wild animals on town property is not only illegal, it is also dangerous. On several occasions domestic animals have been caught in traps set for raccoons, squirrels, and beavers.

What she actually said went something like this:

> Tina was found dead last week—her neck broken by the jaws of a steel trap. I didn't know Tina, and most of you didn't either. But John and Rachel Williamson knew her, and so did their children, Tyrone and Vanessa. Tina had been a beloved member of their family for ten years. She was a Samoyed—a handsome, intelligent dog, pure white with soft, dark eyes. When she died she was only 200 yards from her back door.
>
> Tina had gone out to play that morning as usual, but this time she found something *un*usual—an odd-shaped box with delicious-smelling food inside. She put her head inside the box to get at the food. When she did, the trap closed and Tina was killed.
>
> Unless we crack down on illegal trapping within town property, this tragedy will be repeated. The next time it might be *your* family dog. Or your pet cat. Or your child.

People who listen to a speech like that will not soon forget it. They may well be moved to action, as the speaker intends. The first speech, however, is not nearly so compelling. Listeners may well nod their heads, think to themselves "good idea"—and then forget about it. The story of Tina and the family who loved her gives the second speech emotional impact and brings it home to listeners in personal terms.[25]

Speak with Sincerity and Conviction   Ronald Reagan was one of the most effective speakers in recent U.S. history. Even people who disagreed with his political views often found him irresistible. Why? Partly because he seemed to speak with great sincerity and conviction.

What was true for Reagan is true for you as well. The strongest source of emotional power is the conviction and sincerity of the speaker. All of your emotion-laden words and examples are but empty trappings unless *you* feel the emotion yourself. And if you do, your emotion will communicate itself to the audience through everything you say and do—not only through your words, but also through your tone of voice, rate of speech, gestures, and facial expressions.

Ethics and Emotional Appeal

Over the years much has been written about the ethics of emotional appeal in speechmaking. Some people have taken the extreme position that ethical speakers should stick to reason and avoid emotional appeal entirely. To support this view, they point to speakers who have used emotional appeal to fan the flames of racial hatred, religious bigotry, and political fanaticism.

There is no question that emotional appeals can be abused by unscrupulous speakers for detestable causes. But emotional appeals can also be wielded by honorable speakers for noble causes—by Winston Churchill to rouse the world against Adolf Hitler and the forces of Nazism, by Martin Luther King to call for racial justice, by Mother Teresa to help the poor and downtrodden. Few people would question the ethics of emotional appeal in these instances.[26]

Nor is it always possible to draw a sharp line between reason and emotional appeal. Think back for a moment to the story about Tina, the Samoyed who was killed by an illegal trapper. The story certainly has strong emotional appeal. But is there anything unreasonable about the story? Or is it irrational for listeners to respond to it by backing stronger measures to control illegal trapping? By the same token, is it illogical to be angered by drive-by shootings? Fearful about cutbacks in student aid? Compassionate for victims of child abuse? In many cases, reason and emotion work hand in hand.[27]

One key to using emotional appeal ethically is to make sure it is appropriate to the speech topic. If you want to move listeners to act on a question of policy, emotional appeals are not only legitimate but perhaps necessary. If you want listeners to do something as a result of your speech, you will probably need to appeal to their hearts as well as to their heads.

On the other hand, emotional appeals are usually inappropriate in a persuasive speech on a question of fact. Here you should deal only in specific information and logic. For example, did George Bush, while he was Vice President of the U.S., cover up the facts about his role in the plan to exchange weapons for American hostages in Iran? If you say, "No, because I admire Bush," or "Yes, because I have always disliked Bush," then you are guilty of applying emotional criteria to a purely factual question. The events leading to the arms-for-hostages deal are matters of fact and should be discussed on factual grounds alone.

Even when trying to move listeners to action, you should never substitute emotional appeals for evidence and reasoning. You should *always* build your persuasive speech on a firm foundation of facts and logic. This is important not just for ethical reasons, but for practical reasons as well. Unless you prove your case, careful listeners will not be stirred by your emotional appeals. You need to build a good case based on reason *and* kindle the emotions of your audience.[28]

When you use emotional appeal, also keep in mind the guidelines for ethical speechmaking discussed in Chapter 2. Make sure your goals are ethically sound, that you are honest in what you say, and that you avoid name-calling and other forms of abusive language. In using emotional appeal, as in other respects, your classroom speeches will offer a good testing ground for questions of ethical responsibility.

■ SAMPLE SPEECH WITH COMMENTARY

The following persuasive speech was presented in a public speaking class at the University of Wisconsin.[29] It deals with a question of policy and is a good example of how student speakers can utilize the methods of persuasion discussed in this chapter.

THE DANGERS OF CHEWING TOBACCO

Catherine Twohig

COMMENTARY

The speaker begins with an extended example of a man who died from chewing tobacco. Detailed and graphic, the example does an excellent job of gaining attention and of pulling the audience into the speech.

At this point, the speaker displayed an enlarged color photograph show-

SPEECH

On March 30, Tom, a twenty-three-year-old man from northern Wisconsin, went in for his yearly dental checkup. As far as he could tell, there were no real problems except maybe the one or two usual cavities that the dentist always seems to find. The dentist began poking around at Tom's teeth, but soon became more interested in Tom's lower lip and gums. The dentist noticed an unusual growth on Tom's lower lip and asked if Tom was a regular user of chewing tobacco. Tom answered yes.

After a series of tests, Tom was diagnosed as having a deadly type of oral cancer. Just one week after ing what Tom's face looked like after surgery. The photograph was 11 × 17 inches and had been enlarged for the speaker at a local copy service.

The speaker does a superb job of establishing her credibility. Her combination of professional training and personal experience make her a very believable speaker on this topic.

A clear preview statement lets the audience know what to listen for in the body of the speech.

This speech is structured in problem-solution order. In this paragraph, the speaker begins her problem main point by using statistics to show how widespread the use of chewing tobacco is in American society. Notice how the speaker explains the meaning of her statistics. Her last sentence—"Children are using chewing tobacco before they can even read the warning labels"— is especially effective in this regard.

The speaker shows that chewing tobacco poses a number of dangers. She begins, in this paragraph, with tooth decay and tooth loss.

Tom's dental checkup, he had surgery to remove the cancer. This photograph shows Tom after his surgery. As you can see, a large portion of Tom's lower lip was removed and the area was drawn together by stitches. The surgery left Tom disfigured and looking quite grotesque, but it was not the worst part. Tom died just one month later. Chewing tobacco caused Tom's death.

Due to the fact that I am currently studying to be a dentist, and because my father is a dentist and I have worked for him as an assistant for over four years, I have actually seen cases similar to Tom's which result from chewing tobacco. I have also attended a number of seminars on this topic, and today I'd like to persuade each of you to feel as strongly as I do about the dangers of chewing tobacco.

In my speech, I'd like to show you the many problems that can result from chewing tobacco. Then I'd like to persuade each of you to take action and help change the lenient laws governing the use of chewing tobacco in our society. Let's begin by looking at how widespread the problem of chewing tobacco really is.

Chewing tobacco is more common than you may think. According to the American Cancer Society, one in every twelve Americans is a regular user of chewing tobacco. The average age of first use is just ten years old, which means that many children are chewing tobacco when they are in fourth grade. The American Cancer Society also reports that 40 percent of high-school boys have tried chewing tobacco—and, what's worse, 21 percent of kindergartners have tried it. Children are using chewing tobacco before they can even read the warning labels!

Now you know that chewing tobacco is widespread, but you may wonder what could possibly happen when a person uses chewing tobacco. Well, smokeless tobacco has multiple dangers according to the American Dental Association and the American Cancer Society. First, tooth decay and tooth loss can occur. Chewing tobacco contains grit and sand, which wear away at the teeth. It also contains added sugars to improve the taste—but they also wear away at the teeth, leading to cavities and tooth loss.

In this paragraph, the speaker shows how regular use of chewing tobacco can cause gum disease.

Now the speaker gets to the most serious health problem caused by chewing tobacco—oral cancer. In this paragraph, she uses a series of statistics from the American Dental Association to show how regular use of chewing tobacco is more dangerous than smoking cigarettes. Here, as in other parts of the speech, her statistics are clearly presented and come from a highly credible source.

Coming after the statistics in the previous paragraph, the story of Sean Marsee is extremely effective in driving home the dangers of chewing tobacco. Vivid and richly textured, the story personalizes the statistics and provides strong emotional appeal. This is an excellent example of how emotional appeal can develop naturally out of the content of a speech.

The speaker's concern for the audience here and throughout the speech substantially increased her credibility and persuasiveness.

Another effect of chewing tobacco is gum disease. Regular use of chewing tobacco causes visual gum damage in less than two to three months. According to the American Dental Association, about half of all teenage users have some type of gum problem. But what's wrong with gum disease? Well, it causes the gums to pull away from the teeth, which further increases the risk of tooth decay and loss.

Gum disease and tooth loss are serious enough, but as we saw at the beginning in the story about Tom, chewing tobacco can have more serious consequences. According to the American Dental Association, those who use chewing tobacco just once in a while have four times the risk of developing oral cancer than do nonusers. And if that isn't bad enough, those who use chewing tobacco three or more times a week for over a year have fifty times the risk of developing cancer than do nonusers. This risk is even greater than that of smoking cigarettes. But unlike smoking cigarettes, where cancer develops slowly over time, chewing tobacco can cause cancer in teens and young adults.

For example, Sean Marsee, a nineteen-year-old high-school student from Oklahoma, was one of the most well-liked students in his senior class. Sean used chewing tobacco from age twelve to age eighteen, when he was diagnosed as having oral cancer during his senior year in high school. As a result, Sean had to have a series of disfiguring operations. First three-fourths of his tongue was removed. Then all the muscles and lymph nodes on the right side of Sean's face and neck were removed. And lastly his jawbone was removed from here to here. As you can imagine, Sean was left looking quite grotesque. But this was not the worst part. As extreme as the surgery was, it could not stop Sean's cancer from spreading, and he died just one year later. There can be no doubt that chewing tobacco caused Sean's death.

I know this is a terrible thought, but the point I'm trying to make is an important one. You must be aware of the terrible consequences of chewing tobacco because next time it could happen to you or to someone you love.

Now the speaker moves into her second main point, in which she gives a two-part solution to the problem of chewing tobacco. The first part deals with the laws governing the sale of chewing tobacco to minors. Because the speaker is a student in Wisconsin, she focuses on the laws in that state.

The speaker draws from the experience of California to show the practicality of her plan. Reasoning analogically, she concludes that because a law similar to the one she is proposing has cut chewing tobacco use by 60 percent in California, it would be effective in her state as well.

The speaker presents the second part of her plan. Reasoning causally, she provides testimony from the American Dental Association that children develop an interest in chewing tobacco because they want to emulate sports stars who chew. If professional athletes take a stand against chewing tobacco, she contends, fewer children will take up the habit.

The speaker uses the Kansas City Royals baseball team as an example to show the practicality of her call for a ban on chewing tobacco at professional sporting events. Although the example does not prove that children will stop using chewing tobacco if professional athletes stop, it does show that seeking a ban on chewing tobacco during professional sporting events is within the realm of possibility.

Let's look, then, at what can be done to diminish the use of chewing tobacco. First, the laws in Wisconsin pertaining to the age at which chewing tobacco can be bought must be strengthened. The law in Wisconsin states that chewing tobacco can be purchased at age eighteen, but according to the Department of Law Enforcement, the laws on chewing tobacco sales have been ineffective. To be effective, the laws must be enforced and have adequate penalties.

A number of other states, including California, set the fine for selling chewing tobacco to minors at $1,500 for the first offense and $6,000 for the second offense. According to the American Dental Association, this law has cut the use of chewing tobacco by minors by almost 60 percent. I would like you to help pass a law resembling this in Wisconsin. You must help stop people from selling cancer to our children. You can make a difference. You can write to our legislators urging that a bill like this be created here in Wisconsin.

Second, use of chewing tobacco during all professional sporting events should be banned. According to the American Dental Association, the primary reason children develop an interest in chewing tobacco is because they see their role models doing it. These role models include parents, relatives, and friends, but more importantly, they include sports stars. Children see athletes as role models. Children think if it's all right for athletes to use chewing tobacco, it must be all right for me to do it too. If these role models would stand up and say chewing is wrong, many of our children would change their minds about the drug.

What we need, then, is a ban on chewing tobacco use during professional sporting events. You may think this is impractical, but already one baseball team, the Kansas City Royals, has taken a stand. They have switched from chewing tobacco to bubble gum. You can help influence other teams to do the same. I urge you to write to your favorite team or to your favorite athlete urging them, individually or as a team, to take a stand against chewing tobacco as the Royals did.

Brief and hard-hitting, the conclusion reinforces the speaker's call for action against the use of chewing tobacco. Referring back to the examples of Tom and Sean is especially effective and ends the speech on a strong note.

In conclusion, then, I am pleading with each of you to take action against the use of chewing tobacco. When you think of this subject, remember the problems of chewing tobacco. Remember Tom—and remember Sean. By adopting the measures I have discussed today, you can help stop what happened to Tom and Sean from happening to others.

SUMMARY

People have been studying the methods of persuasion since the days of the ancient Greeks. They have found that listeners accept a speaker's ideas for one or more of four reasons—because they perceive the speaker as having high credibility, because they are won over by the speaker's evidence, because they are convinced by the speaker's reasoning, or because they are moved by the speaker's emotional appeals.

Credibility is affected by many factors, but the two most important are competence and character. The more favorably listeners view a speaker's competence and character, the more likely they are to accept her or his ideas. Although credibility is partly a matter of reputation, you can enhance your credibility during the speech by establishing common ground with your listeners and by letting them know why you are qualified to speak on the topic. You can also build your credibility by presenting your speeches fluently and expressively.

If you hope to be persuasive, you must also support your views with evidence—examples, statistics, and testimony used to prove or disprove something. As you prepare your speech, try at each point to imagine how your audience will react. Anticipate their doubts and answer them with evidence. Regardless of what kind of evidence you use, it will be more persuasive if it is new to the audience, if it is stated in specific rather than general terms, and if it is from credible sources. Your evidence will also be more persuasive if you state explicitly the point it is supposed to prove.

No matter how strong your evidence, you will not be very persuasive unless listeners agree with your reasoning. In reasoning from specific instances, you move from a number of particular facts to a general conclusion. Reasoning from principle is the reverse—you move from a general principle to a particular conclusion. When you use causal reasoning, you try to establish a relationship between causes and effects. In analogical reasoning, you compare two cases and infer that what is true for one is also true for the other. Whatever kind of reasoning you use, you want to make sure that your thinking is sound and valid.

Finally, you can persuade your listeners by appealing to their emotions—fear, anger, pity, pride, sorrow, and so forth. One way to generate emotional appeal is by using emotion-laden language. Another is to develop vivid, richly textured examples that personalize your ideas and draw listeners into the speech emotionally. Neither, however, will be effective unless you feel the emotion yourself and communicate it by speaking with sincerity and conviction.

As with other methods of persuasion, your use of emotional appeal should be guided by a firm ethical rudder. Although emotional appeals are usually inappropriate in speeches on questions of fact, they are legitimate—and often necessary—in speeches that seek immediate action on questions of policy. Even when trying to move listeners to action, however, you should never substitute emotional appeals for evidence and reasoning. You need to build a good case based on facts and logic in addition to kindling the emotions of your audience.

REVIEW QUESTIONS

1. What is credibility? What two factors exert the most influence on an audience's perception of a speaker's credibility?

2. What are the differences among initial credibility, derived credibility, and terminal credibility?

3. What are three ways you can enhance your credibility during your speeches?

4. What is evidence? Why do persuasive speakers need to use evidence?

5. What are four tips for using evidence effectively in a persuasive speech?

6. What is reasoning from specific instances? What guidelines should you follow when using this method of reasoning?

7. What is reasoning from principle? How is it different from reasoning from specific instances?

8. What is causal reasoning? What two errors must you be sure to avoid when using causal reasoning?

9. What is analogical reasoning? How do you judge the validity of an analogy?

10. What is the role of emotional appeal in persuasive speaking? Identify three methods you can use to generate emotional appeal in your speeches.

APPLICATION EXERCISES

1. Research has shown that a speaker's initial credibility can have great impact on how the speaker's ideas are received by listeners. Research has also shown that a speaker's credibility will vary from topic to topic and au-

dience to audience. In the left-hand column below is a list of well-known public figures. In the right-hand column is a list of potential speech topics. Assume that each speaker will be addressing your speech class.

For each speaker, identify the topic in the right-hand column on which she or he would have the highest initial credibility for your class. Then explain how the speaker's initial credibility might be affected if the speaker were discussing the topic in the right-hand column directly across from her or his name.

SPEAKER	TOPIC
Hillary Rodham Clinton	African Americans: The Next Agenda
George Bush	Women in the Mass Media
Barbara Walters	Reforming the American Presidency
Jesse Jackson	Talk Shows: Who Needs Them?
David Letterman	The Amercan Health Care Revolution

2. Identify the kind of reasoning used in each of the following statements. What weaknesses, if any, can you find in the reasoning of each?

   a. According to a study by the American Medical Association, men with bald spots have three times the risk of heart attack as men with a full head of hair. Strange as it may seem, it looks as if baldness is a cause of heart attacks.

   b. Contrary to what the chemical industry argues, limiting pesticide use does not threaten the food supply. Sweden has cut back on pesticides by 50 percent over the last few years with almost no decrease in its harvest. The Campbell Soup Company uses no pesticides at all on tomatoes grown in Mexico, and they reap as much fruit as ever. Many California farmers who practice pesticide-free agriculture have actually experienced increases in their crop yields.

   c. The United States Constitution guarantees all citizens the right to bear arms. Gun control legislation infringes on the right of citizens to bear arms. Therefore, gun control legislation is contrary to the Constitution.

   d. Almost every industrialized nation in the world except for the United States has a national curriculum and national tests to help ensure that schools throughout the country are meeting high standards of education. If such a system can work elsewhere, it can work in the United States as well.

3. Over the years there has been much debate about the role of emotional appeal in public speaking. Do you believe it is ethical for public speakers to use emotional appeals when seeking to persuade an audience? Do you feel there are certain kinds of emotions to which an ethical speaker should not appeal? Why or why not? Be prepared to explain your ideas in class.

4. Analyze the speech in the Appendix by Sandy Hefty ("A Friend in Need," pages 459–462). Pay special attention to how the speaker uses the methods of persuasion discussed in this chapter.

5. Analyze the speech in the Appendix by Mary Fisher ("A Whisper of AIDS," pages 456–459. In your analysis, concentrate on how Fisher builds her credibility, employs evidence and reasoning, and generates emotional appeal. In addition, study how she uses the resources of language discussed in Chapter 11 to bring her message home to listeners.

NOTES

1 Roger Dawson Productions, Incorporated, La Habra, California.
2 See, for example, Kathleen Kelley Reardon, *Persuasion in Practice* (Newbury Park, Calif.: Sage, 1991).
3 Although source credibility can be a factor in shaping the response of readers to written work, it plays a much more crucial role in public speaking. See Steve Booth-Butterfield and Christine Gutowski, "Message Modality and Source Credibility Can Interact to Affect Argument Processing," *Communication Quarterly,* 41 (1993), 77–89.
4 For a review of research on the factors of credibility, see Daniel J. O'Keefe, *Persuasion: Theory and Research* (Newbury Park, Calif.: Sage, 1990), pp. 130–157.
5 James C. McCroskey, *An Introduction to Rhetorical Communication,* 6th ed. (Englewood Cliffs, N.J.: Prentice-Hall, 1993), pp. 82–92.
6 Although it deals primarily with interpersonal communication, an interesting study with implications for credibility statements in public speaking is Lynn Carol Miller, Linda Lee Cooke, Jennifer Tsang, and Faith Morgan, "Should I Brag? Nature and Impact of Positive and Boastful Disclosures for Women and Men," *Human Communication Research,* 18 (1992), 364–399.
7 There is abundant research showing that perceived similarity between speaker and audience enhances the speaker's persuasiveness. For a summary of that research, see Richard M. Perloff, *The Dynamics of Persuasion* (Hillsdale, N.J.: Lawrence Erlbaum, 1993), pp. 145–149.
8 Perloff, *Dynamics of Persuasion,* pp. 170–179; O'Keefe, *Persuasion,* pp. 134–135.
9 A great deal of research has been conducted on the role of evidence in persuasive communication. For an excellent survey of that research, see John C. Reinard, "The Empirical Study of the Persuasive Effects of Evidence: The Status after Fifty Years of Research," *Human Communication Research,* 15 (1988), 3–59.
10 See Mike Allen, "Meta-Analysis Comparing the Persuasiveness of One-Sided and Two-Sided Messages," *Western Journal of Speech Communication,* 55 (1991), 390–404.
11 Reinard, "Empirical Study of Evidence," pp. 37–38.
12 See Donald Dean Morley and Kim B. Walker, "The Role of Importance, Novelty, and Plausibility in Producing Belief Change," *Communication Monographs,* 54 (1987), 436–442.
13 See Perloff, *Dynamics of Persuasion,* pp. 157–158; Reinard, "Empirical Study of Evidence," pp. 34, 36–39.

[14] O'Keefe, *Persuasion,* pp. 159–161.

[15] Adapted from James C. Humes, *A Speaker's Treasury of Anecdotes about the Famous* (New York: Harper & Row, 1978), p. 131.

[16] For an intriguing look at this subject, see Iona Opie and Moira Tatem (eds.), *Dictionary of Superstitions* (Oxford: Oxford University Press, 1992).

[17] In classical systems of logic, reasoning from particular facts to a general conclusion was known as induction. Contemporary logicians, however, have redefined induction as any instance of reasoning in which the conclusion follows from its premises with probability—regardless of whether the reasoning moves from specific instances to a general conclusion or from a general premise to specific conclusion. In this scheme, reasoning from specific instances is one kind of inductive argument—as are causal reasoning and analogical reasoning. See, for example, S. Morris Engel, *With Good Reason: An Introduction to Informal Fallacies,* 4th ed. (New York: St. Martin's, 1990); Howard Kahane, *Logic and Contemporary Rhetoric: The Use of Reason in Everyday Life,* 6th ed. (Belmont, Calif.: Wadsworth, 1992).

[18] Lionel Ruby, *The Art of Making Sense* (Philadelphia: Lippincott, 1954), p. 261.

[19] For centuries, reasoning from a general premise to a specific conclusion was known as deduction. But just as contemporary logicians have redefined induction (see note 17 above), they have redefined deduction as any instance of reasoning in which the conclusion follows from its premises with certainty. Some deductive arguments move from general premises to a specific conclusion, but others move from specific premises to a general conclusion. Many speech textbooks confuse reasoning from principle—which is one form of deduction—with deductive reasoning in general.

[20] The full text of Anthony's speech is in Karlyn Kohrs Campbell (ed.), *Man Cannot Speak for Her: Key Texts of the Early Feminists* (New York: Praeger, 1989), pp. 289–316.

[21] For more detail on methods of reasoning, see George W. Ziegelmueller, Jack Kay, and Charles A. Dause, *Argumentation and Advocacy,* 2nd ed. (Englewood Cliffs, N.J.: Prentice-Hall, 1990); James A. Herrick, *Critical Thinking: The Analysis of Arguments* (Scottsdale, Ariz.: Gorsuch Scarisbrick, 1991); David L. Vancil, *Rhetoric and Argumentation* (Boston: Allyn and Bacon, 1993).

[22] H. E. Butler (trans.), *The Institutio Oratoria of Quintilian* (Cambridge, Mass.: Harvard University Press, 1961), IV, 141.

[23] George Campbell, *The Philosophy of Rhetoric,* ed. Lloyd F. Bitzer (Carbondale, Ill.: Southern Illinois University Press, 1988), p. 77.

[24] For an excellent recent review of communication research on emotion and persuasion, see Alice H. Eagly and Shelly Chaiken, *The Psychology of Attitudes* (Fort Worth, Tex.: Harcourt Brace Jovanovich, 1993), pp. 431–447.

[25] The power of examples to generate strong responses in listeners is well documented. For a recent study, see Dean C. Kazoleas, "A Comparison of the Persuasive Effectiveness of Qualitative versus Quantitative Evidence: A Test of Explanatory Hypotheses," *Communication Quarterly,* 41 (1993), 40–50.

[26] For a strong defense of emotional appeal on ethical grounds, see Craig Waddell, "The Role of *Pathos* in the Decision-Making Process: A Study in the Rhetoric of Science Policy," *Quarterly Journal of Speech,* 76 (1990), 381–400.

[27] This point has been made by a number of recent studies. See, for example, Craig R. Smith and Michael J. Hyde, "Rethinking the 'Public': The Role of Emotion in Being-with-Others," *Quarterly Journal of Speech,* 77 (1991), 446–466; Mary M. Garrett, "*Pathos* Reconsidered from the Perspective of Classical Chinese Rhetorical Theories," *Quarterly Journal of Speech,* 79 (1993), 19–39.

[28] Research on fear appeals, for example, has demonstrated that messages devoted exclusively to arousing fear in the audience are less effective than messages that combine fear appeals with reasonable explanations of how to eliminate or cope with the source of fear. See Kim Witte, "Putting the Fear Back into Fear Appeals: The Extended Parallel Process Model," *Communication Monographs,* 59 (1992), 329–349.

[29] Reprinted with permission of Catherine Twohig. This speech is also available on the videotape supplement to *The Art of Public Speaking.*

Chapter 17

Speaking on Special Occasions

SPEECHES OF INTRODUCTION

SPEECHES OF PRESENTATION

SPEECHES OF ACCEPTANCE

COMMEMORATIVE SPEECHES

AFTER-DINNER SPEECHES

Special occasions are the punctuation marks of day-to-day life, the high points that stand out above ordinary routine. Christenings, weddings, funerals, graduations, award ceremonies, inaugurals, retirement dinners—all these are occasions, and they are very special to the people who take part in them. Nearly always they are occasions for speechmaking. A close friend proposes a toast to the bride and groom; the sales manager presents an award to the sales representative of the year; the President delivers an inaugural address; the basketball coach gives a speech honoring the team's most valuable player; a family member delivers a moving eulogy to the deceased. These speeches help give the occasion its "specialness." They are part of the ceremonial aura that marks the event.

Speeches for special occasions are different from the speeches we have considered so far in this book. They may convey information, but that is not their primary purpose. Neither is their primary purpose to persuade. Rather, they aim to fit the special needs of a special occasion. In this chapter we look at the most common special occasions and the kinds of speeches appropriate for each.

SPEECHES OF INTRODUCTION

"Distinguished guests, the President of the United States." If you are ever in a situation in which you have to introduce the President, you will need no more than the eight words that begin this paragraph. The President is so well known that any further remarks would be inappropriate and almost foolish.

Most of the time, however, a speech of introduction will be neither this brief nor this ritualized. If you are introducing another speaker, you will need to accomplish three purposes in your introduction:

Build enthusiasm for the upcoming speaker.

Build enthusiasm for the speaker's topic.

Establish a welcoming climate that will boost the speaker's credibility.

A good speech of introduction can be a delight to hear and can do much to ease the task of the main speaker. The basic message of such a speech should be "Here is a speaker you will enjoy, and this is why."[1] Usually you will say something about the speaker and about the topic—in that order. Following are some guidelines for speeches of introduction. Most of the points apply also to the other types of special-occasion speeches discussed in this chapter.

Be Brief   During World War I, Lord Balfour, Great Britain's foreign secretary, was to be the main speaker at a rally in the United States. But the speaker introducing Lord Balfour gave a 45-minute oration on the causes of the war. Then, almost as an afterthought, he said, "Now Lord Balfour will give his address." Lord Balfour rose and said, "I'm supposed to give my address in the brief time remaining. Here it is: 10 Carleton Gardens, London, England."[2]

Every speaker—and audience—who has ever sat through a long-winded introduction knows how dreary it can be. The audience is thinking, "Oh, for heaven's sake, get *on* with it." For the speaker, it is even more troublesome. She or he is psyched up. The adrenaline is pumping. But as the introducer drones on, the feeling of readiness begins to drain away. By the time the introducer finally sits down, the speaker may well have lost much of her or his creative energy.

The purpose of a speech of introduction is to focus attention on the main speaker, not on the person making the introduction. Under normal circumstances, a speech of introduction will be no more than two to three minutes long, and it may be shorter if the speaker is already well known to the audience.

Make Sure Your Introduction Is Completely Accurate   Many an introducer has embarrassed himself or herself, as well as the main speaker, by garbling basic facts about the speaker. Always check with the speaker ahead of time to make sure your introduction is accurate in every respect.

Above all, get the speaker's name right. This may seem obvious, but it needs repeating. Remember that nothing is more important than a person's name. When you get a name wrong, you strip that person of identity and importance. If the speaker's name is at all difficult—especially if it involves a foreign pronunciation—practice saying it well in advance. However, don't practice so much that you frighten yourself about getting it wrong. This was the plight of an announcer whose gaffe is now a classic: "Ladies and gentlemen, the President of the United States—Hoobert Heever!"

Adapt Your Remarks to the Occasion   In preparing your introduction, you may be constrained by the nature of the occasion. Formal occasions require formal speeches of introduction. If you were presenting a guest speaker at an informal business meeting, you might be much more casual than if you were presenting the same speaker to the same audience at a formal banquet.

Adapt Your Introduction to the Main Speaker   No matter how well it is received by the audience, a speech of introduction that leaves the main speaker feeling uncomfortable has failed in part of its purpose. How can you make a main speaker uncomfortable? One way is to overpraise the person—and especially to praise him or her for speaking skills. Never say, "Our speaker will keep you on the edge of your seat from beginning to end!" This is like prefacing a joke with the line, "Here is the funniest joke you've ever heard." You create a set of expectations that are almost impossible to fulfill.

Another way to create discomfort is by revealing embarrassing details of the speaker's personal life or by making humorous remarks that are in poor taste from the speaker's point of view. An introducer may think this kind of remark is funny: "Why, I've known Anita Fratello since she was ten years old and so fat that everybody in the class called her Blimpo!" To the speaker, however, the remark will probably not be a bit funny and may be painful.

Adapt Your Remarks to the Audience   Just as you adapt other speeches to particular audiences, so you need to adapt the speech of introduction to the audience you are facing. Your aim is to make *this* audience want to hear *this* speaker on *this* subject. If the speaker is not well known to the audience, you will need to establish his or her credibility by recounting some of the speaker's main achievements and explaining why he or she is qualified to speak on the topic at hand. But if the speaker is already personally known to the audience, it would be absurd to act as if the audience had never heard of the person.

Also, you will want to tell each audience what *it* wants to hear—to give the kind of information that is interesting and accessible to the members of that audience. If you were introducing the same speaker to two different groups, some of the information in the speeches of introduction might be the same, but it would be slanted differently. Suppose, for example, the police commissioner of a certain city is going to address two groups—an audience of elementary-school children and the members of the city council. The introduction to the school children might go something like this:

Children, we have a very important guest with us today. He is the number-one policeman in our city, the head of all the other police officers. Besides knowing a lot about crime right here at home, the police commissioner has also spent time working with Interpol—a special group of police officers who deal with crimes around the world. Today he is going to talk about how all of us can work with our neighborhood police officers to prevent crime. Let's give a big round of applause and listen carefully to Police Commissioner Robert Washington.

But the introduction to the city council would be along these lines:

Members of the city council and distinguished guests: It is my privilege to introduce to you today the police commissioner, who will address us on the subject of the community policing program. Most of you know the commissioner has a distinguished record as head of our police force for more than ten years. However, you may not know that he also holds a master's degree in criminology and studied abroad for a year with Interpol, the international police force.

The commissioner first introduced the community policing program three years ago. The idea behind the program is to get police officers out of their cars and into our neighborhoods, where they can talk directly to merchants and residents about the real dynamics of our city. These officers do more than make arrests. They try to find ways to help solve the problems that contribute to crime in the first place. Often that means hooking people up with services offered by other city agencies—schools, hospitals, housing, drug treatment centers.

And the program seems to be working. Crime is down in the neighborhoods with community policing, and our citizens report that they feel more secure. Today the commissioner is going to tell us how this program can be extended to more of the city and made more effective for all of our citizens. Please welcome Police Commissioner Robert Washington.

Try to Create a Sense of Anticipation and Drama   You may have noticed one detail shared by the two speeches introducing the police commissioner: In both cases the speaker's name was saved for last. This is a convention in speeches of introduction. While there may occasionally be good reason to break the convention, usually you will avoid mentioning the speaker's name until the final moment—even when the audience knows exactly whom you are discussing. By doing this you build a sense of drama, and the speaker's name comes as the climax of your introduction.

Often you will find yourself in the situation of introducing someone who is fairly well known to the audience—a classmate, a colleague at a business meeting, a neighbor in a community group. Then you should try to be creative and cast the speaker in a new light. Try to increase the audience's eagerness to hear the speaker. Talk to the speaker beforehand and see if you can learn some interesting facts that are not generally known—especially facts that relate to the speaker's topic. If possible, interview some of the speaker's close friends or family.

Above all, if you expect to be creative and dramatic, be sure you practice your speech of introduction thoroughly. Even though it is short, there is no excuse for not working out the delivery as fully as possible. You should be able to deliver the speech extemporaneously, with sincerity and enthusiasm.

SPEECHES OF PRESENTATION

Speeches of presentation are given when someone is receiving publicly a gift or an award. Usually such speeches are relatively brief. They may be no more than a mere announcement ("And the winner is . . .") or be up to four or five minutes in length.

As with other kinds of speeches, speeches of presentation need to be adapted to the audience and to the occasion. The main theme of a speech of presentation is to acknowledge the achievements of the recipient. You need to tell the audience why the recipient is receiving the award. Point out her or his contributions, achievements, and so forth. Do not deal with everything the person has ever done. Focus on achievements related to the award, and discuss these achievements in a way that will make them meaningful to the audience.

Depending on the audience and the occasion, you may also need to discuss two other matters in a speech of presentation. First, if the audience is not familiar with the award and why it is being given, you should explain briefly—or at least allude to—the purpose of the award. Second, if the award was won in a public competition and the audience knows who the losers are, you might take a moment to praise the losers as well.

Below is a sample speech of presentation. It was delivered by Gregory Peck in presenting the Jean Hersholt Humanitarian Award to Danny Kaye at the 1982 Academy Awards ceremony in Los Angeles. Because the Hersholt

Award is a special honor bestowed by the academy's board of governors, there are no public competitors for the award. Thus Peck did not need to say anything in recognition of the "losers." His speech focused on Kaye's contributions to UNICEF and to symphony orchestras as the reasons for bestowal of the award.[3]

▬ PRESENTING THE JEAN HERSHOLT HUMANITARIAN AWARD ▬

Gregory Peck

It's a long trip from Brooklyn to Buckingham Palace, and it's a far piece from Beverly Hills to an obscure village in Bangladesh. Danny Kaye has made both journeys, sustained by his remarkable gifts, his grace, and his intelligence. He has been a star of the first magnitude since his remarkable talent exploded on the Broadway stage in *Lady in the Dark* in 1941, and one who has had a high sense of priority: His wife, Sylvia, and daughter, Dena, have always come first in his life—and then, in no special order, his work, the world's children, and great music.

For UNICEF (United Nations International Children's Emergency Fund), he continues to travel the world, bringing joy and hope to children on all the continents, and initiating programs to save them from hunger and give them a better chance in life. He has been doing this for years, with no pay and without fanfare. No trumpets. No headlines. His reward, the laughter of children.

As forbearing and skillful as he is with children, so he is with symphony orchestras, groups of seventy or eighty highly disciplined artists. He cannot read music, yet he has conducted major orchestras all over the world with musicianship that is sensitive, completely serious, and, at times, likely to veer off alarmingly into the hilarious. Danny's irrepressible *joie de vivre* makes his concerts joyous occasions for musicians and audiences alike. Bach and Mozart have no better friend. Nor have the orchestras and their pension funds. Nor have we.

And thus, for his prodigious labors for the children of the world, for the wondrous people who make music, the Board of Governors proudly gives the Jean Hersholt Humanitarian Award to a "Citizen of the World" who does honor to our profession—Mr. Danny Kaye.

■ SPEECHES OF ACCEPTANCE

The purpose of an acceptance speech is to give thanks for a gift or an award. When giving such a speech, you should thank the people who are bestowing the award, and you should recognize the people who helped you gain it.

The acceptance speech that follows is the companion piece to the speech of presentation by Gregory Peck. It was delivered by Danny Kaye in accepting the Jean Hersholt Humanitarian Award at the 1982 Academy Awards ceremony, and it exemplifies the three major traits of a good acceptance speech—brevity, humility, and graciousness.[4]

ACCEPTING THE JEAN HERSHOLT HUMANITARIAN AWARD

Danny Kaye

I am terribly excited to be given this great honor. And I'm so delighted that I find myself, as we say, trembling. If I were any more delighted, I think I'd be in an institution.

However, I feel a little bit guilty about all the praise that Greg lavished on me. It was really no hardship at all. Really. I am crazy about children. I am crazy about conducting. And I am crazy about flying.

I am definitely not crazy about disease or famine or neglect. But, then, neither are any of you. And we, all of us in our profession, share a long and wonderful tradition of doing something about it—of giving of our time and our talent wherever and whenever needed—without prejudice, without stint. That's one of the reasons that I am so very proud of our profession and so proud to be one of you.

I share this award with you, with all of you, and I give thanks to the memory of Dag Hammarskjöld and Maurice Pate, with whom I started to work for UNICEF about twenty-eight years ago. And to Gene Ormandy, who put a baton in my hand, my little nervous hand, and made me an offer I couldn't refuse—to stand in front of a symphony orchestra and conduct. Wow! That's the greatest feeling of neurotic power in the world. You ought to try it!

My special thanks to the Board of Governors. I love this and I love you. Thank you.

COMMEMORATIVE SPEECHES

Commemorative speeches are essentially speeches of praise or celebration. Eulogies, Fourth of July speeches, testimonial addresses, and dedications are examples of commemorative speeches. Your aim in such speeches is to pay tribute to a person, a group of people, an institution, or an idea.

As in an informative speech, you probably will have to give the audience information about your subject. After all, the audience must know *why* your subject is praiseworthy. They will need to know something about the history of the institution or the life of the person being praised. As in other speeches, you may draw on examples, testimony, even statistics to illustrate the achievements of your subject.

Your fundamental purpose in a commemorative speech, however, is not just to inform your listeners but to *inspire* them—to arouse and heighten their appreciation of or admiration for the person, institution, or idea you are praising. If you are paying tribute to a person, for example, you should not compose a biography that simply recounts the details of the person's life. Rather, you should create a speech that goes beyond biography—that penetrates to the *essence* of your subject and generates in your audience a deep sense of respect.

When speaking to commemorate, you do not exhort like the advocate or explain like the lecturer. You want to express feelings, to stir sentiments—joy and hope when a new building is dedicated or a new President is inaugurated; anticipation and good wishes at a commencement celebration; lament and consolation at a funeral or memorial service; admiration and respect at a testimonial dinner. In some ways, a commemorative speech is like an impressionist painting—"a picture with warm colors and texture capturing a mood or a moment."[5]

But while the painter works with brush and colors, the commemorative speaker works with language. Of all the kinds of speeches, perhaps none depends more on the creative and subtle use of language than does the speech to commemorate. Some of the most memorable speeches in history—including Abraham Lincoln's Gettysburg Address—have been commemorative. We remember such speeches—we continue to find them meaningful and inspiring—largely because of their eloquent use of language.

One of the most effective commemorative speakers in our recent history was President Ronald Reagan. After the explosion of the space shuttle *Challenger* in 1986, Reagan delivered a nationally televised eulogy to the astronauts killed in the blast. Below are two versions of Reagan's closing lines. The first is what he *might* have said, stripping the text of its warm emotional content and poignant language:

Like Francis Drake, the great explorer of the oceans, the *Challenger* astronauts gave their lives for a cause to which they were fully dedicated. We are honored by them, and we will not forget them. We will always remember seeing them for the last time this morning as they prepared for their flight.

Here is what Reagan *actually* said:

There's a coincidence today. On this day 390 years ago, the great explorer Francis Drake died aboard ship off the coast of Panama. In his lifetime the great frontiers were the oceans, and an historian later said, "He lived by the sea, died on it, was buried in it." Well, today we can say of the *Challenger* crew: Their dedication was, like Drake's, complete.

The crew of the space shuttle *Challenger* honored us by the manner in which they lived their lives. We will never forget them, nor the last time we saw them, this morning, as they prepared for their journey and waved goodbye and "slipped the surly bonds of earth" to "touch the face of God."[6]

The final words—"'slipped the surly bonds of earth' to 'touch the face of God'"—are especially effective. Drawn from a sonnet called "High Flight" that many pilots keep with them, they ennoble the deaths of the astronauts and end the speech on an eloquent, moving, and poetic note.

When speaking to commemorate, you will deal for the most part with intangibles. Your success will depend on your ability to put into language the thoughts and emotions appropriate to the occasion. It is easy—too easy—to fall back on clichés and trite sentiments. Your challenge will be to use language imaginatively in order to invest the occasion with dignity, meaning, and honest emotion.

In doing so, you may want to utilize the special resources of language discussed in Chapter 11 to enhance the imagery and rhythm of your prose. Metaphor, simile, parallelism, repetition, antithesis, alliteration—all are appropriate for commemorative speeches. A number of highly acclaimed commemorative speeches—including Martin Luther King's "I Have a Dream" and John Kennedy's Inaugural Address—are distinguished by their creative use of such devices.

Confronted with the evocative speeches of a Kennedy or a King, you may decide that the speech of commemoration is far beyond your abilities. But other students have delivered excellent commemorative speeches—not immortal, perhaps, but nonetheless dignified and moving. The following speech was given by Ryan Saurer, a student at the University of Wisconsin, in a public speaking class. The assignment was to give a brief speech paying tribute to a person, an institution, or an idea. Ryan spoke about James "Cool Papa" Bell, an African-American baseball star of the 1930s and 1940s who never played in the major leagues because of his race. As you read the speech, notice how effectively Ryan used the resources of language to give his ideas artistic unity and emotional impact.[7]

JAMES "COOL PAPA" BELL

Ryan Saurer

In 1946 one of the greatest baseball players of all time retired after almost twenty-five years as a pro. No, it wasn't Babe Ruth, Joe DiMaggio, or any other star you've probably heard of. The man was James "Cool Papa" Bell, star of the Pittsburgh Crawfords of the Negro League.

The Negro League was the name of the league where black players were forced to play until 1947, when major league baseball became integrated. The Negro League had some of the best players never to be appreciated, and Cool Papa Bell headed that list.

Many say that Bell was the fastest player ever to play the game. This could very well be true. He led the league in stolen bases almost every year he played until he retired at age forty-one. Satchell Paige, a former teammate of his, said Cool Papa was so fast he could flip the switch and be in bed before the lights went out.

In fact, Jesse Owens, the Olympic sprinter who was known as the fastest man in the world, said he would race and beat anyone around the bases as long as that person wasn't Cool Papa Bell. At five feet, eleven inches tall and only 135 pounds, Bell was thin as a rail. But no one made fun of his slender size as he swiftly and smoothly stole second or scored from first on a single.

And Cool Papa was smooth. In his first game as a pro, the seventeen-year-old, then known as James, came into the game in the bottom of the ninth inning and struck out one of the league's best hitters on three straight pitches. Pretty smooth for a guy who wasn't even a pitcher. For playing with the savvy of a seasoned veteran even though he was only a kid, his manager called him "Cool Papa."

But to say that Cool Papa had style would be an injustice to him. Cool Papa *was* style. Whether in his baseball uniform or his Sunday best, Cool Papa had a flair all his own. Some of you may have seen flip-down sunglasses, a necessity and fashion statement for many major league players today. Flip-down sunglasses weren't unknown to Cool Papa. After all, he invented them.

But despite all of Cool Papa's baseball feats and the style with which he accomplished them, his greatest achievement was that he played at all. You see, James "Cool Papa" Bell was the victim of a disease known as racism—racism that kept him from playing in the same league as white players, racism that kept him from being in the same record books as white players, racism that kept him from earning the same money as white players. In fact, to make ends meet, Cool Papa would race home after each game just so he could change clothes and get to his second job as a nighttime security guard. This kind of thing would be unheard of for players today.

But despite the inequalities he faced, Cool Papa kept on playing the game he loved. He helped pave the way for Jackie Robinson, the first African American in the major leagues, and others who followed him. Cool Papa did this by fighting racism the same way he played baseball—stylishly but effectively. Despite knowing that he would never reach his dream of playing in the major leagues just because of his color, Cool Papa Bell, and many others for that matter, played on, hoping that someday there would be only one league—a league of professional baseball players, regardless of race.

So let's take a few moments, which is longer than it would take Cool Papa to steal second base, to appreciate James "Cool Papa" Bell—the speedy baseball star, the stylish innovator, the man who fought racism just by going to work every day.

AFTER-DINNER SPEECHES

After-dinner speeches may be harder to define than any other kind of speech. While the custom of saying a few words of tribute or celebration following a meal is probably as old as civilization itself, after-dinner speeches as a formal type of speech developed in England during the early nineteenth century.[8] By the 1880s they had become so popular on this side of the Atlantic that one observer called them "the style of oratory most cultivated" in the United States.[9]

At that time they were delivered, literally, after dinner. By the 1920s, however, with the growing popularity of noon meetings for groups such as the Lions and Kiwanis clubs, "after-dinner" speeches could be heard after lunch as well. Because so many organizations now have breakfast gatherings, you are as likely to hear an "after-dinner" speech today at eight o'clock in the morning as at eight o'clock in the evening.

After-dinner speeches are best thought of as a kind of speech to entertain. Whether presented after breakfast, lunch, or dinner—in a formal dining room or at an outdoor barbecue—they usually have a lighter touch than a speech to inform or to persuade. This will obviously have some impact on your choice of topic. AIDS, child abuse, drunk driving, violent crime, toxic waste—all are important, but audiences do not expect to hear about such weighty matters in the relaxed atmosphere of the typical after-dinner speech. For the most part, though, any topic suitable for an informative or persuasive speech can be appropriate for an after-dinner speech, as long as you approach it in a lighthearted manner.

Suppose, for example, that your subject is nutrition. If you were giving an informative speech on this topic, your specific purpose might be "To inform my audience of the four basic nutrients in the human diet." If you were presenting a persuasive speech, your specific purpose might be "To persuade my audience that they should reduce their consumption of red meat in favor of more fish, vegetables, and grains." But if you were giving an after-dinner speech on the topic of nutrition, your specific purpose might be "To entertain my audience by showing them the ridiculous extremes some people go to in following special diets."

Or to take another example, say your subject is meteorology. If you were making an informative speech, your specific purpose might be "To inform my audience of the different methods used by meteorologists to predict the weather." If you were giving a persuasive speech on the same topic, your specific purpose might be "To persuade my audience that the federal government should not reduce the budget for weather-related research." If you were giving an after-dinner speech, however, your specific purpose might be "To entertain my audience by showing them how preposterous it is to talk about the 'typical' weather in our state."

As these examples suggest, after-dinner speeches should not be technical or argumentative. They may contain information that is new to the audience, and they may even have a persuasive impact, but their supporting materials should be chosen primarily for their entertainment value. Audiences for after-dinner speeches are seldom in a mood to follow a close train of reasoning, a complicated set of statistics, or a series of abstract concepts. Rather, they are looking for a good-natured speech that stimulates the imagination by approaching the topic in a novel way, treating it lightly, even whimsically.

This is not to say after-dinner speeches should be rambling or totally frivolous. Like all other speeches, they require careful preparation and organization. They should have a central theme, and they should strive to make a thoughtful point about that theme—whether it be about an aspect of human nature (such as vanity or the desire for immortality), of college life (such as final exams or finding a decent apartment), of sports (such as the similarities between modern football and the ancient Roman gladiators), of family life (such as the perils of summer vacations or the experience of being a parent for the first time), of work (such as putting up with the boss or dealing with weird customers), of travel (such as poor service by the airlines or dealing with unusual customs abroad), or even of current events (such as how we choose presidential candidates or jitters over the stock market).

As you might imagine, humor can be an important part of after-dinner speeches. Some of America's finest after-dinner speakers have been humorists such as Mark Twain and Will Rogers, Art Buchwald and Andy Rooney. This does not mean, however, that you need to be a stand-up comic to be a successful after-dinner speaker. The purpose of humor in an after-dinner speech is more to provoke smiles or chuckles than to convulse the audience with a series of one-liners. Nor is humor used merely to make the audience laugh. In the best speeches, humor grows naturally out of the speech materials and helps the speaker make his or her point by providing special insight into the topic.

One of the best-known instances of humor in a recent public speech occurred in Barbara Bush's 1990 commencement address at Wellesley College. There had been much controversy about the choice of Bush as speaker, and 150 students had signed a petition saying she did not represent the kind of career woman Wellesley seeks to educate.

In her speech, Bush made many serious points about the importance of family and the choices facing modern women, but she softened those points with humor. "Who knows," she said toward the end of her speech, "somewhere out in this audience may even be someone who will one day follow in my footsteps, and preside over the White House as the president's spouse." Then, after a pause, she added, "I wish *him* well!" It was a perfect line, perfectly timed. The audience of 5,400 people roared with laughter and gave Bush a ringing ovation.[10]

Tickling an audience's funnybone, however, can be difficult even for accomplished public speakers. If you don't feel confident working for a laugh, don't worry. Humor can contribute to a successful after-dinner speech, but it is not essential. Indeed, the best approach is usually not to work specifically for laughs. If you deal with the topic creatively, select supporting materials that are interesting in their own right, and use the resources of language to create sharp imagery, vivid descriptions, colorful details, and clever phrasing, you should do just fine.

All of these traits are represented in the following after-dinner speech. It was given by Julie Daggett, a student at the University of Wisconsin, to her public speaking class.[11]

THE HORROR OF IT ALL

Julie Daggett

They never did find his head or hands. I crouched in the corner, peering through my fingers as he moaned and wailed in an endless search for his missing appendages. I was terrified—but not as terrified as poor Bette Davis. They put her in the nuthouse. I simply turned on the light and ran to the safety of my father's lap. As I perched, shuddering, he said the phrase I was to hear over and over through the coming years, "It's okay, it's only a movie." It did not end for me there, however. The movie *Hush, Hush, Sweet Charlotte* was just the beginning of my love/hate relationship with horror movies.

My scaredy-cat tendencies actually began at a very early age. As a young child, I insisted the hall light be kept on when I went to bed—no measly night-light would do for a hard-core chicken. My parents would come upstairs after the news and tell each other to "turn off the l-i-g-h-t." I could be heard miles away screaming, "NO! I know what that spells!" After *The Ghost and Mr. Chicken* with Don Knotts, my bedtime ritual went something like this—look under the bed, look in the closet, turn off the light, and leap into the sack. As time passed, however, this childish nonsense began to subside. I was growing up.

But then it happened. Theater owners offered up *The Exorcist,* a temptation I could not resist. That delicious, horrible feeling of being terrified was renewed. I was hooked. I stayed pretty sane, though, until I read the book, at which time I discovered I was possessed by the Devil. I had six of the ten symptoms, including headaches, nausea, and loss of sleep. It may not have been Satan himself, but there was definitely a demon lurking somewhere.

Over the next several years, the movie industry fed my passion for terror—and my paranoia. The movie *Halloween* ended any possibility of parking on a deserted road after a date. I was not going to fog up the windows making myself a sitting duck for any escaped mental patient. The *Friday the 13th* series put a stop to any thought of camping overnight in the wilderness, while *Night of the Living Dead* put a dent in my car. I was in such a panic to get out of the dark parking lot after viewing this old classic that I slammed into a pole, causing $300 damage to my trusty Chevy.

My fright-flick fanaticism was taking a toll on my everyday life. I began to notice that guys who took me to these movies didn't often ask me out again—apparently my squirming and screaming in the theater embarrassed them a bit. Some people just don't know how to really get into a movie. I no longer took babysitting jobs because I was afraid to be alone in a strange house. I wouldn't do laundry at night because that meant I had to go down to the basement.

My fears weren't even limited to being alone. One Friday night I was home watching HBO with my Mom. Let me explain that our house is situated in the dead center of a very isolated woods. As a kid I remember thinking it would be an ideal place for escaped convicts to hide out and hold hostages. Anyway, there we were, munching away on junk food, when suddenly the lights went out. Keep in mind that this was a calm summer evening—no rain, no lightning, not even any wind. There was only one explanation—we had a madman in the basement.

In my alarm I turned to the woman who had protected me all my life. My Mom looked at me and said the only thing she could say, "Grab the potato chips." Chips and keys in tow, we bolted for the car. But this was not to be the end of our ordeal— no electricity, no electric garage door opener. I looked at my Mom and said the only thing I could say, "Ram it!" Bravely, Mom kept her head. She crept out of the security of the locked car to manually open the garage door and drive us, in our pajamas, to safety. It was then that I knew I was out of control. It was then that I decided to go cold turkey—no more horror films.

It's been two years now, and I can finally look back at these escapades and laugh. It's been two years now, and I pride myself on the fact that I live alone. The only thing that keeps me awake nights these days is writing speeches. I'm not going to end up in the nuthouse like Bette Davis. But I'm not going to get too overconfident, either. Remember all those unsuspecting kids in *Halloween?* They were just out having a good time when, WHAM—and the rest is history.

SUMMARY

Special occasions include weddings, funerals, dedications, award ceremonies, retirement dinners, and the like. Nearly always they are occasions for speechmaking. In this chapter we have considered speeches of introduction, speeches of presentation, speeches of acceptance, commemorative speeches, and after-dinner speeches.

When you make a speech of introduction, your job is to build enthusiasm for the main speaker and to establish a welcoming climate that will boost his or her credibility and confidence. Keep your remarks brief, make certain they are completely accurate, and adapt them to the audience, the occasion, and the main speaker.

Speeches of presentation are given when someone is receiving publicly a gift or an award. The main theme of such a speech is to acknowledge the achievements of the recipient. You need to tell the audience why the recipient is receiving the award.

The purpose of an acceptance speech is to give thanks for a gift or an award. When delivering such a speech, you should thank the people who are bestowing the award and recognize the contributions of people who helped you gain it. Be brief, humble, and gracious.

Commemorative speeches are essentially speeches of praise or celebration. They include Fourth of July speeches, eulogies, testimonial addresses, and the like. Your aim in such a speech is to pay tribute to a person, a group of people, an institution, or an idea. When making a commemorative speech you want to inspire your audience—to arouse and heighten their appreciation of and admiration for the subject. You will deal for the most part with intangibles, and your success will depend on how well you put into language the thoughts and feelings appropriate to the occasion.

After-dinner speeches are best thought of as a kind of speech to entertain, and they usually have a lighter touch than informative or persuasive speeches. Neither technical nor argumentative in nature, they seek to stimulate the imagination by approaching the topic in a novel or unexpected way. Although humor can be an important part of after-dinner speeches, it is not essential. If you do use humor, it should grow naturally out of the speech materials and provide insight into the topic.

REVIEW QUESTIONS

After reading this chapter, you should be able to answer the following questions:

1. What are the three purposes of a speech of introduction? What guidelines should you follow in preparing such a speech?

2. What is the main theme of a speech of presentation? Depending on the audience and occasion, what two other themes might you include in such a speech?

3. What are the three major traits of a good acceptance speech?

4. What is the fundamental purpose of a commemorative speech? Why does a successful commemorative speech depend so much on the creative and subtle use of language?

5. What is the primary difference between an after-dinner speech and a speech to inform or to persuade? What is the role of humor in after-dinner speaking?

APPLICATION EXERCISES

1. Attend a speech on campus. Pay special attention to the speech introducing the main speaker. How well does it fit the guidelines discussed in this chapter?

2. Observe several speeches of presentation and acceptance—at a campus awards ceremony or on a television program such as the Academy Awards, Grammy Awards, Emmy Awards, or Tony Awards. Which speeches do you find most effective? Least effective? Why?

3. Analyze the commemorative speech by Ryan Saurer ("James 'Cool Papa' Bell," pages 409–410). Assess the speech in light of the criteria for commemorative speaking presented in the chapter.

4. Analyze the after-dinner speech by Julie Daggett ("The Horror of It All," pages 412–413). Evaluate the speech in light of the criteria for after-dinner speaking discussed in the chapter.

NOTES

[1] William Norwood Brigance, *Speech: Its Techniques and Disciplines in a Free Society* (New York: Appleton-Century-Crofts, 1961), p. 505.

[2] James C. Humes, *Roles Speakers Play* (New York: Harper & Row, 1976), p. 8.

[3] Reprinted with permission of Gregory Peck and the Academy of Motion Picture Arts and Sciences. Copyright 1982 by the Academy of Motion Picture Arts and Sciences.

[4] Reprinted with permission of Danny Kaye and the Academy of Motion Picture Arts and Sciences. Copyright 1982 by the Academy of Motion Picture Arts and Sciences.

[5] Humes, *Roles Speakers Play* (New York: Harper & Row, 1976), pp. 33–34, 36.

[6] Ronald Reagan, Address to the Nation, January 28, 1986, in Richard L. Johannesen, R. R. Allen, and Wil A. Linkugel (eds.), *Contemporary American Speeches,* 7th ed. (Dubuque, Iowa: Kendall/Hunt, 1992), pp. 398–399.

[7] Reprinted with permission of Ryan Saurer. This speech is also available on the videotape of student speeches that accompanies this edition of *The Art of Public Speaking.*

[8] Chauncey M. Depew, *My Memories of Eighty Years* (New York: Scribner's, 1924), p. 378.

[9] Barnet Baskerville, *The People's Voice: The Orator in American Society* (Lexington: Ky.: University Press of Kentucky, 1979), p. 112.

[10] For the full text of Bush's speech, see the Appendix, pages 447–450.

[11] Reprinted with permission of Julie Daggett.

Chapter 18

Speaking in Small Groups

LEADERSHIP IN SMALL GROUPS
Kinds of Leadership
Functions of Leadership

RESPONSIBILITIES IN A SMALL GROUP
Commit Yourself to the Goals of Your Group
Fulfill Individual Assignments
Avoid Interpersonal Conflicts
Encourage Full Participation
Keep the Discussion on Track

THE REFLECTIVE-THINKING METHOD
Define the Problem
Analyze the Problem
Establish Criteria for Solutions
Generate Potential Solutions
Select the Best Solution

PRESENTING THE RECOMMENDATIONS OF THE GROUP
Oral Report
Symposium
Panel Discussion

417

The president of a small company decided to remodel the office space on her management floor. She assigned her youngest vice president, Greg Anapau, to make a plan for remodeling the offices and to carry through the plan.

Greg was very pleased with his plan. He thought he had taken everyone's needs into account, and he had arranged for most of the remodeling to be done over a long weekend so no one's work would be disrupted. On Monday morning, after the remodeling, Greg settled back in his office waiting for congratulations to pour in.

Instead, a crowd of angry people stormed into his office. "There's no telephone jack in my room," said the advertising manager, "and the telephone company says it can't put one in for three weeks. How can I do business without a telephone?"

Right behind him was the president's administrative assistant. "Do you realize," she said, "how far I have to walk to get to the president's office? It's only 15 feet from my room, but with that partition you put in, I have to walk halfway around the building!"

Next came the research manager, who said, "What am I supposed to do with my library? You didn't leave any space for my library! All the books are packed in boxes, and there's no place to put them."

Angriest of all was another vice president. "For heaven's sake," she said, "why didn't you ask me? The same things happened the *last* time the offices were moved around. I could have told you to watch out for the phone jacks and the research library."

Wearily, Greg went back to his blueprint, making plans to rearrange the offices again.

What went wrong? Greg did not have enough resources on his own to make a successful plan. If a group, instead of a single person, had been assigned to remodel the offices, the problems might have been averted. One person could have taken charge of space needs, another of traffic paths, a third of telephones and other equipment, and so forth. The final plan would have taken *all* factors into account.

Of course, you may have heard the old saying that "a camel is a horse designed by a committee." If you have ever been part of a group that seemed to get nothing done, you may be inclined to say, "Oh, let one person decide and get it over with." The problem in such cases, however, is not that there is a group, but that the group is not functioning properly. A great deal of research shows that if members of a group work well together, they can almost always resolve a problem better than a single person.[1]

This chapter deals with speaking in a particular kind of group—the problem-solving small group. As its name implies, a *small group* has a limited number of members. Most experts set the maximum at eight; others go as high as twelve or more. The important point is that the group must be small enough to allow free discussion among all members. In small-group communication, all participants are potentially speakers *and* listeners. A manageable number of people permits everyone to shift easily between speaking and listening.[2]

A problem-solving small group is formed to solve a particular problem.

Such groups exist in virtually every area of life. Business groups consider ways of increasing sales. Church groups discuss how to raise funds and provide for the needy. Groups of parents work on improving day-care facilities. The President's cabinet debates a foreign policy move. A ski club evaluates proposals for the next outing. You will almost surely be a member of many problem-solving small groups during your life.

Although speaking in a small group is not the same as public speaking, it involves many similar skills. Members of a small group influence one another through communication. At times they inform their fellow members. At other times they seek to persuade them. As a participant in a small group, you might influence your colleagues by giving them important information, by encouraging them to speak, by convincng them to change their minds, by leading them into a new channel of communication, even by getting them to end a meeting of the group. All other members of the group have the same opportunity to influence you through effective communication.[3]

LEADERSHIP IN SMALL GROUPS

We have said that small groups often make better decisions than individuals. But the word "often" should be stressed here. To make sound decisions, groups need effective leadership.

Kinds of Leadership

Sometimes there is *no specific leader*. In such a situation, members of effective groups tend to have equal influence. When a need for leadership arises, any of the members can—and one probably will—provide the necessary leadership. A typical instance might be a class project, in which you and several classmates are working together. From time to time each of you will help the group move toward its goal by suggesting when and where to meet, by outlining the strengths and weaknesses of a certain viewpoint, by resolving disagreements among other members, and so forth.[4]

In some circumstances a group may have an *implied leader*. For example, if a business meeting includes one vice president and a number of subordinates, the vice president becomes the implied leader. The same is true if one member of the group is a specialist in the topic at hand and the others are not. Members will likely defer to the person with the highest rank or greatest expertise, and that person will become the group's implied leader.

Even when a group starts out leaderless, there may be an *emergent leader*. This is a person who, by ability or by force of personality or just by talking the most, takes a leadership role.[5] The emergence of a leader may or may not be desirable. If the group is stalemated or has dissolved into bickering or making jokes, an emergent leader can put the group back on track. There is a danger, however, that the emergent leader may be not the most effective leader but merely the most assertive personality. Ideally, each member of the group should be prepared to assume a leadership role when necessary.

Finally, there may be a *designated leader*—a person elected or appointed as leader when the group is formed. A group that meets for only one session should almost always have a designated leader who takes care of the procedural tasks and serves as spokesperson for the group. Likewise, a formal committee will usually have a designated chairperson. The chair can perform leadership functions or delegate them, but he or she remains in charge of the group.[6]

A group may or may not need a specific leader, but it always needs leader*ship*. When all members of the group are skilled communicators, they can take turns at providing leadership even if the group has a designated or implied leader. As you develop your group communication skills, you should be prepared to assume a leadership role whenever necessary.

Functions of Leadership

An effective leader helps the group reach its goals by fulfilling three overlapping sets of needs—procedural needs, task needs, and maintenance needs.

Procedural Needs   Procedural needs can be thought of as the "housekeeping" requirements of the group. They include:

Deciding when and where the group will meet

Reserving the room, checking the number of chairs, making sure the heat or air conditioning is turned on

Setting the agenda of each meeting

Starting the meeting

Taking notes during the meeting

Preparing and distributing any written handouts needed for the meeting

Summarizing the group's progress at the end of the meeting

If there is a designated leader, she or he can attend to these needs or assign one or more group members to do so. Otherwise, members of the group must devise ways to split the procedural responsibilities.

Task Needs   Task needs go beyond procedural needs and are substantive actions necessary to help the group complete the particular task it is working on. They include:

Analyzing the issues facing the group

Distributing the workload among the members

Collecting information

Soliciting the views of other members

Keeping the group from going off on a tangent

Playing devil's advocate for unpopular ideas

Formulating criteria for judging the most effective solution

Helping the group reach consensus on its final recommendations

Most members will help the group satisfy its task needs. Leadership becomes necessary when some task needs are not being fulfilled adequately, as in this example:

A group of students had undertaken to solve the parking problems on their campus. The group had held several meetings, and most of its task needs had been met. Members had done a good job polling students for their opinions, discussing alternative solutions with the administration, and considering the relative merits of each solution. However, one member of the group, Alaysha, noticed that two items had not been given enough attention: No one had investigated potential sources of money for new parking facilities, and no one had studied the environmental impact of constructing additional parking spaces. Therefore, Alaysha briefly took a leadership role to perform a task need for the group. She pointed out that these two areas had been neglected and recommended that the group explore them further.

The effective leader—whether permanent or temporary—has a realistic notion of the group's task needs and of how to meet them.

Maintenance Needs   Maintenance needs involve interpersonal relations in the group. They include such factors as:

How well members get along with one another

How willing members are to contribute to the group

Whether members are supportive of one another

Whether members feel satisfied with the group's accomplishments

Whether members feel good about their roles in the group

If interpersonal problems dominate discussion, the group will have a difficult time working together and reaching a decision. This is one of the more important areas calling for effective leadership. A leader can do much to create and sustain supportive communication in the group. By helping group members handle conflict, by working out differences of opinion, by reducing interpersonal tension, by encouraging participation from all members, by being alert to personal feelings, and by promoting solidarity within the group, a leader can make a tremendous contribution toward helping the group achieve its goals.[7]

Small groups require effective leadership to accomplish their goals. In a class project, all members of the group have an opportunity to exercise leadership by fulfilling task needs, procedural needs, and maintenance needs.

■ RESPONSIBILITIES IN A SMALL GROUP

Every member of a small group must assume certain responsibilities, which can be divided into five major categories: (1) commit yourself to the goals of your group; (2) fulfill individual assignments; (3) avoid interpersonal conflicts; (4) encourage full participation; (5) keep the discussion on track. Some of these responsibilities involve leadership roles, but all five are so important that each participant should take them as personal obligations, regardless of the group's leadership. Let us look more closely at each of these responsibilities.

Commit Yourself to the Goals of Your Group

For a group to succeed, members must align their personal goals with the group's goal. This sounds obvious, but it is not always easy. When you are working with other students on a class project, the group goal—and most likely the goal of each member—is to get a good grade, which should ensure a positive attitude toward the group. There is a strong incentive for members to cooperate and commit themselves to completing the task.

Problems arise when one or more members have personal goals that conflict with the group's goal. Here is the kind of situation that can occur:

Irene Messner is a member of her church's committee to buy new equipment for the parish house kitchen. Because the budget is very tight, the committee's goal is to get the best equipment for the lowest price. But unknown to the other members of the group, Irene's son-in-law is a salesman for a distributor of high-priced kitchen appliances. Privately, Irene has reasoned that if she can sway the committee toward that company, her son-in-law will get a large commission. Irene does not mention this fact to the group. Instead, she argues that *quality*—not price—should be the determining factor in the purchase. The group process breaks down because Irene will not surrender her private goal.

This is an extreme example, but there can be more subtle kinds of private goals, as in the following case:

Jeff and Rachel are part of a group, and Jeff would like to be on closer terms with Rachel. In order to impress her, he may agree with everything she says, regardless of whether he really shares her views. Consequently, Jeff's expressed views are not his actual views. In short, Jeff has a *hidden agenda* in the group meeting. The group's agenda is to solve the problem, but Jeff's agenda is to get a date with Rachel.

Group members may have all sorts of hidden agendas. One may be experiencing personal problems—lowered grades, a breakup with a friend, trouble at home, or just a bad day. Another may have a commitment to a different group whose goals conflict with those of the present group. A third may want to take charge of the group for reasons of personal power, regardless of the group's task.

Remember that what one member of a group does affects all the other members. You should not try to advance your own interests or boost your own ego at the expense of the group and its goals. Beware of hidden agendas— whether yours or someone else's—and participate with a positive spirit. If a group is to work effectively, all members must commit themselves to the goals of the group and cooperate to achieve them.

Fulfill Individual Assignments

As mentioned earlier, one of the advantages of the group process is that it divides the workload among several people. Work assignments might involve gathering information, making arrangements for a meeting, researching a particular aspect of the group's topic, taking notes at a meeting, and so forth. Unless every member fulfills his or her assignments, the group's entire project may fail—as in the following example:

Several years ago, one student group decided that as a class project they would bring Easter baskets to the patients in the children's ward of a local hospital. After the project had been approved, assignments were given out. Marcus would coordinate with the hospital authorities, Corrine would handle fund-raising for the needed supplies. Peter would supervise the egg-decorating team. Maria would be responsible for buying baskets and chocolate bunnies. Josh would arrange for transportation to the hospital.

Everybody completed their assignments except Josh, who was busy writing a term paper. He asked a friend to pick up a bus schedule and assumed everything would be fine. On Easter morning the group assembled at the bus stop, loaded down with baskets for the children. And they waited and waited. After an hour Josh called the bus company, only to discover that the buses did not run on holidays. By the time Josh had made other arrangements to get to the hospital, visiting hours were over, and the group could not get in.

No matter what other assignments they may have, *all* members of a group have one very critical assignment—listening. If you tune out the person who is speaking, or if you concentrate entirely on what *you* plan to say next, the group is not going to make much progress.

Effective listening is vital to small-group communication. First, it helps you understand what is happening in the group. And unlike a public speaking situation, you can stop the speaker and ask for clarification on any point about which you are confused. Second, listening helps you evaluate the merits of the speaker's position in relation to your own. Third, listening provides support for the speaker and helps establish a positive climate for discussion. In group discussion, as in other kinds of situations, listening is crucial to effective communication.[8]

Avoid Interpersonal Conflicts

If groups were made up of robots, there would be no problem with interpersonal conflicts. But groups are made up of people—people with likes and dislikes and animosities and prejudices and very different personalities. It is vital to the group process that disagreements be kept on a task level, rather than on a personal level.

Suppose you disagree with another member's idea. Disagreement on the personal level could sound like this: "That's the most stupid idea I ever heard of! Do you realize how much money it would cost to do that?" But on the task level, disagreement is aimed at the *idea,* not the person: "Potentially that's a very good solution, but I'm not sure we have enough money to accomplish it."

When disagreements are allowed to become personal, some members may start to see the group as a kind of debating society. Rather than focusing on the task, they may spend their time getting even with other participants, defending themselves, trying to score points, and jumping on people's ideas. Other members—especially those who are shy or soft-spoken—may recoil from the verbal combat and withdraw from active participation in the group's deliberations.

No matter what the group, personal antagonism leaves a bad taste in everyone's mouth and harms the performance of the group. It is essential that someone take a leadership role and bring the discussion back to the relevant issues. Let's say your group is considering the practicality of adding a vegetarian section to the dormitory cafeteria. The discussion might go like this:

DENISE: It seems to me a waste of time, money, and space to make a special section for vegetarians. There are plenty of vegetables on the menu now. Anyone who doesn't want to eat the meat doesn't have to.

JALIL: You're not getting the point. Vegetarian menus have to be *balanced* with enough vegetable protein. It's not enough to say, "Don't eat the meat." We need a special section where the menus are planned for a nutritious vegetarian diet.

DENISE: Oh, for pity's sake, you food freaks are all alike. You think you've got the true faith and all the rest of us are sinners just because we eat a hamburger now and then.

JALIL: If you want to kill innocent animals to eat, that's none of my business. Go ahead, ruin your health, load yourself up with cholesterol. I don't care. But don't stand in the way of people who really care about their bodies.

LEADER: Just a minute. Before we go on with this part of the discussion, don't we have some figures on how many students would actually use the vegetarian section? Lisa, I think that was your department. What did you find out?

None of this is to say that members of a group should never disagree. In fact, a serious problem occurs when members get along so well and are so concerned about maintaining the harmony of the group that they will not disagree with one another about anything. Whenever one member makes a suggestion, everybody else thinks it's a wonderful idea. When this happens, the group misses the benefit of having a group in the first place. There is no chance to reach the best decision by exploring an array of perspectives, opinions, and information. A group that is concerned above all with dodging disagreement will not be any more effective than one that dissolves into personal quarreling.

The point, then, is not that groups should avoid conflict but that they should keep it at the task level and not allow it to degenerate into personal feuding. There is usually little achievement—and even less feeling of satisfaction—when a group is consumed by personal bickering and antagonism.

Encourage Full Participation

If a group is to work effectively, all members must contribute fully and share their ideas with one another. Every member of a group should take responsibility for encouraging other members to participate. You can do this, first of all, by listening attentively. Listening provides support for the speaker. After all, how would you like to speak in a group where everybody else appears bored or distracted?

If there are one or two quiet members in the group, you can draw them into the discussion by asking their opinions and showing your interest in their ideas and information. For instance, you can say something like, "We haven't heard from Jerald in a while, and he has some personal experience in this matter. Jerald, can you tell the others what you told me about this plan?"

Another way to encourage participation is to help build a supportive environment. When a member speaks, you can say, "That's an interesting idea." Or, "I never knew that; can you tell us more about it?" Conversely, try to avoid negative comments that will squelch a speaker before she or he has finished— comments like "Oh, no, that never works" or "What a dumb idea." Supportive comments create good will among group members and make everyone feel free to discuss their ideas without ridicule or embarrassment.

If you are shy or afraid your ideas will be taken too critically, you may be unwilling to participate at first. To overcome your diffidence, try to remember that your contribution is necessary to the group. This is why you are there. At the very least, you can help provide a supportive environment for discussion by listening, reacting, and encouraging the free exchange of ideas.

Keep the Discussion on Track

In some groups the discussion proceeds like a stream-of-consciousness exercise. Here is a hypothetical example in which a town planning board is considering installing a new traffic light at a busy intersection:

AHMED: You know, we're going to have trouble getting cars to come to a full stop even if we do put in a traffic light.

DIANA: Tell me about it! I came through there yesterday and hit my brakes, and the car just kept going. Maybe I need the brakes adjusted, though.

HANNS: Get ready to pay through the nose. I had a brake job on my car last week, and it was nearly twice as much as last time.

RICO: That's nothing. Have you looked at lawnmowers lately? And if you think lawnmowers are high . . .

JILL: Who mows lawns? I had my yard planted with ground cover and put gravel over the rest. It's . . .

LEADER: Excuse me, folks, but weren't we talking about the *traffic light?*

It is the responsibility of every member to keep the discussion on track and to intervene if the group wanders too far afield. There is nothing wrong with a little casual conversation to break the tension or provide a brief respite from work, but it shouldn't be allowed to get out of hand. When working in a problem-solving group, make sure the group's ultimate goal is always in the forefront. Do your best to see that discussion proceeds in an orderly fashion from one point to the next and that the group does not get bogged down in side issues.

On the other hand, you need to guard against the tendency to progress to a solution too quickly, without thoroughly exploring the problem. This concern can be especially serious when members of a group are tired or discouraged. If you feel your group is taking the easy way out and jumping at an easy solution, try to make the other members aware of your concern. By suggesting that they talk about the problem in more detail, you may bring out vital information or ideas. One classroom group found out the perils of making a snap decision:

> The group's first job was to decide what they should do for a class project. Near the beginning of their first meeting, someone suggested that they observe an established small group—the city council of their community—to see how the group worked. Everyone thought it was a splendid idea, and the class group wrapped up their session, congratulating themselves on having disposed of the problem so quickly.
>
> But what looked at first like a great idea proved to have some crucial drawbacks. First, it turned out that the city council would not meet again until after the group's class project was due. Second, the city council had twenty people on it—not really an appropriate number to study as a small group. Finally, city council meetings were not always open to the public. The quick solution turned out to be no solution at all.

Fortunately, there are systematic ways to keep the discussion on track and to avoid hasty group decisions. If your group follows a tested method of decision making, it will have a much better chance of reaching a satisfactory decision.[9] We turn, therefore, to the most common decision-making technique for small groups—the reflective-thinking method.[10]

◼ THE REFLECTIVE-THINKING METHOD

The reflective-thinking method is derived from the writings of the famous American philosopher John Dewey. It offers a logical, step-by-step process for discussion in problem-solving groups. The method consists of five steps: (1) defining the problem; (2) analyzing the problem; (3) establishing criteria for solving the problem; (4) generating potential solutions; (5) selecting the best solution. By following these steps your group will make its work much easier.

Let us take a closer look at the reflective-thinking method. As we do so, we shall illustrate each step by following a single group through the entire process.

Define the Problem

Before a problem-solving group can make progress, it must know exactly what problem it is trying to solve. Defining the problem may seem easy, but it is not always so. In a sense, defining the problem for group discussion is akin to settling on a specific purpose for a speech. Unless it is done properly, everything that follows will suffer.

The best way to define the problem is to phrase it as a question of policy. We discussed questions of policy in Chapter 15 (see pages 346–357). Here it is enough to note that questions of policy inquire about the necessity and/or practicality of specific courses of action. Questions of policy typically include the word "should." For example:

What measures should our school take to deal with racial tension on campus?

What steps should our city take to deal with the growing number of homeless people?

What should the policy of the United States be with respect to terrorism against American citizens?

In phrasing the question for discussion, your group should follow several guidelines.[11] First, make sure the question is as clear and specific as possible. For example:

Ineffective: What should be done about the federal budget deficit?

More Effective: What should the U.S. government do to balance the federal budget within five years?

Second, phrase the question to allow for a wide variety of answers. Be especially wary of questions that can be answered with a simple yes or no. For example:

Ineffective: Should the city build a new elementary school?

More Effective: What steps should the city take to deal with increasing enrollment in the elementary schools?

Third, avoid biased or slanted questions. For example:

Ineffective: How can we keep the campus bookstore from ripping off students?

More Effective: What changes, if any, should be made in the pricing policies of the campus bookstore?

Fourth, make sure you pose a single question. For example:

Ineffective: What revisions should the college consider in its admissions requirements and in its graduation requirements?

More Effective: What revisions should the college consider in its admissions requirements?

More Effective: What revisions should the college consider in its graduation requirements?

To clarify this first step of the reflective-thinking method, let's see how our model problem-solving group defined the problem:

As a class project, the group set out to discuss the problem of sharply rising costs for attending college. Following the reflective-thinking method, they began by defining the problem. After several false starts they phrased the problem this way: "What steps should our school take to reduce student costs for attending college?"

Analyze the Problem

After the problem has been defined, the group begins to analyze it. Too often, groups (like individuals) start mapping out solutions before they have a firm grasp of what is wrong. This is like a doctor prescribing treatment before fully diagnosing the patient's ailment. If your group investigates the problem as thoroughly as possible, you will be in a much better position to devise a workable solution.

In analyzing the problem, pay particular attention to two questions. First, how severe is the problem? Investigate the scope of the problem. Determine how many people it affects. Assess what might happen if the problem is not resolved. Second, what are the causes of the problem? Check into the history of the problem. Learn what factors contributed to it. Ascertain its major causes.

As you might imagine, analyzing the problem requires research. Effective group decisions depend on having the best information available. You can get this information in the same way you gather materials for a speech. Sometimes you can rely on your own knowledge and experience. More often, you need to get information from other sources—by writing away for it, by interviewing someone with expertise on the topic, or by working in the library (see Chapter 6). When meeting with your group, make sure you have done the research assigned to you so you can offer complete and unbiased information.

Let's return now to our sample group and see how it analyzed the problem of rapidly escalating student costs for attending college:

The group talked first about the severity of the problem. Tuition had risen dramatically, as had outlays for books and incidentals. One member offered statistics to show that the cost of attending college had doubled in the past ten years. Other members noted that the problem was affecting not only students. Merchants within the college community were being hurt because students had less money to spend on such items as clothes and entertainment. The institution itself was affected since rising costs were driving away students who might otherwise have applied.

To determine the causes of the problem, the group researched articles in the library about the rise in student costs for attending college across the nation. They also interviewed an economics professor and the head of the student aid program on campus. After studying the matter thoroughly, the group identified several major causes, including administrative costs, faculty salaries, the rising price of textbooks, and increased living expenses.

Establish Criteria for Solutions

If you planned to buy a car, how would you proceed? You would probably not just walk into a dealer's showroom and buy whatever appealed to you on the spur of the moment. You would most likely decide ahead of time what kind of car you wanted, what options it should have, and how much money you could afford to spend. That is, you would establish *criteria* to guide you in deciding exactly which car to buy.

You should do much the same thing in group discussion. Once your group has analyzed the problem, you should not jump immediately to proposing solutions. Instead, you should take time to establish criteria—standards—for responsible solutions. You should work out (and write down) exactly what your solutions must achieve and any factors that might limit your choice of solutions. If, for example, a committee is authorized to spend a maximum of $1,000 on a club's annual banquet, one of the criteria for the committee's decision will be that the banquet cost no more than $1,000.

A common failing of problem-solving groups is that they start to discuss solutions before agreeing on criteria for the solutions. When this happens, a group runs into trouble. Some people will propose solutions based on one set of criteria, while others will propose solutions based on different criteria. You can avoid such conflicts by making sure the group sets up criteria before proposing solutions.

To give a better idea of how this stage of the reflective-thinking method works, let's look at the cost-cutting group we have been following:

After some discussion, the group established these criteria for possible solutions: (1) The solution should significantly reduce students' costs. (2) The solution should come into force at the start of the next school year. (3) The solution should not hurt the prestige of the college. (4) The cost of the solution should be minimal and should be paid by the administration. (5) The human resources needed to implement the solution should come from administrative personnel already working on the school's staff. (6) The solution should involve only actions the college had authority to control—not matters controlled by outside individuals or agencies.

Generate Potential Solutions

Once your group has the criteria firmly in mind, you are ready to discuss solutions. Your goal at this stage is to come up with the widest possible range of potential solutions—not to judge the solutions. That comes later. At this stage you are only suggesting possibilities. One member of the group should be responsible for writing down all the solutions proposed at this time.

Many groups find the technique of *brainstorming* helpful in this stage. Brainstorming allows a group to generate a variety of solutions without prematurely evaluating them. In Chapter 4 we discussed how brainstorming can work for an individual in choosing a speech topic. Here brainstorming is expanded to the whole group.

The best approach is to begin by having each member of the group list all the possible solutions he or she can think of. One member of the group should then consolidate all of these individual lists into a single master list. The group as a whole should discuss the master list to make sure potential solutions have not been overlooked. At this stage members often "piggyback" new ideas onto ideas on the master list. For example, if one suggestion on the master list is "Establish food co-ops," a group member might say, "Yes, and we could establish clothing co-ops, too." One member should be responsible for writing down these new ideas and adding them to the master list. The brainstorming process continues until the group cannot think of any more solutions.

Brainstorming in this fashion has two advantages. First, it encourages creativity. There is a great deal of research to show that beginning with written lists produces more and higher-quality ideas than when a group tries to generate potential solutions by oral discussion.[12] Second, this method of brainstorming encourages equal participation. Having each member create his or her own list of potential solutions makes it less likely that one or two members will dominate the process or that anyone will hold back ideas for fear of being hooted down.

Let's see how our cost-cutting group handled this stage:

By brainstorming, the group came up with the following possible solutions: (1) reduce the number of required books for each course; (2) cut some of the "fat" from the administrative staff; (3) make all professors teach more courses; (4) approach landlords about stabilizing rent and utility costs; (5) establish food and clothing co-ops; (6) increase financial aid; (7) decrease the amount of money available for faculty research; (8) boycott businesses around the campus where price markups are highest; (9) increase out-of-state tuition; (10) decrease dormitory expenses; (11) organize fund-raising programs with the student union; (12) redirect some money from construction of new buildings to student aid. This was a good yield from a brainstorming session—twelve solid suggestions.

Select the Best Solution

After all potential solutions have been listed, it is time to evaluate them and choose the best solution or solutions. The best way to proceed is to take a particular solution, discuss it with regard to the criteria established earlier in the group's deliberations, then move on to the next solution, and so on. This orderly process ensures that all potential solutions receive equal consideration.

As each potential solution is discussed, the group should make every effort to reach *consensus*. A consensus decision is one that all members accept,

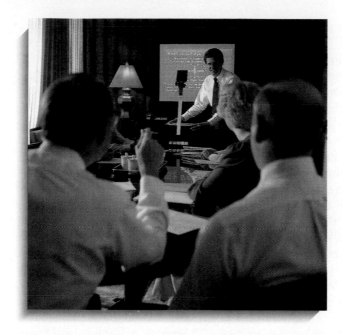

Speaking in a small group requires many of the same skills involved in public speaking. Group members may even make formal presentations as part of the group's deliberations or when presenting the group's report.

even though the decision may not be ideal in the eyes of every member. In other words, consensus may range from full approval of a decision to "Well, I can live with it." Because it usually results in superior decisions as well as in a high degree of unity within the group, consensus is the ideal of group decision making. It comes about when members have been so cooperative that they reach a common decision through reasoning, honest exchange of ideas, and the full examination of issues.[13]

Like most ideals, consensus can be difficult to achieve. If there are different viewpoints, members of the group will often try to find the easiest way to resolve the differences. Sometimes a member will call for a vote, which is very agreeable to those holding a majority opinion (since they will win) but not so pleasant for those in the minority. Resorting to a vote does resolve the immediate conflict, but it may not result in the best solution. Moreover, it weakens unity in the group by fostering factions and perhaps by creating bitterness among the members who lose on the vote. A group should vote only when it has failed in every other attempt to find a solution agreeable to all members.

What kind of final decision did our model cost-cutting group reach? Let's see:

The cost-cutting group had twelve possible solutions to evaluate. Three were rejected because they violated the group's criterion that an acceptable solution must involve only actions controlled directly by the college. Redirecting building money to student aid could be done only by the state legislature. Approaching landlords about stabilizing rent and boycotting campus businesses were also outside the jurisdiction of college administrators.

Three more solutions were rejected because they were economically impractical. Increasing financial aid would hurt many students because the funds would have to come from student fees. Raising out-of-state tuition would drive away 10 percent of the college's out-of-state students. And decreasing dorm costs would make it impossible to provide minimally acceptable services.

The proposal to reduce funds for faculty research was also rejected since most research money comes from government, corporations, and foundations. Besides, research was recognized as a primary means of maintaining the college's prestige. Finally, the suggestion to reduce administrative "fat" was rejected as too costly because a group would have to be established to audit all administrative duties.

After refining the remaining suggestions, the group finally reached consensus on a solution that included the following provisions: (1) A student should not have to spend more than $80 on required books for any single course. (2) The university should authorize the student union to organize food, book, and clothing co-ops. (3) The student union should conduct five fund-raising projects each academic year. (4) Each professor should teach one more class a year.

Once consensus has been reached on a solution or solutions to the problem, the group is ready to present its findings.

■ PRESENTING THE RECOMMENDATIONS OF THE GROUP

The work of a problem-solving group does not end with the last stage of the reflective-thinking process. Once a group has agreed on its recommendations, it usually needs to present them to somebody. A business group might report to the president of the company or to the board of directors. A special committee of the city council will report to the full council. A presidential commission will report to the President and to the nation at large. A classroom group reports to the instructor and to the rest of the class. The purpose of such reports is to present the group's recommendations clearly and convincingly.

Sometimes a group will prepare a formal written report. Often, however, the written report is supplemented with—or replaced by—an oral report, a symposium, or a panel discussion.

Oral Report

An oral report is much the same in content as a written report. If the group has a designated leader, she or he will probably deliver the report. Otherwise, the group will have to select one person for the job.

If you are picked to present your group's report, you should approach it as you would any other speech. Your task is to explain the purpose, procedures, and recommendations of your group. As with any speech, your report should have three main sections. The introduction will state the purpose of the report and preview its main points. The body will spell out the problem addressed by your group, the criteria set for a solution, and the solution being recommended. The conclusion will summarize the main points and, in some cases, urge that the group's recommendation be adopted.

Also, as with any speech, you should adapt your report to the audience. Use supporting materials to clarify and strengthen your ideas, and consider whether using visual aids will enhance your message. Make sure your language is accurate, clear, vivid, and appropriate. Rehearse the report so you can deliver it fluently and decisively. Afterward, you—and possibly other members of the group—may be called on to answer questions from the audience.

Symposium

A symposium consists of a moderator and several speakers seated together in front of an audience. If the group presenting the symposium has a designated leader, he or she will typically be the moderator. The moderator's job is to introduce the topic and the speakers. Each speaker in turn delivers a prepared speech on a different aspect of the topic. After the speeches, there may be a question-and-answer session with the audience.

The symposium is often used for group reports in speech classes. One way to organize it is to have each member of the group present a brief talk sketching the group's work and decisions during one stage of the reflective-thinking process. Another way is to have each speaker deal with a major issue relating to the discussion topic. A group dealing with capital punishment, for example, might have one speaker present the group's conclusion on the issue of whether capital punishment is an effective deterrent to crime, another speaker present the group's position on the morality of capital punishment, and so forth.

No matter what kind of symposium your group presents, all the speeches should be carefully planned. They should also be coordinated with one another to make sure the symposium reports on all important aspects of the group's project.

Panel Discussion

A panel discussion is essentially a conversation in front of an audience.[14] The panel should have a moderator, who introduces the topic and the panelists. Once the discussion is under way, the moderator may interject questions and comments as needed to focus the discussion. The panelists speak briefly, informally, and impromptu. They talk to each other, but loudly enough for the audience to be able to hear. As with a symposium, a panel discussion may be followed by a question-and-answer session with the audience.

Because of its spontaneity, a panel discussion can be exciting for participants and audience alike. But, unfortunately, that spontaneity inhibits systematic presentation of a group's recommendations. Thus the panel discussion is seldom used by problem-solving groups, although it can work well for information-gathering groups.

If you are a participant in a panel discussion, beware of the common fallacy that no serious preparation is required. Although you will speak impromptu, you need to study the topic ahead of time, analyze the major issues, and map out the points you want to be sure to make during the discussion. An effective panel discussion also requires planning by the moderator and panelists to decide what issues will be discussed and in what order. Finally, all panelists must be willing to share talking time. One purpose of a panel is to have all participants voice their ideas, not to have one or two members monopolize the discussion.

Whatever method your group uses to present its findings, you can benefit from the public-speaking guidelines given throughout this book. The techniques of effective speech need refinement for different situations, but the principles remain the same whether you are one person addressing an audience, part of a small group of people working to solve a problem, or a participant in a symposium or a panel discussion.

SUMMARY

A problem-solving small group consists of three to twelve persons assembled to solve a particular problem. When such a group has effective leadership, it usually makes better decisions than do individuals by themselves. Most groups have a designated leader, an implied leader, or an emergent leader. Some groups do not have any specific leader, in which case all members of the group must assume leadership responsibilities. An effective leader helps a group reach its goals by fulfilling procedural needs, task needs, and maintenance needs. As you develop your skills in group communication, you should be prepared to assume a leadership role whenever necessary.

Apart from leadership, all members of a group have five basic responsibilities. You should commit yourself to the goals of your group, fulfill your individual assignments, avoid interpersonal conflict within the group, encourage full participation by all members, and help keep the group on track. Meeting these responsibilities is vital if your group is to be successful.

Your group will also be more successful if it follows the reflective-thinking method, which offers a logical, step-by-step process for decision making in problem-solving groups. The method consists of five steps: (1) defining the problem as clearly and specifically as possible; (2) analyzing the problem to determine its severity and causes; (3) establishing criteria to guide the group in evaluating solutions; (4) generating a wide range of potential solutions; (5) selecting the best solution or solutions.

Once your group has agreed on its recommendations, it usually has to present them to somebody. Sometimes this will require a written report. Often, however, it will involve some kind of oral presentation—a report by one member of the group, a symposium, or a panel discussion. Whichever kind of oral presentation your group gives will call for the skills of effective speechmaking explained throughout this book.

REVIEW QUESTIONS

After reading this chapter, you should be able to answer the following questions:

1. What is a problem-solving small group?

2. What are the four kinds of leadership that may occur in a small group? Explain the three kinds of needs fulfilled by leadership in a small group.

3. What are the five major responsibilities of every participant in a small group?

4. What are the stages of the reflective-thinking method? Explain the major tasks of a group at each stage.

5. What are the three methods for presenting orally the recommendations of a problem-solving group?

APPLICATION EXERCISES

1. Identify the flaw (or flaws) in each of the following questions for a problem-solving group discussion. Rewrite each question so it conforms with the criteria discussed in the chapter for effective discussion questions.

    a. Should all students be required to take two years of a foreign language to graduate from college?
    b. What should be done to prevent the outrageously cruel and inhumane treatment of animals in laboratory experiments?
    c. What should be done about child abuse?
    d. What should our state government do to control the cost of welfare and to combat unemployment?
    e. Should the federal government institute a system of standardized national tests for all schoolchildren?

2. If possible, arrange to observe a problem-solving small group in action. You might attend a meeting of your city council, the school board, the zoning commission, a local business, a church committee. To what extent does the discussion measure up to the criteria of effective discussion presented in this chapter? What kind of leadership does the group have, and how well does the leader (or leaders) fulfill the group's procedural needs, task needs,

and maintenance needs? How do the other members meet their responsibilities? What aspects of the meeting are handled most effectively? Which are handled least effectively?

3. Identify a relatively important decision you have made in the last year or two. Try to reconstruct how you reached that decision. Now suppose you could remake the decision following the reflective-thinking method. Map out exactly what you would do at each stage of the method. Do you still reach the same decision? If not, do you believe the reflective-thinking method would have led you to a better decision in the first place?

4. Attend a symposium or panel discussion on campus. Prepare a brief analysis of the proceedings. First, study the role of the moderator. How does she or he introduce the topic and participants? What role does the moderator play thereafter? Does she or he help guide and focus the panel discussion? Does she or he summarize and conclude the proceedings at the end?

   Second, observe the participants. Are the speeches in the symposium well prepared and presented? Which speaker (or speakers) do you find most effective? Least effective? Why? Do participants in the panel discussion share talking time? Does their discussion appear well planned to cover major aspects of the topic? Which panelist (or panelists) do you find most effective? Least effective? Why?

NOTES

[1] For a recent review of research on the value of groups, see Charles Pavitt and Ellen Curtis, *Small Group Discussion: A Theoretical Approach,* 2nd ed. (Scottsdale, Ariz.: Gorsuch Scarisbrick, 1994), pp. 25–62.

[2] John K. Brilhart and Gloria J. Galanes, *Effective Group Discussion,* 7th ed. (Dubuque, Iowa: Brown, 1992), pp. 11–13.

[3] The importance of communication to effective group discussion is stressed by Dennis Gouran, Randy Y. Hirokawa, Kelly M. Julian, and Geoff B. Leatham, "The Evolution and Current Status of the Functional Perspective in Decision-Making and Problem-Solving Groups," in Stanley A. Deetz (ed.), *Communication Yearbook 16* (Newbury Park, Calif.: Sage, 1993), pp. 573–600. For a review of research on communication in small groups, see John F. Cragan and David W. Wright, "Small Group Communication Research of the 1980s: A Synthesis and Critique," *Communication Studies,* 41 (1990), 212–236.

[4] See J. Kevin Barge, "Leadership as Medium: A Leaderless Group Discussion Model," *Communication Quarterly,* 37 (1989), 237–247.

[5] Donald G. Ellis and B. Aubrey Fisher, *Small Group Decision Making: Communication and the Group Process,* 4th ed. (New York: McGraw-Hill, 1994), pp. 202–207. For an interesting study of the communication processes through which group leaders emerge, see Deborah C. Baker, "A Qualitative and Quantitative Analysis of Verbal Style and the Elimination of Potential Leaders in Small Groups," *Communication Quarterly,* 38 (1990), 13–26.

[6] Brilhart and Galanes, *Effective Group Discussion,* pp. 210–218, provide a helpful summary of the responsibilities of designated group leaders.

[7] On the interaction of internal harmony and other factors in effective group discussion, see Wendy M. Williams and Robert J. Sternberg, "Group Intelligence: Why Some Groups Are Better Than Others," *Intelligence,* 12 (1988), 351–377.

[8] See Larry L. Barker, Kathy J. Wahlers, Kittie W. Watson, and Robert J. Kibler, *Groups in Process: An Introduction to Small Group Communication,* 4th ed. (Englewood Cliffs, N.J.: 1991), pp. 74–98.

[9] Michael J. Beatty, "Group Members' Decision Rule Orientations and Consensus," *Human Communication Research* (1989), 279–296.

[10] For other decision-making techniques, see Pavitt and Curtis, *Small Group Discussion,* pp. 429–467.

[11] Julia T. Wood, Gerald M. Phillips, and Douglas J. Pedersen, *Group Discussion: A Practical Guide to Participation and Leadership* (New York: Harper & Row, 1986), pp. 136–141.

[12] See, for example, Michael Diehl and Wolfgang Stroebe, "Productivity Loss in Brainstorming Groups: Toward the Solution of a Riddle," *Journal of Personality and Social Psychology,* 53 (1987), 497–509.

[13] Ellis and Fisher, *Small Group Decision Making,* pp. 141–142; John F. Cragan and David W. Wright, *Communication in Small Group Discussions: An Integrated Approach,* 3rd ed. (St. Paul, Minn.: West, 1991), pp. 20–21.

[14] Loren Reid, *Speaking Well,* 4th ed. (New York: McGraw-Hill, 1982), p. 360.

Appendix: Speeches for Analysis and Discussion

A REEL DOCTOR'S ADVICE
TO SOME REAL DOCTORS

Alan Alda

An actor giving a commencement speech at a medical school? Many people must have asked themselves this question when it was announced that Alan Alda would address the 210th graduating class of New York's Columbia College of Physicians and Surgeons in May 1979.

Of course, Alda is not just any actor. He is known to millions as Army surgeon Captain Hawkeye Pierce in the classic television series "M*A*S*H." He has won Emmy awards as an actor, writer, and director. Public-opinion polls have shown him to be among America's most respected public figures. *Time* magazine once called him "perhaps America's favorite doctor."

Still, the idea of an actor offering advice to doctors is so unusual that Alda begins his speech by asking, "Why get someone who only *pretends* to be a doctor when you could get a real one?" Note how skillfully Alda answers this question, builds his credibility, and establishes common ground with his audience *before* offering them advice. Also note how Alda uses humor both to lighten his speech and to reinforce its message. Finally, to get a fuller sense of the speech's impact, try to "hear" Alda delivering it.

Alda's speech was greeted enthusiastically by his listeners and received much favorable comment in the press. It is reprinted here with permission from the Columbia College of Physicians and Surgeons.

1 Ever since it was announced that a nondoctor, in fact an actor, had been invited to give the commencement address at one of the most prestigious medical schools in the country, people have been wondering—why get someone who only *pretends* to be a doctor when you could get a real one?

2 Some people have suggested that this school had done everything it could to show you how to *be* doctors and in a moment of desperation had brought in someone who could show you how to act like one.

3 It's certainly true that I'm not a doctor. I have a long list of nonqualifications. In the first place I'm not a great fan of blood. I don't mind people having it, I just don't enjoy seeing them wear it. I have yet to see a real operation because the mere smell of a hospital reminds me of a previous appointment. And my knowledge of anatomy resides in the clear understanding that the hip bone is connected to the leg bone.

4 I am not a doctor. But you have asked me, and all in all, I think you made a wonderful choice.

5 I say that because I probably first came to the attention of this graduating class through a character on television that I've played and helped write for the past seven years—a surgeon called Hawkeye Pierce. He's a remarkable person, this Hawkeye, and if you have chosen somehow to associate his character with your own graduation from medical school, then I find that very heartening. Because I think it means that you are reaching out toward a very human kind of doctoring—and a very real kind of doctor.

6 We didn't make him up. He really lived as several doctors who struggled to preserve life 25 years ago during the Korean War. In fact, it's because he's based on real doctors that there is something especially engaging about him.

7 He has a sense of humor, and yet he's serious. He's impertinent, and yet he has feeling. He's human enough to make mistakes, and yet he hates death enough to push himself past his own limits to save lives. In many ways he's the doctor patients want to have and doctors want to be.

8 But he's not an idealization. Finding himself in a war, he's sometimes angry, sometimes cynical, sometimes a little nuts. He's not a magician who can come up with an instant cure for a rare disease without sweating and ruining his make-up. He knows he might fail. Not a god, he walks gingerly on the edge of disaster—alive to his own mortality.

9 If this image of that very human, very caring doctor is attractive to you—if it's ever touched you for a moment as something to reach for in your own life—then I'm here to cheer you on. Do it. Go for it. Be skilled, be learned, be aware of the dignity of your calling—but please, don't ever lose sight of your own simple humanity.

10 Unfortunately, that may not be so easy. You're entering a special place in our society. People will be awed by your expertise. You'll be placed in a position of privilege. You'll live well. People will defer to you, call you by your title—and it may be hard to remember that the word "doctor" is not actually your first name.

11 I know what this is like to some extent because in some ways you and I *are* alike. We both study the human being. And we both try to offer relief— you through medicine, I through laughter; we both try to reduce suffering. We've both learned difficult disciplines that have taken years to master, and we've both dedicated ourselves to years of hard work. And we both charge a lot.

12 We live in a society that has decided to reward my profession and yours, when we succeed in them, very highly. It can sometimes be easy to forget that the cab driver also works 14 or 15 hours a day and is also drained of energy when he's through. It's easy to think that because our society grants us privilege we're entitled to it.

13 Privilege feels good, but it can be intoxicating. As good doctors, I hope you'll be able to keep yourselves free of toxins.

14 It's no wonder, though, that people will hold you in awe. I know I do.

15 You've spent years in a grueling effort to know the structure and process of human life. I can't imagine a more difficult task. It has required the understanding of complexities within complexities, and there has been more pressure placed on you in four years than most people would be willing to take in a lifetime. I stand here in utter amazement at what you've accomplished. And I congratulate you.

16 I only ask one thing of you: Possess your skills, but don't be possessed by them.

17 Certainly your training has encouraged you to see the human side of your work, and you've examined the doctor-patient relationship. But still, the

enormity of your task has required you to focus to such an extent on technique and data that you may not have had time enough to face your feelings along the way.

18 You've had to toughen yourself to death. From your first autopsy, when you may have been sick, or cried, or just been numb, you've had to inure yourself to death in order to be useful to the living. But I hope in the process you haven't done too good a job of burying that part of you that hurts and is afraid.

19 I know what it's like to be absorbed in technique. When I write for *M*A*S*H* I'm always writing about people in crisis with what I hope is compassion and feeling. And yet one day I found myself talking to someone who was in a real crisis and real pain—and I remember thinking, "This would make a *great* story."

20 Both of these things—becoming set apart and becoming your skill—can make it tough to be a compassionate person.

21 All right, that's my diagnosis of the problem. Here's my prescription.

22 I'd like to suggest to you, just in case you haven't done it lately, that this would be a very good time to give some thought to exactly what your values are, and then to figure out how you're going to live by them. Knowing what you care about and then devoting yourself to it is just about the only way you can pick your way through the minefield of existence and come out in one piece.

23 It can be a startling experience when you try to rank your values, though. Just ask yourself what's the most important thing in the world to you. Your work? Your family? Your money? Your country? Getting to heaven? Sex? Alcohol? What? (I don't need a show of hands on this!)

24 Then, when you get the answer to that, ask yourself how much time you actually spend on your number-one value—and how much time you spend on what you thought was number five, or number ten. What in fact is the thing you value most?

25 It may not be easy to decide. We live in a time that seems to be split about its values. In fact it seems to be schizophrenic.

26 For instance, if you pick up a magazine like *Psychology Today,* you're liable to see an article like "White Collar Crime: It's More Widespread Than You Think." Then in the back of the magazine they'll print an advertisement that says, "We'll write your doctoral thesis for 25 bucks." You see how values are eroding? I mean a doctoral thesis ought to go for at least a C-note.

27 The question is, *where* are their values? *What* do they value? Unfortunately, the people we look to for leadership seem to be providing it by negative example.

28 All across the country this month commencement speakers are saying to graduating classes, "We look to you for tomorrow's leaders." That's because today's leaders are all in jail.

29 Maybe we can afford to let politicians operate in a moral vacuum, but we can't afford to let doctors operate under those conditions.

30 You know how we're feeling these days, as the power and fuel monopoly has its way with us. Well, you people graduating today are entering a

very select group. You have a monopoly on medical care. Please be careful not to abuse this power that you have over the rest of us.

31 You need to know what you care about most and what you care about least. And you need to know now. You will be making life-and-death decisions, and you will often be making them under stress and with great speed. The time to make your tender choices is not in the heat of the moment.

32 When you're making your list, let me urge you to put people first. And I include in that not just people, but that which exists *between* people.

33 I suggest to you that what makes people know they're alive—and in some cases keeps them alive—is not merely the interaction of the parts of their bodies, but the interaction of their selves with other selves. Not just people, but what goes on between people.

34 Let me challenge you. With all your study, you can name all the bones in my body. You can read my x-rays like a telegram. But can you read my involuntary muscles? Can you see the fear and uncertainty in my face?

35 If I tell you where it hurts, can you hear in my voice where I ache? I show you my body, but I bring you my person. Can you see me through your reading glasses?

36 Will you tell what you're doing, and in words I can understand? Will you tell me when you don't know what to do? Can you face your own fear, your own uncertainty? When in doubt, can you call in help?

37 These are things to consider even if you don't deal directly with patients. If you're in research, administration, if you write—no matter what you do—eventually there is always going to be a patient at the other end of your decisions.

38 Now, of course, everyone is for this in principle. Who's against people? But it gets harder when you get specific.

39 Will you be the kind of doctor who cares more about the *case* than the *person*? ("Nurse, call the gastric ulcer and have him come in at three." "How's the fractured femur in Room 208?") You'll know you're in trouble if you find yourself wishing they would mail you their liver in a plain brown envelope.

40 Where does money come on your list? Will it be the sole standard against which you reckon your success? How much will it guide you in relating to your patients? Do patients in a clinic need less of your attention than private patients? Are they, for instance, less in need of having things explained to them?

41 Where will your family come on your list? How many days and nights, weeks and months, will you separate yourself from them, buried in your work, before you realize that you've removed yourself from an important part of your life?

42 And if you're a male doctor, how will you relate to women? Women as patients, as nurses, as fellow doctors—and later as students. Will you be able to respect your patient's right to know and make decisions about her own body? Will you see nurses as colleagues—or as handmaidens? And if the day comes when you are teaching, what can young women medical students expect from you?

43 Questionnaires filled out by women at 41 medical schools around the country have revealed a distressing pattern. The women were often either ignored in class or simply not taken seriously as students. They were told that they were only there to find a husband and that they were taking the places of men who would then have to go out and become chiropractors. (Logic is not the strong point of sexism.)

44 They were often told that women just didn't belong in medicine. And at times they were told this by the very professors who were grading them. They would be shown slides of *Playboy* nudes during anatomy lectures—to the accompaniment of catcalls and wisecracks from male students. And in place of discussions about their work, they would often hear a discussion of their appearance. These are reports from 41 different medical schools.

45 I'm dwelling on this because it seems to me that the male-female relationship is still the most personal and intense test of humane behavior. It is a crucible for decency.

46 I hope you men will work to grant the same dignity to your female colleagues that you yourselves enjoy.

47 And if you're a female doctor, I hope you'll be aware that you didn't get where you are all by yourself. You've had to work hard, of course. But you're sitting where you are right now in part because way back in 1848, in Seneca Falls, women you never knew began insisting you had a right to sit there. Just as they helped a generation they would never see, I urge you to work for the day when your daughters and their daughters will be called not "A woman doctor," or "My doctor, who's a woman," but simply "My doctor."

48 It may seem strange to rank the things you care about. But when you think about it, there isn't an area of your work that won't be affected by what you decide to place a high value on and what you decide doesn't count.

49 Decide now.

50 Well, that's my prescription. I've given you kind of a big pill to swallow, but I think it'll make you feel better. And if not—well, look, I'm only human.

51 I congratulate you, and please let me thank you for taking on the enormous responsibility that you have—and for having the strength to have made it to this day. I don't know how you've managed to learn it all.

52 But there is one more thing you can learn about the body that only a nondoctor would tell you—and I hope you'll always remember this: The head bone is connected to the heart bone—and don't let them come apart.

THE HIDDEN WORLD OF PERFUMES
Kyle Knoeck

"Ointment and perfume rejoice the heart." Part of an ancient biblical proverb, these words are as fitting today as when they were written centuries ago. The international perfume market generates sales of $10 billion a year. Perfumes can be found in thousands of products from soap and cologne to insecticides and cattle feed. Some businesses have even dispensed perfume through air conditioning ducts to boost the productivity of workers.

In the following informative speech, Kyle Knoeck, a student at the University of Wisconsin, explores these and other facts about the production and uses of perfume. As you read the speech, study how clearly Kyle organizes his ideas and how he employs a wide range of supporting materials to provide an entertaining, as well as instructive, look at his subject.

This speech is printed with permission from Kyle Knoeck. It is also available on the videotape of student speeches that accompanies this edition of *The Art of Public Speaking.*

1 Few would dispute the importance of petroleum to the world economy. In fact, some argue that in 1991 the United States and its allies fought a war in the Persian Gulf over this liquid that, at current prices, costs less than half a cent per fluid ounce and doesn't even smell all that good.

2 Imagine the lengths one might go to protect access to a liquid that, in some cases, costs over $100 per ounce—20,000 times the cost of crude petroleum. Wars may be fought again—advertising wars—this time to claim a portion of the international perfume market, which, according to *Smithsonian* magazine, has sales of $10 billion each year.

3 Ever since the ancient Mesopotamians first used perfume in burial rites over 4,000 years ago, humankind has developed an obsession with scent and is willing to pay amazingly high prices for something as intangible as a smell.

4 Puzzled by my own inexplicable fondness for aftershave, I've spent some time researching our culture's partiality to perfume. Even if you're someone who doesn't especially like to dabble Chanel or Polo behind your ears, you probably smell someone else's fragrance every day. Or maybe you use a product made with perfumes—such as soap, facial tissue, insecticides, or even cattle feed.

5 With that in mind, we'll first discuss the ingredients of perfume and then we'll examine some of the new commercial applications of perfume. Let's start with the ingredients.

6 Quite likely, you think of perfume only as a smelly liquid. But many connoisseurs of the stuff would disagree. In fact, perfume is a complex mixture of many ingredients.

7 The most important ingredients of any perfume are a variety of aromatic oils, usually called essential oils. According to Edwin Morris in his book *Fragrance,* essential oils have two important properties—they easily evaporate and become gas at room temperature, and they are detectable to us as fragrance in unimaginably minute quantities. The essential oil of the vanilla bean, for example, can be detected as a fragrance when present in the air at amounts of just two parts per million.

8 Some essential oils are found in animal products. According to Diane Ackerman in her book *A Natural History of the Senses,* the best known of these may be musk, a red, jelly-like secretion found in the gut of an East Asian deer.

9 As *Smithsonian* magazine reports, however, most essential oils are extracted from one of 2,000 different species of flowering plants. These plants may be as exotic as the fragrant ylang-ylang tree that grows on the Comoro Islands, or as common as the rose.

10 But even oils from common plants may be difficult to come by. The finest rose oil in the world can only be found in roses grown near the town of Kazanlâk in Bulgaria. It takes nearly 800 pounds of jasmine flowers to produce just one pound of the oil found in its petals. And oils can be expensive. Iris absolute, an essential oil tortuously extracted from the root of the iris, costs nearly $437 per ounce.

11 Not all perfume ingredients come from natural sources. Synthetic ingredients can imitate or enhance the smells of natural essential oils and can greatly reduce the cost of a perfume. In the case of the perfume classic Chanel No. 5, an artificial aldehyde provides the perfume with its signature scent. But Chanel may be the exception that proves the rule. Synthetic ingredients rarely compare in quality to natural ingredients. As French perfumer Françoise Marin explains, "It's like silk against polyester. You cannot replace the touch of nature."

12 When creating a new fragrance, a perfumer will usually draw upon the scents of between 30 and 50, and sometimes up to 500, different oils, hoping to find the perfect blend of smells. Of course, the perfume or cologne you buy in the store isn't just a bottle of essential oils. When marketed, the oils are dissolved in alcohol. A high-quality perfume will contain up to 25 percent essential oils and 75 percent alcohol; an inexpensive *eau de toilette,* just 2 to 4 percent essential oils. If the perfume is to be used in a product other than a cosmetic fragrance, the oils may be dissolved in something other than alcohol, but these fragrant oils remain the key ingredient in any manufactured scent.

13 Having explored the ingredients that go into creating these pricey odors called perfume, it's important to remember that perfumes are found in more places than wrists and ears. Researchers are learning how perfumes can affect human behavior, and we will now examine the new commercial applications of perfume that this research is bringing.

14 Doctors William Dember and Joel Warm at the University of Cincinnati have found that people who receive regular puffs of perfume can perform much better at tasks that require sustained attention. The scents of peppermint and muguet can spark alertness, and *New Scientist* magazine reports that applications of this research could find the best use in jobs like air-traffic control, quality-control inspections, and long-distance truck-driving, where a lapse of concentration could prove fatal.

15 Don't let it be said that any enterprising businessperson would let this opportunity slide by. The *Los Angeles Times* reveals that some companies in Japan are already delivering small doses of perfume via the air-conditioning ducts to improve worker productivity. Tokyo's Kajima Corporation uses a lemon scent in the morning to wake workers up, rose to calm them during lunch, and tree-trunk oil to perk them up in the afternoon.

16 Businesses may also one day use perfume to complement Muzak. As last January's issue of *American Demographics* reports, one shopping mall in Minneapolis has experimented with the idea of using perfume in the air to increase sales, and an experiment at a Philadelphia jewelry counter found that a floral scent in the air seemed to make prospective customers linger longer.

17 The new commercial applications of perfume do raise some thorny issues, however. *American Demographics* points out that workers and customers may not like the idea of being subconsciously influenced by smell. Other issues arise because, in some people, perfumes can trigger allergic reactions. According to the National Center for Environmental Health Strategies, the Food and Drug Administration has acknowledged that perfumes can cause reactions, including headaches, sore throats, confusion, and dizziness.

18 The issue is starting to come to public attention. *The Wall Street Journal* reports a movement afoot in Los Angeles to ban perfume from certain public places. Perfume wearers are learning that they have to consider those around them who might suffer from reactions to their fragrance. This issue is sure to be one with which businesses will have to contend as well if they decide to use perfume in their air systems.

19 As we have seen, perfume is much more than a smelly liquid. These complex mixtures of aromatic oils may make us work harder and spend harder, if they don't trigger an allergic reaction first. Today we have explored perfume's pungent ingredients and some new uses for these fragrant creations.

20 It seems almost absurd to think that perfume is thousands of times more expensive than a precious energy resource like petroleum. But on the other hand, no matter how far you can drive your car on petroleum, oil is not the kind of fragrance you would want in your cologne, hair spray, room deodorizer, or even, I suppose, in your cattle feed.

CHOICES AND CHANGE

Barbara Bush

Barbara Bush's commencement address at Wellesley College on June 1, 1990, appears destined to become one of the best known speeches of recent years. Bush was invited to speak by the senior class when their first choice, Alice Walker, author of *The Color Purple*, could not attend. In protest, 150 Wellesley seniors—about one-fourth of the graduating class—signed a petition charging that Bush was not a good role model for career-oriented students at a women's college and had been chosen because of the man she married rather than for her own achievements.

The petition touched off a storm of controversy. Throughout the month before Bush's speech, educators, newspaper columnists, and others debated the petition and the larger issue of women's role in American society. The media spotlight became even more intense when Bush invited Raisa Gorbachev, whose husband would be in the United States for summit meetings on the day of the Wellesley commencement, to join her at Wellesley and also to speak to the graduates.

In her speech, Bush dealt with one of the most important issues facing modern women—how to balance their careers with their commitments to friends and family. She urged her audience to respect difference, to get involved in social issues, and to cherish human relationships as "the most important investments you will ever make." She capped off the speech by suggesting that someone in the audience might follow in her footsteps as the President's spouse. "I wish *him* well," she added, to thunderous cheering and applause.

Bush's blend of humility and humor won many accolades. NBC News anchor Tom Brokaw called her address "one of the best commencement speeches I've ever heard," while the *New York Times* judged it "a triumph." Many Wellesley students who had been skeptical about Bush's appearance also said they were pleasantly surprised by the speech. "She was wonderful and funny," one of them stated. "I think she could have addressed more women's issues. But she was sincere and she touched our hearts."

The text of this speech was taken from a videotape supplied by Wellesley College, and it includes several impromptu comments and other changes from the version published in the press. The speech is also included in the videotape supplement to *The Art of Public Speaking.*

1 Thank you very, very much President Keohane, Mrs. Gorbachev, trustees, faculty, parents, and, I should say, Julia Porter, class president, and certainly my new best friend, Christine Bicknell—and of course the Class of 1990. I am really thrilled to be here today and very excited, as I know all of you must be, that Mrs. Gorbachev could join us. These are exciting times— they're exciting in Washington, and I had really looked forward to coming to Wellesley. I thought it was going to be fun; I never dreamt it would be this much fun. So thank you for that.

2 More than ten years ago when I was invited here to talk about our experiences in the People's Republic of China, I was struck by both the natural beauty of your campus and the spirit of this place.

3 Wellesley, you see, is not just a place, but an idea, an experiment in excellence in which diversity is not just tolerated, but is embraced.

4 The essence of this spirit was captured in a moving speech about tolerance given last year by a student body president of one of your sister colleges. She related the story by Robert Fulghum about a young pastor who, finding himself in charge of some very energetic children, hits upon the game called "Giants, Wizards and Dwarfs." "You have to decide now," the pastor instructed the children, "which you are—a giant, a wizard or a dwarf." At that, a small girl tugging at his pants leg asks, "But where do the mermaids stand?"

5 And the pastor tells her there are *no* mermaids. And she says, "Oh yes there are—I am a mermaid."

6 This little girl knew what she was and she was not about to give up on either her identity or the game. She intended to take her place wherever mermaids fit into the scheme of things. Where *do* the mermaids stand—all those

who are different, those who do not fit the boxes and the pigeonholes? "Answer that question," wrote Fulghum, "and you can build a school, a nation, or a whole world."

7 As that very wise young woman said, "Diversity, like anything worth having, requires effort." Effort to learn about and respect difference, to be compassionate with one another, to cherish our own identity, and to accept unconditionally the same in others. You should all be very proud that this is the Wellesley spirit.

8 Now I know your first choice today was Alice Walker—guess how I know!—known for *The Color Purple.* Instead you got me—known for the color of my hair! Alice Walker's book has a special resonance here. At Wellesley, each class is known by a special color. For four years the class of '90 has worn the color purple. Today you meet on Severance Green to say goodbye to all of that, to begin a new and a very personal journey to search for your own true colors.

9 In the world that awaits you beyond the shores of Lake Waban, no one can say what your true colors will be. But this I do know: You have a first-class education from a first-class school. And so you need not, probably cannot, live a "paint-by-numbers" life. Decisions are not irrevocable. Choices do come back. And as you set off from Wellesley, I hope that many of you will consider making three very special choices.

10 The first is to believe in something larger than yourself, to get involved in some of the big ideas of our time. I chose literacy because I honestly believe that if more people could read, write and comprehend, we would be that much closer to solving so many of the problems that plague our nation and our society.

11 Early on I made another choice which I hope you'll make as well. Whether you're talking about education, career, or service, you're talking about life, and life really must have joy. It's supposed to be fun!

12 One of the reasons I made the most important decision of my life, to marry George Bush, is because he made me laugh. It's true, sometimes we've laughed through our tears, but that shared laughter has been one of our strongest bonds. Find the joy in life, because as Ferris Bueller said on his day off: "Life moves pretty fast. You don't stop and look around once in a while, you're gonna miss it!" (I'm not going to tell George you clapped more for Ferris than you clapped for George!)

13 The third choice that must not be missed is to cherish your human connections: your relationships with family and friends. For several years, you've had impressed upon you the importance to your career of dedication and hard work—and of course that's true. But as important as your obligations as a doctor, a lawyer, a business leader will be, you are a human being first, and those human connections—with spouses, with children, with friends—are the most important investments you will ever make.

14 At the end of your life, you will never regret not having passed one more test, not winning one more verdict, or not closing one more deal. You will regret time not spent with a husband, a child, a friend, or a parent.

15 We arc in a transitional period right now, fascinating and exhilarating times, learning to adjust to changes and the choices we, men and women, are facing. As an example, I remember what a friend said, on hearing her husband complain to his buddies that he had to babysit. Quickly setting him straight, my friend told her husband that when it's your own kids, it's not called babysitting!

16 Now, maybe we should adjust faster; maybe we should adjust slower. But whatever the era, whatever the times, one thing will never change: fathers and mothers, if you have children, they must come first. You must read to your children, and you must hug your children, and you must love your children. Your success as a family, our success as a society, depends not on what happens in the White House, but on what happens inside your house.

17 For over 50 years, it was said that the winner of Wellesley's annual hoop race would be the first to get married. Now they say the winner will be the first to become a C.E.O. Both of those stereotypes show too little tolerance for those who want to know where the mermaids stand. So I want to offer a new legend: the winner of the hoop race will be the first to realize her dream—not society's dream, her own personal dream. And who knows? Somewhere out in this audience may even be someone who will one day follow in my footsteps and preside over the White House as the president's spouse. And I wish him well!

18 Well, the controversy ends here. But our conversation is only beginning. And a worthwhile conversation it has been. So as you leave Wellesley today, take with you deep thanks for the courtesy and the honor you have shared with Mrs. Gorbachev and with me. Thank you. God bless you. And may your future be worthy of your dreams.

I HAVE A DREAM
Martin Luther King, Jr.

Martin Luther King's "I Have a Dream" speech is widely regarded as a masterpiece. It was delivered August 28, 1963, to some 200,000 people who had come to Washington, D.C., to participate in a peaceful demonstration to further the cause of equal rights for African Americans. King spoke from the steps of the Lincoln Memorial, in the "symbolic shadow" of Abraham Lincoln, and the crowd filled the vast area between the Memorial and the Washington Monument. In addition, millions of Americans watched the speech on television or listened to it on the radio.

Like most ceremonial addresses, "I Have a Dream" is relatively short. Although it took King only sixteen minutes to deliver the speech, he prepared it more carefully than any other speech in his career to that time. His purpose was to set forth as succinctly and as eloquently as possible the guiding principles of the civil rights movement, and to reinforce the commitment of his listeners to those principles.

One of the most interesting features of this speech is King's use of language to make the abstract principles of liberty and equality clear and compelling. Throughout, King relies on familiar, concrete words that create sharp, vivid images. He uses many more metaphors than do most speakers, but they are appropriate to the occasion and help to dramatize King's ideas. Finally, King makes extensive use of repetition and parallelism to reinforce his message and to enhance the momentum of the speech.

If you have heard a tape recording of "I Have a Dream," you know its impact was heightened by King's delivery. In his rich baritone voice, marked by the fervor of the crusader and modulated by the cadences of the Southern Baptist preacher, King gained the total involvement of his audience. As William Robert Miller says, "The crowd more than listened, it participated, and before King had reached his last phrase, a torrent of applause was already welling up."

The text of this speech was taken from a tape recording and is reprinted with permission of Joan Daves. Copyright 1963 by Martin Luther King, Jr. The speech is also available on the videotape supplement to *The Art of Public Speaking*.

1 I am happy to join with you today in what will go down in history as the greatest demonstration for freedom in the history of our nation.

2 Five score years ago, a great American, in whose symbolic shadow we stand today, signed the Emancipation Proclamation. This momentous decree came as a great beacon light of hope to millions of Negro slaves, who had been seared in the flames of withering injustice. It came as a joyous daybreak to end the long night of their captivity.

3 But one hundred years later, the Negro still is not free. One hundred years later, the life of the Negro is still sadly crippled by the manacles of segregation and the chains of discrimination. One hundred years later, the Negro lives on a lonely island of poverty in the midst of a vast ocean of material prosperity. One hundred years later, the Negro is still languished in the corners of American society and finds himself an exile in his own land. And so we've come here today to dramatize a shameful condition.

4 In a sense we've come to our nation's Capitol to cash a check. When the architects of our republic wrote the magnificent words of the Constitution and the Declaration of Independence, they were signing a promissory note to which every American was to fall heir. This note was a promise that all men— yes, black men as well as white men—would be guaranteed the unalienable rights of life, liberty, and the pursuit of happiness.

5 It is obvious today that America has defaulted on this promissory note insofar as her citizens of color are concerned. Instead of honoring this sacred obligation, America has given the Negro people a bad check—a check which has come back marked "insufficient funds."

6 But we refuse to believe that the bank of justice is bankrupt. We refuse to believe that there are insufficient funds in the great vaults of opportunity of this nation. And so we've come to cash this check—a check that will give us upon demand the riches of freedom and the security of justice.

7 We have also come to this hallowed spot to remind America of the fierce urgency of now. This is no time to engage in the luxury of cooling off or to take the tranquilizing drug of gradualism. Now is the time to make real the

promises of democracy. Now is the time to rise from the dark and desolate valley of segregation to the sunlit path of racial justice. Now is the time to lift our nation from the quicksands of racial injustice to the solid rock of brotherhood. Now is the time to make justice a reality for all of God's children.

8 It would be fatal for the nation to overlook the urgency of the moment. This sweltering summer of the Negro's legitimate discontent will not pass until there is an invigorating autumn of freedom and equality. Nineteen sixty-three is not an end, but a beginning. Those who hope that the Negro needed to blow off steam and will now be content will have a rude awakening if the nation returns to business as usual. There will be neither rest nor tranquility in America until the Negro is granted his citizenship rights. The whirlwinds of revolt will continue to shake the foundations of our nation until the bright day of justice emerges.

9 But there is something that I must say to my people, who stand on the warm threshold which leads into the palace of justice. In the process of gaining our rightful place, we must not be guilty of wrongful deeds. Let us not seek to satisfy our thirst for freedom by drinking from the cup of bitterness and hatred.

10 We must forever conduct our struggle on the high plane of dignity and discipline. We must not allow our creative protest to degenerate into physical violence. Again and again we must rise to the majestic heights of meeting physical force with soul force.

11 The marvelous new militancy which has engulfed the Negro community must not lead us to a distrust of all white people. For many of our white brothers, as evidenced by their presence here today, have come to realize that their destiny is tied up with our destiny. They have come to realize that their freedom is inextricably bound to our freedom. We cannot walk alone.

12 As we walk, we must make the pledge that we shall always march ahead. We cannot turn back. There are those who are asking the devotees of civil rights, "When will you be satisfied?" We can never be satisfied as long as the Negro is the victim of the unspeakable horrors of police brutality. We can never be satisfied as long as our bodies, heavy with the fatigue of travel, cannot gain lodging in the motels of the highways and the hotels of the cities. We cannot be satisfied as long as the Negro's basic mobility is from a smaller ghetto to a larger one. We can never be satisfied as long as our children are stripped of their selfhood and robbed of their dignity by signs stating "For Whites Only." We cannot be satisfied as long as a Negro in Mississippi cannot vote and a Negro in New York believes he has nothing for which to vote. No, no, we are not satisfied, and we will not be satisfied until justice rolls down like waters, and righteousness like a mighty stream.

13 I am not unmindful that some of you have come here out of great trials and tribulations. Some of you have come fresh from narrow jail cells. Some of you have come from areas where your quest for freedom left you battered by the storms of persecution and staggered by the winds of police brutality. You have been the veterans of creative suffering. Continue to work with the faith that unearned suffering is redemptive.

14 Go back to Mississippi, go back to Alabama, go back to South Carolina, go back to Georgia, go back to Louisiana, go back to the slums and ghettos of our Northern cities, knowing that somehow this situation can and will be changed. Let us not wallow in the valley of despair.

15 I say to you today, my friends, so even though we face the difficulties of today and tomorrow, I still have a dream. It is a dream deeply rooted in the American dream.

16 I have a dream that one day this nation will rise up and live out the true meaning of its creed, "We hold these truths to be self-evident, that all men are created equal."

17 I have a dream that one day on the red hills of Georgia the sons of former slaves and the sons of former slaveowners will be able to sit down together at the table of brotherhood.

18 I have a dream that one day even the state of Mississippi, a state sweltering with the heat of injustice, sweltering with the heat of oppression, will be transformed into an oasis of freedom and justice.

19 I have a dream that my four little children will one day live in a nation where they will not be judged by the color of their skin but by the content of their character. I have a dream today.

20 I have a dream that one day, down in Alabama, with its vicious racists, with its governor having his lips dripping with the words of interposition and nullification, one day right there in Alabama little black boys and black girls will be able to join hands with little white boys and white girls as sisters and brothers. I have a dream today.

21 I have a dream that one day every valley shall be exalted, every hill and mountain shall be made low, the rough places will be made plane and the crooked places will be made straight, and the glory of the Lord shall be revealed, and all flesh shall see it together.

22 This is our hope. This is the faith that I go back to the South with. With this faith we will be able to hew out of the mountain of despair a stone of hope. With this faith we will be able to transform the jangling discords of our nation into a beautiful symphony of brotherhood. With this faith we will be able to work together, to pray together, to struggle together, to go to jail together, to stand up for freedom together, knowing that we will be free one day.

23 This will be the day—this will be the day when all of God's children will be able to sing with new meaning, "My country 'tis of thee, sweet land of liberty, of thee I sing. Land where my fathers died, land of the pilgrim's pride, from every mountainside, let freedom ring." And if America is to be a great nation, this must become true.

24 So let freedom ring from the prodigious hilltops of New Hampshire. Let freedom ring from the mighty mountains of New York. Let freedom ring from the heightening Alleghenies of Pennsylvania!

25 Let freedom ring from the snowcapped Rockies of Colorado! Let freedom ring from the curvaceous slopes of California!

26 But not only that. Let freedom ring from Stone Mountain of Georgia!

27 Let freedom ring from Lookout Mountain of Tennessee!

28 Let freedom ring from every hill and molehill of Mississippi. From every mountainside, let freedom ring.

29 And when this happens, when we allow freedom ring—when we let it ring from every village and every hamlet, from every state and every city— wc will be able to speed up that day when all of God's children, black men and white men, Jews and Gentiles, Protestants and Catholics, will be able to join hands and sing in the words of the old Negro spiritual, "Free at last! Free at last! Thank God almighty, we are free at last!"

FAMILY MEDICAL HISTORIES: A PROVEN LIFESAVER

Steven Harris

Of all the medical breakthroughs of recent years, few are more important than the discovery that many diseases are hereditary in origin. In the following persuasive speech, Steven Harris, a student at the University of Wisconsin, seeks to convince listeners that they should create a family medical history to help deal with the threat of hereditary diseases.

As you read the speech, study how the speaker uses statistics, examples, and testimony. Does he convince you that hereditary diseases pose a significant risk? Does he present a workable solution to the problem? How could he have made the speech more convincing?

This speech is printed with permission from Steven Harris and is also available on the videotape supplement that accompanies this edition of *The Art of Public Speaking.* If you view the speech on videotape, you will see that Steven used a striking visual aid in the solution section of his speech to help explain how to create a family medical history.

1 Actress-comedian Gilda Radner, alias Roseann Roseanna Danna as she's well known to long-time *Saturday Night Live* fans, gave us laughter and enjoyment for decades before her death at the age of forty-two from ovarian cancer. She suffered through a year of intense pain before her doctors finally diagnosed the problem. If detected early, the survival rate for ovarian cancer is 85 percent, but that drops to 15 to 20 percent if the cancer spreads. Doctors and Radner's husband, Gene Wilder, believe she died a premature death that could have been prevented had she known that her grandmother, aunt, and a first cousin all suffered from the same disease.

2 The importance of knowing your family's medical history is becoming increasingly urgent, as more and more diseases are found to have genetic links. Researchers at the National Institutes of Health are working to isolate all of the body's 50,000 to 100,000 genes and match them to specific diseases, a project they hope to complete by the year 2004. It may be only a matter of

time before scientists locate the genes that cause such common illnesses as diabetes and high blood pressure. But unfortunately, time is not on our side. Hereditary diseases are a crisis potentially affecting everyone in this room.

3 In order to better understand this, we'll discuss the scope of this threat, the medical community's reaction or inaction, and finally indicate an easy solution to help you deal with the threat of hereditary diseases.

4 First we'll look at the problem hereditary diseases pose to all of us. The number of diseases with a genetic link is staggering, and these are only the diseases scientists know have a hereditary component. *U.S. News and World Report* states that if a member of your family had ovarian cancer, your risk of contracting the disease increases by 20 to 40 percent. If a family member had breast cancer, your risk increases by up to 50 percent. And if lung cancer runs in your family, your risk increases by 300 percent.

5 The *U.S. News and World Report* article gives several examples of diseases found to have genetic links—diabetes, stroke, mental illness, alcoholism, allergies, arthritis, sickle-cell anemia, and high blood pressure. Even birth defects and a predisposition for miscarriages can be inherited. Researchers at the University of Utah found that men under age forty in families with histories of heart attack had twelve times the risk of early heart disease, while women from such families had eight times higher risk.

6 Now you may be thinking that your doctor is your best chance of early detection, but unfortunately the medical community has put us at even greater risk, accentuating the problem.

7 The problem lies not only with the severity of the diseases themselves, but also with an historic belief by the medical community that family history is of minimal importance. Doctors have traditionally taken meager medical histories, failing to recognize their importance. Ask yourself if your doctor updated your family history during your last physical. Most likely he or she did not. This leaves a gaping hole in your diagnosis.

8 The *New York State Journal of Medicine* describes a recent study in New York City designed to determine if data on the family history of cancer patients were being recorded by hospitals. They found that only four of sixty-four hospitals indicated familial recurrence of cancer on medical charts, and no hospital accrediting agency required that this information be recorded.

9 Another study by the same researchers investigated 200 cancer patients undergoing treatment in an oncology clinic. These cases showed numerous examples of hereditary cancer syndromes, but their clinical charts demonstrated that the family history of cancer had either been completely omitted or reported as "negative," despite substantial evidence to the contrary. There are doctors, of course, who do take into account hereditary factors, but unfortunately they are still a small minority, as reported by the Hereditary Cancer Institute at Creighton University.

10 Having heard the problems, we must now look at some solutions. Obviously, one step is for doctors to take better account of medical history in order to ensure that we receive quick treatment and proper diagnoses. But what I want to focus on is what we as individuals can do.

11 You can help your doctor and yourself by making a medical family tree. To assist you in making a medical family tree, *U.S. News and World Report* offers this chart as a guide. List all medical conditions contracted by close relatives—especially parents, siblings, grandparents, aunts and uncles, and cousins. Include important information about each relative in the space provided, such as age, height, weight, personal habits, and any medical conditions they have contracted.

12 In addition, list the age when each relative contracted that condition; this will inform your doctor of the best time to begin testing for a disease or to begin preventive medicine. Don't hesitate to overelaborate your medical family tree. Trained physicians may see patterns that you cannot.

13 Getting this information is not that difficult. Simply speak to your relatives and include every medical condition they recall having. Not only heart disease and high blood pressure, but even such things as migraines and allergies should be included. Even if you think your family is in good health, a little probing may uncover hidden problems. Consider the few hours required to make a detailed medical family tree as an investment in your health future.

14 Today we learned what an important issue and just how big a threat hereditary diseases are and how you can protect yourself by making a medical family tree. The first item mentioned in the UCLA School of Public Health's book *50 Simple Things You Can Do to Save Your Life* is to know your family history. Had Gilda Radner and her doctor known her family's medical history, she might be alive today. The knowledge you gain by investigating your family's medical history may help you fend off future problems and possibly save your life.

A WHISPER OF AIDS
Mary Fisher

As we saw in Chapter 1, Mary Fisher's emergence as an AIDS activist demonstrates how the need for public speaking can touch anyone sometime in her or his life. Only a year before Fisher rose to give the following speech to the Republican National Convention in Houston, Texas, she learned that she had contracted the HIV virus from her ex-husband. Resolving to do all she could to fight the disease, she became an outspoken advocate of the need for public understanding and resources in the battle against AIDS.

After telling her story to the Republican Platform Committee in May 1992, Fisher, a former staff assistant to President Gerald Ford, was invited to address the party's national convention that summer. Feeling, as she said later, like "the only HIV-positive Republican," she was deeply concerned about how her message of compassion and awareness would be received.

It did not take long, however, for Fisher's audience to realize that they were hearing a very special speech. Within a few minutes, the Astrodome turned eerily silent as the delegates stopped their chatting and gave Fisher their undivided attention. Some were moved to tears. Across the United States, millions watched on television, captivated by Fisher's somber words and heartfelt delivery. The *New York Times* deemed the address "exceptional for its deep emotion and sharp message."

One of the most admired public speeches of recent years, Fisher's address has been widely reprinted. The text here is from Fisher's book, *Sleep with the Angels: A Mother Challenges AIDS*, and is presented with permission from Moyer Bell Publishers, Wakefield, Rhode Island. Copyright 1994 by Family AIDS Network, Incorporated.

1 Less than three months ago, at platform hearings in Salt Lake City, I asked the Republican Party to lift the shroud of silence which has been draped over the issue of HIV/AIDS. I have come tonight to bring our silence to an end.

2 I bear a message of challenge, not self-congratulation. I want your attention, not your applause. I would never have asked to be HIV-positive. But I believe that in all things there is a good purpose, and so I stand before you, and before the nation, gladly.

3 The reality of AIDS is brutally clear. Two hundred thousand Americans are dead or dying; a million more are infected. Worldwide, forty million, or sixty million, or a hundred million infections will be counted in the coming few years. But despite science and research, White House meetings and congressional hearings, despite good intentions and bold initiatives, campaign slogans and hopeful promises—despite it all, it's the epidemic which is winning tonight.

4 In the context of an election year, I ask you—here, in this great hall, or listening in the quiet of your home—to recognize that the AIDS virus is not a political creature. It does not care whether you are Democrat or Republican. It does not ask whether you are black or white, male or female, gay or straight, young or old.

5 Tonight, I represent an AIDS community whose members have been reluctantly drafted from every segment of American society. Though I am white and a mother, I am one with a black infant struggling with tubes in a Philadelphia hospital. Though I am female and contracted this disease in marriage, and enjoy the warm support of my family, I am one with the lonely gay man sheltering a flickering candle from the cold wind of his family's rejection.

6 This is not a distant threat; it is a present danger. The rate of infection is increasing fastest among women and children. Largely unknown a decade ago, AIDS is the third leading killer of young-adult Americans today—but it won't be third for long. Because, unlike other diseases, this one travels. Adolescents don't give each other cancer or heart disease because they believe they are in love. But HIV is different. And we have helped it along—we have killed each other—with our ignorance, our prejudice, and our silence.

7 We may take refuge in our stereotypes, but we cannot hide there long. Because HIV asks only one thing of those it attacks: Are you human? And this is the right question: Are you human? Because people with HIV have not entered some alien state of being. They are human. They have not earned

cruelty and they do not deserve meanness. They don't benefit from being isolated or treated as outcasts. Each of them is exactly what God made: a person. Not evil, deserving of our judgment; not victims, longing for our pity. People. Ready for support and worthy of compassion.

8 My call to you, my Party, is to take a public stand no less compassionate than that of the President and Mrs. Bush. They have embraced me and my family in memorable ways. In the place of judgment, they have shown affection. In difficult moments, they have raised our spirits. In the darkest hours, I have seen them reaching not only to me, but also to my parents, armed with that stunning grief and special grace that comes only to parents who have themselves leaned too long over the bedside of a dying child.

9 With the President's leadership, much good has been done; much of the good has gone unheralded; as the President has insisted, "Much remains to be done."

10 But we do the President's cause no good if we praise the American family but ignore a virus that destroys it. We must be consistent if we are to be believed. We cannot love justice and ignore prejudice, love our children and fear to teach them. Whatever our role, as parent or policy maker, we must act as eloquently as we speak—else we have no integrity.

11 My call to the nation is a plea for awareness. If you believe you are safe, you are in danger. Because I was not hemophiliac, I was not at risk. Because I was not gay, I was not at risk. Because I did not inject drugs, I was not at risk.

12 My father has devoted much of his lifetime to guarding against another holocaust. He is part of the generation who heard Pastor Niemoeller come out of the Nazi death camps to say, "They came after the Jews and I was not a Jew, so I did not protest. They came after the Trade Unionists, and I was not a Trade Unionist, so I did not protest. They came after the Roman Catholics, and I was not a Roman Catholic, so I did not protest. Then they came after me, and there was no one left to protest."

13 The lesson history teaches is this: If you believe you are safe, you are at risk. If you do not see this killer stalking your children, look again. There is no family or community, no race or religion, no place left in America that is safe. Until we genuinely embrace this message, we are a nation at risk.

14 Tonight, HIV marches resolutely towards AIDS in more than a million American homes, littering its pathway with the bodies of the young. Young men. Young women. Young parents. Young children. One of the families is mine. If it is true that HIV inevitably turns to AIDS, then my children will inevitably turn to orphans.

15 My family has been a rock of support. My 84-year-old father, who has pursued the healing of the nations, will not accept the premise that he cannot heal his daughter. My mother has refused to be broken; she still calls at midnight to tell wonderful jokes that make me laugh. Sisters and friends, and my brother Phillip (whose birthday is today)—all have helped carry me over the hardest places. I am blessed, richly and deeply blessed, to have such a family.

16 But not all of you have been so blessed. You are HIV-positive but dare not say it. You have lost loved ones, but you dared not whisper the word AIDS. You weep silently; you grieve alone.

17 I have a message for you: It is not you who should feel shame; it is we. We who tolerate ignorance and practice prejudice, we who have taught you to fear. We must lift our shroud of silence, making it safe for you to reach out for compassion. It is our task to seek safety for our children, not in quiet denial but in effective action.

18 Some day our children will be grown. My son Max, now four, will take the measure of his mother; my son Zachary, now two, will sort through his memories. I may not be here to hear their judgments, but I know already what I hope they are.

19 I want my children to know that their mother was not a victim. She was a messenger. I do not want them to think, as I once did, that courage is the absence of fear; I want them to know that courage is the strength to act wisely when most we are afraid. I want them to have the courage to step forward when called by their nation, or their Party, and give leadership—no matter what the personal cost. I ask no more of you than I ask of myself, or of my children.

20 To the millions of you who are grieving, who are frightened, who have suffered the ravages of AIDS firsthand: Have courage and you will find comfort.

21 To the millions who are strong, I issue this plea: Set aside prejudice and politics to make room for compassion and sound policy.

22 To my children, I make this pledge: I will not give in, Zachary, because I draw my courage from you. Your silly giggle gives me hope. Your gentle prayers give me strength. And you, my child, give me reason to say to America, "You are at risk." And I will not rest, Max, until I have done all I can to make your world safe. I will seek a place where intimacy is not the prelude to suffering.

23 I will not hurry to leave you, my children. But when I go, I pray that you will not suffer shame on my account.

24 To all within sound of my voice, I appeal: Learn with me the lessons of history and of grace, so my children will not be afraid to say the word AIDS when I am gone. Then their children, and yours, may not need to whisper it at all.

25 God bless the children, and bless us all.

A FRIEND IN NEED

Sandy Hefty

Every year millions of Americans give their time and energy as volunteers to help people less fortunate than themselves. In the following speech, Sandy Hefty, an undergraduate at the University of Wisconsin, urges students to get involved by volunteering to help the elderly. A volunteer herself, Sandy focuses on the difficulties faced by less fortunate people of advanced age who do not get the care and companionship they need to live independently in their homes.

Because this speech deals with a question of policy, be sure to assess how convincingly the speaker defines the problem and how well she defends her solution. Also consider how she uses the methods of persuasion discussed in Chapter 16. Does she establish her credibility and good will? Is her evidence clear and convincing? Does she relate the topic to her audience and take account of potential objections to her plan? How does she seek to generate emotional appeal? What could she have done to make the speech more effective?

This speech is printed with permission from Sandy Hefty and has been edited slightly for publication. It is also available on the videotape supplement that accompanies *The Art of Public Speaking*.

1 Loretta Olson sometimes gets confused and does some pretty bizarre things. For instance, sometimes she puts her ice cream in the refrigerator instead of the freezer, and sometimes she feeds her cat chocolate chips instead of cat food. You see, Loretta is an 85-year-old woman who suffers from Alzheimer's disease. She was preceded in death by her husband and only child and now is trying to live on her own the best that she can. You may be wondering how somebody as confused as Loretta could possibly keep living on her own, but she does.

2 During my freshman year, I volunteered six hours a week to help Loretta remain independent in her home. Due to the forgetfulness associated with Alzheimer's disease, my main duty as a volunteer was to help Loretta with her cooking and house cleaning, which she often forgot to finish on her own.

3 Since I started volunteering time with Loretta, I've learned that there are millions of elderly Americans who need help to remain independent in their homes. According to the United States Census Bureau, our elderly population is the fastest growing segment in the nation. This trend is even seen in my class survey, in which all but two of you said you have living grandparents and seven of you said you have grandparents living alone.

4 Although the elderly are no longer the poorest segment of American society, according to the Poverty and Wealth Branch of the United States Census Bureau, 1.8 million Americans in the 75-plus age group fall below the poverty line. One point eight million—that's roughly the populations of Seattle, Indianapolis, and Boston combined.

5 Today, I would like to persuade each of you to help solve the problems facing more advanced and less fortunate elderly Americans by volunteering time to help them remain independent in their homes. Let's begin by addressing the problems that can occur among this group of people.

6 There are two problems that can occur when elderly people living alone do not get the companionship and care they need. The first problem is that elderly people may not be able to meet all of their physical needs. Before I met Loretta, I was a caregiver for an 87-year-old woman who suffered from arthritis. This woman often needed help buttoning her blouse and tying her shoes, as well as needing help cutting vegetables for meals and doing light house cleaning. This is not unusual for many people of advanced age. Like

Loretta, they can continue living at home, but need help with certain physical tasks such as house cleaning, food preparation, and transportation.

7 Not only is there the problem of elderly people not meeting all of their physical needs, but there is a second, more tragic problem that can occur. That second problem is suicide. According to the National Center for Vital Statistics, persons age 75 and older have the highest rate of suicide compared to all other age groups. Anthony Boxwell, author of the article entitled "Geriatric Suicide: The Preventable Death," says that suicide among the elderly stems from three main causes—helplessness, hopelessness and haplessness. Helplessness describes the feelings of impotence some elderly people feel after retirement or upon realizing they're losing their physical and mental vigor. Hopelessness is associated with depression caused by the realization of the onset of old age. And haplessness refers to a series of repeated losses, such as loss of earnings, friends, and family.

8 Now that we have talked about the two major problems facing elderly people who do not get the companionship and care they need, let's talk about what we can do to help solve these problems.

9 We as individuals can't do everything, of course. Some responsibility lies with families, government, and charitable agencies. But there is something we can do, and that is get involved with a volunteer program that assists elderly people who need help living at home. Here in Wisconsin, we have a Community Options Program, which is an individually tailored financial assistance method to help keep the elderly and people with disabilities out of nursing homes. Right here in Madison, Independent Living has a Friendly Visiting Program in which volunteers provide companionship and household assistance for elderly people who live at home. You can contact Independent Living by calling the number on this handout, which I will be giving you after my speech.

10 Now I'm sure you have some questions about this kind of work. For instance, how much time does it take? It takes as much time as you want to put into it. You can volunteer as little as one to two hours a week or as many as forty hours a week. You decide how much time you want to volunteer based on your own schedule. But no matter how much time you spend, you will certainly experience great personal gratification. I know I have. I have been a volunteer for six years, and volunteering time with people who are less fortunate than I makes me feel good about myself. Volunteering time with the elderly has also taught me unique ethnic traditions, as well as American history.

11 You should also know that this kind of volunteer work can have benefits for you beyond feelings of personal gratification. Some volunteer organizations such as the state-run Community Options Program and the federally funded Title 19 Program offer financial assistance to people who participate. This can run from reimbursement of your travel expenses to an actual salary for certain kinds of work.

12 In closing, I am urging you to volunteer time to help needy elderly people remain independent in their homes. Remember that spending time

with elderly people living alone can help them meet their physical and emotional needs. You can adjust the time spent to fit your needs, you can get great personal gratification, and you can even receive monetary benefits as well. But most important, Loretta Olson—and millions like her—will be forever thankful for your efforts.

Index

Photo Credits